WAR COMES TO AACHEN

PHILIP W. BLOOD

War Comes to Aachen

*The Nazis, Churchill and the
'Stalingrad of the West'*

HURST & COMPANY, LONDON

First published in the United Kingdom in 2024 by
C. Hurst & Co. (Publishers) Ltd.,
New Wing, Somerset House, Strand, London, WC2R 1LA
© Philip W. Blood, 2024
All rights reserved.

Distributed in the United States, Canada and Latin America by
Oxford University Press, 198 Madison Avenue, New York, NY 10016,
United States of America.

The right of Philip W. Blood to be identified as the author
of this publication is asserted by him in accordance with the
Copyright, Designs and Patents Act, 1988.

A Cataloguing-in-Publication data record for this book
is available from the British Library.

ISBN: 9781911723691

This book is printed using paper from registered sustainable
and managed sources.

www.hurstpublishers.com

Printed and bound in Great Britain by Bell and Bain Ltd, Glasgow

This book is dedicated to my grandma: Gwendoline Casasola (neé Henshaw, parachute seamstress) and all the family members of the generation who had their lives changed forever in the age of total war:

Great War: Rowland Casasola (Royal Engineers), Wilfred Henshaw (Royal Army Service Corps), Tom Henshaw (Manchester Regiment—killed in action 29 August 1916), Jack Henshaw (Tank Corps—died of wounds) and Joe Scholes (Kings' Regiment).

World War II: Eric Blood (Royal Navy), Peter Blood (child during the Manchester Blitz), Pamela Blood (née Casasola, child during the Manchester Blitz), Charles Casasola (Royal Artillery), Lena Casasola (munitions worker), Joseph Casasola (Volunteer Fire Services and Police Auxiliary), Jimmy Darlington (Army), Michael Fallon (RAF Bomber Command), Anne Henshaw (ambulance driver), Arthur Henshaw (Princess Louise's Regiment), Evelyn Henshaw (ATS), Jack Henshaw (Conscientious Objector), James Henshaw (7th Armoured Division), Joan Henshaw (WRNS), Stanley Henshaw (Border Regiment—Chindits), Joseph Scholes (Lancashire Fusiliers—died of wounds) and Joseph Sykes (Royal Navy).

CONTENTS

Maps	ix–xiv
List of Illustrations	xv
Abbreviations	xvii
Acknowledgments	xix
Introduction	1

PART ONE
THE AGE OF TOTAL WAR

1. Metropolis	9
2. Letting Go of Democracy	31

PART TWO
TOWARDS AN ANTHROPOLOGY OF BOMBING

3. In Defence of the Community	53
4. Warlord	83
5. Frying Elver	115

PART THREE
WAR OF DESTRUCTION

6. The Paralysed City	141
7. The Stalingrad of the West	167
8. Restoring Democracy	197

PART FOUR
POSTMODERN WAR AND SOCIETY

9. British Military Occupation	227
10. Imposing the Raj	255
11. Ordinary People	285
Reflections	321
Notes	331
Select Bibliography	355
Index	361

MAPS

Map 1: (*see* Ch. 3): RAF Bomber Command, Battle of Germany—drawn from Mercator Projection Map of Europe, circa 1941, located in TNA AIR 14/233—Routing of Bomber Aircraft—Tactical. Copyright Ben Skipper.

MAPS

Map 2: (*see* Ch. 5): Aachen, Arson Raid, 12/13 July 1943. Drawn from TNA Air 24/257, Aachen air raid July 1943. Copyright Ben Skipper.

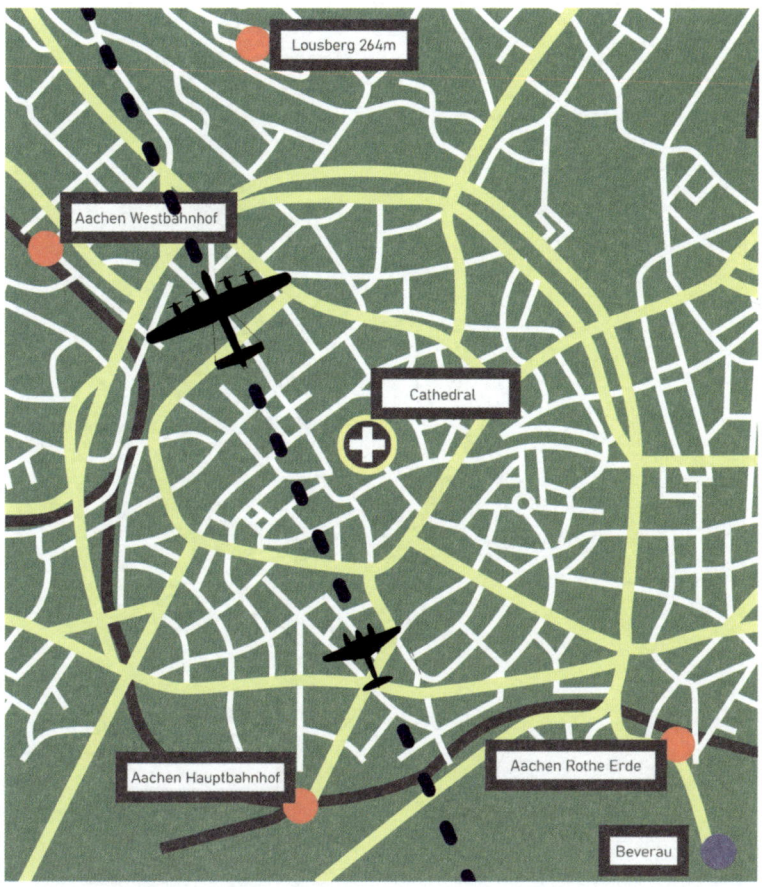

Map 3: (*see* Ch. 6): Aachen Blitz Raid, 11 April 1944, drawn from TNA 20/5952 Zone Maps, target sheets 1944, Air 24/270 and AIR 24/270 Operations Research, April 1944. Copyright Ben Skipper.

MAPS

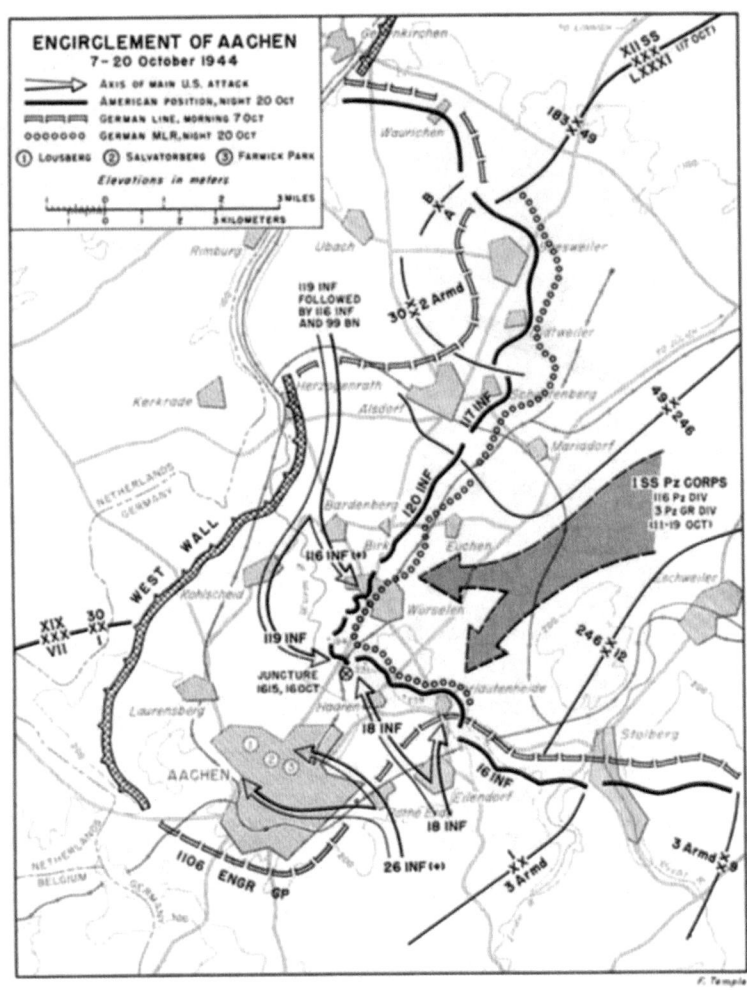

Map 4: (see Ch. 7): Encirclement of Aachen 7–20 October 1944. Source: Charles B. MacDonald, *The Siegfried Line Campaign* (U.S. Army Center of Military History, CMH Pub 7-7-1, 1963).

MAPS

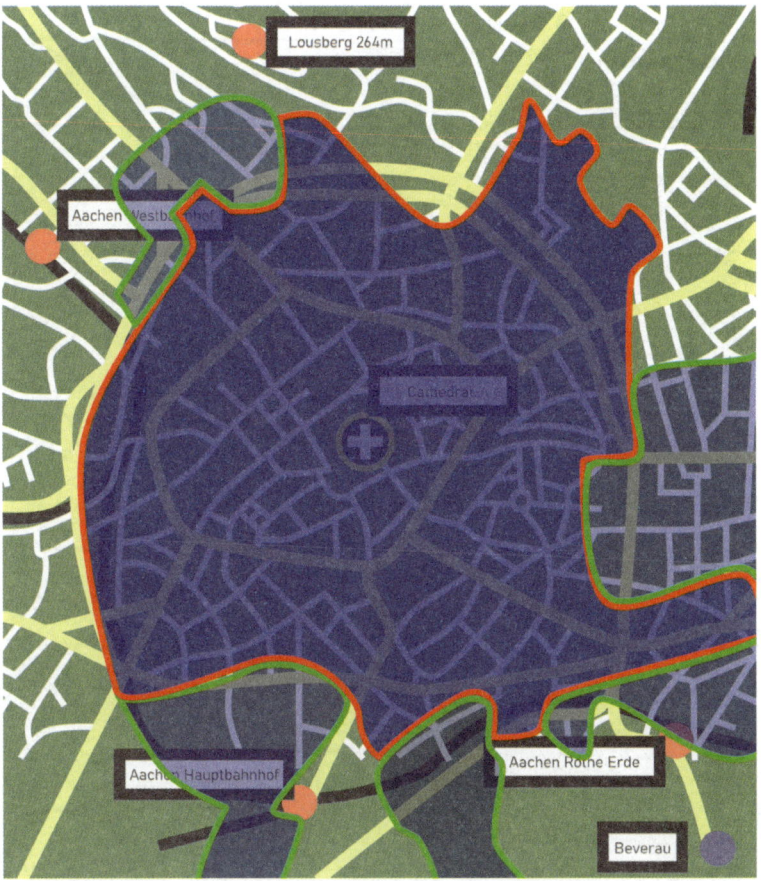

Map 5: (*see* Ch. 9): Illustration from over-layering an RAF zone target area map (red) and the final destruction area map (green)—identifying total area of 650 acres of destruction. Based on TNA AIR 20/5952, Aachen target sheets and maps—zone one targeting; AIR 14/3760, K Reports, bombing interpretation reports, AIR 14/2952, Report on Aachen Air Raid Shelters (February 1945), and AIR 14/3682, Damage Diagrams, Headquarters Bomber Command, September 1945. Copyright Ben Skipper.

MAPS

Map 6: (*see* Ch. 10): Official map of Aachen ruins, destruction and rubble as recorded in 1947. Courtesy of Stadtarchiv Aachen.

LIST OF ILLUSTRATIONS

Introduction: the Aachen City plaque commemorating the end of Nazism and the beginning of democracy. Once fixed to the massive German Army bunker, it was removed and the bunker demolished in 2014. (Author collection)

The Great War: memorial to the fallen Jewish soldiers in the Synagogue; RWTH-Aachen University Aula auditorium with the doors framed by the roll of honour of names of students and faculty etched in marble; memorial to fallen German soldiers from Kelmis, a neighbouring community now in Belgium; Aachen war memorial erected on a turret of the old walls after the Great War. Destroyed in 1944, it was reconstructed sometime after 1946. (Author collection)

Letting Go of Democracy: Aachen Nazi Party and SA leader Eduard Schmeer. (NARA, Hoffmann Collection, courtesy Michael Miller); Ordensburg Vogelsang, the Nazi political school for future leaders, today a museum in the Eifel National Park. (Author collection)

In Defence of Aachen: Hochbunker, Sandkaulstrasse, the first bunker in 1941 and demolished in 2014. The demolition exposed the housing cells used into the 1950s; Hochbunker Kasinostrasse, in proximity to where two American airmen were beaten and stoned, encouraged by Aachen police officials. (Author collection)

Frying Elver: the area where the RAF's target indicator flares were dropped and the centre of Zone 1 fires; the 14th-century *Rathaus*

LIST OF ILLUSTRATIONS

(town hall) with its coronation hall was seriously damaged during the air raids and all the surrounding municipal buildings were destroyed. (Author Collection)

The Paralysed City: Aachen Burtscheid area after the heavy bombing raids against the railway lines; destruction to the *Hauptbahnhof* after the battle. (US Army Signals Corps, NARA); an image of Adalbertstrasse in October 1944, and in 2004, before the redevelopment. (Author collection)

The Stalingrad of the West: American Sherman tanks in Rolandstrasse after the firefight; American anti-tank gun team in the city centre; German soldiers surrendering; Captain Bobbie E. Brown, received the Medal of Honour for acts of bravery on 8 October 1944, during the encirclement battle. (US Army Signals Corps, NARA)

Restoring Democracy: civilians being evacuated after the battle; women and children being fed with US Army rations in Brand; Aachen's first post-Third Reich police force November 1944; Franz Oppenhoff, Aachen's first post-Third Reich Oberbürgermeister. (US Army, NARA)

Defiance and Disorder: soldier and smuggler, Heinrich Schreiber, 1923–2020. (Author collection); Aachen city centre, believed to be 1954. (NARA)

Ordinary People: Aachen's ornate synagogue destroyed by arson in November 1938. (Aachen Stadtarchiv); former Gasborn police precinct designated as the collection point for the units and personnel assigned to the destruction of the synagogue on Kristallnacht; one of the Judenhaus in the university district that served in the ghettoisation of Aachen's Jews; memorial plaque decorated with candles and flowers during Kristallnacht memorial service in November 2023. (Author Collection)

Conclusion: the civilian dead air raid, 11 April 1944, buried in military style by the Nazis and under the watchful gaze of the Bismarck tower from 1905. (Author Collection)

ABBREVIATIONS

As used throughout the book:

BBRM	British Bombing Research Mission 1944–5, superseded by the BBSU.
BBSU	Report of British Bombing Survey Unit, 'The Strategic Air War Against Germany 1939–1945', 1946.
BCD	Martin Middlebrook and Chris Everitt, *The Bomber Command War Diaries: An Operational Reference Book 1939–1945* (Hinckley, 1995).
BC-ORS	RAF Bomber Command Operational Research Section.
CMH	Center for Military History, US Army (Pennsylvania, USA).
CWGC	Commonwealth War Graves Commission.
FMS	US Army Historical Branch, Foreign Military Studies (German army).
HstaD	Haptarchiv Stadt Düsseldorf.
IHK	Industrie- und Handels Kammer (Chamber of Commerce), Aachen/Cologne.
KKG	Kaiser Karls Gymnasium.

ABBREVIATIONS

McSherry Papers	The Frank J. McSherry Papers, Civil Affairs 1944–5 (Germany), Box 50, CMH.
MGO	Military Government Organisation.
NARA	National Archive, College Park annex, Washington DC.
Poll-Chronicle	Bernhard Poll (Hrsg), *Geschichte Aachens in Daten*, Teil 1: bis 1964 (Aachen, 2003).
RB Aachen	*Regierungsbezirk Aachen*—the name of the British military occupation.
StaA	Stadt Aachen, city archives.
TNA	The National Archives, London.

ACKNOWLEDGMENTS

This book is the culmination of countless inspirations and motivations. To begin, I extend my deepest gratitude to Aachen, Germany, for embracing me, and to the rich cultural tapestry that defines our community. To the friends and associates in Aachen who contributed in various capacities, your support has been invaluable. Whether artists, medical professionals, musicians, or Alemannia Aachen football fans, their opinions were greatly appreciated.

I dedicate this book to the resilience of my grandparents, my family's wartime generation and to the vibrant community of our former home in Manchester, lost during the tumultuous 1970s Victorian housing clearances. Their stories serve as a poignant reminder of the importance of preserving our cultural heritage.

The inception of this project was in 2001, initiated by colleagues at RWTH Aachen University: Professor Paul Thomes, his team of scholars and, in particular, the enthusiasm of my former research assistant Michael Birklein. Special thanks to Dr Roger Cirillo, former US army Lieutenant Colonel, for generously providing the invaluable US Army combat reports for the Battle of Aachen. I fondly remember the insightful conversations about pre-1945 Aachen society with the late Heinrich Schreiber, a former veteran soldier, whose wisdom enriched this endeavour.

I am profoundly grateful to the authors and scholars whose seminal works have served as guiding lights throughout this journey: Len Deighton, Professor Wilhelm Deist, Martin Francis, Professor Richard Holmes, Frederick Taylor, Sir Max Hastings,

ACKNOWLEDGMENTS

Dr Bernd Lemke, Dr Declan O'Reilly, Dr Alexandra Richie, Dr Nick Terry, Wolfgang Trees, Professor Nicholas Stargardt and W.G. Sebald.

A special note of appreciation goes to Matthew Ford and Dr Mark Fenemore for their invaluable feedback on the earliest drafts. A special thanks to Michael Miller (@AxisBiographic1) for his generous research assistance. Also, Paul Woodadge (@WW2TV) for hosting a tour of the wider Aachen battlefield in November 2022. Lastly I extend my appreciation to Michael Dwyer and the dedicated team at Hurst Publishers for their commitment to bringing this project to publication. Your hard work has transformed vision into reality, and for that, I am immensely grateful.

Philip W. Blood
Aachen, May 2024

INTRODUCTION

German soldiers, I am speaking to you at a painful moment; I was forced to surrender because we ran out of ammunition, food, and water. I saw that the further fight was worthless. I was acting against orders; I was supposed to fight to the last man. At this time, I have to remind you, that you are German soldiers, and please behave as such. I also wish you the best of health, and a fast return to your Fatherland after the ceasing of hostilities and to help rebuild Germany. I was refused by the American authorities to give a *Sieg Heil* and *Heil Hitler*, but we can still do it in our minds.[1]

At noon on 21 October 1944, as the German commander of Aachen addressed his troops one last time after surrendering to the US Army. The Americans had expected a desolate city razed by strategic bombing and ground warfare but found themselves amidst an eerie aftermath. Aachen was a dead city. The lethal combination of high-explosive bombs, phosphorus fires, napalm, artillery barrages and tank shells had left Aachen seemingly lifeless, its ancient structures defenceless against the onslaught of modernity. Even after the departure of German PoWs, the city remained a haunting spectre, inhabited only by the entombed dead and fleeting waves of US troops. For weeks, Aachen was treated as a ghost town by Allied forces. Twenty-six years earlier, on 9 November 1918, the end of the Great War in the west unfolded under less traumatic circumstances. With Kaiser Wilhelm's abdication and the subsequent armistice signed by the Imperial German Army, fears of chaos reminiscent of Napoleon's retreat stirred within the local populace. The arrival of the 4th Army, under General Sixt von Arnim, calmed fears and stirred memories of past parades. Once again, the city's streets were adorned with black-red-white imperial flags. However, as one orderly army departed for Cologne, a swarm of soldiers, deserters and civilian refugees flooded the city in a chaotic rout. The Oberbürgermeister raised a Soldiers and Workers Council for self-defence and to police the city. Then the Belgian Army arrived to occupy the city and imposed martial law. The symbolic transition from German defeat to Belgian victory was captured in a military victory parade before Charlemagne's cathedral, which was immortalised by a Belgian artist to commemorate the historic moment. The contrast between the ending of the two wars reflected the escalation of violence that marked the age of total war.

Losing one world war was a disaster; losing another in quick succession was a catastrophe, a sentiment encapsulated in those wry observations of Sellar and Yeatman about history as a 'bad thing'. In 1930, the world was gripped by global depression, but their satire was insightful: 'Though there were several battles in the War, none were so terrible or costly as the Peace which was signed afterwards in the ever memorable Chamber of Horrors at Versailles'.[2] Satire thrived in the era of 'total war', born out of the immense devastation and suffering witnessed across the first half of the twentieth century. Amidst the staggering death tolls, entire communities vanished, consumed by the relentless barrage of shelling and bombing that left villages, towns and cities obliterated. Yet, amidst the ruins, survivors endeavoured to rebuild their shattered lives, though for many, returning to normalcy proved elusive. *War Comes to Aachen* recounts the tale of a city pronounced 'dead' in October 1944, its streets emptied and its buildings reduced to rubble, as witnessed by one British military intelligence officer who remarked on the impossibility of finding any undamaged buildings. Amidst the debris, the *Trümmerfrau* (the rubble women), the subject of both myth and satire in German literature and media, toiled for sustenance, while former Nazis, once ubiquitous, receded into the shadows, their pasts viewed as alien enti-

INTRODUCTION

ties. Weaving together these disparate narratives illuminates a unique history of Aachen in the age of total war.

The impetus behind this book stems from my academic immersion in the field of modern socioeconomic and cultural history at a German university that profoundly reshaped my perspective of war. Exploring Aachen's societal evolution since 1804 revealed the enduring impact of war and total war. Simon Winder's introspective narrative in *Lotharingia* (2019) served as a poignant reminder of how regional experiences can mould a worldview, although my understanding pales in comparison to the profound local knowledge possessed by local historians like Herbert Ruhland. Amidst the student enthusiasm for archival exploration, scepticism has persisted among Aachen's citizens about an outsider's portrayal of their city's history, in a society framed by anti-militarism and war aversion. My purpose remained constant over two decades: crafting a nuanced social-cultural history of Aachen from the dual perspectives of a foreign resident and a historian. Navigating the city's complex relationship with its modern history—marked by tensions about the erasure of the past—can prove challenging. An example from one of my historical tours that addresses Aachen's total war legacy:

Wilck's surrender in Hansemannplatz, just steps away from my home, holds a poignant significance in the narrative of modern Aachen. Today, the statue of David Hansemann, prominently positioned at a bustling crossroads and flanked by bus stops, commands attention in local discourse. Yet few passers-by are aware that across the street lies the former site of Anne Frank's grandmother's home—a hidden relic of historical importance overshadowed by the bustle of daily life. Continuing the journey towards the Quellenhof hotel, a cornerstone of Aachen's history since 1900, one encounters the solemn silence of an abandoned cemetery, where a memorial stone pays homage to the Heimat 1945. A stroll through Fawick Park along Rolandstrasse serves as a poignant reminder of the fierce clashes between German and American soldiers in October 1944. Pausing at the crossroads, one can trace the haunting path of RAF bombers that ignited the city in flames during July 1943. Following the ancient battlements leads to a solemn war memorial nestled within a reconstructed turret, the city's tribute to those who perished in the Great War. Across Feldmannplatz, where tragedy befell two teenagers at the hands of a compassionless German officer, stands the former gravesite of soldiers laid to rest after the October 1944 battles. Nearby, an imposing air raid shelter stands as a testament to the city's resilience in the face of relentless bombardments. Concluding the journey at Ponttor, a medieval gatehouse seamlessly integrated into the modern urban landscape, one glimpses the housing quarters once inhabited by Belgian soldiers in 1920. This is modern Aachen—a city steeped in history, bearing the indelible scars of total war.

Total war remains awkward to define. From a study of total war in the 1970s, 'The years 1870 to 1945 were the period in which Europe feared Germany. Before that it was France, afterwards the Soviet Union. In this perspective the Second World War is the end of an era.'[3] For the authors, especially Peter Calvocoressi, who had served in Ultra intelligence, it was their total war. Richard Overy maintained that 'The Second World War was a war of extremes.' He concluded that, 'Paradoxically the effort to wage total war between 1939 and 1945 created the conditions which would make it possible to return to the tradition of war fought with limited resources by armed forces.'[4] Ian Beckett argued that total war implied a 'far wider global conflict than previous wars'.[5] After a decade of scholarly research and discourse, in 2003 Roger Chickering and Stig Förster concluded that the age of total war was over, implying it was a twentieth-century phenomenon.[6] A few years before they had questioned: 'how total was the Great War?' They recognised that 'current interest in the "Great War" had been the currency from new methodologies in historical research'.[7] From a different perspective, Hugh Bicheno warned, 'Total war is one in which the whole population and all the resources of the combatants are committed to complete victory and thus become legitimate military targets ... becomes ideological in nature at an early stage ... to increase the power of the rulers. It is thus a term to be used sparingly.'[8] In their last volume, Chickering and Förster accepted that they had not defined total war, and that it continued to defy measurement.[9]

The pervasive nature of extreme violence during periods of all-encompassing warfare expands the boundaries of violence as a political tool, implicating civilians in decision-making processes. This escalation inevitably leads to massacres, mass death and geno-

INTRODUCTION

cide. The interplay of political, military, economic and cultural dynamics exacerbates violence in total war, heightening the risk of genocide. Modern total warfare, fuelled by industrialisation, urbanisation and modernity, has thrust cities into the forefront as strategic hubs, as both vital resources and vulnerable targets for bombing and conquest, risking their wholesale destruction. The extreme violence of total war blended ideas and created memories and beliefs. Ian Garner has observed that 'the Battle of Stalingrad is widely associated with death and destruction on an unimaginable scale, for these Russians the battle still summons memories of immense sacrifice and renewed belief in utopian potential'.[10] In Aachen, the notions of sacrifice and utopia were swept away by defeat, generating a contradiction to the Stalingrad experience—but where did those ideas go? Its unlikely we will ever know. In the twenty-first century, the realities of postmodern warfare have starkly demonstrated that cities, with their dense populations, have become prime targets for devastation, irrespective of declarations of general war. The convergence of micro-technology and heightened destructive capabilities has rendered cities inevitable theatres of mass death. From Grozny to Srebrenica to Mariupol, the twenty-first century is already reshaping total war, with cities bearing the brunt of its ferocity.[11]

PART ONE

THE AGE OF TOTAL WAR

It is astonishing how little the bulk of the native [German] population know of the actual happenings in occupied French and Belgian territory. The demobilized [German] soldiers naturally are aware of what went on, but it goes without saying that they do not speak in many cases about the oppression of the French and Belgians had become so much a matter of routine that it ceased to produce any impression on the invader...

ATTITUDES OF CIVILIANS

(a) In the area occupied recently, especially near the Rhine, civilians are becoming less agreeable than formerly billeting it has been found difficult to secure rooms for officers in the better houses.
(b) A German officer made the following statement: "The German people thoroughly understand how the civilians in Belgium and France were treated and they will not afford you the excuse or opportunity to treat then likewise. You need not expect any trouble whatsoever from the German population as they realize that might is against them, and they are powerless".

TNA, Fo 608/268, Situation in Germany,
Foreign Office (Military Section), 25 January 1919.

1

METROPOLIS

The mobilisation is ordered, the Kaiser has called the people to arms. We are convinced in the justice of our cause. We have confidence in the people, and we trust in our beloved Kaiser. The war will ask for huge sacrifices, huge sacrifices in blood and finance. The people will carry the sacrifice and Aachen will preserve the fame of the old Kaiserstadt.

The resonance of Oberbürgermeister Veltmann's proclamation echoed through the streets of Aachen. On the fateful day of 31 July 1914, Kaiser Wilhelm II's voice, emanating from the grand halls of the Neues Palais in Berlin, declared Germany to be in a state of siege. With the swift decree of a 'general mobilisation' the following day, Imperial Germany was thrust into the throes of war. In the wake of this announcement, Dr Wallichs, the Rector of the esteemed Technical University, rallied the student body and faculty, invoking a sense of patriotic duty: 'We are surrounded by enemies ... trust in the strength of the Fatherland and the student volunteer.'[1] His impassioned plea extended even to underage students, urging them to join the ranks of volunteers by enlisting at recruiting centres scattered throughout the city. As the calendar turned to 4 August 1914, the streets of Aachen bore witness to the mass assembly of troops, their formation signalling the commencement of a journey westward. The fervour of local enthusiasm for the war spilled onto the thoroughfares, immortalised in a photograph that graced the pages of the *Eupen Echo*, capturing the jubilation of the moment. Waving crowds, bedecked in garlands of flowers, danced alongside the marching soldiers, their spirits lifted by the promise of patriotic duty.

Yet beneath the surface of this jubilation lay the indelible imprint of history, woven into the fabric of Aachen's collective memory. The legacy of the Franco-Prussian War of 1870–1 loomed large, its echoes reverberating through the city's streets. Battle honours such as Gebweiler, Schlettstadt and Lisaine adorned memorials, serving as tangible reminders of past conflicts.[2] Notably, on 4–5 June 1913, the *Königliches Preussiches Infanterie-Regiments von Lutzow (1.Rheinisches)* Nr.25 paraded through Aachen, commemorating the centenary of its formation. This storied regiment, born amidst the tumult of the Napoleonic Wars, had weathered numerous conflicts, from the fields of Ligny to the plains of Waterloo.[3] As Aachen stood on the precipice of war, its significance as a strategic city became increasingly apparent. Positioned at a critical juncture, with burgeoning medical facilities and industrial infrastructure, the city found itself thrust into the forefront of geopolitical manoeuvring. The advent of modernity, epitomised by the proliferation of railways and industrialisation, transformed Aachen into a bustling metropolis, primed for the challenges that lay ahead.

During the Great War, Aachen emerged as a pivotal strategic hub, owing to its advantageous geopolitical location, extensive medical infrastructure and the array of civilian resources vital to military operations. By 1905, the railway network in Aachen underwent a comprehensive modernisation and rationalisation process, part of a strategic rationalisation. These construction initiatives were in line with the Schlieffen Plan.[4] Aachen's railway network was meant to function as a strategic bridgehead for operations in the west. The stations, marshalling yards, depots and army garrisons were theoretically capable of handling increased traffic efficiently.[5] In August 1914, the reality and fantasy of mobilisation caused a logistic nightmare. At one end of the military system, the armies marched out of the city to the cheers of the crowds, but further down the lines the rail system was gridlocked. If this was

METROPOLIS

war by timetable,[6] it stalled in a massive gridlock across the entire railway network west of the Rhine.[7] Four years later, the trains again became gridlocked between Aachen and Cologne as soldiers and civilians alike fled the advance of allied armies. Rail bridges across the Rhine were clogged with non-railway traffic as long lines of troops, horse-drawn carts and motor vehicles formed an unusual convoy of refugees. During the allied occupation of the demilitarised Rhineland, the local German railways were employed to carry the reparations traffic. In December 1929, when the last Belgian occupation army departed Aachen, they rode in German trains that were never returned.[8]

Though no longer heavily militarised, the city had evolved into a bustling *Grossstadt*, a modern industrial metropolis, propelled by the progress of railways and industrialisation. This era marked a watershed moment in railway history, witnessing their widespread utilisation as indispensable logistical arteries supporting global warfare efforts. From mobilisation to troop deployment, railways played a vital role, facilitating the transportation of troops, supplies and casualties with unparalleled efficiency, effectively sustaining the relentless demands of warfare. Furthermore, they served as conduits for returning soldiers, prisoners of war and war reparations, while also facilitating the clean-up efforts in the aftermath of total destruction post-1918. Amidst this broader historical narrative, the Great War catalysed the empowerment of railways and industry, reshaping societies and bolstering the march towards democracy. However, for Aachén and its borderlands, the conflict proved devastating.[9] Local folklore from the *Dreiländereck* (three borders region) recounts tales of Aachen's railways being repurposed to meet the military demands of the Schlieffen Plan, highlighting the transformation of German railways from symbols of conservative-liberalism to instruments of imperialist warfare. Other narratives recount the harsh realities faced by civilians, including allegations of German military atrocities during the march towards Liège, juxtaposed with myths portraying the German occupation of the Low Countries as benign and devoid of geopolitical ambitions. This chapter delves into the multifaceted impact of the Great War on Aachen, exploring its ramifications on society, infrastructure and historical memory.

I. 1914: the Battle of Liège

German literature immediately historicised the opening phase of the war, which was continually revised and embellished. By 1918, Germany had propagandised and embellished the myths and legends of the first battles. The Imperial German Army planned to invade Belgium, in an act of aggressive war and violating Belgian neutrality. The army leaders had tried to circumvent the neutrality before the war. During a royal visit by the Belgian king, in November 1913, the Germans requested that, in the event of war, German armies would be granted the right of free passage through Belgium.[10] Holger Afflerbach also noted that the French high command had requested the right to violate Belgian neutrality on 9 January 1912.[11] Both requests were denied. Meanwhile, the German high command took the strategic decision to capture Liège in a *coup de main*. Annika Mombauer argued the Liège decision was the difference between Moltke's plan and the Schlieffen Plan, placing a massive concentration of over 600,000 troops in the narrow Aachen corridor.[12] Afflerbach noted that Liège became the key strategic position under Moltke's plan.[13] Alexander Watson observed, 'The first combat operation then began early on 4 August, when after an ultimatum demanding free passage an assault force of 39,000 men crossed into Belgium, violating the Kingdom's neutrality, and marched towards the fortified city of Liège.'[14] The German high command's decisions had a profound impact on Aachen and the *Dreiländereck*.

Following the outbreak of war, the German Second Army was tasked with rapidly capturing Liège (Lüttich in German) in a *coup de main*. The Second Army formed the Xth Corps, also known as the *Maas-Armee* (Meuse Army), under the command of General Otto von Emmich (1848–1915). The Quartermaster-General, Major-General Erich Ludendorff, was assigned to the staff of X Corps to ensure the success of the mission. The *Maas-Armee* was assigned three cavalry divisions (9th, 4th, 2nd) and six infantry brigades

(11th, 14th, 27th, 34th, 38th, 43rd), each with two infantry regiments, a total force of 60,000 troops with more than 100 artillery and siege guns. The brigades were concentrated in the Aachen-Eupen area start lines covering a thirty-mile front from Aachen to Malmedy. The march direction was towards Verviers, Spa and Visé. On 4 August, *Maas-Armee* crossed the Belgian frontier. The 34th Infantry Brigade marched due west from Aachen via Gemmenich, Warsage to Visé. The 27th Infantry Brigade followed the road to Kelmis but then broke off to drive west through Plombières, Hombourg and on towards Herstal. The 14th Infantry Brigade, commanded by Major General von Wussow, set out from Aachen marching through Kelmis (the state of Neu-Morsenet) then through Henri-Chapelle and Clermont on towards Battice and Herve to attack the fort at Fléron. On the left flank, the 14th Infantry Brigade had set out from Eupen to attack the fort at Chaudfontaine.[15] The *Königliches Preussisches Infanterie-Regiments von Lutzow (1.Rheinisches) Nr.25* marched with the 29th Infantry Brigade (First Army) on the farthest flank of the right wing of the invasion.

The brigades of the *Maas-Armee* followed the routes along railway lines and tramways, including part of Aachen's transport network. The Catholic grammar school encouraged the pupils to join the cheering crowds as the army marched along Lütticherstrasse towards Belgium. Local myths refer to school pupils scouting the route for the army, which was unfamiliar with the terrain. They also helped bring up supplies and rations to the front. The demographics of the army's order of battle might explain why this was necessary. The four regiments of the 34th Infantry Brigade came from Alsace-Lorraine, Schleswig-Holstein, Mecklenburg and Hannover. The three regiments of the 27th Brigade, all reservists, were from Westphalia. The three regiments of the 14th Brigade originated in Hannover and Magdeburg.[16] Consequently, imbued with fears of the *Franc Tireur*, the advancing German soldiers had little sympathy for the Belgians. In the first weeks, there were massacres of Belgian and French civilians on the spurious grounds of combatting the *Franc Tireur*. The fantasies of 1870 were not being replayed in 1914, but Germans maintained the claim for decades after the war.[17] Bitter street fighting or shootings erupted in frontier towns like Welkenraedt or Herstal. A vicious cycle ensued as trigger-happy young German soldiers injured comrades, which led to more German reprisals against the Belgians. In August 1914, a group of American war correspondents came to Aachen under German army supervision to test the veracity of allied claims of atrocities. The reporters came from the Associated Press and the *Chicago Daily News*, but the German army censored the reports before they were released. There were counterclaims of German soldiers brutalised by Belgians lying in Aachen's hospitals, but these were unsubstantiated. On 8 August, an Aachen civil court sentenced four Belgians to death for shooting German soldiers.[18]

Liège finally surrendered on 16 August, but the atrocities continued. Aachen's Belgian neighbours were embittered by the betrayal and slaughter of more than 360 civilians.[19] Belgians from the Dreiländereck have not forgotten the atrocities and the lists of dead are recorded on war memorials as in Welkenraedt.[20] During the centenary of the Great War many communities in the border regions hosted fascinating exhibitions of their local histories. In *Liège Expo 14–18*, held at the main railway station, an exhibition took an anti-war stance but depicted the atrocities in 1914, and brutal scenes form the German occupation.

Belief that there was enthusiasm for war in 1914 was exaggerated that later became a myth of the war. The reality was less clear-cut; perhaps a more realistic opinion would argue that support was sporadic.[21] The city's Roman Catholic grammar school was founded by the Jesuit Order (1601) and became the *Kaiser-Karls Gymnasium* (KKG) in 1886. The school record indicates the pupils and teachers were encouraged to serve in the army. School Director Scheins pushed 'patriotic enthusiasm' and in February 1915 defined the war as both legal and ethical: 'Germany had to counter English envy, the French quest for revenge for 1870, and Russia's greed for German lands.' The national curriculum was accelerated to advance the *Arbitur* (A levels) to release students into the recruitment system. The September 1914 examination board recorded thirty-four pupils already in army uniform. By February 1915, fifty-nine senior pupils had enlisted, leaving behind eight seniors. Eleven teachers had enlisted by 1915: two had been killed and one seriously wounded. Dr Karl Pschmadt was enlisted on 8 October 1914 into *Ersaztbataillon des 25 Infanterie Regiment*. He received basic training in Aachen and in November transferred to France. He suffered 'trench foot' but once recovered was transferred to the 65th Infantry Regiment. On 16 December, Pschmadt returned to the 25th Infantry in time for the Christmas battles defending against the French offensive. He was promoted to corporal. He tried to assist a wounded comrade but was killed from being shot in the neck. His family were informed with the comfort of being advised that he was 'a reliable and patriotic soldier'.[22]

Not all pupils were overcome by war enthusiasm. Peter Wamich, born on 21 April 1895 in Aachen, was the third child of a wine merchant. He attended the KKG from 1905 until Easter 1914, when he took the *Arbitur*. His class composed of thirty-two pupils with a curriculum of Greek and Latin. His school attendance was spotless, and his teachers assessed him as 'industrious'—an intense and diligent student. He was required to repeat a year, which was not uncommon before the war. Wamich selected a written examination in German, Ancient Greek, Mathematics and Latin, and an oral examination in Religion. He was graded 3.0, regarded as low today and was required to re-sit History—a re-sit was not frowned on. He elected the priesthood alongside ten of his classmates. The other pupils became teachers, doctors and lawyers. Wamich read Catholic Theology at Bonn University. In June 1915, he was called up for a one-year enlistment and posted to the *16.Reserve-Division des Reserve-Infanterie Regiments Nr.68*. Neither his religious calling nor his faith allowed him to avoid military service and he completed his training in Koblenz. Letters and family correspondence revealed a reluctant soldier. On 14 June 1915, he wrote about being prepared to do his duty but preferred to avoid the war. He was posted to the front on 28 August and arrived in Epernay (France) on 5 September 1915. He wrote to his parents describing a nearby village as a pile of rubble, that he was sleeping in a cot with straw in a dilapidated barracks and had dug trenches for three continuous nights. On 23 September 1915, he was killed in a grenade attack. On 5 October 1914, Wamich's commanding officer, Oberleutnant Flaskamp, wrote to his parents about his 'heroic death' and explained that he was buried where he was killed. In their grief, his parents held a memorial service and issued a death notice with his picture in the local newspaper.[23]

II. 1915–17: hard war

The war escalated into a bitter struggle of national survival. Aachen made a powerful contribution to Germany's form of hard war as the nation became gripped with paranoia about security. The Aachen municipal authorities made a formal request to the army for the removal of all Belgians from within the city limits.[24] German atrocities continued into 1915. Diana Preston has mapped six weeks in 1915 when the Germans employed gas warfare, introduced unrestricted submarine warfare and began bombing British cities. The complexion of war had changed, with gas warfare on the Western Front and Zeppelin airship raids on London in the first blitz that started on 8 September 1915.[25] By November 1918, the British public mood was bitterly hostile towards Germans, not just because of the events in 1915 but due to the trail of atrocities that began within days of the outbreak of war.[26] In 1914, the *Königliches Preussiches Infanterie-Regiments von Lutzow (1.Rheinisches) Nr.25*, departed from the *Gelbe Kaserne* in Aachen. The first major action was in the Battle of Neufchâteau on 22–3 August. The regiment was redeployed to the Vosges region of Alsace-Lorraine and quickly became sucked into the carnage of the Hartmannsweilerkopf Campaign that raged between January and April 1915. The regiment suffered eight officers and 306 ORs killed, and many more unknown wounded—this represented approximately 10 per cent of its total losses for the entire war.[27] Later the regiment served on the eastern front in 1916–17 and was disbanded in 1919.

In order to prevent frontier violations, the German army constructed an electrified fence along the Belgium-Holland border in 1915. The troubles had continued since the atrocities in 1914 and many Belgian civilians fled to Holland. Some joined the Belgian army, some smuggled black-market goods and others were outlaws from the German military police. The work on the electrified fence began in the spring: 180 kilometres long, from nearby Vaals

(Holland) close to Aachen and on to Bruges. Three fences ran in parallel: the electrified fence with a regular current of 2,000 volts, running between two normal barbed-wire fences. Interspersed along the fence were signals wires, searchlights and transformer points to maintain a constant current. The fence was completed by the autumn, paid for and built with Belgian money and labour. The fence killed about 3,000 people and many more were injured. The would-be evaders adopted ingenious means to traverse the fence: pole-vaulting, rolling through the fence in a barrel or levering a wooden jack to create an insulated gap in the wire.[28] Walking the fence route with local historian Dr Herbert Ruhland, in 2000, he explained how memories of the fence continued into the 1960s but receded until 'rediscovered' in the 1990s.[29]

In 1914, the results of a business survey taken of nine hundred German industrialists identified deep concerns over serious shortfalls in raw materials for industry. The results suggested the supply of raw materials and Germany's strategic reserves would only last six months of war. The illusion of military superiority and the blind faith in planned rapid victory (Schlieffen Plan) were not supported by realistic wartime planning or stockpiling strategic reserves of raw materials.[30] In August, the *Kriegsrohstoffabteilung* (KRA), Raw Materials Section, was established within the War Ministry, to resolve the problem.[31] Twenty-eight months later, Germany entered 1917 determined to see the war to its bitter end. The Hindenburg-Ludendordff military dictatorship had 'remobilised' the army and the state. The allied blockade and the wasting effects of frontline stalemate forced critical shortages in raw materials and food supplies.[32] The standard of living in homes across Germany deteriorated rapidly. The food shortage affected soldiers and civilians alike. The deprivations and alternative rationing measures came to be bitterly referred to as the 'hunger winter' or 'turnip winter'.[33] Industrial firms had to compete with municipalities for food for their workers, and both went to the black market.[34] Inflated prices, shortages and discord between town and country were symptoms of the larger problem—the state. As Roger Chickering summed up, 'The state was the public arbiter of hunger. It was also the symbol of the problem'.[35] In their hour of need, the Aacheners tuned once again to smuggling and the black market.

Aachen's war began with high hopes of victory but soured with hardship, graft, corruption and disappointment. The textiles, weaving and cloth industries were initially producing uniforms, but military orders shrank by 75 per cent. The collective memory, after 1916, was the fixation with hunger and supplementing rations.[36] On 11 January 1917, rationing was extended to potato shortages with the ration reduced to 1,500 grammes per week and the balance from turnips. Concern grew over the fall in calorie intake. In 1916, the daily count was 1,344 calories, with 130 grammes of protein made from egg whites. In spring 1917, the count was reduced to 1,100 calories and 30 grammes of protein. The normal level was set at 2,569 calories per day. The authorities were growing concerned at the rising infant mortality rates in the ages of 6–15, which had risen by 55 per cent in 1917, and later the ministry attributed 763,000 deaths to the Royal Navy's blockade. On 10 July 1917, the state ordered a ration of eleven pounds in weight of potatoes weekly.

The day before the *Eupen Echo* had told its readers to run to the forest to collect berries and leaves. Soon there were hundreds of berry collectors and some local authorities had to ban collecting to save the trees. The Sparkasse Bank opened a stall selling iron for gold in the city centre. The initiative also appealed to women for their jewellery. In return for giving up their gold, customers received a certificate—'I gave gold for iron'—and an iron coin. A socialist leader from Aachen observed the deterioration at the front and recorded in his diary:

> 1 August 1918, the mood of the troops is heated, with tensions everywhere. The troops stand together in groups discussing politics. There is no fighting spirit, it's gone and their strength is broken.
>
> 8 September 1918, the socialists at the front lose their reluctance to promote politics and distribute *Vorwarts* in the trenches. Officers lack the courage to stop their morale from decaying. The subordinate officers and enlisted men are working together and support

each other, waiting for something to happen while pulling at their chains. Only a few weeks before the men were loyal to the Kaiser but now they behave like wild people and have to be restrained.[37]

The first air raid on Aachen came on 19 May 1918, and another followed on 1 November when the aircraft flew over the *Ostfriedhof* (the city's east cemetery). People panicked and children were dragged away screaming. On 4 November, there was an air raid on Herbestal, and seven bombs were dropped on a field. Two women and a man were killed in neighbouring Welkenraedt. To better hear approaching aircraft, the priesthood stopped ringing the church bells. As the war came to an end there was a bitter realisation of the odious position of the Aacheners standing vis-à-vis their neighbours: Belgium, Holland, France and Luxembourg. Many long-standing ties had been cut, fuelled by Aachen's arrogance of victory. The war cost Aachen heavily and in 1921 the working population had reduced to 44,779. The regional micro-economy was utterly devastated, and the armistice-imposed restrictions. The collapse of the German Army, in 1918, was a crisis that almost overwhelmed Aachen. The violent impact of the war was disastrous for the city, with military fatalities estimated at 3,500, but the figure is not accurate and there are doubts about casualty levels. To compound the effects of the war, economy and casualties from 1 October to 26 October 1918, the Great Influenza epidemic killed 285 people. The city closed the schools, and the gas works was placed on short time due to staff absences.[38] The German medical association recorded the first outbreak of the *grippe* (flu) the year before, in October 1917. Prior to the flu epidemic, the medical authorities were mostly concerned with the alarming rise in sexually transmitted diseases, syphilis and gonorrhoea, and the continuing battle against tuberculosis (TB).[39]

III. Aachen's Anglo-German relations

The German invasion of Belgium led Britain to declare war. The Anglo-German conflict sparked a bitter propaganda war with the rhetoric of hatred from both sides. Arthur Marwick has argued that the war became 'the ultimate expression of the German challenge to British supremacy', while the German atrocities stirred an acute and profound national revulsion in Britain.[40] Typical of the animosity that arose between Britain and Germany was the case of Edith Cavell (1865–1915), arrested by the German security services in Belgium and charged with espionage. She was imprisoned in a civilian internment camp in Aachen. Every day, she travelled by train to Brussels for her trial before a military court and was escorted by an Aachen *Landsturm* detachment. Cavell was found guilty and sentenced to death by firing squad. Cavell's trial and execution was witnessed by Captain Dr Gottfried Benn, the chief medical officer of the German military government in Brussels. In 1930, he wrote about Cavell's execution and described her as the 'daughter of a great nation'.[41]

Remarkably, against the carnage of war and the bitter rhetoric of propaganda, Britain and Germany orchestrated acts of human kindness. In particular the PoW exchanges, the repatriation of soldiers on medical grounds—the severely wounded, the sick or disabled soldiers. Prisoner exchanges, paroles and repatriation of wounded was not new to war and had been routinely practised in the early years of the American Civil War. Britain and Germany negotiated many prisoner exchanges. The mechanics involved long, drawn-out diplomatic negotiations, filed in extensive collections of archived Foreign Office records. The system, from the British side, was administered at a ministerial level, and Foreign Minister Sir Edward Grey was responsible for the policy. The exchanges were managed through diplomatic negotiations between Britain, Germany and the neutral countries of the USA, the Netherlands and Switzerland (through the Red Cross). Aachen, because of its frontier location, was selected as an exchange station for PoWs and civilian internees to be handed over to neutral Dutch representatives. The city was inundated with hospitals, field hospitals and at least five prisoner camps in the vicinity. As a consequence, the German Army doctors could conduct final examinations before release. Holland became the exchange country, with ships sailing from London to Rotterdam and trains travelling to and from Aachen, crossing the border at Maastricht, and arriving in Vlissingen (aka Flushing) for embarkation.

The system of exchanges involved indirect communication between the belligerents; all correspondence was passed via neutral agencies, which was then translated, interpreted and officially presented to the other side. Unfortunately, the system was also dependent upon good faith and trust, not only between the belligerents, but also with the neutrals, which was not always forthcoming. Suspicion of the 'other' trying to encourage escapes or unequal numbers in exchange led to long delays because of internal ministerial discussions and the passing of further diplomatic correspondence for confirmations at the last moment. The system was also prone to local interference from medical officials or army officers who seemingly intervened to stop soldiers being exchanged—this happened in May 1916. In January and April 1916, the War Office had sent lists of British PoWs in Germany regarded as suitable for repatriation.[42]

On 19 May 1916, the German foreign ministry in Berlin passed a note to the American Embassy confirming a verbal agreement for the exchange of 100 severely wounded British soldiers.[43] The next day, the US Embassy in Berlin communicated the details of the note to the US Embassy in London; both notes were passed to the FO. On 25 May 1916, the train with the British PoWs arrived in Aachen but the Germans removed three officers. Ernest von Loon, the representative of the Dutch Red Cross, was annoyed by their removal but travelled with the rest through Holland. On arrival, he informed the British that one officer was a colonel and had requested release to travel to Brussels to meet his wife. The hospital ship (HMHS) SS *St Denis* released ten German officers in the exchange and confirmed taking on board 100 soldiers and 3 officers 'suffering from mental complaints'. The legation in Holland, however, confirmed it was to receive 93 British soldiers but no officers. They then confirmed that 96 had arrived in Flushing. On 26 May 1916, the FO received official notice from the Royal Navy that 95 British soldiers had embarked on the HMHS *St Denis*.[44] They were also informed that several NCOs and the officers were detained in Aachen because the Germans believed they were capable of military training.[45] Sir Edward Grey, probably in exasperation at the different estimates, sent an official request to the US Ambassador for clarification from Berlin and for the 'real reason for the detention of officers and Non-Commissioned officers'.⁴⁶ The case files ended without any written explanation.

The correspondence briefly took a strange path. The British diplomat in Holland was Ernest G.B. Maxse (1863–1943), based in Rotterdam, and he wrote to Sir Rumbold in London.⁴⁷ The FO official was less than convinced by Ernest van Loon's integrity. Regarding a complaint about the Dutch Red Cross, the official denied hearing any, but claimed: 'The person who is dissatisfied is that snob E. van Loon, who has, to the great disgust of the FO, obtained a decoration from the German Emperor, and who actually had the cheek to delegate a friend of his to come to me and ask in his name if I could not procure a British decoration for him'. The FO refused Loon the permission to wear his German medal. The official had subsequently written to Loon: 'we highly appreciate his good works, and that the consciousness of them would have to be his principal reward'.⁴⁸ Maxse was a gossip and in subsequent letters claimed the German soldiers and medical orderlies on the train were all fed up with the war and wanted it over. In a private letter from October 1916, he referred to a claim by a friend, whose cousin was married to a German general, that the Kaiser and the General Staff knew the war was over and were trying to inform the public with unsettling the dynasty or ruling elite. In his subsequent reports about conditions in Germany, he referred to Austria being close to financial collapse, the growing sense of war weariness, distress about air raids and compulsory conscriptions to war loans.⁴⁹

A second group of prisoners were repatriated through Aachen. On 19 June 1916, the FO received a list of the prisoners to be repatriated in agreement with the Germans. Of all the men repatriated, two had been hospitalised in Aachen. In the Marien Hospital, Lieutenant J.F.C. Raikes (1st Monmouthshire Regiment) was listed as 'seriously wounded in the head'. Drummer R.J. Hookway (4th Grenadier Guards) was in another Aachen hospital with a 'wounded right leg, left thigh and pelvis'. The rest were located in hospitals, specialist clinics or field stations across Germany— Berlin, Munich, Rostok and places in the east. They had suffered a number of injuries, from broken or fractured limbs to the loss of limbs and eyes. There were also more serious wounds, including shot in the liver, bullet wounds to the abdomen, double amputations, loss of both eyes, prolapse of the large intestine, total loss of the lower jaw, loss to the entire side of the face and frost bite. In addition to the physical wounds, many were also suffering from diseases, including tuberculosis, consumption, bronchitis, angina, Bright's disease and nephritis. One poor soldier was simply diagnosed 'insane', while another was described as suffering '*paramoia erisypele*, mental disease, lunacy'. Their regiments represented a cross section of British servicemen, with guardsmen, light infantry, riflemen, engineers, Highlanders, Irish, Canadians, Welsh, the home counties, Yorkshire, Lancashire, an officer serving with the Royal Flying Corps and a seaman from the Royal Naval Division.[50] The list of soldiers and their injuries are a reminder of the deep suffering that lies behind that glib term 'wounded-in-action'.

On 28 July 1916, the Government Committee on the Treatment by the Enemy of British Prisoners of War wrote to the War Office, in which the fate of the British soldiers had become a major concern. Dame Adelaide Livingstone (1881–1970) was an American who arrived in England in 1914 and set about working to repatriate British civilians in German captivity. Livingstone was appointed to the committee by the British government, and in that capacity, she had written to the FO. She had observed that, over a period of eighteen months, a number of officers and men identified for repatriation had been given a final examination in Aachen by a board of German medical officers. Livingstone had learned 'privately' that the men held back had been previously rejected by the Swiss Red Cross as too ill for internment in a neutral country. In her opinion:

> It must be recognised that to return prisoners of war to their places of confinement in Germany, after they have got so far on their journey as Aachen, and so crush suddenly the hopes of seeing the termination of their captivity, is heart breaking to the individuals overtaken by this misfortune, and tends to induce deep depression and discouragement even in men whose spirit has borne up against the trials of lengthy imprisonment.

Livingstone proposed that all soldiers rejected by the Aachen medical board should be automatically sent to Switzerland.[51] On 31 July,

Horace Rumbold wrote on the FO file cover: 'The suggestion seems an excellent one. It is monstrous that the unfortunate officers and men rejected at Aix [Aachen] should fall between 2 stools.' Another scrawled that, 'this is a most inhuman proceeding on the part of the Germans' and suggested placing the case before the press. British civilians were also interned in Germany, and became subject to repatriation. In June 1915, the brother of a prisoner wrote to the Sir Edward Grey to gain his release. Francis Badham, a sickly 56 year-old, and resident in Aachen, was deported to Ruhleben civilian internment camp. He had returned to Aachen but there was no news of him. The FO wrote to the US Embassy to receive clarification regarding the case and whether the Germans would release him.[52] The final outcome of the case was not recorded.

IV. 1919–29: hard peace

On 9 November 1918, Kaiser Wilhelm abdicated, bringing about the end of hostilities, and Germany descended into chaos. The city's fathers reacted quickly, fearful that the city lay in the path of a number of withdrawing front armies. The German army, for so long the symbol of law and order, had fallen under suspicion, with a breakdown of discipline. The question on everyone's mind was how the troops would behave during the retreat. Concern over the mounting chaos led the city assembly to raise a Soldiers and Workers Council (SWC) on 9 November 1918. This was formed by soldiers garrisoned in the city and industrial workers, and was commanded by *Oberbürgermeister* Fawick, police president von Hammacher (1858–1936) and officials from the Aachen Chamber of Commerce (hereafter IHK). The SWC issued a declaration on 11 November that warned the community about the hardships to come and the need for heightened security measures. Fawick declared martial law on 11 November 1918, applying a regulation from the Prussian state code (1854). The SWC organised vehicles, guns, rations, armbands and even the ubiquitous paraphernalia of German bureaucracy—rubber stamps and identity cards. Routines were introduced for rationing, street patrols and investigations of disturbances of the peace. The troops in the garrisons, mostly local formations, were placed on standby.[53]

The atmosphere was dense with looming catastrophe. The German army began to disintegrate almost as soon as the armistice was agreed. The pandemonium began as German deserters flocked to the plethora of narrow-gauge military trains and tramways to escape. The 4th Army, under the command of General Sixt von Arnim, formed an orderly march through Aachen. Von Arnim held a short parade before the *Elisenbrunnen*. The streets were draped with the old black-red-white imperial flags. The masses were euphoric, garlanding the soldiers with flowers and offers of wine, but there were tensions and fears for the future. The army marched through Lütticherstrasse and Krefelderstrasse, the same roads taken by Napoleon's armies, and they were chock-a-block with endless columns of over 500,000 men and 100,000 horses. Elsewhere, the numbers of troops continued to swell in the city; many were wounded, desperately waving useless travel permits. Hundreds of wounded were taken off trains and left on stretchers as the weather deteriorated. Carl Delius, a textile manufacturer and IHK board member, opened up his empty factory floors to the wounded and issued rations. The numbers of soldiers overwhelmed the officials' ability to process their demands for immediate demobilisation. Among the soldiers were thousands of German civilians, refugees from Belgian retribution. The army's suspicions about the sailors' revolt in Hamburg sparked an incident on the military training grounds, and a naval field battery was disarmed. The panic levels were fuelled by the expected arrival of the allied armies. The army corps' garrisons were ordered to leave, adding more panic among the populace. Soldiers lost all discipline and committed petty crimes—stealing food, money and train permits. Two soldiers donned French uniforms to rob the city's main bookstore.

Fears mounted about foreign occupation and revolution. On 18 November (nine days after the abdication and a week since the armistice), Fawick wrote to State Secretary Erzberger in Berlin to inform him that in eight days the city would fall under Belgian military control. He was concerned with the threat of Bolshevik revolution since the Germans were disarmed. Hammacher, Aachen police president, wrote to Erzberger two days later warning of riots, plundering and the threat of Bolshevism. The last German troops departed on 27 November, largely to avoid becoming PoWs under the Belgians. The Belgians arrived the next day; they honoured mounted British troops that rode through the city on 1 December, and the French army on 11 December. The Belgian Army held a full victory parade on the Katzschof, the square before the cathedral on 1 December. The scene is immortalised in a painting displayed in the Royal Army Museum in Brussels. The Belgians billeted troops on the homes of well-off Aacheners and seized other properties. Aacheners were warned they would finance and serve the occupation. The Belgian commander established his headquarters in the *Alte Kurhaus* (the casino today) by the Hotel Quellenhof, with a suite of rooms in the fashionable Heinrichsallee. In 1920, the city was forced to build tenement housing, and by 1922 the Belgians had acquired 54 houses and 4,060 rooms.[54] The Belgians imposed routine army patrols and the mounted gendarmerie carried out police duties. Aacheners were made to step off the pavement and doff their hats to Belgian soldiers. There were acts of kindness. Belgian soldiers were largely friendly towards the locals, but the curfew reduced fraternisation. French soldiers distributed bread to German children in Eupen, for many the first decent food since the allied blockade.

News eventually filtered into Aachen about the demands of the Treaty of Versailles. The entire frontier section, including Eupen, Malmedy and parts of Monschau—59,945 or 8.7 per cent of the regional population—was mandated to Belgium. There were sporadic protests, with public readings of the treaty terms. Church congregations turned into protests for secret plebiscites. At 10.30 on 14 April 1920, a general strike was called in Eupen. It began with leaders of the Christian trade unions but gradually the larger population had joined the protest. Richard Pontzen, the leader, was arrested and tried. He was found not guilty, but the Belgian authorities kept him in prison. On 17 April 1920, there was a larger protest march through Aachen. Many protesters were aggrieved at losing access to the Aachen–Monschau railway. There were local negotiation and compromise. Fawick was able to retain control of the Lichtenbusch district even against a determined Belgian attempt at annexation. A new border was drawn on 1 November 1921. This effectively ended the 'old' Aachen regional community that had formed under the Holy Roman Empire.

The city received some relief once the allied naval blockade was lifted on 12 July 1919, but shortages continued. Cardinal Schulter called for help and the Dutch raised four truckloads of food—two for Aachen and two for Cologne. However, rising prices, inflation, unemployment and border controls encouraged extensive smuggling. According to the IHK's 1922 annual accounting, the city was a *Grossstadt* of 153,000 people. The unemployment figure had reached 20 per cent but in 1929 the Great Crash brought extensive closures in textiles and weaving, causing further pressure on employment. The devastation of weaving was so severe that the Weaver's Association closed in 1932. In a desperate attempt to stem the decline, the city opened labour camps with the basic right of food for work. Smuggling escalated into strategic proportions, with 1932 being marked as a high point. The smugglers worked in teams of more than a hundred men, using armoured vehicles and engaging in frontier battles. In 1931, a fire fight led to fifteen smugglers and an official being killed and more than a hundred injured on both sides. There were 5,000 trials with widespread confiscation contraband, including 1,452,000 cigarettes, 14,000 kilos of coffee and 1,743 kilos of tobacco.[55]

Relations between the Germans and Belgians broke down on 22 March 1922 in Hambon (Duisburg). Belgian Lieutenant Joseph Graff was on a tram when an assassin approached. He was shot at point blank and killed instantly. Graff was born in Bressoux (Liège), the son of a Lieutenant General of the Belgian army.[56] A strict curfew was imposed in Aachen from 10.00 to 16.00, which was enforced until May 1922. In Düsseldorf, a French army officer was stabbed to death; a soldier and a sergeant were badly beaten in the same incident. On 29 April 1922, the allied occupation of the Rhineland introduced martial law. Smuggling, among Aacheners, is sometimes treated light-heartedly as a local lifestyle, but it had a darker side. On 22 April 1923, Johann Greber, a German customs official, was found shot dead in Aachen state forest. The murder investigation was handicapped by the developing political crisis. The German police displayed notices for information, but the curfew stifled the investigation. The Belgian administration began to remove senior police officers and expelled officials from the city under martial law. A court martial sentenced Oberbürgermeister Fawick to a month in prison, with a fine of a million Reichsmarks, and to be expelled from the city. Belgian gendarmes raided police offices and precincts. The central customs house by the main railway station was occupied and the frontier officials expelled from the city. The murder of Johann Greber was never solved.[57]

Two political factions emerged in the chaos that offered a choice of Rheinish Republicanism. The first was a proposal to create a Rheinish-Westfalisch Republik, a region of twelve million people with the ambition to operate like Bavaria but remain within the German federal state. On 6 November 1918, over 5,000 people gathered in Cologne to hear speeches and proclamations that harked back to a time before 1815. Berlin accused the separatists of being traitors. The movement never really advanced, probably because the supreme allied occupation headquarters saw no benefits for the allies. A second group was the Rheinish separatist movement that gained some traction from the Belgian and French authorities. On 5 August 1923, in Düsseldorf, the separatists announced their goals of free Rhineland with independence guaranteed by the League of Nations. Belief in the prospect for success, the Belgian authorities began arresting political representatives (refer to Fawick, noted previously) identified as potential obstacles. On 21 October 1923, Leo Deckers proclaimed the Rheinish Republic and attempted to seize Aachen town hall. A crowd of locals, trade unionists and civil servants were angrily opposed to the proclamation. Fighting started when the separatists fired shots into the crowd, starting the short-lived battle of the Rathaus. The uniformed and armed Schutzpolizei stormed the Rathaus, forcing the separatists to flee to the rooftops. They were disarmed and five were beaten, but the police were forced to protect them from being lynched by the crowd. The Belgians, having encouraged the movement, stood back once the fighting erupted.[58] Later, Konrad Adenauer, the future chancellor of West Germany, explained why he had briefly advocated the *Rheinish-Westfalisch Republik* as a viable option in the 1920s. He disowned his support by claiming a separatist buffer state between Germany and France was destined to fail. The Belgian military occupation ended in November 1929 and all ideas of separatism disappeared until 1946.[59]

2

LETTING GO OF DEMOCRACY

There is a photograph of a motley crew of Nazis marching through Aachen. They had crossed the old girder bridge that spanned the platforms of the main railway station and were marching along Burtscheider Strasse towards Kasinostrasse. While their banners were prominently displayed, they appeared to be wearing civilian clothing, possibly dating the picture to March 1931, when the Prussian state imposed a ban on wearing Brownshirt uniforms. In the faded black-and-white photograph, they looked no different from any other group. In 1930, President Hindenburg made an official visit to Aachen and he was treated like a monarch. Romantically, the old city pretended to identify with monarchy, but post-war politics had shifted the balance of power towards the working class. The German working class had been the beneficiaries of Weimar democracy, which was teetering by 1933. In 1931 or 1932, the Aachen Nazi Party had perhaps 1,100 fully paid-up members. A year later, a local newspaper, *Echo der Gegenwort*, headlined '*Hitler Reichskanzler*', and a few weeks afterwards reported '*Der Reichstag in Flammen*' (Reichstag fire). On 25 June 1933, the *Grenzecho* from Eupen, the German-Belgian newspaper, headlined '*Auf der Flucht erschossen*' (a suspect shot while running away)—that Nazi euphemism for all political and racial murders. Arthur May, a known Communist and editor of *Aachener Arbeiterer*

Zeitung, was arrested and harshly treated. He was murdered while under police custody transporting him to Jülich on the night of 21–2 June 1933.[1]

How the Nazis assuaged Aachen's reluctance towards Nazism and persuaded the citizens to conform to the concept of the *Volksgemeinschaft* has no straightforward explanation. The citizens had denied the Nazis or Hitler an electoral mandate. Local histories have struggled with this conundrum. In 1958, Bernhard Poll's *Geschichte Aachens in Daten* served as a chronicle of the city's timeline dating back to antiquity. Poll, as a director of the city's archive, between 1948 and 1966, restored the remnants of the records seriously damaged by the war and pillaged during the occupation. In many ways this was a remarkable achievement, but in keeping with local histories, if there is no record then it never happened. Poll recorded the July 1932 Reichstag election in which Aachen had 113,705 eligible voters—94,207 voted (82.9 per cent), the Centre Party received 39,908 (42.6 per cent) and the Nazis received 16,973 votes (18.1 per cent). Poll's only comment was that the election had placed 18 parties in the Reichstag. Poll's record for 23 June 1933 referred to the ban imposed on the SPD, but not the shooting of Arthur May. Poll referred to the smuggling and the condition of the state theatre. He itemised church and religious events including seminars, grand missions of pastors and the passing of elderly clergy. In November 1932, the Minister of Finance opened an exhibition about air-raid defence held in the *Kaiserhof*. He mentioned a new institute at the Technical University, but also added that the student body had recovered, with 1,500 students after so many had been killed in the Great War. The question of unemployment was disrupting city institutions, with 10–15,000 persons claiming welfare assistance or hardship allowances.[2] Poll did not comment on how welfare might be distorting Aachen's politics.

Fifty years later, Holger Dux published a photographic collection that set a less formal tone than Poll. His page of photographs for 1932 included a street parade of local companies and their latest products. The local economy and companies were still struggling against the ramifications of the Great Crash. Dux identified

LETTING GO OF DEMOCRACY

smuggling, as almost an Aachen vocation, and the most prolific social crime in 1932. A hundred-strong band of smugglers were using motorcycles and armoured vehicles to smuggle contraband to the black market. The smuggling had turned into social banditry, with 5,066 arrests, and sixteen persons were killed in serious acts of violence. He mentioned the Reichstag election in March and the Nazi failure to convince the citizens. In public events, the Eighth International Horse Tournament saw *Oberleutnant* Momm on *Baccarat* win the *Kampf der Nationen* prize.[3] For Dux, the smuggling was a significant signpost of society, but social crime can have many interpretations—the romance of social banditry or evidence of a serious social-political issue. Michael Römling's survey of Aachen history skipped through the Nazi period. He judged smuggling to be at its height in 1930 and the city had created construction schemes to alleviate the pressure of unemployment. Römling also referred to the corruption of the local Nazis and mentioned that fanatical Nazi students in the university spat at and assaulted Jewish academics and students.[4]

Aachen masks its political mysteries, as the results from Hitler's referendum of 19 August 1934 illustrate. Poll identified a total of 113,706 eligible voters—one more than in 1932. A total of 107,860 (94.9 per cent) voted and the Nazis received 74,756 (71.7 per cent)—with abstentions there were almost 40,000 persons who had not voted for Hitler. Even the 71.7 per cent approval was well below the national average of 89.93 per cent, and these two indicators point to a continuing reluctance, with upwards of 25 per cent of citizens opposed to the Nazis. There was a consensus for Hitler, but also a significant segment were prepared to defy the Nazi intimidation at the ballot box. For many of Poll's readers, the elections were part of their memories, albeit a representative of the city's bureaucratic elite. Dux presents a study in nostalgia, a classless record with romantic overtones. Römling's conservatism is protective of the city's traditions and reputation. These interpretations cannot explain the history of a city in the age of total war. Aachen's elites shared power with the Nazis, largely for profit and economic gain. The losers were the working class, denied the vote and trade union representation, and politically neutralised as a social

33

class. This story only came to light during the US army occupation of Aachen when Saul Padover, a US army psychological warfare officer, questioned Kurt Pfeiffer (a city official) on 2 February 1945. This chapter is shaped by the details from that interrogation report (refer to chapter eight for the interrogation).[5]

I. Industrialisation and democracy

To better comprehend Aachen and Nazism we must turn back history toward another of Aachen's historical threads. Industrialisation formed a city within a city, like the modern 'railopolis', where the railways are the sinews connecting Europe and the industries were its economic power. The railways skirted the old fortifications, bringing urban sprawl and industrial urbanisation, which absorbed the rising population. Within the old fortifications lay the centre, which retained a mixed cultural heritage of medieval and baroque structures. If Aachen was a railopolis, it came from the endeavours of three pioneers. William Cockerill (1759–1832), a skilled mechanical engineer, was instrumental in designing engines tailored for the textile industry. The Cockerill family, hailing from Lancashire, England, made their mark when they relocated to Liège, Belgium, in 1807. His machinery found its way to Aachen's textile factories, breathing new life into their production processes and profitability. His son, John Cockerill (1790–1840), possessed a keen business acumen. He steered the family's engineering enterprise towards innovations such as blast furnaces and the use of coke in steel production. Additionally, he played a pivotal role in establishing, in 1835, the Banque de Belgique, which raised commercial investment for the railway and industry.

On a similar trajectory was David Hansemann (1790–1864), a Hamburg Protestant who began his career at a textile factory in Monschau in 1810. Hansemann had a strong entrepreneurial spirit and founded the *Aachener Feuer-Versicherungs-Gesellschaft* (1825), a highly successful insurance institution. He became president of the Aachen IHK, a socioeconomic chamber but also a political lobby, having been introduced in 1804 during Aachen's time in the French Republic. In 1837, he became vice president of the *Rheinischen*

Eisenbahngesellschaft, overseeing the construction of the Cologne–Aachen–Liège–Brussels railway line.[6] In 1848, Hansemann joined the Frankfurt parliament and took on the role of Minister of Finance under Ludolf Camphausen. Despite being politically criticised by Karl Marx and viewed with suspicion by Prussian elites, he later distanced himself from politics, founding the *Disconto-Gesellschaft* in 1851 and passing away in Berlin in 1864.[7] A third pioneer was at the cutting edge of twentieth-century aviation, Hugo Junkers (1859–1935). Born in nearby Rheydt, he had studied engineering at Aachen's Technical University.[8] In 1897, he was offered a professorship and taught at the university until 1912. He embraced entrepreneurship and founded a company for advanced aircraft designs and patents. In collaboration with Hans Reissner (1874–1967), a mathematical engineer, Junkers began working on an all-metal aircraft design in 1909 at his factory in Dessau. Prior to war, the university established an aviation science and engineering research faculty. In 1916, he designed the Junkers J.1, an all-metal ground-attack aircraft that influenced several later designs.

Railway fever had a profound impact upon Aachen. A series of new lines extended the city's reach: the Aachen–Düsseldorf railway (1853), with connections to Mönchengladbach and Rheydt, and the Aachen–Maastricht railway (1853), extended to Hasselt and Landen (Belgium).[9] By 1856, Aachen's railway stations were advertising connections to Rotterdam, Amsterdam, Antwerp, Paris, Hannover, Hamburg and Berlin. The railway's regional infrastructure continued expanding, to Eifelbahn (1865), Ahrtalbahn (1880), Vennbahn (1885), Eifelquerbahn (1895) and Vennquerbahn (1912).[10] The railway infrastructure formed economic zones beyond the region (Aachen-Land), with strong links to Cologne, Koblenz, Trier, Luxembourg, Liège, Belgium and Maastricht. In 1880, Aachen's first horse-drawn tramway was established *Aachener Kleinbahn Gesellschaft*, and it was electrified in 1894. The services brought low-price travel and served industry's demands for cheaper workers' transport.[11] The tram network increased to twenty-eight lines connecting Aachen to Vaals (Dutch border town), Altenberg (Moresnet), Eupen (Belgium), Herzogenrath and Baesweiler, adding to the local transport infrastructure.[12] Local traffic was further increased by industrial and private railways—*Aachener Industriebahn AG* (1870–82), connecting to Stolberg, Würselen, Hoengen and Jülich. The Alsdorf coalfields—'Anna' and 'Maria'—with their furnaces requiring a constant flow of heavy freight traffic, maintained large private fleets of locomotives and waggons; they operated a scheduled service of workers' trains to meet shift work.[13] The railway station Templarbend terminus (1846) was situated on the fringe near the Pontor, the old gatehouse of the city walls. That station was replaced by the present-day Hauptbahnhof in 1905 and Aachen-Westbahnhof with extensive marshalling yards and a goods station in 1910. The city's railway stations became cultural sites with memorials. In front of the Hauptbahnhof stood the *Tritonenbrunnen*, designed by Carl Burger (1875–1950). This fountain included Aachen's memorial to those who had fallen in the wars of unification from 1866 to 1871, sculpted by Friedrich Drake (1805–1882).

Aachen's transformation to modernity, as with many cities in the nineteenth century, was the consequence of unregulated industrialisation. The first textile steam engines, in July 1822, marked the start, and by 1900 the *Tuchfabrik* (textile manufacturing) and the *Nadelfabrik* (needle industry) were fully mechanised. The rise of Aachen's affluent clothocracy was reminiscent of Manchester's cottonocracy, created by influential figures from the *haute bourgeoisie* and the landed aristocracy and closely tied to the Church. The Aachen industrialists were not a backward-looking feudal elite, but a class that ushered in modernity, driven by cash profits, and to a degree paternalistic towards the working class. The industrial modernisation generated businesses with prominent names; founded in the eighteenth century, some were still operating into the late twentieth century. For example, Carl J.M. Nellessen was founded in 1760 and continued in operation until 1930. In contrast, Joseph van Gülpen, J.H. Kesselkaul Enkel, J. Cüpper & Söhne, Süskind & Sternau and Heinrich Gustav Croon were important businesses that shaped Aachen's economic landscape, some surviving into the 1970s. The industrial pharmacist Leonard Monheim had specialised in colonial pharmaceuticals but turned to confectionery, establishing the city's first chocolate factory in 1903. The Rothe-Erde district and railway station formed an industrial park, further underscoring Aachen's economic rise, which was epitomised by the needle factory erected by Walter Hesse in 1911. Despite its closure in 2004, the factory's legacy endures, housing the city's central archive and museum. Industrial growth spawned a new elite to supplant the old guard, ushering in a bureaucratic ethos that prioritised the concentration of political power and wealth. Carl Mehler exemplified this change, his trajectory after military service leading to the founding of Nolten & Mehler GMBH. By 1900, Aachen had evolved into an industrial city.

Aachen's railway and industrial barons had small beginnings. Carl Delius epitomised the political clout wielded by the clothocracy, with a large factory by the railway line. The business passed to his son, Carl, but the Great Crash of 1929 forced the concern into bankruptcy in 1932, with thousands made unemployed. Pierre Pauwels, a Belgian railway engineer, and Hugo Jacob Talbot (1794–1850), a German industrialist, joined forces to establish Pauwels & Co., specialising in the manufacture of freight wagons. As the railway infrastructure expanded, crisscrossing international frontiers, the coal transported by Talbot's wagons played a pivotal role in boosting commerce. This enterprise was later renamed *Waggonfabrik Talbot*, solidifying its status as one of Aachen's influential industrial families. Aachen's business culture at the time saw success translate into elevated social status, and the Talbot family became part of the elite bourgeois-industrialist class. The Talbot brothers—Eduard, Julius and Gustav—carried the business into a second generation, spanning from 1829 to 1899. In 1890, Gustav was honoured with Prussia's *Roten Adlerorden IV Klasse*, a monarchist award recognising his achievements in industry and commerce. In 1860, Talbot constructed a new factory on Jülicher Strasse, complete with a purpose-built residential complex for the workforce. This reflected the paternalistic approach that characterised labour management in Germany during that era. The monarchy-church-industry power complex granted Aachen a unique place in *Kaiserreich* (Imperial German) society. The era saw the emergence of industrial paternalism as a response to working-class political activism. Industrialisation caused serious social problems beyond the scope of this book.

II. Rudderless Weimar

An ignored aspect of Great War history was Germany's drive for colonisation within Europe. The German occupation of neighbouring Belgium encouraged colonising fantasies among Aachen's municipal and business elites—in particular, regional expansionism along the lines of a German-Belgium customs union, driven from Aachen. The IHK yearbook for 1914 shows no evidence of pre-existing expansionist plans. The foreword referred to the war, but mostly reviewed industrial and commercial progress during 1913, the most notable item being the Vennbahn railway, which had had finally reached Stavelot and Malmedy.[14] During the war, the board of the IHK and city aldermen were instrumental in the administration of the German military government of Belgium and northern France. This wartime political administration was partly dictated by Imperial German Army military ordinances from the 1870s known as the *Etappen*, or rear-area system, which effectively mobilised civil institutions into the military government system. The primary purpose of these 'lines of communications' doctrines were to sustain the army in conquered territory. They followed the Napoleonic rationale of exploitation and plunder. Aachen effectively took control and governed Brussels and Liège. The takeover of Belgian businesses, manipulation of the financial system, the theft of patents and slave labour following from mass arrests of civilians were all part of a harsh occupation. Although the archives are lost, evidence of the *Etappen* in Belgium can be found in memoirs and industry *festschrifts*. Talbot's centennial *festschrift* includes a citation from Hindenburg, in 1927, alluding to the company for its war effort, the work with the IHK and the occupation.[15]

In 1917, expectations for victory were still running high, and ambitions flourished. Professor Heinrici from the Technical University set forth plans for an expansion of the city, to be funded with reparations from France. The strategic aim was to transform Aachen into the industrial metropolis of Western Europe. There were two parts to the plan: an extensive increase in the rail network and the construction of a Rhine–Meuse canal, with a harbour in Soers (the northern district of Aachen). Since the construction of the Manchester ship canal in Britain, Aachen business leaders pushed initiatives to construct a canal link to the Rhine. Cologne, recognising the threat, as had happened to Liverpool, went to great effort to prevent such plans from being realised. To raise the population density required to serve the metropolis, the planners envisioned entirely new housing schemes from extensive construction programmes.[16] The planning for the colonisation of the Low Countries was fuelled by Germany's war propaganda and local ambitions for expansion, with echoes of Charlemagne's empire.

Germany's defeat ended the colonisation. Aachen's frontier was pushed back with the loss of territory to Belgium.[17] There was also the sequestration of financial assets and capital from many German companies. The Aachener-Münchener Fire Insurance Company in particular suffered a sudden shortfall in its capital assets. The company had sold a range of insurance products in Strasbourg and the Alsace-Lorraine region. In 1904, a 'magnificent regional office' was opened in Strasbourg, designed by Georg Frentzen (1854–1923), a famous Aachen architect who also designed Cologne's main railway station and the controversial *Bismarckturm*. Defeat closed the business. In 1920, the Germans valued the Strasbourg office at 715,000RM, but the French auctioned the building for 450,000 Francs, crediting the sale against Germany's war reparations bill. In addition, the company lost all its general insurance business from the region. In 1924, the company placed a claim before the Cologne reparations court, a German compensation scheme to alleviate the impact of reparations on businesses. The claim was upheld and a settlement rate of one-in-thirty-two-thousand, minus costs, was applied to the compensation. The company received 900RM, booked in nine instalments. In the anniversary festschrift (1925), the company dryly concluded, 'the unlucky end of the war led to a negative impact on our scope of business'.[18]

Aachen's demographics fluctuated during a critical ten-year period: falling from 160,803 (1914) to 145,941 (1919) and slightly increasing towards 155,816 (1925). The post-1815 demographic increases that continued up to 1900 had slowed significantly by the time Hitler came to power: from 160,803 in 1914 to 162,774 in 1933. The city remained Catholic, representing 90 per cent of the population. The combination of the Belgian occupation and global crash brought the pressure of mass unemployment. An example was the case of the *Hüttengesellschaft der Rothen Erden*, a large steel works in the Rothe Erde industrial park. The site was first developed in 1845 by a consortium of four businessmen and engineers for the production of iron and steel. The business was purchased by Carl Ruetz in 1851 and the site increased as the company expanded through mergers and acquisitions. In 1921, the IHK advertised the industrial park as a massive viable concern for investment and included the steelworks.[19] However, by 1926 the steelworks had ceased trading, and 4,800 workers became unemployed. The entire site was demolished in 1927. The real cause of the company's collapse was the break-up of Aachen's former geo-economic structure. The trade links with Alsace-Lorraine were severed, and freight movements were hindered by Belgian military controls. In effect, raw materials could not supply the work and produce could not be distributed.[20] The Belgian authorities claimed the business was not viable. The problem stemmed from the Belgian occupation. German and foreign investors outside the occupation zone were reluctant to invest in Aachen's companies, which caused a breakdown in production processes, due to ageing machinery, which in turn had reduced operational competitiveness and falling profits. Regardless of the cause, the Aachen community remembered this as a spiteful act of Belgian retribution. The city purchased the land and later O. Engelbert Fils & Co. (Liège), a Belgian tyre company, opened a business on the site in 1929.

The Aachen economy remained diversified between the older inner-city industries and the outer zones of engineering works and coalmines, which employed 55.5 per cent of the working population. Aachen remained the hub of a vast and integrated transport network, retaining the international connections with France, Belgium and Holland. Economic gloom was already descending on Aachen long before the Great Depression. In December 1928, the city recorded about 10,000 unemployed registered for benefits (6.45 per cent), 6,373 received welfare and 2,654 received either welfare from the Catholic Church or charitable assistance.[21] The Great Crash had a domino effect on collapsing businesses, generating the dual effects of skyrocketing unemployment and rampant inflation, which gripped the city in deep depression. In August 1931, over 22 per cent of the Aachen community was receiving welfare assistance and emergency benefits.[22] By 1933, Aachen's economy had experienced twenty years of low levels of investment, poor capitalisation, sustained periods of boom and bust, the uncertainty of continuing depression, the loss of a significant communal/economic sector and declining markets. The three political parties of Weimar Aachen, the Catholic Centre Party (*Zentrum*), the Social Democratic Party (SPD) and the Communist Party (KPD), were not equipped to politically cope with the economic crisis. In the 1924 national election, the Centre Party received 37,710 votes, which represented 51.6 per cent of the total. Twelve years before, this was 60 per cent. From the surrounding districts, the Centre Party reached 86.2 per cent of the vote. The SPD, the KPD and other parties increased their votes.

On 20 May 1928, the Centre Party received 31,264 votes (42.7 per cent), which reflected Aachen's large pocket of working-class conservatism. The SPD increased its votes from 6,900 in 1924 to almost 10,000 in 1928. The Nazis received 761 votes (1.0 per cent). The election of 14 September 1930 reflected the global meltdown. The Centre Party received 32,208 votes (36.2 per cent). The KPD made gains to 14,456 votes (16.3 per cent) and the SPD made gains with 11,257 (12.7 per cent). The largest swing was to the Nazis, with 11,391 (12.8 per cent). The results of the 1930 election undermined the old political status quo. In the election of 6 November 1932, the turnout was 5 per cent down, and the political complexion changed slightly. The Centre Party held 43.1 per cent and the KPD held 20 per cent. The Nazis received 13,019 votes, rising to 14.6 per cent but set against a lower turnout. The momentum of the Nazi vote had stalled, and this was attributable to embarrassing local party scandals (discussed later).[23]

In Aachen, the frustration with the status quo of the political party system and the continuing crisis led to some political or ideological experimentation, during Belgian occupation, setting an electoral diversity and avoiding single-party domination. This ranged from leftist anarcho-syndicalism to regional interest politics of the Rhenish separatist movement, alongside the broad support for the left through the SPD and KPD. In 1933, the Aachen economic zone still included the neighbouring towns of Stolberg, Eschweiler and Düren, and the five land districts including Monschau.[24] When Hitler came to power on 30 January 1933, there were no significant spontaneous marches or protests. On 3 March 1933, in the referendum on the Nazi government, the Aachen electorate gave no indication of ballot box intimidation: the Nazis received 27,717 votes (27 per cent), while the Centre retained 38.3 per cent against intolerable pressures, the KPD took 16.4 per cent and the SPD 9.4 per cent. Aacheners simply refused to freely grant the Nazis a mandate for power.

III. Anatomy of a clique

A collective of colonial dogma was central to Nazi notions of *Lebensraum*. The party's ranking system displayed regional and national identity, similar to how the British Empire introduced High Commissioners. The position of Nazi *Gauleiter* (regional leader) emerged within Nazi ideology in 1925, coinciding with the creation of the *Gaue*, which were political subdivisions for local administration. This term wasn't merely an alternative to the state system of the Kaiserreich; the *Gau* had deep-rooted cultural connections within German history, which the Nazis exploited as an act of *Volkisch* dogma. The *Gauleiter* served as local party bosses, and in nearly all instances, their personal loyalty and allegiance went direct to Hitler. They oversaw local party administrations that embodied the dogma of the political soldier and operated as parallel structures to municipal administrations. Prior to gaining power, several Nazi *Gau* officials were elected to municipal positions, thus establishing their dual power grab. It was through administrative functions like the *Gau* that the Nazis smoothly transitioned into power. After gaining power, Hitler created the position of *Reichsleiter* from a segment of senior *Gauleiters*, granting them national responsibilities encompassing education, defence and labour.[25]

LETTING GO OF DEMOCRACY

Josef Grohé (1902–1987) hailed from the Rheinish Palatinate in the Kaiserreich and became Hitler's *Gauleiter* for Aachen-Köln. Similar to many senior Nazi officials, he was an outsider to the local community but was parachuted in to lead the party. Grohé was too young to serve in the war, attended a school for trades and commerce in 1919 and later worked as a clerk in a hardware firm starting in 1921. He joined the Nazi party in 1922 and actively engaged in terrorism against the French occupation of the Ruhr. After the ban was lifted on the Nazi Party, Grohé re-joined and rose to the position of deputy *Gauleiter* of Southern Rheinland in 1926. In the same year, he became the editor/publisher of the *Westdeutscher Beobachter*, a Nazi newspaper with a substantial regional readership.

In 1929, Grohé was elected as a councillor for the city of Cologne. Three years later, he secured a position in the *Prussischer Landtag*, a representative assembly for the Kingdom of Prussia (abolished in 1934). Once the Nazis assumed power, Grohé initiated the removal of Konrad Adenauer as Oberbürgermeister of Cologne. Being a staunch anti-Semite, Grohé, once in power, endorsed boycotts against Jewish businesses and encouraged personal attacks on Jews. This zealous radicalisation of Nazi ideology set precedents for other *Gaue* to follow, with Aachen-Köln being one of the first to implement near total Aryanisation across all state institutions by the end of 1934. Grohé continued to expand his influence from Köln to Aachen. In July 1944, he assumed the role of Reichskommissar for Belgium and northern France, once again reflecting the geopolitical ambitions for the Low Countries. When the US Army approached in March 1945, Grohé fled Cologne. As an *Alter Kämpfer*, Grohé remained a steadfast Nazi until his death in 1987.

Adolf Frömbken is believed to have been the first Nazi, in 1921, but he was not from Aachen.[26] It was the Schmeer brothers who took control of Aachen's Nazi party under Josef Grohé's patronage. They typified the corruption of the Nazi cliques. The first was Rudolf Schmeer (1905–1966). Born in Saarbrücken, he played a pivotal role as the senior member of a mafia-like gang. He joined the party in 1922 and arrived in Aachen the same year. Schmeer organised acts of terrorism against the Belgians and received a five-year prison sentence. From 1926 to 1931, he organised meetings with the old industrial elites.[27] Max Mehler, the son of Carl Mehler of C. Mehler, GMBH Aachen, was born in Aachen in 1874 and studied engineering at the university. During the Great War, he served as a reserve captain in the field artillery, earning both classes of the Iron Cross for bravery. After the war, he became a commercial lawyer in the company, expanded the company's production to include machinery for working with resin and hydraulic pumps, specialising in coal dust-burning systems based on US patents. He joined the Nazi Party.[28]

Mehler encouraged Quirin Jansen (1888–1952), the company bookkeeper, to join the Nazi Party in 1928, and Jansen became the party organiser. In 1933, Jansen assumed the role of commissar-director of the city's labour department. In September 1933, Hermann Göring appointed Jansen as *Oberbürgermeister*, a position he held until September 1944. The socio-political connections between the Nazis, the local industrial elites and the city's municipal authorities were already established before 1922. Schmeer was promoted to *Hauptdienstleiter*, a special rank in the party hierarchy, partly due to his expertise in administering workers and work organisations under *Reichsleiter* Robert Ley, who led the Nazi labour organisation. Eduard Schmeer (1900–1967), Rudolf's older brother, attended the machine-engineering school in Aachen (1923–7). In September 1925, he joined Aachen's Nazi clique, acquiring the social standing of *Alter Kämpfer* (old fighter) with party No. 18,940. In 1930, Eduard joined *SA-Standartenführer der Standarte 25*, the city's Nazi Stormtrooper detachment. In March 1932, he lost his position to a rival and was dismissed by the successor. In April 1932, Josef Goebbels (a Rhinelander) visited Aachen in his official capacity and during the ceremonies Eduard turned up, causing confusion among the organisers. He publicly attacked his rival as a homosexual, though an internal investigation later proved the allegation false. In 1938, Eduard became the *Kreisleiter* of Aachen, reporting to the Aachen-Cologne *Gauleiter* (explained later). He remained the leading Nazi stooge, living off the community until 1944. He drew a party salary of 4,000RM, which was increased in excess of 25,000RM with his state salary and other benefits in kind.[29] Hugo Schmeer, the younger brother, became Eduard's deputy with the rank of *Ortsgruppenleiter* (local group leader), though little is known of his activities.

IV. Commodifying racism through Aryanisation

The beat police were one of the first institutions to be Nazified. The police were infiltrated by the SA and SS. The Nazis formed the *Wehrbände* (armed bands) and mobilised members of the politische *Kampfbünde* (political combat leagues) to serve as auxiliary police forces. The police were central to the Holocaust in Aachen; this is discussed in greater detail in chapter eleven.[30]

The institution most pivotal to the Nazi powerbase in Aachen was the IHK. On 21 June 1929, the IHK celebrated its founding with the 125th anniversary celebrations. By 1933, apart from Georg Talbot, most of the 1914–15 board were replaced. The new men were moulded by the post-war society; they included Dr Kurt Pfeiffer, discussed in chapter seven. Typical was Hans Croon from the clothocracy. He became a leading figure in the economic affairs of the city. From 1933, Croon was president of the *Wirtschaftskammer*—the Nazi organisation that superseded the IHK—and brought Nazism and industry into a working partnership. In June 1954, the IHK's 150th anniversary *festschrift* carried the history forward from 1929, with Croon and the board portrayed as noble business leaders working towards the betterment of the community.[31] Industry had fallen a long way since Hansemann's liberalism had failed. The *Führerprinzip* (Nazi leadership dogma) was the managerial culture of the IHK by December 1933. The IHK's 'new' culture began to imitate the culture of the Nazi order. In 1891, George Talbot (1864–1948) had taken the family into a third generation of railway rolling stock, known for 'the self-discharging wagon'—one is on display before the former Talbot factory entrance. After George, Herbert (1906–1977) and Richard (1896–1987) carried the business into a fourth generation. The company continued to thrive and expand, with the construction of the *Tannhäuserhalle* (main factory hall) in 1930, underscoring its significance to Aachen, and employing 2,000 workers.[32] In 1938, a Talbot company *festschrift* boasted of a factory guard mustered from the work force, perfectly illustrating the notions of industrial self policing under the Nazis.[33] The IHK practised Nazi kleptocracy through 'Aryanisation', which led to the sequestration of all Jewish businesses and the disqualification of their owners from membership. By 1935, the IHK could boast it was 'Jew-free', one of the first in the Third Reich, as will be discussed in chapter eleven.

Under the Nazis, the Technical University (TU) followed a squalid path of careerism without moral leadership. The TU was a highly visible supporter of the Nazi regime, from the lowest student fraternities through to the senior academics of the faculties and on to the levels of institutional governance. In 1946, the British identified 27 per cent of academic staff had joined the Nazi stormtrooper (SA) organisation with upwards of a further 70 per cent having joined other Nazi organisations, and 59 per cent were full Nazi Party members.[34] There is evidence that students hurled abuse at Jewish classmates or demonstrating against Jewish lecturers long before Hitler came to power. Hugo Junkers came under pressure by the regime to dispose of his business. He lost the struggle and died in 1935, but *Veltrup Werke*, in Aachen, profited from the shift in ownership. Otto Blumenthal (1876–1944), a former professor of mathematics, had worked with Junkers. In 1933, he was forced out of the TU and moved to Holland but was later rounded up by the Nazis and died in Theresienstadt beside many of Aachen's Jews (discussed in chapter eleven).[35]

In terms of Catholicism and state politics, the Church and the Nazis were locked in an ideological struggle over the 'hearts and minds' of the community. Both were fundamentally opposed to each other, and both tried to impose absolutes on the other. In June 1933, the Nazis signed the Concordat with the Catholic Church that was supposed to guarantee its independence. Hitler initiated the *Ordernburgen* (Order Castles), designed to provide a four-year advanced political education to the future Nazi leadership elite. There were four main complexes: Krössinsee (Pomerania), Vogelsang (Eifel), Sonthofen (Bavaria) and Marienburg (Poland). Work on the Vogelsang began on 22 September 1934, and the construction programme granted contracts to local enterprises, especially for the supply of building materials and the employment of 1,500 labourers. There were two phases of construction, the first to 1936 and the second 1936–8, but work was suspended in 1941. There were labour shortages caused largely by the construction of the nearby Siegfried Line defences.[36] The education programmes started in 1936, a critical year in Nazi Germany, when Hitler's leaders consolidated their power bases and began to militarise their organisations. On 20 November 1936, Hitler and Robert Ley visited the complex to honour the first graduates. A month later, a local newspaper showcased the moment—'in the early hours of a cold autumn day, there was great activity in the streets with masses arriving in coaches, and cars, or marching groups of farmers, workers, RAD personnel, youths and to greet their führer with public cheers; especially for the security and welfare he brought to the borderlands'.[37] The political education programme ceased in 1939 with the outbreak of war, but the complex continued to educate German youth attending the Adolf Hitler Schools.[38]

The local response to the *Vogelsang* was propagandised by Hitler to further press Catholicism's Rhineland stronghold. There was a period of conciliation between Catholic teachings and Nazi dogma. Then, from 23 July 1935, the Nazis began calculated attacks with plans to dissolve organisations, close convents and intimidate congregations. The Hitler Youth targeted the Catholic youth organisations for vandalism and bullying. The mounting tensions led Pope Pius XI to issue the *Mit brennender Sorge* encyclical, accusing the Nazis of fomenting suspicion, and hostility towards the Church. Copies were smuggled into Germany, and some priests read them from the pulpit. The Nazis responded by closing religious facilities across Germany, and a Church publishing house was closed down after it tried to print the letter. In the *Heiligtumsfahrt* of July 1937, the pilgrimage and procession of relics went ahead against concerted Nazi opposition. The Nazis banned the railways from providing special trains, pilgrims were denied access to rooms in hostels and the Nazi police chief, Carl Zenner, refused authorisation of several processions. However, an estimated 800,000 Catholics participated in the pilgrimage. Problematically, not all

Church leaders were critical of the Nazis. Bishop Wiekan announced during his sermon that 'we owe it to the Führer that we come together tonight'.[39]

The Aachen working class, during the period 1914–39, suffered serious privations. This was expressed in their decline of faith as recession turned into depression. The city's financial reserves buckled under the dual strain of depression and mass unemployment. The working class, shackled by poverty, began to seek alternative political solutions. Small farmers, on Church lands, faced crippling rent increases, and many gave up their livelihoods to seek work in the city. In 1936, church attendance was estimated at 63.2 per cent, but it's difficult to isolate motivations between faith or welfare. The Church was partly responsible for its rigid Ultramontanism ideas and abandoning the masses without proper leadership or guidance during the Nazi abuses. The Nazis exploited the divided loyalties between church and state and applied pressure on persons of faith. In 1939, all Catholic schools were required to remove crucifixes from classrooms. The Bergdreisch convent, in central Aachen, was forced to close and sell up its assets. With the onset of war, priests were conscripted to serve in the Wehrmacht, while church bells were melted down for recycling. The Church also paid a financial contribution to the war effort. On 11 December 1939, a Gestapo report noted that there had been a subtle intensification of Catholic propaganda distributed at religious meetings and events.[40]

On 7 March 1935, the Rhineland and Aachen were remilitarised. The *Poll-Chronicle* described the troop movements in detail, identifying the transfer of the second battalion of the 39th Infantry Regiment from Münster to Aachen. Accommodation was located in a mechanical engineering school and later in the *Gelbe Kaserne*. More troops were garrisoned in the *Theodor-Körner-Kaserne*, in the Gallwitz barracks and the *Lützowkaserne* on Trierer Strasse.[41] There followed several years of military rebuilding and the construction of the Siegfried Line. In 1936, there were upwards of 20,000 troops garrisoned in Aachen, the 39th was renamed 78th Infantry Regiment, and there were more than double in recruitment than in Aachen-Land districts.[42] The influx of soldiers and workers on the *Westwall* or Siegfried Line added to city's populace.

LETTING GO OF DEMOCRACY

The regime became a garrison state, like the Kaiserreich, as German militarism once again became the *leitmotiv* of culture and society. Remilitarisation temporarily reduced unemployment by state-funded defence construction schemes. This was especially popular in the border localities along the Siegfried Line fortifications, creating jobs and contracts for the construction industry. The construction plans called for two belts of the defence fortifications running north and south through the city. The construction programme caused an unexpected double whammy for the economy. Initially, there was a mini-boom period for local pubs, restaurants, guesthouses and truck owners because of the injection of cash from the daily rate system. However, the constant transport of heavy loads damaged roads, while the construction sites ruined landscapes and blighted places of interest. The older established industries also suffered from labour shortages, unable to compete with the state's heavily subsidised wages. There were also never enough living quarters for the massive influx of outside workers that descended on Aachen. Social militarisation imposed civil defence regulations on the populace, with preparations for mass evacuation. The cathedral's treasures, including Charlemagne's relics, were packed away, and there was a sudden withdrawal of cash from the banks. Rationing was introduced in August 1939 and Aachen became home to 40,000 soldiers.[43]

Was Aachen a Nazi city? Despite the presence of a powerful ruling Nazi clique, the widespread implementation of Aryanisation and the religious protest in favour of Hitler, the available evidence still does not indicate Aachen was a Nazi city. In 1939, the Nazi Party initiated a national questionnaire aimed at collecting formal data on its members. Aachen, a city with a population ranging from 110,000 to 160,000, saw 9,605 questionnaires completed and surviving the war. In 1939, the city was divided into twenty political districts (*Ortsgruppe*), a division replicated in all German cities. The questionnaire gathered basic information such as age, date of party enrolment, hometown district, religious affiliation and occupation. Age profiles were segmented into ten-year intervals: 1851–60 (11 respondents), 1861–70 (81 respondents), 1871–80 (737 respondents), 1881–90 (1,895 respondents), 1891–1900 (2,707 respondents), 1901–10 (2,987 respondents) and 1911–20

(1,187 respondents). Crucially, the key age groups within the party in 1939 were as follows: 49–58 years represented 19.73 per cent, 39–48 years represented 28.18 per cent and 29–38 years represented 31.10 per cent, underscoring the significance of middle-aged individuals within the party's membership. Despite the Nazi regime's anti-clerical stance, religious affiliation was notable, with 5,832 Catholics (60.72 per cent) and 1,362 Protestants (14.18 per cent), although approximately 25 per cent did not acknowledge any religious affiliation. In terms of occupations, white-collar workers outnumbered blue-collar workers. This division included civil servants (25.57 per cent), office workers (26.28 per cent) and the self-employed (22.38 per cent).[44] The available evidence suggests that the Nazis were unable to shed their petty bourgeois character, and it can be cautiously inferred that Aachen was not a city with widespread support for Nazism on the eve of the Second World War.

PART TWO

TOWARDS AN ANTHROPOLOGY OF BOMBING

Aachen is an important railway junction on one of the main routes from north-west Germany into Belgium and France. It is the centre of a large coal-mining area, and many companies exploiting these mines have administrative offices in the town. In peace-time textiles formed the main industry in Aachen proper. There are a large number of spinning and weaving mills, many of which were closed early in the war. The leading firms of Aachen's engineering and rubber are mentioned in the report. The town has been heavily damaged by bombing, and the production of several of these firms reduced, but much of the industrial damage, particularly to the main factories, has been repaired ... The central part of the town is closely built, and has largely preserved its mediaeval character.

TNA, FO 837/1313 *The Bomber's Baedeker*, Guide to the Economic Importance of German Towns and Cities, Foreign Office and Ministry of Economic Warfare, Part 1 Aachen—Küstrin, May 1944, pp. 1–4.

A memorial to the officers and airmen of Nos. 2, 3, 8 and 100 Groups, Royal Air Force Bomber Command. Who lost their lives during the war will be unveiled in Ely Cathedral on Remembrance Day, November 6, by the Senior Air Staff Officer of Bomber Command. The memorial will be a stained-glass window with four lights or panels in the north side of the nave. The left-hand light will show the figure of a member of aircrew in flying clothing above the badge of No. 2 Group. The right-centre light portrays St. George and the Dragon above the badge of No. 8 Group. The design also Includes the Lion of St. Mark the Patron Saint of the Royal New Zealand Air Force. The right-hand light shows the figure of an airman above the badge of No. 100 Group. At the bottom of each Light are scenes showing Wellington bombers during different phases of on operational bombing sortie, ... At the bottom of the two centre lights is written 'In honour and memory of the members of Nos 2, 3, 8 and 100 Groups who served in the Ely district during the Second World War, 1939–45.'

> TNA, AIR 14/4017 preparations for the Memorial Service in Ely Cathedral on Remembrance Sunday, 6 June 1955.

3

IN DEFENCE OF THE COMMUNITY

At noon on Saturday, 7 October 2017, a haunting wail pierced the air of Aachen, reverberating across the city in a ten-minute cycle of sound and silence. While many residents carried on with their daily routines, the atmosphere at a local elderly care facility was transformed into pandemonium. Within its walls, a community of long-term patients, most afflicted with incurable dementia, found themselves thrust into a state of terror and confusion. Minutes before the eerie sound began, nurses and caregivers bustled about, attending to their usual tasks. However, as the wailing commenced, panic swept through the facility like wildfire. Patients convulsed with fear, some collapsing to the ground in a frenzy of screams, while others sought refuge under tables or in corners, their faces contorted with anguish. The distress was palpable, the air filled with the unsettling sounds of whimpering and sobbing. The alarm triggered deep-seated psychological trauma reminiscent of wartime air-raid sirens. Medical staff, caught off guard by the unexpected reaction, struggled to comfort and calm the terrified patients. Psychiatrists, baffled by the extreme response, found themselves confronting underlying wartime neuroses previously overlooked in their patients. Trapped in a world of their own worst nightmares, the elderly residents were rendered incapable of articulating their fears, leaving caregivers feeling helpless in the face of such profound distress.¹ Decades before, Len Deighton wrote, 'I wanted to emphasise the dehumanising effect of mechanical warfare. I like machines but in war all humans are their victims.'²

The origins of this trauma harkened back to 3 September 1939, when Britain and France declared war on Nazi Germany following Hitler's invasion of Poland. At that time, the looming conflict seemed distant to the citizens of Aachen, as detailed in Hans Siemons' study of the city during wartime.³ Yet, geopolitically, Aachen was far from a neutral bystander to the events unfolding in the west. Annexed lands within its state boundaries, mandated by the Treaty of Versailles, tied the city's fate to the broader geopolitical landscape. Additionally, Aachen's proximity to Belgium and its involvement in the construction of the Siegfried Line underscored its strategic significance. When war erupted on 10 May 1940, Aachen found itself thrust into the midst of the conflict. While no longer the linchpin it once was in 1914, the city nonetheless played a role in the swift and intense battles along the border. The capture of Fort Ében Émael by German airborne forces heralded a new era of technologically advanced warfare, marking the beginning of a series of triumphs for the German army. As German forces swiftly gained control of key districts, including Eupen, Moresnet and Malmedy, jubilation erupted in Aachen, fuelling a resurgence of imperial hubris among its leaders. Yet, beneath the surface of apparent victory lay a deeper reality of military inferiority masked by the myth of Blitzkrieg. The success of German armoured and airborne units belied the underlying weaknesses of a largely antiquated military apparatus reliant on outdated transportation methods.⁴ A similar situation existed in air-raid precautions and defence.

Aachen, as a *railopolis*, was immediately elevated to the status of a strategic target for RAF Bomber Command in May 1940. Official RAF doctrine was implemented from 13 May 1940 as per Plan W.A.5, the pre-war doctrine for bombing energy plants, and Plan W.A.4 (C) marshalling yards, both covering the Rhineland. From 9 July 1941, railways in the Rhineland 'especially in congested areas', in a 'policy to dislocate German transportation system and destroy of civilians particularly industrial workers'. On 20 August

IN DEFENCE OF THE COMMUNITY

1941, 'small towns on railways' were identified 'to divert part of the effort to less heavily defended objectives.' From 14 February 1942, the priority shifted to 'industrial cities in Ruhr and Rhineland', with 'operations ... "focussed" on enemy civil morale'. On 5 May 1942, a new directive on industrial cities in the Rhineland: 'primary aim is destruction of industrial cities and undermining German morale'.[5] The first area bombing of a German city was Monchengladbach on the evening of 11–12 May 1940. The raid involved thirty-seven aircraft and killed three Germans and an Englishwoman.[6] David Edgerton has written that 'the early years, a time of defeat, have become the subject of an almost obsessive fascination: evacuation, Dunkirk, the Battle of Britain, the Blitz, being "alone"—all are at the centre of national narratives of the war in which a new inwardly focused nation was born'.[7] Edgerton argued that memorialising the early years and understating the final victory enabled Britain to exaggerate its part in the war. In contrast to Britain, the early years of victory are forgotten in Germany, while the final years have amplified a sense of victimhood. Aachen's war in the west began with the allied bombing campaign in May 1940, which would continue until August 1944. As Noble Frankland wrote: 'That night [15 May 1940], ninety-nine aircraft of Bomber Command were despatched to attack oil and railway targets in the Ruhr. The strategic air offensive had begun.'[8] Some of those bombs landed on Aachen. This chapter reconstructs the initial phases of the bombing war and its social impact on Aachen.

I. 1940: British bombing

At one time, the usual comparisons between the Royal Air Force Bomber Command and Hitler's Luftwaffe concentrated upon bombing strategies, the bomb loads and the bomber aircraft. Increasingly, there has been debate about the role of the Luftwaffe in Hitler's war. In 2021, with strong archival evidence, I reconstructed the Luftwaffe's involvement in the Holocaust and Hermann Göring's role as a leading perpetrator.[9] In military operations, the criminal Luftwaffe and the victorious RAF shared similar doctrines and methods for bombing civilians. Regardless of Nazi war crimes, in the application of ruthless brutality, the evidence shows that RAF Bomber Command was not morally exceptional. This story is a complex web of truths and myths. Between them, the RAF was first to bomb German cities, but the scale of destruction was less visible due to aircraft obsolescence and the limited bomb loads. The Luftwaffe revealed its fighting power, first at Guernica (1938), Warsaw (1939), Rotterdam (1940), London (1940) and Coventry (1940). Nonetheless, the RAF had a willingness to bomb civilians as an expression of its national will, but not to avoid the attrition losses on the scale of the Great War, as has been claimed. RAF strategic doctrine was driven by RAF officers for the RAF to deliver, and there were no references to cooperation with the other services in regard to bombing Germany.

RAF strategic doctrine determined the Ruhr and Rhineland would be its strategic battleground prior to the outbreak of war. In March 1939, the RAF drafted a strategic plan designated W.A.5(b) for bombing the Ruhr. The plan's introduction explained the RAF's operational thinking:

> The targets selected for attack in Plan W.A.5 are those whose destruction is calculated to bring industry in the Ruhr to a state of dislocation, this being the method offering the best chance of reducing Germany's war potential as rapidly and economically as possible. This is more especially true of the targets selected for day attack in that plan. Because of the inaccuracy of night attack, as foreseen by Bomber Command, the objectives for night bombers could not be scientifically selected with a view to the destruction of the most vulnerable points in the Ruhr industrial system. They had perforce to consist of targets large in area and comparatively easy of identification, and the aim of attack on them was rather to disorganise their proper functioning than to destroy them.[10]

The plan concluded: 'the increased importance and congestion of the Transportation systems in the circumstances under review justifies greater attention being paid to the interference of railway traffic by sustained raids against traffic centres by night'. The problem with the plan was its absence of any realistic assessment of Bomber

IN DEFENCE OF THE COMMUNITY

Command's capability in 1939–40. The plan's appendices referred to bombing viaducts. The expected average bombing error in an attack on a viaduct was believed to be 300 yards, the number of bombs required was upwards of 200, the number of aircraft in the region of 40 (allowing 20 per cent casualties) and a total commitment of four bomber squadrons. This was compared with: 'The number of heavy squadrons calculated to put a coking-plant out of action for 2–3 months by high level bombing is 4 squadrons (48 aircraft).' From these assessments, it is not difficult to draw the conclusion that theory was out of sync with capability.

The first indication that the RAF was to push the limit of the laws of war emerged in bomber doctrine. An Operational Instruction was penned by Air Vice Marshal Bottomley issued in his capacity as Senior Air Staff Officer. On 30 June 1940, Bottomley issued Instruction No. 37 on the 'burning of German forests'. Attached was Appendix A (appendix 'B' and 'C' were only maps), which set out the doctrine for burning the forests: 'Forest fires are feared by mankind throughout the world and cause considerable psychological effect on inhabitants in their vicinity due to fear.' To avoid the localisation of fires it was recommended to bomb 'near large centres of population' and that 'panic is more likely in the thickly populated areas'. The appendix also referred to Germany's use of wood in timber and pulp forms, and its importance to the synthetic industry. The character of the forests, the resin, needles, twigs and dry soil were described as prone to fire hazard. The coniferous forests, of mixed ages, were also vulnerable to fire hazard. The weapon of choice was the 25lb parachute incendiary, designed purposefully to set fire to forests: 'as each fire pot ejected from the 25lb incendiary bomb develops sufficient heat to start a considerable fire if the terrain in its vicinity is inflammable, the more widely dispersed the bombs, the greater the chance that some of them will fall on suitably inflammable ground.' The instructions identified seventeen forest targets and listed the woods south-east of Aachen, as being an 'industries and communications' target.[11] British doctrine was set towards waging a strategic campaign against civilians early into the war, but the policies were in advance of capability and that would remain the case until 1942, when the heavy bombers began to roll off the production line.

The doctrinal language adopted in the allied strategic bombing campaign points to the culture war that arose from the bombing of British and German cities in 1940–1. In an article about the attempts to break German morale, Richard Overy has discussed the relationship between the British political warfare offensive and RAF Bomber Command. He identified how the PWE and Bomber Command cooperated in the propaganda campaign dropping millions of leaflets and news sheets over Nazi Germany and occupied Europe. He questioned whether exploiting air power could be used to secure a political dividend from war.[12] Overy has consistently argued that the leaflet was the weapon of propaganda warfare, and has examined the documents of Ritchie Calder, director of plans and propaganda, in the Political Warfare Executive.[13] Better known for his sympathetic observations as a journalist recording the impact of the London Blitz,[14] Calder had redirected his experience of morale into psychological warfare. While propaganda was Calder's primary directive, the language he adopted for reports framed bombing in the realm of the politics of violence and the drive towards a culture war. His filing system identified a prominent classification of his brand of political warfare—'Morale Warfare—Fear 1940–41'. In July 1941, Calder issued a report about air raids and explained:

> The effect of any raid can be magnified by a morale assault. The nerve tension which follows a night of raids and of sleeplessness makes any community extremely sensitive to rumour and suggestion; salt must be rubbed into the wound, since judged by Nazi standards (Warsaw, Rotterdam and Belgrade), the RAF attacks have not assumed the proportions of terror raids, in which they themselves complete the morale assault. (Even Coventry, where a town was deliberately disembowelled, fell short of a terror raid.)[15]

Calder advised that 'the German in any target area, must be made to feel that as a civilian is being sacrificed, that it is not really his war and that he is just trapped in it'. He claimed the small number of neurosis cases after the German blitz was partly associated with the public sense of 'all being in it together'. He compared this with the German way to suppress feelings, their 'feelings are bottled up; our criticisms find full expression'. It was a remarkably shallow interpretation of cultures. Calder was also aware of the delayed effects of the bombing; months or weeks later came the appearance of 'naked fear', which he described as if 'It was as though a clean gash had been made in their minds, without "suppuration", but re-opening like an old wound every time they hear a bomb or siren.' Nothing can be done; they have to be taken away from the bombs or sirens. Compounding the sense of fear, the 'lull' between bombing raids caused a spike in the cases of fear when the bombing returned. He underlined: <u>'This should be borne in mind when the RAF return to the attack on a town which has been neglected for some time.'</u>

The public reaction to the bomber at 15,000 feet: 'It was a dehumanised machine, a symbol of Hitler or war ... From extracts from German letters, it seems that the bombers have become "Tommy" ... I have come to the conclusion that the logic of their attitude is "If our boys arc heroes when they fly through German flak, those chaps must have guts to fly through ours." This seems to me to be most important, if we think that the Germans are pretty much like ourselves in this. It would pay us to keep on boosting the courage of the German pilots—with the double effect of telling them how fearsome our defences are, and what courage the pilots must have to face it all ...' There was a chilling prediction: 'It is enough for them to know that we could if it suited us burn them out.' Summer drought and water shortage at a time when the R.A.F. is doing its present raiding makes emphasis at the moment all the more opportune. Neutral observers quoted as talking about the anxiety in Berlin or Nuremburg over the water-supply would provide a minor nerve war, without committing the Air Ministry to anything. In a subsequent report, Calder recommended the employment of 'demonstrational raids'. An important priority was to show the occupied populations that 'the Germans are not the masters of the sky'. As a part of his comments and points, Calder deemed it was essential that Political Warfare was represented on the Target Committee.[16]

WAR COMES TO AACHEN

II. War journalism

From the Air Ministry records, there is a detailed summary of all the Bomber Command raids on Aachen. The records indicate consecutive raids in May, on 13–14, 14–15, 15–16, 16–17 May and then 21–2 and 24–5 May—overall twenty-two aircraft 'attacking' about thirty tons of high-explosive bombs.[17] One of the few comments about those raids came from Arthur E. Slater, a former Air Ministry senior civil servant and Air Chief Marshall Sir Hugh Dowding's private secretary; he wrote that the raids on the evening of 15–16 May 1940 were an attack on the marshalling yards. He may have meant 14–15 May.[18] The BCD has no references to Aachen but notes eighteen Wellingtons raided the communications in the Rhineland or Ruhr on 14–15 May. However, there is no confirmation in the *Poll-Chronicle*. The *Poll-Chronicle* lists: 11 May 1940, an RAF aircraft flew over the city for the first time at 17.00 hours. The next day, Sunday 12 May, a raid dropped nine bombs on Hasselhölzer Weg, a district in the south-west of the city, killing a child. A child was the city's first civilian fatality from bombing. Bomber Command claimed three aircraft attacked the city on 13–14 May 1940, but the city has no record of the raid. The *Poll-Chronicle* refers to the arrival of long columns of allied PoWs in the district of the Brander Heide on those days. One aircraft flew over the city on 16 May, dropped parachute flare over a cloister within the city limits, and then flew off.[19] There was a significant difference of interpretations about the raid of 21–2 May 1940. The Air Ministry recorded nine attacking aircraft that delivered almost thirteen tons of bombs. Martin Middlebrook identified 'German Railways' 21–2 May with 124 aircraft sent to multiple targets including Aachen. The *Poll-Chronicle* for 22 May 1940 itemised twenty-two aircraft attacked Kaiserallee (today Oppenhoffallee—south-east city limits), with three dead and nineteen injured.[20]

There are few records of the early raids on Aachen, but William Shirer, the famous author, who was serving as war correspondent for an American newspaper, witnessed that raid. In the *Berlin Diary* (1946), he had observed allied bombing from May 1940:

IN DEFENCE OF THE COMMUNITY

War on civilians started ... The other side reported German planes had killed many. Tonight the Germans claimed three Allied planes dropped bombs in the middle of Freiburg, killing twenty-four civilians. ... As a taste of what this phase of the war is going to be like, a German communiqué tonight says that 'from now on, every enemy bombing of German civilians will be answered by five times as many planes bombing English and French cities'.[21]

Shirer's observations from the 'other' side leave an impression of random damage caused by RAF bombers seemingly lost in the dark. He was surprised by what he saw: 'the night bombings of the British have done very little damage. I thought the night bombings of western Germany, the deadly efforts which the BBC had been boasting since the big offensive began, would have affected the morale of the people.' He believed that the BBC's claims of extensive damage and the decline of German morale were exaggerated. In Hannover, they visited a house where twenty people had been killed. The group was then taken to see the wreckage of a crashed Handley Page bomber. It was shot down by anti-aircraft fire; the crew had bailed out, four surrendered but a fifth was on the run.[22] Luftwaffe mechanics were busily removing parts from its fuselage, while 'hundreds of peasants' looked on, engrossed by the aircraft's mangled fuselage.

The correspondents were taken to Aachen, in darkness; there was a full moon and the tree-lined road stirred ominous feelings. They came across 'endless columns of troops, in trucks and on foot ... moving up to the front, singing and in good spirits'. They arrived in Aachen on the evening of 19 May, guests of the International Hotel (36 rooms) at 11–13 Römerstrasse (long since gone) opposite the main railway station. His room was in the attic, an 'unpleasant room to be in if the British bombers come over tonight'. At 01.00 hours there was no indication of a raid as he wrote up his notes but drifted off to sleep. At 02.50 hours, 'I awoke to the crashing of anti-aircraft cannon and the rat-tat-tat of a machine gun on the roof across the street.' The British were attacking the rail yards, but there had been no alarm raised. He was shocked, 'no air raid alarm. We got our first warning from the sudden thunder of the *flak* guns.' He went to the lobby and watched

German reactions, 'a half-dozen frightened women were frantically rushing downstairs in their nightgowns, fear frozen on their faces'. Several German officers sauntered along after them. The journalists joined them; there was no 'false bravery' but everyone was being cautious. Shirer was tired and faced the prospect of a 05.00 hours start. Sleeplessness was to become endemic to Aachen life during the war years, and this was the beginning.

On 21 May, after spending the day visiting battlefields the correspondents returned to Aachen. It was too late for Shirer to broadcast and he began writing his story. He was writing when the British arrived at 00.20 hours. He moved from his room to continue writing in the dining room on the ground floor. At 00.40 hours, the air-raid siren started wailing—twenty minutes *after* the guns began firing. He felt the concussion of bombs and heard their explosions. 'Our little hotel is a hundred yards from the station,' Shirer wrote, 'the British are obviously trying to get the station and the railroad yards.' At 00.45 hours, larger-calibre guns began firing, and five minutes later they could hear the gunfire of the fighters. At 00.50 hours, he thought he could distinguish between the sounds of large British aircraft and the smaller chasing German fighters. At 01.00 hours, the light flak around the main railway station began firing. Twenty minutes later, he received his telephone call, but could barely hear the caller through the cacophony of noise. The raid continued for four more hours, ending at 04.00 hours, whereupon he immediately fell asleep.[23] Thus was Shirer's account for the raid on 19–20 May; however, it does not tally with British or German records. Not surprisingly, there was little coverage about the raids in the *Aachener Anzeiger Politiches Tageblatt* (AAPT). The newspaper published a bulletin from Berlin, which claimed the allies had indiscriminately bombed civilians deep inside Germany. The Air Ministry issued a Bomber Command intelligence report for the period 02.00–10.00 hours of 22 May 1940: 'Six Wellingtons attacked marshalling yard N.W. Aachen in target area between 23.19 and 00.20 hours and 95 250lb bombs were dropped. Thirty-five bursts were registered on marshalling yard and 24 bursts straddled yard and 11 bursts on road of yard and six on main railway.'[24]

IN DEFENCE OF THE COMMUNITY

The levels of operational confusion included the tracking of single aircraft losses. On 23–4 May 1940, the raid of 122 aircraft included 50 Hampden bombers. A Handley Page Hampden (No. L4171) from No. 44 Squadron based at Waddington crashed near Aachen. On 24 May, the Air Ministry received a signal from No. 44 Squadron that the aircraft was 'missing'. On 11 June 1940, the Red Cross in Geneva advised the Air Ministry in London that a 'heavy bomber was shot down and the four occupants killed'. The bodies were recovered from the crash site in Merzbrück, about eight miles from Aachen centre. The crew: Acting Squadron Leader Johnson (pilot), Pilot Officer Barker, Sergeant Collins (air observer) and Corporal Crook (air crew); all were pronounced killed in action on 24 May 1940. The German records show the aircraft was shot down near Aachen and the crew remains taken to a nearby reserve military hospital. The hospital chief was able to identify Barker and Collins but marked the other remains as 'unknown'. The bodies were then released for burial on 31 May 1940. The crew were buried with full military honours in Aachen's *Ehrenfriedhof* (since renamed *Waldfriedhof*) beside the dead of nations from the Great War. The crew's families finally received confirmations of their deaths on 26 June 1940.[25]

If there is a nobility in war, it soon disappears when confronting how people died. In June 1940, a Handley Page Hampden (P1178) from the No. 83 Squadron based at RAF Scampton attacked German communications and crashed near Aachen. The BCD also referred to a Hampden lost when forty-eight aircraft were sent to raid across northern and western Germany on 4 June 1940.[26] The Air Ministry were advised at 19.00 hours on 4 June that the crews were missing, since expected time of arrival was 17.00 hours. A telegram from the Under Secretary of State was immediately sent to the next of kin of Haydon and Greenwell; his father was in Rhodesia. Soon after, Greenwell's father received a letter from Department F4 of the Air Council explaining what 'missing' meant: 'I am to explain that this does not necessarily mean that he is killed or wounded and that if he is a prisoner of war he should be able to communicate with you in due course. Meanwhile enquiries will be made by this department through the International Red

Cross.' On 9 July, the families of Haydon and Greenwell received telegrams confirming their deaths. Sergeant Charles Evans of Department F4 wrote to the relatives to explain that the International Red Cross confirmed their deaths, they were buried on 7 June 1940 in the *Ehrenfriedhof* (today Waldfriedhof) and further letters would follow.[27] On 27 July 1940, Harry Broadhurst wrote to the RAF Personnel Services confirming their deaths. There is no record on file of Sergeant Thomas's family being informed until 22 December 1941, but that was probably due to clerical error. On 9 January 1942, the director of personnel services advised his mother 'it is therefore concluded his death was instantaneous'. Haydon's father informed the RAF that his son's wife had remarried and was no longer the next of kin. The story was reactivated when Greenwell's mother wrote to the RAF on 21 December 1945 requesting a photograph of the grave. In January 1946, she was advised photographs were to be made and issued to families.

In Germany, in 1946–7, the RAF began plans to exhume personnel buried in German cemeteries and bury them in Commonwealth War Graves. The process revealed how the Germans had conducted a post-mortem of the crew. Dr Kurohof conducted the post-mortems on 5 June 1940 and completed the death certificates; the bodies were given a funeral with full military honours on 7 June. British post-mortem followed exhumation on 23 April 1947. Flying Officer Haydon (pilot), from Hertfordshire, from a German post-mortem: his head was crushed and body shattered. The British exhumed his body, but his head was missing, fingers and hands missing, parachute harness, Mae West, white socks aircrew issue, short civilian aertex pants, shirt with attached collar, service drill trousers, officers drill jacket. Pilot Officer Greenwell, from Rhodesia: it is possible that he died in the German hospital on or about 4 June. Shattered body but no burns, an incomplete record states he died in a German hospital. A smashed skull, buried with braces. Sergeant Perry (air observer), Bristol, head crushed body shattered and seriously burned. British post-mortem, lower half of body decomposed, hair reddish brown, no fingers or hands, service drill tunic with sergeant rank, shirt with collar, service dress belt, fur-lined flying jacket, complete flying suit, Mae West and parachute harness. Sergeant Thomas (air crew), Manchester, body burned and smashed, in advanced state of decomposition. Burned message pad, two Royal Sovereign pencils, flying suit, airman's blouse and trousers, blue socks, white stockings, cotton singlet, khaki scarf and flying suit. He had a Jersey coin in his pocket. Mrs Tomas passed away in September 1942. Thomas's body was shattered in the remains of the aircraft and seriously burned. After the exhumations and post-mortems, the bodies were transferred to Rheinberg cemetery. The final correspondence from the RAF to the families was sent on 18 April 1950, with photographs of the temporary crosses on the graves.[28]

III. Becoming a troglodyte society

The citizens, though somewhat psychologically prepared for air raids, found themselves profoundly shaken by the 1940 bombings, sparking widespread questioning of safety measures. Despite relatively low civilian casualties, the tumultuous raids instilled an exaggerated fear of vulnerability. A report from 23 May 1940 by the Gestapo in Aachen squarely blamed the Luftwaffe for deficiencies in defence planning, openly criticising delayed alarm signals and sirens. Particularly damning was the failure of anti-aircraft fire to down enemy planes, despite their prolonged presence within searchlight beams for three hours, unimpeded by interception. Subsequent to a significant raid, the Gestapo's report on 30 May 1940 lamented a palpable decline in public morale, fuelled by rampant rumours and diminished labour productivity due to sleep deprivation. Contrasting the populace's pre-bombing confidence in defence capabilities with post-bombing disillusionment, the Gestapo highlighted the abrupt realisation of vulnerability. The Luftwaffe's warning system, criticised for its silence until enemy bombers audibly neared the city, further eroded trust. Local apprehensions over the efficacy of the air-raid warning system prompted civilians to adopt self-protective measures.[29]

On the evening of 28 and 29 May, according to a Gestapo report, alarms were triggered without any sign of enemy aircraft, causing widespread disturbance among the population. People were observed rushing to air-raid shelters at the mere sound of passing automobiles or the flickering of searchlight beams. Persistent rumours circulated, suggesting that future alarms might not be forthcoming, a notion reportedly started by the city's own air-raid personnel. The Gestapo identified a breakdown of trust between the populace and security services. By 10 June, the Gestapo acknowledged that public confidence in both the air-raid warning system and anti-aircraft defences had been completely eroded. Once again, incorrect alarm activations were attributed to organisational chaos within the Luftwaffe and confusion over responsibilities. Industrial facilities were compelled to sound the 'end of raid' alarm due to absenteeism among workers, causing further disruptions. The simultaneous alarm systems for the city and industrial zones led to widespread sleep disturbances, with civilians resorting to setting alarm clocks for midnight and seeking refuge in cellars like automatons. To address the issue, civilian groups formed impromptu volunteer air-raid warning teams to safeguard their neighbourhoods. In a July 1940 report, the Gestapo noted significant civilian congregations in shelters between 00.30 and 03.00, even in the absence of alarms. In response to the sleep deprivation issue, city officials agreed to adjust school start times to 09.00.[30]

The defensive preparations in Aachen during World War II present a complex narrative, often obscured by the scarcity of air-raid precaution and administration records. Many of these crucial documents were lost, while some were seized in 1944 and sent to the UK for translation by the Foreign Office. Others were utilised to compile research reports. In March 1945, the Research & Experiments Department under the Ministry of Home Security dispatched a survey team to Aachen to assess the air-raid shelters. This mission fell under the purview of the British Bombing Research Mission, established by Bomber Command in 1944. Assisted by officers from the American Military Government, the team gained access to a former member of the NSDAP, who had held a position of authority in the Nazi ARP organisation but was now believed to be cooperating with the Americans. This individual elucidated that, prior to 1940, the only provisions for raid protection were reinforced basements repurposed as shelters. Across the city, basements were inspected and converted into *Luftschutzraum* (public basement shelters). Approximately 150 such shelters were identified and registered in Aachen's city centre. These spaces underwent transformation with the installation of gas-proof doors, basic first-aid kits and sanitation facilities. Bricked-up doorways were replaced by regulation emergency exits and lighting, while walls and timbers were reinforced to enhance structural integrity and mitigate collapse risks. Additionally, a limited number of private basements underwent similar reinforcement and conversion into shelters. Despite the meticulous efforts of the survey team, all records pertaining to private shelters had vanished. Moreover, the team was surprised to find no provisions akin to the Anderson shelters commonly found across Britain.

In 1941, in response to mounting public criticism, the decision was taken by the Nazi authorities to construct large public shelters. The shelters, or bunkers, came in different designs, and nineteen were completed or in the progress of completion when the city capitulated in October 1944. There were fourteen multi-storey bunkers at different stages of construction. In addition to these shelters, there was a tunnel system (under construction) and a second smaller tunnel in preparation. The survey team examined in detail the post-1941 facilities. The first construction they surveyed was 'a large single-storey concrete shelter sunk with roof just below the ground'. There was a poor use of space and decorations, and it was assumed the design was influenced by propaganda rather than practical purpose. The multi-storey bunkers were positioned to the north of the central zone along the ring road—Ludwigsallee, Monheimsallee, Heinrichsallee and Wilhelmstrasse—and to the south by the main railway line. They were aligned in 'a rough circle round the central zone at a distance approximately 800 metres from the town centre (Münsterplatz)'. This effectively meant people required a fifteen-minute warning to reach the bunkers safely. The report also hypothesised that the reason the sites were chosen was, firstly, open spaces in congested areas, and secondly, the Germans 'may have assumed that allied attacks would aim at the town centre and that the chance of a direct hit would decrease if the shelters were removed a little distance from the centre of the target'. The first sub-surface concrete shelter was in the Römerplatz, although it's possible the report confused the address with Römerstrasse and Bahnhof, close by the main railway station. This was the same street and district where William Shirer's International Hotel had been in May 1940. This was a concrete construction, a single storey lying just below ground level covering a space of 212 feet by 68 feet. The roof and walls were 5 feet thick, and the 'interior was divided into two by a heavy spine wall down the centre'. On one side there was a series of small cubicles, and on the other an open space for 500 citizens. The bunker in Monheimallee was made up of four sections, placed end to end, making a total area of 466 feet by 58 feet with a roof thickness of 5 feet plus 2 feet of earth. It had a central passage with small rooms on both sides. These shelters 'were both complete, well-built, dry and in good condition'. There was no indication of bomb or shell damage.

There were fourteen large multi-storey concrete shelters. Two surface concrete shelters were inspected: Sandkaulstrasse (the first of the smaller bunkers) and Hohenzollernplatz (representing the larger construction). Sandkaulstrasse bunker was completed in 1941—50 feet by 48 feet 8 inches, with a wall thickness of 3 feet 8 inches along the sides and 2 feet by 2 inches at the ends, and with a roof thickness of 5 feet 7 inches. The concrete used in the construction was regarded as good quality and samples were taken back to Britain for testing. The survey team described the appearance: 'It had three floors and a pitched camouflage roof, consisting of tiles laid on in-situ concrete slabs which were supported by concrete posts. Each entrance had the usual double steel doors with a small chamber between, forming a gas seal.' There was a ventilation shaft of 4 inches diameter that weaved through each compartment. The shafts were 'dog-legged' to prevent fragments from injuring people and there were other means to prevent gas from entering the shelter. The Sandkaulstrasse shelter had not been identified in photo-reconnaissance photographs.[31] The Hohenzollernplatz bunker was still under construction at the time of the city's capitulation. In terms of construction, the bunker was an exception from the tunnel policy that dominated from 1943. The remnants of plans, discovered in an on-site waste bin, indicated 8-feet-thick walls, increased from 6 feet based on corrections to a drawing from May 1942. Another drawing from November 1943 indicated a ceiling of 5 feet and 'a concrete buster slab was envisaged at ground level round the shelter but there is no evidence that this was ever constructed'.

The bunkers were subject to concealment measures, and some had 'a pitched tiled roof erected on top of the real roof'. The purpose was to make the bunkers blend into neighbourhoods. Other bunkers, adjoining flat-roof houses, also had flat roofs. The British report noted: 'A certain amount of exterior decoration, eagles, swastikas etc., had also been used, and some of the shelters had architectural pretensions.' The report also conjectured that if the roof measures were meant for concealment from air reconnaissance, they had failed. The Germans could not disguise bunkers under construction and the RAF were able to identify their development. The bunkers had been reinforced by including steel meshes or hooked bars in a U shape. The reinforcing was intended to reduce internal spalling (flying chips of masonry or mortar) from an external explosion, and for weight bearing purposes. Roof reinforcing estimates were made based upon the Rütscherstrasse bunker, which had 'a uniform cubical mesh' almost half-an-inch thick in the interior. The internal walls were not reinforced but mostly partitions of 5-inch brick and plaster cover. There was no consistency to reinforcing with Hohenzollernplatz fully reinforced and Rütscherstrasse with none, excused as caused by the shortage of materials. The quality of the concrete was ordinary 'beach aggregate' and a sample produced a 'compressive strength ... slightly over 7,000 lb/sq.in. maximum aggregate'.

The overall scale of bomb damage to the bunkers was low, with only some fragmentation scars. The roofs had been damaged but not as badly as neighbouring buildings. The Rütscherstrasse bunker had received two 'direct hits'—one 'merely chipped the extreme edge of the roof' and the other went 'through' at the same place. The bomb had struck a concrete partition wall and had caused it to be demolished to the ground floor—'the absence of fragmentation on the inside indicated that the bomb may have been 1,000lb M.C. (or American G.P. types)'. The report confirmed: 'Only two rooms were in any way affected by this hit, and even in these rooms a good proportion of the occupants would probably have escaped unhurt.' The bunker in Zeppelinstrasse had been hit but was fully repaired, with the hole filled with a 'large patch', making it more resistant to perforation. It was believed two persons were killed, although the bunker was not full at the time.

One tunnel bunker was located in Ludwigsallee, excavated into a sandy clay hillside. The entrance was a 'massive concrete portal' on the same scale as the surface bunkers. The bunker was reached through two alternative flights of stairs, through a brick-lined tunnel almost 13 feet wide and 10 feet high with a 'circular arch roof'. There was an emergency spiral staircase but it was unprotected on the surface. The tunnel bunker was 'distinctly worse off' in amenities and less elaborate compared with the other bunkers. The occupants had wooden benches, and its smaller space was crowded, with even less space for toilets and first-aid facilities. The second was the enormous Kamperstrasse tunnel bunker with an expected 30,000-person capability. By September 1944, only an eighth of the planned construction was completed. It was planned to have three entrances/exits, lined in concrete and 14 feet wide by 11 feet high. The excavation was used to increase cover over the crown of the tunnel, making 30 feet, but the plans envisaged 45 feet depth of cover, rising to 55–60 feet. The tunnel was open to public inspection and several thousand had taken shelter by the capitulation even without offering protection. The overall capacity of the shelters was not calculated by the surveyors, but they estimated each person had 6 square feet ground space and 35 cubic feet air space. In practice it seemed there was serious over-crowding in all bunkers. Space wasn't wasted, and in heavy air raids space reduced to less than 3 square feet per person.

The report noted the entire construction programme had suffered from labour shortages. However, the survey team were not concerned the labour assigned to build the bunkers. In 2004, a university research project examined Nazi slave labour in Aachen, which included a bunker construction programme. Until 1941,

IN DEFENCE OF THE COMMUNITY

Aachen had not experienced labour shortages because its industries were not part of the general armaments programme of the war effort. Some factories had closed, and their labour dispersed. Aachen's traditional labour market had drawn on Dutch and Belgium workers, and many were still commuting to their jobs with German companies. In 1941, Aachen's entire labour force was 80,533, with about 4 per cent foreign labourers including PoWs. Then from 1942, slave labour from the east, Soviet Russians and Poles, gradually replaced Dutch workers who were becoming increasingly irritated by German work regulations. In addition, since 1940 large numbers of allied PoWs passed through Aachen, and in 1941 French PoWs were still in Rhineland camps.

An assortment of documents were collected from the Luisenhospital and state hospitals, city utilities and outside *Luftschutz* agencies that referred to the employment of PoWs in the bunker construction programme. Oberbürgermeister Jansen had ordered PoWs to remove rubble from the entrances to bunkers. The *Kriegschaedenamt* (War Compensation Agency) assigned Soviet PoWs as slave labour to remove debris from bomb-damaged building and to save family belongings. The home registration agencies also used Soviet PoWs to assist in rehousing people. There were two labour camps in Aachen, financed by the municipality; both the Gestapo and the labour exchange exploited the inmates. A city official was involved in the decision to employ French PoWs on bunker construction. Dr Kurt Wiendieck was responsible for a work programme that included setting time schedules, working hours, supplies, shelter and rations. From August 1941 to April 1944, the city's official involvement in the exploitation of PoW labour extended to the construction of *Tiefbunkers* (in cellars) and *Hochbunkers* (large building shelters).[32]

The conditions, given usual Nazi measures, were remarkably lenient. The daily work schedule was set at nine-hour shifts, Monday to Friday, five hours on a Saturday and Sundays off. The PoW Camp was in Belvedere, and they were transported to worksites in buses supplied by the city. The bunker in Ludwigsallee was relatively close to the camp, and this allowed the officials to raise the daily work rate to ten hours. The exception to the standard hourly rate was when work involved pouring and working the cement. On 1 March 1943, a meeting held between city officials and different agencies raised the hourly rate to ten hours in the summer months. In August 1941, there were 200 PoWs assigned to bunker construction labour. These men were organised into *Kriegsgefangenen Bau- und Arbeitsbataillons 25* (PoW Construction Battalion 25), but on 17 July 1942 they became part of PoW Construction Battalion 35. The numbers fluctuated between 150 and 200 PoWs until September 1944. The first company of Battalion 35 was assigned to Bochum in May 1943 to clear bomb damage and returned five months later. During work shift, the PoWs were strictly segregated from all other workers, although civilians were increasingly conscripted to serve in the battalion.

IV. Terror from above

In the last three months of 1941, the Foreign Office received a stack of captured German letters and learned of indications of the stiffening attitude against British raids. One letter stated, 'The English do not come so often now, they are gradually tiring; they do not accomplish much at any rate, but many of them are shot down, thanks to our strong defence; we all feel much calmer now.' Several letters referred to the dislocation and interruption of children's schooling. Although one letter from 22 December 1941 referred to failing German morale: 'They cannot "take it" like the British people, and if the RAF would send only a few planes every night, even without dropping bombs, the air raid alarms alone and the continuous spending the nights in the shelters would have a tremendous effect on the morale of the people, especially the Berliners.'[33] The period January 1941 to December 1942 saw a significant upgrade in the fighting power of RAF Bomber Command. The period opened with light and medium bombers still dominating operations, but by the end of 1942 the new heavy bombers were increasing in numbers and the older aircraft being taken out of service. The average weight of bomb load had reached from 3,405lb (1.5 tons) bombs per aircraft in 1942 to 6,903lb (3.1 tons) by 1943.[34]

IN DEFENCE OF THE COMMUNITY

The Air Ministry account listed thirty-five RAF raids on Aachen in 1941. There was a general increase in the numbers of aircraft, an increase in bomb loads and a large number of nuisance raids. A significant milestone was reached on the evening of 9–10 July, when the city's sirens sounded for the hundredth time. The bomber stream passed overhead at 01.30–02.39 hours and bombed in what is generally treated as the first large raid on Aachen. The Air Ministry counted sixty-six 'attacking aircraft' had dropped 78.3 tons of high explosives and 15.6 tons of incendiaries. The BCD identified eighty-two aircraft assigned to the raid, with 1,698 homes destroyed, de-housing 3,450 people, and serious damage to prominent cultural buildings—cathedral, Rathaus and churches. The *Poll-Chronicle* identified a *Grossangriff* against the city centre; more than 30 bombers had dropped 176 bombs and 3,000 incendiaries. They accounted for total casualties: 60 killed and 85 injured; extensive structural damage to the cathedral, the city archive, two central high schools, several churches and the Alexianer cloister. Several flak batteries maintained a steady barrage, supported by a railway flak detachment that was firing while shuttling between the main station and Rothe Erde station.[35]

According to the *Poll-Chronicle*, the Engelbert tyre factories were bombed on 31 July 1942, in the early hours between 01.43 and 3.05 hours. The RAF dropped 62 bombs and 500 incendiaries, which caused 1 dead and 15 injured. The BCD has no reference to this raid, but page 186 refers to an attack on Cologne in the evening of 30–1 July, with 116 aircraft. There had been foul weather warnings that evening, and the crews reported 'Cologne believed hit'. Aachen was either bombed in error or had been dumped on. According to a local account, the raid brought home the reality of the war as the Nazis increased the ration of coffee beans and peas to cook *Eintopf* (yellow-pea stew). There were no further raids on Aachen until 27 November, when the centre was bombed between 20.38 and 21.30 hours. The RAF dropped 30 bombs, 150 incendiaries and a mine. The casualties were: 20 dead, 22 injured and the old *Kurhaus* (health resort) was destroyed. This raid recorded the first use of a mine and a 30lb phosphorus bomb. The Air Ministry data identified no raid on Aachen and BCD listed a raid on Düsseldorf by 86 aircraft, although Cologne also reported damage and casualties. The raid caused casualties and destruction but was another error. For 8 December 1941, the *Poll-Chronicle* recorded a raid against the Westbahnhof district at 04.27–05.30 hours—five bombs and nine incendiaries. The Air Ministry claimed 68 aircraft had dropped 85.8 tons of high explosives and 10.7 tons of incendiaries. The BCD entry for 7–8 December (page 224) referred to an error in the RAF report as incorrectly dated 8–9 December. The BDC noted 130 aircraft were assigned to the raid and Aachen's Nazi Party headquarters was the aiming point. In difficult weather only sixteen of sixty-four aircraft bombed; three bombs hit the railway yards.

The next large raid was 5–6 October 1942. The RAF assigned 257 aircraft—101 Wellingtons, 74 Lancasters, 59 Halifaxes and 23 Stirlings. Ten aircraft were lost, making it 3.9 per cent, but another 6 aircraft crashed due to thunderstorms. The weather had been a problem from the start and the Pathfinders were ineffective. In twenty minutes (22.35–22.57 hours), an unspecified number of aircraft dropped four parachute-mines, seven bombs, one firebomb, 329 incendiaries and fourteen phosphorus canisters on Burtscheid, an area known for its healthcare and religious institutions; three hospitals including Roman Catholic Marienhospital were all seriously damaged. They killed five and injured thirty-nine. The Dutch town of Geleen, seventeen miles away, suffered the loss of 800 houses, eighty-three killed, twenty-two injured and 3,000 homeless.[36] The raid included four Wellingtons from RCAF No. 425 (Alouette), their first operation, and 'bombed what was believed to be Aachen'. No. 425 began flying in August 1942 and became operational in October. During the 5–6 October raid the squadron also suffered from severe icing and electric storms—two crews returned early, one crashed at Debden, which killed all on board, but all five according to the official history reached the target but made no claims about their bombing accuracy.[37] Crews from No. 405 (RCAF) bombed Mechelen, instead of Aachen, and the crews blamed an electrical storm for knocking out their 'Gee' navigation system.[38]

In December 1945, Arthur Harris delivered his final despatch for Bomber Command, and described the doctrine he inherited. On 23 September 1941:

IN DEFENCE OF THE COMMUNITY

The ultimate aim of the attack on a town area is to break the morale of the population which occupies it. To ensure this we must achieve two things; first, we must make a town physically uninhabitable and, secondly, we must make the people conscious of constant personal danger. The immediate aim, is therefore, twofold, namely, to produce (I) destruction and (II) the fear of death.

He was also at pains to reiterate, 'my primary authorised task was therefore clear beyond doubt: to inflict the most serious material damage on German industrial cities'.[39]

V. The last hope

In 1948, the British Air Ministry published a study of the Luftwaffe, which examined the capability of the German home defence system. The flak, searchlight and prediction systems were initially regarded as a reasonable standard, with the flak regiments 'considered to be the elite of the German Air Force'. There was some over-confidence placed in the capability of flak to defend cities, and faith in Göring's speech from August 1939 that no enemy aircraft would penetrate the Ruhr area. The early raids of May 1940 exposed the futility of Nazi claims and ushered in the emergence of night fighter forces. By 1942, the Luftwaffe had raised an efficient level and a serious threat to the RAF.[40] On 19 July 1940, Göring pressed forward with a night fighter and a defence system later called the Kammhuber Line. Lw-Oberst Josef Kammhuber had devised a system of sectors, each with dedicated radar, searchlights and a night fighter, making a long line stretching from Schleswig-Holstein running along the German-Dutch border and then extending into northern France. The system was successful until Bomber Command devised 'the stream' countermeasure, which proved successful in the heavy raid on Cologne in May 1942. *Kammhuber line* was a geospatial box system of grids placed on a map of Germany made up of many boxes, each forty miles square, with radar, searchlights and anti-aircraft guns assigned to support the system.

The air defence of Nazi *Gau Aachen-Köln* were centralised under 7th Flak Division (Cologne), with flak-groups sited in Aachen, Brühl, Leverkusen, Köln and Wuppertal. The *Gefechtsstand der*

Kölner Luftabwehr, based in Fort IV of Cologne's nineteenth-century fortifications, was the control centre for the defence of the *Gau*. The facilities included plotting rooms, fire control systems, mess-hall, communications and barracks. The flak batteries included heavy and medium flak artillery—ranging in calibre from 20 to 105mm guns. The flak emplacements were placed across Cologne and under the central command of the tactical headquarters. There was also an *Eisenbahn-Flak Longerich*, which was next to Fort IV, and the trains were sent to support Aachen flak defences during air raids. There is an account that Oberbürgermeister Jansen confronted the Luftwaffe representatives of *Luftgau VI* (the Luftwaffe's regional organisation that incorporated the Ruhr and *Gau Aachen-Köln*) over the withdrawal of heavy flak defences from Aachen. The Luftwaffe agreed to ring Aachen with flak defences and raised a flak unit: the officer cadre was raised in Berlin, the 514th Reserve Heavy Flak Detachment and the 5/889 Reserve light flak detachment were transferred to Aachen. Generally referred to as *Flakgruppe Aachen*, it was supplied with 88mm flak guns (believed to have served with the *Africa Korps*) for the heavy batteries and 20mm or 37mm guns for the light batteries. *Flakgruppe Aachen* established its headquarters in Villa Springsfeld on the Salvartorberg, the area of high ground to the north overlooking the centre.[41]

In autumn 1941, a battery of railway flak was drawn from Cologne's defences and stabled in Eilendorf on the Vennbahn (the German-Belgian border railway). This initially formed the first battery in *Flakgruppe Aachen* but served both Aachen and Cologne during respective air raids. Post-war memories claimed different details about the batteries. For example, one person claimed the second battery was emplaced in Eilendorf and known as *Batterie Eilendorf*, while another recalled the second was emplaced in the Siegfried Line, the concrete bunker system between the Lousberg hill and Vaals on the Dutch border. Another, possibly the third battery, was emplaced in Richterich in the grounds of Schloss Schonau, north-north-west of the city. A heavy battery was positioned in the Westpark, covering Hanbruch and Venskyhäuschen, in the western suburbs. A fourth battery was deployed in Beverau in the town of Burtscheid, which is a south-eastern district. The fifth and sixth batteries were placed on the golf course (about three miles to the west) and Turnierplatz (the show jumping arena a mile north of the city centre). The guns of the light flak detachment 5/889 were positioned on the roofs of taller buildings. Several batteries were served by Soviet Russian *Hilfswillige* (HIWIs); the Russian PoWs were offered work by the Germans, mostly hard labour for miserable rations. During the raids they formed shell lines, passing the shells by hand to the gunners. During the rest of the time, they carried out menial duties such as cleaning the guns and barracks and working as hard labour digging trenches or carrying out other heavy duties.

On 26 January 1943, Hermann Göring announced *Kriegshilfdiensteinsatz der Jugend* (youth assistance to the war effort), and from 8 February the Luftwaffe mustered the 1926–7 age groups (16–17-year-olds) and later the 1928 age group. They were designated by the Luftwaffe as auxiliaries, *Luftwaffenhelfer* (LH), to serve in the anti-aircraft defences. The policy allowed the transfer of fully trained Luftwaffe troops to combat formations.[42] The *Luftwaffenhelfer* had three ranks, *Helfer*, *Oberhelfer* and *Mannschaftsführer*, and were required as auxiliaries to continue their schooling. The collected recollections of Aachen's former *Luftwaffenhelfer* represents insight of life among the youth. The youths were mustered from schools dating back to 1601 as in the case of *Kaiser Karls Gymnasium* (KKG), or 1818 with the Hindenburg-Schule (Couven-Gymnasium), and others included *General Litzmann School* (today Rhein-Maas Gymnasium), the *Kaiser Wilhelm Oberschule* (Einhardt-Gymnasium) and members of the Walloon community in Malmedy, who were ordered to remove their children from schools and send them to Aachen.

Many recalled the first draft of 12 January 1943, when the entire school class was ordered to parade before Luftwaffe NCOs. The NCOs strolled through the ranks selecting candidates. One pupil recalled they did not select those youths from Nazi families. When the youths were marched away, one mother marched alongside in tears. The first muster of youths was 1926–7 age bracket and were ordered to attend the headquarters of *Flakgruppe Aachen*. The light flak detachment 5/889 acquired sixty-seven auxiliaries and they were quartered in barracks on the golf course. Each section of nine youths was allocated twenty square metres of barrack space. The rooms were cold; they shared a washbasin and the ration included bread, sausages and tomatoes. A Catholic priest was assigned to live with them in their barracks. A local monastery supplied bread and parents visited every Sunday. Recollections of training were quite disjointed; some were fascinated with the flak system of guns and radar, while others recalled basic military training, and a few recalled how the railway flak units continually travelled between Aachen, Jülich and Monschau. Those assigned to Jülich, the nearby garrison town, received basic infantry training with a rifle. The general opinion of all former pupils was their happiness at escaping the drudgery of school.[43]

One former pupil (GLS) said his friends enjoyed joining up; they had reached manhood and removed their despised Hitler Youth armbands. A former pupil from Jülich claimed the enthusiasm was not so much an expression of Nazism but the opportunity to participate in the war with real guns, searchlights and military equipment. Some believed serving as *Luftwaffenhelfer* elevated their self-esteem, while others imagined themselves as *Landesknechts*. The Luftwaffe insignia was removed and replaced them with an HJ armlet, black shoulder straps with light-blue piping and an eagle emblazoned with the letters LH. The boys removed the Hitler Youth badges and restored the Luftwaffe insignia. Resigned to the situation, some parents moved closer to where their sons were assigned or visited them daily. The Luftwaffe NCOs did not like their presence, and this added to the tensions between the military and the parents. A former pupil from Eschweiler recalled how parents tried to make the most of it by supporting their sons. One mother was frantic over her son's safety because her husband and both her other sons were soldiers at the front. She was bombed out and moved to the Lousberg area to be near to her son's flak battery. Other parents protested publicly, which attracted the suspicions of Nazi officials, and there were a number of denunciations against the protestors. Some parents dubbed the LH the *Letzte Hoffnung*—the last hope—possibly light-heartedly or as an act of passive resistance.

IN DEFENCE OF THE COMMUNITY

The *Luftwaffnhelfer* came at the turning point of the war, when the crescendo of violence and destruction reached boiling point. The father of one pupil blamed the GLS for planting patriotic ideas in their heads. The militaristic training of Hitler Youth made it impossible to influence their sons. In the end, parents were powerless in handling their children. Neighbours showed no interest in the plight of parents once the bombing raids increased, which added to a sense of powerlessness, isolation and fear. Parents tried to persuade family doctors to issue unfit-for-service medical certificates. Some parents placed sons in apprenticeships for essential war work or got them to fail the school year, which forced a resit. Several former KKG students claimed the schools was deeply conservative and Catholic, which formed a secret resistance to the call-up of pupils. There were conflicting claims: one recalled the presence of a Jesuit priest who was a member of the anti-Hitler resistance, but another claimed the presence of Nazi teaching staff, making resistance impossible. Most recalled that their flak duties continued long into the early hours, but they were still required to attend school at 09.00 hours. The strain caused lethargy and most fell asleep at their desks. The battery commanders were sometimes quite caring and allowed the boys to oversleep, as did some teachers.[44] If there was a dilemma for German youth under Nazism it was to be too young to be soldiers and too old to be treated as children. How German youth behaved when offered an opportunity to fight back is perhaps a difficult story. Perhaps Nicholas Stargardt has best summed up the cost of their dilemma: 'What it cost these teenage boys to summon up such cool poise is impossible to calculate, but they did so in the self-image of having finally grown up and entered the world of men.'[45]

4

WARLORD

> The German civilian population might be expected to be psychologically more susceptible to air raid attack than the British people. The British people were from the start prepared for the worst, whereas the German people had been assured by their leaders, and believed that they would be safe from enemy bombs. The British people had confidence that conditions must soon improve whereas the German people fear that conditions can only deteriorate. The British people had no thought of any end to the war save victory; the German people, on the other hand, when the heavy raids hit them, were war weary and suffering from great nervous strain.[1]

There is a general sense of gratitude towards Winston Churchill for his leadership in confronting the tyrannical ambitions of Adolf Hitler and the Axis powers. Churchill's foremost strategic objective was to uphold liberty, freedom and democracy. He perceived total war as indispensable to safeguard Britain's sovereignty, protect the empire and thwart the spread of tyranny across Europe. Recognising Churchill's leadership aptitude, the House of Commons rallied behind him in May 1940. As prime minister, he also created the post of Minister of Defence, taking charge of the war at a critical moment in history. However, history also has a convenient way of overlooking the part played by others, as in the case of the Secretary of State for War, held successively by Anthony

Eden (May–December 1940), David Margesson (December 1940–February 1942) and James Grigg (February 1942–July 1945). Eden's time in office was the most turbulent, marked by military setbacks and the Battle of Britain, while Margesson's tenure was cut short following the fall of Singapore, leading to his replacement by Grigg. These historical dynamics underscore the challenges liberal democracies face when confronting expansionist and genocidal totalitarian regimes. The decisions made by political leaders and diplomats during this period profoundly shaped history and underscore the intricate ethical considerations intertwined with wartime strategies.[2]

In his memoirs, Churchill depicted himself, like the wartime propaganda, as Britain's Warlord, the champion of Westminster democracy and defender of the empire. Hindsight and memory distort history, more so when certain key aspects are missing from a memoir. The initial year of the warlord's leadership was fraught with defeats and setbacks as he mobilised all national security resources to defend the British Isles. This strategy frustrated Hitler's ambitions and disrupted the German army's plans. However, a strategic dilemma emerged afterwards: how to frame the political imperative of defeating Nazi Germany and at the same time build the necessary military resources for victory. There were painful lessons learned in 1940 that came from the scale of effort required to wage modern warfare successfully. The military resources were not available, and the nation wasn't geared up for total war. As warlord, Churchill was forced to set priorities. In effect he synthesised his long-held faith in the power of intelligence, both political and military, with the bomber and the doctrines of strategic bombing, into his tool for victory. This was a risky venture since the bomber's potential was still unproven, albeit offering a considerable promise as a weapon.

In 1940, while intelligence was relatively straightforward to mobilise, RAF Bomber Command entered the fray with muddled doctrines, overly ambitious targets and inadequate aircraft. Frederick Taylor has described how Churchill confronted the stark reality revealed in the Butt Report during the summer of 1941: the bombers were not only missing their targets but also bombing indiscriminately. By November 1941, all bomber operations ceased temporarily, leading some, like Taylor, to interpret it as an acknowledgment of failure. However, Churchill remained steadfast as Taylor summarised, 'Bomber Command was too important a propaganda symbol, and its promise as a weapon, against the German war machine and against the German homeland, too attractive.'[3] Recognising the shortcomings of Bomber Command reporting, as highlighted by the Butt Report, Anthony Eden set about representing an alternative political intelligence, based upon Foreign Office sources, about the effects of bombing. By centralising all intelligence—gathering data, conducting research and analysis, and formulating reports—Eden could present expert reports to the War Cabinet, for collective consideration, or approval. In 1942, the group began formulating an opinion of the success or failure of the new directives to bomb German civilians to break their morale. After ten months without recognisable success the group began considering alternative paradigms, including a sudden defeat scenario as per 1918. While this chapter does not directly address the bombing of Aachen, through examples, it is intended to explain the political discourse about the bombing campaign at cabinet level. It also places in context the political background to the massive fire raid of Aachen in July 1943 (the subject of the next chapter).

I. Anthony Eden's strategic initiative

There is a small collection of British Foreign Office records, erroneously tagged under a general catalogue 'Conditions in Germany and occupied countries, 1942'. Within each file there are as many as ten files, each covering a range of subjects including 'German morale', 'the effects of bombing', 'German public opinion' and more. Before the advent of focus groups and Delphi groups, the political intelligence departments of the Foreign Office came under the control of a Central Department (FOCD) and the Joint Intelligence Committee (JIC). The FOCD and JIC arranged ad hoc interdepartmental groups of specialists to focus on a range of intelligence, propaganda and political warfare subjects. The FOCD spearheaded civilian-based political initiatives, such as researching German morale and monitoring signs of an impending German collapse. Pre-war political research heavily relied on initiatives like Mass-Observation, a social science endeavour launched in 1937 to provide accurate observations of everyday life and public moods, filling a void overlooked by media, politicians and scientists.[4] The concept of mass observation was ingeniously adapted by the Foreign Office to monitor German morale, resembling a focus group approach in market research. Functioning as an ad hoc research think tank, the FOCD coordinated intelligence gathering, sifting through 'informed' gossip from embassies and diplomatic circles, distinguishing between valuable information and uninformed rumour or gossip. The process of information appraisal operated within an echo chamber of similar social classes. The data or information was often accepted on face value because it emanated from a demographically parallel social group to the diplomats, primarily comprising middle- or upper-class individuals: civil servants, diplomats, academics, senior military officers and business executives. Despite the social parallels, a distinction remained, with British diplomats acquiring information while anonymous 'informants' offered expert opinions or rumours. Following thorough analysis and appraisal, reports circulated for discussion before final presentations to the War Cabinet and the king. However, inherent within this system was a subtle inclination towards class superiority in information treatment and a sense of national superiority, particularly in the context of belligerents at war.

The FOCD became the engine room of Churchill's civilian intelligence initiative, but it would be a mistake to assume it was non-military or passive. This office was highly efficient, collecting and coordinating intelligence across a wide spectrum of civil-military interests. The office served the Foreign Minister and the diplomatic service, but coordinated reports on behalf of the War Cabinet, the Chiefs of Staff, the JIC and other agencies. The coordinator of the FOCD was Sir Frank Roberts (1907–1998), previously a secretary of the Anglo-French Supreme War Council operations (1940–1), and thereafter the senior officer of the FOCD. From the levels of War Cabinet and committees, he coordinated agendas, meetings and the contents of reports, which he then distributed. Roberts passed opinion on most content and was not a silent secretary. Technically, Roberts reported to Sir Anthony Eden (1897–1977), elevated to Foreign Secretary on 22 December 1940. Under Eden were Sir Alexander Cadogan (1884–1968), the Permanent Under Secretary for Foreign Affairs, and Sir Orme Sargeant (1884–1962), Deputy Under-Secretary of State for the Foreign Office. He had joined the Foreign Office in 1906 after leaving Radley College. From July 1942, they were joined by Sir Geoffrey Harrison (1908–1990), as Acting First Secretary in the Foreign Office.[5] The Foreign Office was also responsible for the Political Warfare Executive (PWE) under Sir Bruce Lockhart (1887–1970), who served as the director-general.[6] Roberts also coordinated intelligence affairs with the Minister of Economic Warfare (MEW), under Roundell Palmer (1887–1971), the 3rd Earl of Selborne. The MEW was also responsible for the Special Operations Executive (SOE); its director, Henry Moore the Earl of Drogheda (1884–1957), was regularly addressed in FOCD correspondence. The Political Intelligence Department (PID) was raised as a secret Foreign Office department in 1939. From 1943, it merged with the Royal Institute of International Affairs, in Oxford, to serve as the Foreign Office Research Department. The leading analyst was Dr John Hawgood (1905–1971), a historian.[7] Roberts also cooperated and coordinated with the Joint Intelligence Committee (JIC), an interagency committee raised in 1936 by the Committee of Imperial Defence to coordinate intelligence assessment.[8] Victor Frederick William Cavendish-Bentinck, 9th Duke of Portland (18 June 1897–30 July 1990), was chairman of the JIC and council on the Services Liaison Department of the Foreign Office.

During the war, British embassies in neutral countries functioned as vital 'listening posts', gathering all pertinent information related to Germany—a dimension of diplomacy often relegated to a secondary role in the annals of wartime history but of profound strategic significance during that period. The role of diplomats during wartime typically evokes varied impressions, ranging from those engaged in pre-war negotiations to those involved in drafting armistices at war's end. However, diplomats played a crucial role in shaping national strategy and conducting diplomacy throughout the conflict. A depiction of the diplomat at war was briefly captured in the film *The Battle of Britain* (1969), through Sir Ralph Richardson's portrayal of Sir David Kelly (1891–1959), the Envoy Extraordinary and Minister Plenipotentiary in Berne, Switzerland, from 1940 to 1942. In a pivotal scene, Richardson's character receives the German ambassador, referred to as 'Max Richter', bearing a peace offer from Hitler. Tensions escalate as Max presents Hitler's guarantees, only to be countered by Kelly's scepticism: 'the Führer's guarantees, guaranteed nothing'. Their exchange turns heated as Max questions Churchill's resolve, prompting Kelly's defiant retort: 'don't dictate to us until you're marching up Whitehall, and even then, we won't listen'. The scene encapsulates British stereotypes of stoicism and resolve, intertwined with the cultural imagery of the 'bulldog spirit', the cup of tea, the unforgivable raising of his voice.[9] Switzerland held immense strategic importance for British diplomacy during the war, a fact later acknowledged by Churchill, who praised its contribution to the cause of freedom. Throughout the conflict, British embassies in neutral countries, including Sweden under ambassador Sir Victor Mallet (1893–1969), Spain under ambassador Samuel Hoare, First Viscount Templewood (1880–1959), Portugal under Sir Ronald H. Campbell (1883–1953) and Turkey under ambassador Sir Hughe Knatchbull-Hugessen (1886–1971), played crucial roles in gathering intelligence and conducting strategic diplomacy.[10]

Very early on in their work, the group were instructed to examine what the British press preferred for their headlines. Interestingly, one report was a discussion about the British press but dressed up as another 'situation in Germany memorandum. Harrison had written a draft report which opened:

> Since just before Christmas the British press have been carrying a great number of items on the plight of the German army, on German internal dissensions and on the deterioration in German morale. So much so, that, not without apparent justification the British public is not far from beginning to think in terms of an early German collapse and even an end to the war in. Europe before summer is out. This is a dangerous state of affairs.[11]

The working papers provide a more nuanced back story. Cavendish-Bentinck thought the editors of newspapers wanted either 'optimistic reports which will give pleasure to their readers' or 'hair-raising stories which will excite them at the same time make them think that the newspaper printing these stories is doing wonderful work by revealing facts'. He accepted German morale was low but all the more remarkably, predicted a 'volcanic' German collapse by December 1942.[12] Harrison also made a file on 15 January, claiming 'The American press has been a bad offender in the matter of reproducing exaggerated reports of conditions in Germany. Several news clippings were included to illustrate the problem. An example was an article from the Diplomatic correspondent of *The Times* (15 January 1942), who had written of Germany, 'Among the people at home some of the dark mood of the last war is descending ... This time they have had still greater sacrifices without the victory.'[13] There is no indication of what happened after the report; like many of the group's projects they were disregarded without explanation.

II. Termination of railways as a strategic target

In the previous chapter, the focus was on the bombing of Aachen as a *railopolis* in May 1940, from Plan W.A.4 (C) and marshalling yards to 9 July 1941 'railways in the Rhineland' and the 'policy to dislocate German transportation system and destroy of civilians particularly industrial workers'. In 1942, an RAF target report referred to the layout of the city: 'Aachen is a compact circular shaped city, encircled by boulevards and railways, with the main factories on its outskirts, notably along the two main railways to the north east and east ... The roads and the railways radiate from Aachen like the spokes of a wheel, and surround the town to the west and south. On these routes are situated several small marshalling and good yards.'[14] However, the same report identified four civilian areas—'city-centre, an area of 100 acres, a fully built up mixed area of 350 acres, an area of about one square mile'. The area was noted as small but 'highly vulnerable to high explosive and incendiary bomb attack'. Monitoring the impact of the war on the German railways offered an impression of ordinary everyday life.

The raid on Rostock on 26 April 1942 caused a flurry of police signals. The railway station was burnt out, and 2,000 houses were destroyed. In April 1942, an Axis Strength and Policy report presented to the War Cabinet included a brief summary about railways:

> The German railway organisation has on the whole been able hitherto to cope adequately with the difficulties caused by the Russian campaign. This has entailed the transfers of locomotives and rolling-stock to the East, where gauge conversion has been efficiently carried out; but the demand has been met by restrictions on unnecessary travel, increased use of inland waterways and intensive construction of new rolling-stock and locomotives. Shortage of personnel appears to be the main problem. Reports during recent months show an accentuation of difficulties greater than during any previous period of the war.[15]

A member of the Swedish press bureau informed Stockholm embassy officials about a railway journey. From the window of a train, he had seen the damage caused to the railway yards of Rostock; all the towers were destroyed in the town. There was an additional note about the bombing:

> At least 250 Danish workers were killed in Rostock. The Germans were very angry about the recent British raids. During the second and third British raids on Rostock there was panic among the population and many people drowned in the canals. The police forced the population into the air raid shelters with revolvers. Later the men were forced out again to help with the fire fighting.[16]

On 11 June, Sir Samuel Hoare, Ambassador in Madrid, hosted an after-dinner meeting with various officials from Vichy France: 'As regards transport German railways and rolling stock were strained far beyond capacity and the Germans had lost a considerable amount of rolling stock through bombing and on the eastern front. They had taken 50 per cent of France's rolling stock and did not dare to take any more from her or any other occupied country for fear of internal collapse.'[17]

In July 1942, PWE compiled a report on German rail travel from German newspapers. The report began with the Nazi wartime slogan for the railways, *Rädar mussten rollen für den Sieg* (The Wheels Must Turn for Victory). There was considerable over-crowding, with carriages bursting to overflowing. The worst region for over-crowding was in the Rhineland. The railway authorities claimed upwards of 40 per cent of journeys were wasteful and unimportant. Trains were delayed from ten to thirty minutes, which caused further crowding on platforms. Passengers suffered torn clothing from the unrepaired broken windows in carriages. There was a sense of panic and chaos in stations due to the absence of working timetables. The increase in war salaries had made second-class tickets more accessible. The male train guards were replaced by women, which added to the problems of order, because no one listened to them. This had caused a 'traveller's morale', whereby passengers shouted and abused female guards. Some travellers risked arrest for travelling without permits—only military passes and travel warrants guaranteed a complete journey. On 21 June 1942, the *Völkischer Beobachter* advised that permits would be required for all train travel. All travellers on inspection had to prove their journey was of national or vital importance. Some newspapers reported that, since the ruling, there had been an upsurge of black-market tickets and permits.[18]

A Stockholm informant for a PID report had observed trains with special carriages for mothers travelling with children. The source assumed they were meant for evacuees. There was still a large number of persons travelling on the trains even after a travel ban, and the ordinary carriages were jam-packed with soldiers and civilians.[19] The PID's links to Social-Democrat exiles in Sweden added to stories about the railways. In Dresden, there were noticeable changes due to travel restrictions, with fewer trains and mostly all mixed stock of goods wagons and passenger carriages. This was causing further delays in running times, as trains were required to shunt wagons for dropping off or collection along their journeys. The general fall in staff numbers meant fewer men were available to work the shunting. The consequence of these changes resulted in a normal four-hour journey taking an entire day. The shortages of labour had seen women take up driving trams; the five-minute intervals between trams were increased to fifteen minutes, and others had been curtailed. This meant that 'Many workers had to walk great distances to their place of work; they had no time for anything but the journey from home to work and back again ... All this has a depressing effect on people's spirits, in spite of all the reports of the victories in the east.'[20] Although there was no specific FOCD file on the end of bombing railways, it is evident that the bombing had failed to stop the trains or break German morale. However, in 1946, a review of Harris's decision to move away from communications and railways would be regarded as a significant failing (refer to chapter nine).

III. Mass observation of German morale

The change from bombing military targets to targeting civilians and morale has been thoroughly studied and researched. On 18 August 1941, the Butt Report found that, irrespective of aircrew claims, they were not hitting their targets.[21] The report had three important outcomes. In August, RAF Bomber Command formed an Operational Research Section under Dr B.G. Dickins, based in High Wycombe, with 'its ultimate purpose being to assist in getting the maximum number of bombers over their targets with the minimum of losses'.[22] Between 5 and 12 February, Bomber Command introduced a series of directives that constituted the Area Bombing Directive, and on 22 February, Sir Arthur Harris became Commander-in-Chief of RAF Bomber Command. On 30 March, Professor Lindemann presented a paper to Churchill on 'dehousing' based on evidence drawn from studies of the German blitz of Britain 1940–1. The 'morale' question reset agendas and narratives, which set a high intensity among the FOCD groups which fluctuated through 1942.

One of the earliest reports, from January, originated from an informant who had travelled to Germany: 'The mentality of the German masses has undergone a marked change since last year. Spirits are sinking everywhere. The inhabitants of Greater Germany are tired of war, tired of work, tired even of so-called

German victories ... The detonations of British bombs and the glow of the fires in Northern and Western Germany are at last bringing the deaf and the blind German masses to their senses.'[23] On 16 January, the British consulate in Barcelona informed London of an article, *'Näher Gerückt der front!'*, published in the German weekly newspaper *Das Reich* five days before. The consular report noted that 'the people at home are told that they can no longer expect the succession of easy victories which had been their fortune in the past ... The Germans are today not in the third year of war but in the 28th year of war and must be prepared to make sacrifices accordingly.' The article also asserted:

> The Leitmotiv is no longer the joys and delights of a victorious advance; emphasis is laid on the sufferings of the troops, the cancellation of all leave, the longer death rolls, and the ruthlessness with which the Russians are fighting.[24]

In response to the group perception of rising German war pessimism, Roberts added a cautionary file note, 'There is no doubt a good deal of useful information here, but I cannot help feeling that the German difficulties in the East are perhaps exaggerated.'[25]

On 8 February 1942, the Stockholm office received a German informant they designated 'S'. She had returned from a trip to her former family home in Germany and met her brother, serving in the Luftwaffe on leave from southern Russia. He had told her of 'indescribable suffering and great casualties'. There was 'grumbling against party men, but in her opinion fear of Bolshevism and hatred of Russia will keep them united and they will go on fighting'. There was a decline in Hitler's popularity with regular officers. There was a rumour circulating that the famous fighter pilot, Werner Moelders, had returned his medals two weeks before his fatal flying accident in 1941. Russian aircraft had caused casualties and Luftwaffe aircraft were ill suited and poorly equipped for severe winter conditions. Families were far better off than 1916–17.[26] The most constant form reporting was about German morale usually included in the Joint Intelligence Sub-Committee reports. An 'Axis Strength' report for 13 February 1942 concluded: 'There are no signs as yet of a break in German civilian morale, nor of the emergence of any organised opposition in the country. Apathy is widespread but is beginning to give place to uncertainty and doubt about the future.'[27]

In April 1942, Bentinck revised and submitted the report as final:

> The prospect that the war may be long is perhaps now coming to be accepted, most reluctantly, by the German people. But what dominates the thoughts of all is the immediate threat of the Red Army, whose annihilation this summer Hitler has promised. Provided the spring offensive does not fall far short of its objective, it would be rash to count on any development favourable to ourselves on the German home front. But if it does, the endurance of the German people may approach breaking point.[28]

Hawgood issued a PID second quarter report for 1942 that was approved for printing and submission as a 'blue paper' for circulation to the War Cabinet. The report was concerned with the 'political situation and public morale in Germany' and opened: 'After a slight recovery in German morale during February 1942, the downward trend which had been discernible at the turn of the year was resumed in March'. Hawgood explained that Hitler's speech on 26 April on becoming 'Supreme Law Lord' and 'free from all ties imposed by existing rules of legal procedure', was the language of a serious domestic crisis. Fritz Sauckel was made responsible for organising the roundup of foreign labour and there had been investigations into civil servants dealing on the black market. Albert Speer, the Minister of Armaments, was granted draconian powers over manufacturers guilty of sabotage from making false returns. But, Hawgood conceded:

> It was obvious, however, that nothing in the condition of Germany at the end of April pointed to an imminent breakdown either in civilian morale or in administrative machinery, and the measures above referred to no doubt had the object of gearing up the whole German war machine to the highest pitch of efficiency for the coming critical months.

Reactions to Hawgood's report among members of the FOCD, while in draft prior to submittance, was varied and provide an insight into the groupthink. On 9 April, Roberts added the file note, 'thought it covered the ground very adequately'. Cavendish-Bentinck added, 'I think this appreciation excellent' and wanted it printed immediately. However, on 11 April, Roger Makins (1904–1996), a career diplomat, complained: 'I find Mr. Hawgood's production very verbose but as it is almost the sole visible result of his activities in the Political Intelligence Department I agree that it might be printed.'[29] Two months later, Hawgood concluded:

> At the beginning of June, therefore, there were probably very few Germans who had high hopes of any spectacular successes in the immediate future, or anything that could happen before the month was out to make to make them feel that there was some prospect of achieving final victory or securing a satisfactory peace fairly soon.

Class had a significant influence over both participants and in measuring the value of information. For the source and nature of the information to be received as valuable qualitatively it was assumed the informant was above reproach, socially acceptable on class grounds. Foreign informants were treated as equals because they were mostly on the same social level as the British diplomats. Class cut across the boundaries of belligerent nations, since all involved were middle or upper class or higher, which added a social endorsement of information. In one case, from Switzerland, the British official concluded:

> I recognise that one must discount much of this kind of talk. I simply pass it on for what it is worth but should like to remind you once again that my informant is a first-class witness, both from the technical standpoint and that of general reliability and straightforwardness.[30]

On 25 April, the British ambassador in Bagdad sent a report to London on comments made by the Swiss Consul from Cairo after his visit to Berlin. In the seven months since a previous visit, he noticed a significant deterioration in morale. The consul claimed, 'The people were beginning to realise that while many victories had been won, nothing decisive had been accomplished since the defeat of France in 1940.' He also thought the Japanese victories in the Far East 'had furnished German morale with an invaluable tonic during the winter'.[31]

On 30–1 May, Bomber Command carried out its first 'thousand-bomber raid', which generated a certain flurry of activity and discussion. In June, the intercepted letters were quite intense with comments about the bombing. A letter from Cologne contained the line, 'there are no electric trains'. An actress from Stockholm wrote that 'things are daily becoming worse' and a dancer recently arrived in Switzerland thought, 'this war cannot last much longer for we are approaching the end of our strength'. A letter from Gelsenkirchen mentioned that the 'Conditions are such that those at home are in just as much danger as those at the front, only not so well protected.' A baron from Berlin writing to his daughter referred to the war against the Soviet Union as the 'man-swallowing Eastern Front'. Aware of the German censor, many letters contained oblique references to the bombing. For example, one woman wrote of avoiding the summer's thunderstorms. The air raid on Rostock was examined from captured German correspondence. An intercepted letter from 11 June 1942 written by a German girl to a PoW in Canada told how it took her four days to arrive in the city. She 'found her mother, who had been alone for four nights with nerves completely shattered'. The house was a shell with no roof, doors or windows; she made the temporary repairs alone and, in the evening, went on duty. The absenteeism among women on flak duties had caused the commanding officer to shout at them, saying if they had been men they would have been shot. But many of the women had young children and were greatly concerned over their safety. Electricity and water were working again but there was no cooking because the gas was still switched off. Looters were being shot and the names placed on billboards. A vehicle with a loudspeaker travelled the town announcing the latest news, and bombs could be heard exploding.[32]

On 20 June, Stockholm hosted a special meeting for a leading Swedish businessman recently returned from Germany. The businessman had met a person from Cologne who told him after the

'1,000 bomber raid' that there was severe damage to the centre and 25 per cent of housing destroyed. Utilities and the telephone network were out of use. Fire was the main cause of damage, with a report circulating that German regulations had not prevented the spread of fires. The Germans observed the bomber waves at different heights, regarded as an effective method. The first wave at maximum ceiling had attracted the searchlights, then a second wave came in attracting anti-aircraft batteries and many of them were overwhelmed by the third wave of bombers. The British interviewer introduced a note of doubt about the bombing: 'I have asked him whether he thought the morale in German cities was likely to be broken by bombing any more than ours had been by German bombing, and he was rather doubtful about this.' There was an unfavourable tone about bombing, which had thus far not disrupted civilian morale. There was no indication of serious damage after a recent air raid on Essen and more destruction had been caused to smaller cities along the Rhine River.[33]

There was an avalanche of comments about the bombing of defenceless women and children:

> Four nights the English raided it; one can find no words with which to express what happened. How these "death-burners" worried themselves over the civil population. Extinguishing the rescue work on the houses in the residential quarter, and the inhabitants were hindered by fire-bombs. Those who have never experienced can have no idea of what it was like. As there was no military objective the old art gallery was destroyed in blind fury, also the residential quarter was ploughed by thousands of fire and high explosive bombs, and, on the third night, even land mines, too. That is not war, that is plain madness. An outrage and an abomination, that such a thing is possible in the 20th Century. I would rather be among the savages they have more pity on defenceless humans! Out of 7 towers, only two are left to greet you ... words are too weak describe what has been done to helpless women and children. (After raid on Rostock)[34]

A Swedish engineer visited Berlin in June 1942, and attended the 'Soviet Paradise' exhibition held in the *Lustgarten*. Some German visitors were shocked at the size of Soviet war machines and began demonstrating against the war in the east. The Nazi organisers had displayed some ugly truths:

> There was a large panorama composed of life-sized figures of the mutilated corpses of civilians cut out and pasted on cardboard. Parents and their young children wandered about, wallowing in these atrocities. There was a hall lit with a kind of dull reddish light, giving the impression of an inferno, full of grotesque caricatures of Jews who occupy important positions throughout the world. There were two large figures of Roosevelt and Churchill in this hall, but their faces had been retouched to give them a distorted and demoralising appearance.[35]

In June, Cavendish-Bentinck published the JIC 'Axis Strength' report for the War Cabinet. Regardless of the increased flow of information indicating a disturbance in German morale, he selected to make a cautious statement on morale:

> There are no signs as yet of a break in German morale, nor of the emergence of any organised opposition in the country. Apathy is widespread, but there is now considerable uncertainty and anxiety about the future. There is depression and war weariness, especially among the older people. There are signs of some deterioration in German morale as a result of the deterioration in the food situation, the extreme measures taken in labour mobilisation, and of heavier R.A.F. raids.[36]

In July 1942, a Turkish diplomat, during a visit to the British embassy in Ankara, gave details of his visit to Berlin. He was surprised the famous Adlon Hotel suffered from food shortages. He thought the shortages were attributable to disorganised transport or poor agricultural productivity due to labour shortages, but to a lesser extent British bombing. There was an absence of German men in villages, only male PoWs working the fields. He assumed: 'the German capitalist and bourgeois classes are beginning to fear that they are faced by a menace owing to the fact that productive labour, both in agriculture and in industry, is foreign and very strongly anti-German'.[37] From Portugal, a cypher received by Lockhart claimed the Germans had made some despondent remarks about the progress of the war. He claimed the air raids 'had done no substantial military damage but were producing an unsettling effect on civilian population'. The informant also observed 'that he was much struck by the dejected mood of the Minister in contrast with his buoyant expectation of victory a year ago'.[38] In July 1942, a German diplomat, described as 'belonging to the aristocracy and official class', had said: 'The general unpleasantness of life in Germany including even air raids is not yet a demoralising factor.' He also thought incendiaries dropped on the harvests and forests would succeed if the right time was chosen.[39] In July, Hawgood concluded a 'situation in Germany' report as follows:

> Public morale, after continuing to sag through April and May, recovered toward the end of June under the impetus of better news from the battlefronts, but was prevented from rising to any very marked extent by the impact of heavier air raids, and by the realisation of difficulties on the home front notably in food supplies and transport, which were likely to become much more pronounced if a fourth winter of war had to be faced.[40]

In August 1942, General Azcarate, the Mexican minister to Germany, informed British diplomats that the German officer corps would fight to the bitter end. 'Apathy' was also identified as significant and appeared in the reports. In a diplomatic note received from Mexico, there were no signs of a break in German civil morale but there was widespread apathy, a war-weary apathy and a deep apathy among the elderly.[41] In August, a member of the Swedish press visited Berlin and penned the following opening of a report: 'The spirit of the population is less depressed than in the autumn of last year. The food is extremely bad.'[42] We can assume it was unlikely that he had come into contact with many working-class Germans.

A report from the telecommunications service isolated the rising 'indignation' towards the bombing of defenceless women and children found in intercepted letters. The British were blamed for 'wantonly attacking residential districts egged on by Russian influence'. From Lübeck someone wrote, 'whoever has not seen it cannot imagine the destruction ... the English have let loose their

Bolshevistic methods. They cannot achieve any success at the front, and they vent their rage upon the defenceless civilian population.' A person from Hamburg wrote of an 'unholy war' where 'England becomes increasingly Bolshevised' making it impossible to 'talk of honourable warfare'. From Duisburg a survivor of the bombing quipped, 'churches, children, and hospitals they can hit sometimes, but never what they want to hit. ALL our factories and bridges are intact.' Another person from Hamburg wrote, 'The English machine-gunned the fire-fighters and ARP workers.' Some wanted revenge; a letter from Cologne exclaimed: 'The English—they are and remain a pack of swine and they have a shock coming to them.' The British also extracted comments that they dubbed the 'war of nerves'. A person from Mannheim wrote, 'The thought of the coming days and nights often frightens me.' A similar sentiment came from a person in Essen, 'Hell cannot be much worse. To sit in the cellar listening to that for 4 or 5 hours with whistling of the bombs, often drowned by the noise of the anti-aircraft fire is very upsetting to the nerves.' The letters also included observations of how the German were coping after the raids. After the bombing of Cologne, the city's refugees were taken to Aachen and Paris. In May, looters were shot in Rostock. Many of the letters supported the air defences, with jubilant comments about enemy aircraft shot down, especially if it was more than twenty. After a large raid on Cologne, a woman wrote, 'The willing spirit of the helpers was quite marvellous ... The help organisation worked very well. Transport of salvaged furniture was at once arranged; and also, for those people who could be housed outside the town.'[43]

A report was received from the Istanbul legation concerning information received from a woman described as 'born in German but neutral by marriage'. She was a diplomat's wife and had been warned by friends and acquaintances not to visit Germany in the summer because of the bombing. She was informed that the 'material and moral disintegration of family life in Germany where the fathers were in the army while the growing children, both boys and girls, take part in all kinds of army auxiliary services—the family circle is thus divided, and the children subjected to every kind of thoroughly demoralizing influences'. Many diplomats from other neutral countries referred to how the middle and upper class were suffering from Nazi measures. The shared backgrounds formed a common empathy that pinpointed the rising fears of general insecurity and specifically Gestapo scrutiny of diplomats and senior officials. They felt the middle/upper classes especially suffered because with the 'rationing and restrictions the richer people are constantly infringing the regulations and thus expose themselves to denunciations and penalties'. This had set a gloomy atmosphere among the privileged classes. A senior German official on a mission to Turkey complained to the British that 'his family were placed under special observation of the police and that such things have now become a general practice'. From his impression, there was serious despondency among the 'highly educated and socially privileged classes'.[44]

In September, there was a sense that the moment of 'shock and awe', from the implementation strategy of bombing civilians to undermine German morale, had passed. Anthony Eden presented a memorandum to the War Cabinet: Morale in Germany, 26 September. Eden began by asserting that civilian morale had been shaken in the winter of 1941–2. This was due to Soviet resistance and the entry of the USA into the war. Hitler had stemmed the slide by taking overall command. German victories and efforts to soothe German morale had only marginal results. He argued: 'While it is difficult at present to assess the general influence on morale of the greater weight of air raids there is no doubt that they are increasing the physical and nervous strain on the population.'[45] However, he did not expect a visible decline of morale with ramifications for the German effort in the near future. Cavendish-Bentinck shared his opinion:

> The morale of the German army and air force is still high and there are no signs of any deterioration as yet. German naval morale also remains high. There is no general dissatisfaction with service conditions in the navy, but there are incipient signs of anxiety about conditions at home. The fear of retribution and vengeance if Germany is defeated is strong among naval prisoners.[46]

Alexander Cadogan raised a 'margin note' that referred to the shortage of rations. Cavendish-Bentinck outlined a summary of German morale for the period January–August 1942:

As compared with any period prior to 1942 the decline in morale was clearly marked. There was more anxiety about the progress of the war, more dissatisfaction with service conditions, and more political criticism. On the other hand, within the period under review German successes in Russia appeared temporarily to have brought about some slight rise in morale. And the will to resistance was also strengthened by fear of the consequences of defeat.

On 9 September 1942, a diplomatic cypher arrived from Lisbon marked secret concerning a Portuguese diplomat from Turkey. The diplomat had recently engaged in a conference with Franz von Papen (1879–1969), Hitler's former Vice-Chancellor (1933–4) and Nazi Germany's ambassador to Turkey. During their meeting, Von Papen had claimed events in the Rhineland were 'a tragedy':

> The devastation resulting from our bombardments was appalling, thousands of persons were destitute and homeless, and the bulk of the population was now demanding peace at any price. Von Papen was at pains to represent the Rhinelanders as less able to stand up to punishment than other Germans but declared that unless Russia could be defeated before the winter he feared for the future of the Nazi regime.

The Foreign Office observed an increasing tendency of sources to refer to 'fear' as a prominent feature of German civilian morale. A Mrs Rose, Franz von Papen's secretary in Turkey, was overheard to mention 'fear'. There was 'fear' everywhere, but the most damaging cause was news from the troops in Russia and their treatment of Russian civilians. She claimed, 'The Germans understand that, if Russia were ever in a position to take revenge, they would kill off the whole German race.' The report triggered a paper trail of 'margin notes' on the file. One official noted, 'There seems little doubt that fear is the dominant factor in German minds.' Harrison added, 'It seems to me a time may come when we shall be able to demoralise Germans today by fear of air-raids. fear of Russians, fear of Poles and Czechs without necessarily withdrawing the hope of a future for Germany tomorrow.'[47]

At the month end, the frustration between the increasing air raids and the lack of intelligence was reflected in Roberts's letter to Hawgood (PID), three weeks after the first draft paper, 'I think it will be generally agreed that the most urgent problem facing us is to try and amplify the very brief remarks about air raids made in our first paper and to consider whether it is yet possible to provide a more positive and reasoned assessment of their effects on civilian morale.' Roberts noted 'the information so far available in the Foreign Office is rather fragmentary and, in some ways, conflicting and it is difficult to judge the relative weight to be given to varying accounts from isolated sources'.[48]

In October, the FOCD received a report collected on 17 September, from Emmanouil Tsouderos, the Greek Prime Minister, based upon information he had received from an informant who had recently visited Germany. The report included details of shortages in Germany, including coal, petrol and communications. Transport difficulties were believed to extend to the collection of that year's harvest, adding to further shortages in food. The loss of military momentum had carried over into 1942, and Germany's overall casualties were reaching 2.5 million. The informant believed the air raids were making a huge difference by causing interruptions to industrial production, not just in physical damage but causing sleeplessness and drowsiness to the work force. He also recommended an attack should last three days and nights in succession. There was evidence the working class were war weary. During his visit to Cologne, the informant witnessed graffiti scrawled on the ruins: 'we thank the Führer'. The black market was in full-scale operation and with massive price increases even for staple foods.[49]

On 3 October, an informant, unnamed but regarded as an important source, made the following observation that was passed to London:

> He thought that we over-estimated the effect on industry of our bombardments which he regarded as not being very great. Disorganisation of transport was the most important result but even here the effect as yet was far from decisive. Destruction of dwelling houses was important and the morale of the bombed out and other evacuees was low and contagious. He thought the effect on morale might be almost "decisive" in the long run if bombard-

ments increased much in frequency and range. Volume of bombing was in any case insufficient as yet.[50]

On 4 October, Roberts noted the time would be right, 'when the German armies are held up by the Russian winter, when our own bombing of Germany is achieving even greater proportions through the winter, and when the United Nations may hope to be achieving military successes elsewhere'. Cavendish-Bentinck added, 'Ever since the Treaty of Versailles the Germans have been taught that we did not fulfil the promises which were made when their plenipotentiaries signed the Armistice in November 1918.' In his opinion, the fear in propaganda had failed and at an opportune time, when the Germans suffered defeat, then the theme of hope should be applied to propaganda. A final note drew more caution, 'We await developments, military, climatic psychological with a watchful and hope discerning eye.'[51]

In October 1942, a telegram from Berne confirmed both the consul and the military attaché had approached an informant separately. There were few discrepancies, each corresponding closely, and as a consequence the report was sent to London. The first point referred to the question of opposition in Germany. The report announced, 'There is not a vestige of conspiracy in Germany today. Ruling factor is terror and there is no party, class or other element courageous enough to struggle against it.' The public was tired of war but the morale of the army remained high. To preserve the high morale, the army reduces the level of contact soldiers and wounded men have with the homeland. There was malnutrition due to mismanagement, which had undermined civilian morale and efficiency, which was worsened by overwork and lack of sleep due to air raids. The report went on to estimate six million foreign workers in Germany, which had diluted skilled labour and reduced output, especially in the mines. The report noted that Britain overestimated the effects of air raids on German industry. The real success of bombing was that directed at Germany's transportation network. However, 'Destruction of dwelling houses was important, and the morale of the bombed and other evacuees was low and contagious.' In the long run, it was felt the civilian morale might be decisive given that the level of bombing was still 'insufficient'. The war in the east may yet contribute to the decline of morale. Big business and industrialists were increasingly aligning themselves with the regime because they would be lost in the event of a German defeat, and they also doubted that the material power of the United Nations could ever be deployed effectively enough to bring about allied victory.[52] There was a handwritten comment from 5 October, 'This fits in pretty closely with our own assessment.' Roberts added, 'This strikes me as a well-balanced judgement. It will be noted that the potentialities of our air raids are very great, although their moral and material results have not yet been very great.'

On 3 October 1942, Harrison drafted a report for a morale committee in which he opened with several key questions about assessing the air raids:

1. Their effect on the ability and willingness of the German people to continue the war;
2. Their effect on the attitude of the German people towards the Nazi regime.

The first caveat was that the British people had been expecting the worse, whereas the Germans had been promised there would be no bombing and had become war weary after ten years of Nazism. The heavy air raids caused the Germans to begin 'to be haunted by the fear of possible defeat.' 'The light raids with the objective of causing sleeplessness, unless they are interspersed with really heavy attacks, are in danger of defeating their object by producing the feeling of immunity and even stiffening morale.' The heavy raids had caused temporary panic, breakdown in administration and even anti-Nazi demonstrations. 'The German far more than the British people are inclined to throw all their responsibility on the government for building an effective ARP organisation.' Heavy raids cause

— The dislocation of essential services, gas, water, electricity and transport
— Housing problems
— Friction with refugees from foreign slaves or other Germans

WAR COMES TO AACHEN

– Shortages of bombing
– Loss of possessions.

'When the raids become more widespread and when full effect becomes apparent under conditions of winter, there may be a different story to tell.'[53]

On 2 October 1942, the 'Morale in Germany' committee agreed to issue an official statement about the effects of air raids. The Foreign Office draft memorandum set the format: 'While it is difficult at present to assess the general influence on morale of the greater weight of air raids, there is no doubt that they are increasing the physical and nervous strain on the population.' On 8 October 1942, PID Dr Hawgood issued a Third Quarter discussion paper: 'Air raids alone are not likely to produce a catastrophe breakdown in German morale on a national scale, but they play a very real part in worsening the situation.'[54]

On 21 October, after some discussion and cosmetic alterations, the paper was turned into a Foreign Office minute and circulated to the War Cabinet by Eden.[55] A draft report from 21 October summarised: 'No really new significant tendencies have manifested themselves and therefore the picture as a whole requires little modification.' The report observed: 'Goebbels, in particular, has intensified his campaign to persuade the German people that their alternative is "Sieg oder Vernichtung", and most vigorous efforts are being made to instil into them greater hatred of the British enemy.' The Nazi terror was being tightened against 'grumblers, saboteurs and rumour-mongers', and a 'frontal attack upon those "clericals" who were hampering the war'.[56]

On 27 November, from a major report about 'Germany on the Eve of the Fourth War Winter' a section covered RAF air raids. The report opened: 'The effect of air-raids on civilian morale is already such as to constitution in the eyes of German rulers a direct menace to the prosecution of the war, there are indications that the position will deteriorate rather than improve.' The report added: 'The possibly growing belief of civilians that the RAF is deliberately aiming at them, and that Germany cannot be defeated if civilian morale stands firm, has so far acted on the whole as a strengthening factor.' There was a note that the report had not included an assessment of the German soldiery. However, the most significant summary was in a paragraph under a sub-heading of 'Nervous Strain':

> Heavy bombing has directly contributed to nervous strain in three important ways, and indirectly in many others. Directly, it has produced a great aggravation of the daily worries—particularly housing. It has strongly contributed to the fear that these worries will not end within any foreseeable future and may even become worse. Thirdly, raids are a major factor in creating sleeplessness. A fourth kind of effect is known to exist, but its extent is not yet known. This is the psychological shock experienced by those who have been 'near misses' as opposed to 'remote misses'.[57]

In December, there was a final assessment for the year from the post and telecommunications censor of German letters intercepted. The report received a mixed reception. One reader used a blue crayon to highlight the key factors. There had been more than five hundred letters translated and the summaries were: July was the month of confidence in victory, August saw a reduction in confidence and 'to keep faith in Hitler', whereas in September confidence had reduced with a rise in war-weariness, and October was the month 'to hold out and let us hope we shall be able to'. One letter from Düsseldorf noted that RAF leaflet raids in the Rhineland were being treated with 'ridicule and abuse and the contents make even the children laugh'. In another letter (Wiesbaden): 'That warfare has taken this form and that such targets should have been sought out is to be regretted, since the unfailing reprisal will destroy English cultural organisations which it would have been better to preserve. Following the thousand bomber raid on Cologne, several discussed the destruction of Cologne's heritage. One was resigned: 'the horror of such a war can only be realised by those who have experienced it—as it is indescribable'. There was no crayon highlighting these comments.[58]

On 4 December, a research section of PWE issued a report on German 'morale factors' but was treated with indifference and Cavendish-Bentick pointed to the 'law of diminishing returns' of making assumptions from isolated opinions. The report drew evidence for German publications to claim German morale was cracking with signs of 'nervous strain'. The report claimed the strain was causing inefficiencies due to carelessness at work and the general lack of 'vitality', along with sleeplessness, decline in productivity, absenteeism, fatigue and other 'mental factors'.[59]

On 21 December, previous correspondence between Ambassador Mallet (Stockholm) and Eden was transformed into a Foreign Office minute for War Cabinet consideration. The importance of the minute was the consensus it generated from all representatives in the inter-departmental group. Mallet's informer had recently spent four days in Berlin and had observed how the three social classes responded differently to war. The 'high ups' were well informed; they understood the strategic calamity of Hitler's failure to take Stalingrad. The Germans from that category were deeply concerned how they would be treated by the allies. The professional middle classes were hypnotised by Goebbels' propaganda and showed themselves susceptible to Nazi politics and believed the war was still winnable. The working class were difficult to assess, and they were very cautious about discussing politics, especially when bosses were about. They were generally 'fed up with the war' and were well informed, probably through returning German soldiers, about life at the front. The issues depressing morale most were 'air inferiority, the hard work in the factories, and the war in the east. Hitler remained popular and it was believed he had surrounded himself with capable leaders and few had heard of the atrocities committed by the Nazis.'[60]

A final 'Morale in Germany' memorandum for the year was issued by the War Cabinet on 24 December 1942.[61] The paper opened by suggesting it was too early to include the effects from the war in the east or the latest Russian offensive on any assessment of morale. There had been an increase in rations and a cessation of bombing of Germany: 'Consequently, the general trend of morale, which is dominated by the two factors of nervous strain and war-weariness, remains at present fundamentally unaffected.' The strain on the population had not relaxed due to concerns over housing, clothing and overwork; the troops at the front and rising casualties; the apprehension over increasing numbers of foreign workers; and the lack of hope in the future. The consequences were: 'damage to the war effort is, in fact, likely to result from organised opposition among the masses, but from un-coordinated, widespread and involuntary inefficiency resulting from overstrain'. The psychological condition of the German people was beginning to solidify: 'War-weariness and general apathy are now established traits of German morale.' This condition appeared to leave the German people mute in regard to both victories or defeats, or alternative governments or to 'a New Order in Europe'. While the future was clearly bleak, the Nazis were holding the country together through terror or what was dubbed the 'strength through fear' campaign. There were some signs of working-class opposition in Austria, Silesia, as well as in some northern and western cities. The paper concluded: 'in the army there is as yet no sign of a decline in morale'.[62]

IV. Towards a 1918 syndrome

On 23 October 1942, Cavendish-Bentick issued a request to Hugh K. Grey, of the Foreign Office library, to use 'internal resources' for a report on why Germany collapsed in 1918. The collapse had caught the allies by surprise and had led to a rapid end of the Great War. The first draft, from 20 November 1942, examined the historical evidence and concluded the Imperial Germany Army's morale was in decline but the collapse of home-front morale accelerated matters. The report noted that victory for the central powers solely depended upon Germany. The post-war assertion that Germany was militarily undefeated was denied in the report, claiming defeat was hinged upon the failure of the 1918 offensive, and the reluctance to continue defensive war. The home-front morale collapsed due to severe rationing, poor clothing and the allied blockade. The cracks in the home front opened after the army proved it could not secure victory. The report argued there was no specific date when the morale started to break but decided on the Battle of Amiens in 1918. Then followed the disintegration of alliances, with the surrender of Bulgaria an indication of imminent collapse. The arrival of Austrian troops on the western front indicated German reserves were depleted. The falling morale of the German troops came from captured documents and growing numbers of mass surrenders. The final collapse in the relationship between the kaiser and the generals was another crack, but the demand for unconditional surrender probably prolonged the war. All evidence pointed to the collapse on the home front as most prominent. The disillusionment was made public, and the report referred to the *Kölnische Zeitung* and its articles about distrusting the General Staff. The General Staff began to lose control over the home front. The ensuing debates in the Reichstag also accelerated the demoralisation. From all this evidence, the British military intelligence decided there would be decisive victory in 1919. All planning and discussion addressed 1919. The German proposals for peace were first discussed in October 1918. The allied armies were in an exhausted state, and nobody was aware of Germany's impending collapse. Military intelligence was in a difficult position, but Grey was diplomatic in his criticism.[63]

Grey's report was well received, and the FOCD file received numerous comments and observations. The most common assumption was that Nazi Germany was more prepared for long war than in 1914–18. In 1942, there was no indication of collapse; the only parallel was that German collapse would come as a surprise. There were signs that all the panaceas of an early victory had worn thin, and several comments warned of indulging in over-confidence and wishful thinking. One comment that proved insightful noted there was no sign of a German collapse before summer 1943 and the last offensive in the east. Hitler, Goebbels' propaganda, and the Nazi state were seen as more prepared for war. The group discussion concentrated upon the need for a revised draft that compared the 1918 situation with 1942. There was an observation arguing that the historical parallel was artificial: firstly because the U-boat menace was still a serious problem; and secondly, Hitler could compel the populace to his will, unlike the kaiser. In the instructions for the second draft, Cavendish-Bentick wrote: 'History does not necessarily repeat itself in all matters but a picture of the indications of the Germans' collapse in the last war may enable useful deductions to be drawn today.' In the notes and comments, he also cautioned, 'do not rely entirely on the opinion of the military advisors as to the state of the enemy' and 'it's too much to expect the cabinet will read and act upon the report'. The second draft report was issued on 9 December, which opened with Cavendish-Bentick's observation about history.[64]

The agreed parallels between 1918 and 1942 included the high casualties, growing doubts over victory, war weariness, rationing and the absence of consumer goods, the drabness and drudgery of everyday life and growing manpower shortages. One major factor was the bombing, which was assumed to be damaging German morale, just as the home-front problems in 1918 had caused the collapse. The differences in 1942 were significant. Germany had become a totalitarian state and was both psychologically and physically better prepared for war. Hitler was a more powerful dictator than Hindenburg during the Great War. German politics had also changed under Nazism, with a compliant press and no opposition. The working class were no longer represented and without power but had been regimented for war. The Nazi propaganda and Goebbels were recognised as formidable. There was a general acceptance that in 1918 the generals could voice opposition but in 1942 they were silenced. There was an assumption that opposition politics was shattered, but in 1918 there had been nothing comparable to Heinrich Himmler, the SS and the Gestapo. In regard to the question, was Germany slowly breaking?, there was a consensus that the accumulated evidence and the mounting problems pointed to some form of collapse—someone had written in pencil 'military operations' perhaps alluding to the battle unravelling at Stalingrad. In one note, Harrison referred to the war on the eastern front and concluded: 'Another year in Russia and bigger and better raids on German towns of all sizes may get the German soldiers worried.'

This revised assessment was the eureka moment for the diplomatic 'listening posts'. Finally, the diplomats received a series of questions or points that could be raised in interrogations or interviews. A range of points included: references to defeat, the appearance of 'peace feelers', the departure of Germans from the occupied zones, shortages (especially fuel oils), willingness to surrender, open opposition to Nazis, decline in morale, issues among the workforce and rising defections.

WAR COMES TO AACHEN

On 28 December, Frank Roberts began sending copies of the revised documents to embassies under secret correspondence. He advised in the covering letter for diplomats to be watchful for:

1. 'Signs of strained relations between civilians and members of the armed forces …'
2. 'Evidence of conflict between military and civilian authorities over the allocation of manpower.'
3. 'Signs of positive thinking about an alternative regime.'

In addition, they were instructed to be mindful of strained relations between foreign and German work forces, murmurings that victory by the allies would be less punitive and dissatisfaction over rationing.

If we paraphrase Len Deighton, the language of the bombing was dehumanising. In this chapter we have observed how civil servants and members of the government discussed the mass destruction of civilians under the rubric of 'morale'. Today, we better understand genocide and why it's not only practised by totalitarian or 'evil' states. We also know that German morale wasn't broken by the bombing; that came with military defeat on the ground. In an autobiography, Cavendish-Bentinck was cited from a report in 1944, 'There is no evidence to suggest that the Allied bombing may shortly foment any effective opposition to the regime, or that the stamina and discipline of the German people have deteriorated to such an extent that a collapse may be considered likely within the next two weeks.'[65] By the end of 1942, the participants in the FOCD groups, the inter-departmental groups, the War Cabinet, the government, Churchill and the king knew where the bombing of Germany was leading. The mass destruction of Germany extended to industry, residential areas, cultural centres, civilians and the military. It was indiscriminate killing, and the results achieved nothing.

By turning civilians and morale into strategic targets, the British government stepped across the threshold of morals and ethics, which was why they had gone to war in the first place. The government had transformed the war from a moral cause to defend Poland, into mass civilian killing, thereby becoming the purveyors of political violence. Since morale was an ephemeral concept, ground in vague concepts of civilian character and German national qualities, the conventional conflict was turned into a culture war. Some scholars might claim revenge or retribution for the Blitz or the Holocaust, or even a form of war realism. However, this was no eccentricity on 'Bomber' Harris's part; the wholesale destruction of German cities and the mass killing of civilians had no military value, did not shorten the war, or make allied victory inevitable. By the end of 1942, victory was inevitable, hence why the FOCD began examining the possibility of a German collapse. The experiment of morale bombing had failed by the end of 1942, the 'shock and awe' of the bombing had passed by September, and yet the crime was to continue, with bombing until April 1945. Every month since 1942, Harris had submitted his gruesome bombing reports with aerial pictures of destroyed German cities for the cabinet, there was collective silence which confirmed collective responsibility toward his actions. On 26 July 1943, the War Cabinet received the summary report of the burning of Aachen, in which it was noted that, 'apart from the direct industrial damage, this is a substantial contribution to the "housing blockade of the Reich," which German propaganda admits is being imposed by persistent bombing. Direct industrial damage is very severe. ... The Cathedral, which has naturally figured largely in German reports of the attack appears undamaged.'[66] The veracity of Harris's July 1943 raid report is examined in the next chapter.

5

FRYING ELVER

On the morning of 13 July 1943, RAF Bomber Command's teleprinter operators were feverously issuing secret orders and instructions to the bomber groups. The raid was planned for that evening, with 374 aircraft allocated—214 Handley Page Halifaxes, 76 Vickers Wellingtons, 55 Short Stirlings, 18 Avro Lancaster and 11 De Haviland Mosquitoes. Precise instructions were issued to five of six bomber groups. One set of orders was received by No. 6 (RCAF) Group: they were to contribute sixty-nine aircraft to a raid on Aachen that evening. The group's squadrons were based at RAF Middleton, RAF Leeming and RAF Linton. The plan advised there would be five waves of bombers, with the group's aircraft set to join the first, fourth and fifth waves. The instructions ordered a specific load for the Wellingtons of incendiaries and the Halifaxes to carry a mixed load (HE bombs and incendiaries). The attack plan was 'Musical Parramatta', which meant Mosquito aircraft from Pathfinder force would drop target indicators (TIs) of yellow on the preliminary point, red at the aiming point and further green TIs would be dropped on the aiming point during the raid. A decoy raid of six Mosquito aircraft were planned for an attack on *Whitebait* in 'a diversion and drive the sorely tried inhabitants into the shelters once more in anticipation'. HQ Pathfinder Force sent a teleprint to No. 139 Squadron ordering six aircraft to carry out an anti-morale attack on *Whitebait*.[1]

115

WAR COMES TO AACHEN

The story of the RAF bomber offensive against Aachen took a different turn in July 1943. The raid differed from all the previous twenty-six air raids on Aachen that year because the mission was to commit arson. By 1943, Churchill's politics of violence against the German people escalated. Throughout 1942, Churchill's Foreign Office focus group had tried a mass observation to collect indications of success, or whether the bombing was failing. The reference to 'arson' in an order from a British military document brings the story of Aachen in the age of total war to a very dark place. Arson in English common law, in 1940, was a serious act of criminal destruction and an offense punishable by the death penalty. The *mens rea*, or the guilty mind, was implicit in the RAF order, which is confirmed by the *actus rea* (guilty act) of the orders. Criminal orders in civil law are not the same as immoral but not criminal orders in wartime. Arson was not a war crime, in the context of the practices and precedents already set by the Second World War, but there was a moral question of restraint. While it was not illegal, to rain fire on civilians was immoral, and there would be long-term ramifications, but they were not considered by Churchill as important in 1943. The absence of strategic oversight at that critical moment in the war set Bomber Command on a genocidal path—the use of 'criminal' means to destroy a population, a culture and Germany's cities.

A set of orders was received at No. 4 Group, 'to carry out Musical Paramatta on Elver' during the hours of darkness—a total of 168 aircraft from RAF Driffield, RAF Holme, RAF Pocklington and RAF Snaith. Under 'Bomb Loads', the message referred: 'The "Arson" load is to be as per postagram from this headquarters 9 July 1943'. No. 3 Group in RAF Mildenhall were advised: '<u>Arson</u>. Except that the Lancaster II's are to carry the maximum BX number of 8,000LB. Bombs available.' There can be no doubt the aircrews knew they were carrying mostly incendiaries for a fire mission to burn Aachen.[2] The bomber swarm was set for a round trip from their bases to Noordwijk (Netherlands) to Aachen (Germany) to Cayeux (France) back via Beachy Head. The weather en route was mixed clouds with '7/10ths cloud tops and 9,000ft visibility over the North Sea' and 'at Aachen 10/10ths stratus cumulous tops approx. 6,000ft with breaks west and northwest'.³ In his memoirs, Harris described why he selected Air Vice-Marshal Robert Saundby (1896–1971) as the senior air staff officer (SASO): 'his ideas about bombing were absolutely sound and naturally I relied enormously on his experience ... He was a keen fisherman, which was why all the main German towns that were our targets had the names of fish for code names, Whitebait for Berlin, Trout for Cologne'.⁴ *Elver* are young eels that weave their way upstream, from the sea, through brackish water. Why Aachen was designated *Elver* is open to speculation. Regardless of the unusual application of fish codes, there was a much more serious set of issues driving the bombing of Aachen. Bomber Commands' politics of violence was directed at German civilians, which today would be classified as a war crime.⁵

I. Codename: Elver

> Aachen lies in a fertile countryside of gently rolling hills, two or three miles from the Dutch or Belgian frontiers. To the south of the town there is a continuous belt of woodland, to the north there are a few scattered coal mines. A narrow-forested ridge overlooks the town on the north. Aachen is an ancient city and contains many historic buildings, but it is today primarily an industrial town, with modern iron foundries and machine workshops, and old established industries, producing glass, needles and pins and cloth. It is the frontier station on the east-west railway route from Brussels to Cologne.⁶

On 5 June 1942, Bomber Command issued a revised target assessment. Aachen was defined as an ancient city, with old and modern industries, and the main railway line. There was no detail about the military or strategic priorities. The assessment also focused on the city's geographical and environmental dimensions: 'a compact circular shaped city, encircled by boulevards and railways, with the main factories on the outskirts'. The 'inner town' was 'the site of the medieval town. Its streets are narrow and winding ... there are many ancient public buildings'. Many buildings were known to have been constructed in the latter half of the 1800s, with 'several storeys, and it has a high density of population'. The centre was congested with prominent residential quarters. The mixed tenement areas were identified as primarily for artisan residents, in particular the eastern districts of the city. The Burtscheid district (to the south-east) was included, with its old cloth and needles manufacturing industries. The report concluded: 'the compact residential area ... is small, but has fairly high vulnerability'. The report advised the bombing of the city centre and the working-class areas—the area believed to hold the best prospect of undermining the morale of the masses.

The industrial section summarised the small factories and workshops dispersed throughout the city. The larger factories were on the outskirts, in particular the north-east area where the gas works and power station were located, in a total area of 300 acres. The iron and steel plant at Rothe Erde in the east covered an area of 150 acres, while to the north-west there was another district covering 25–30 acres for smaller factories. In regard to the railways, the report noted they 'radiate from Aachen like the spokes of a wheel', surrounding the town to the south and west. The report concluded with an assessment of the potential target zones. The list began with zone 1, the city centre (covering 100 acres); then zone 2a, which included the fully built-up mixed area (covering 350 acres) and the tenement area to the east (covering 150 acres); followed by 2b, the partially built-up residential area (covering 500 acres); and the list was completed with the industrial acreages mentioned previously listed as zone 4. The recommendations were stark: 'the Inner Town (zones 1 and 2a) and the railways enclosing it have an area about one square mile. Though small, this area is highly vulnerable to H.E. and I.B. attack.' This area would increase to two square miles if zone 2b were included. The industrial area was dismissed because 'they would demand precise attack and owing to their removal from residential areas there would probably be little effect on morale'. An attack on the railway station and goods yards, it was believed, would obstruct through communications.[7]

By September 1942, RAF Bomber Command restructured the rationale for targeting German cities. The first category of target was its distance from RAF Mildenhall in Suffolk: 'Section A' targets were within 400 miles, while Section B targets lay between 400 and 600 miles. The cities of the Ruhr and Rhineland lay in Section A. The second category was the city's population size: above 100,000 but below 200,000; above 200,000 but below 500,000; and above 500,000. Aachen was listed in the first tranche, with a given population of 170,000, while Cologne's population was 750,000. These target classifications determined the size of raids, the mix of bomb and the tonnage.[8] Size was only one categorisation. The references to Aachen's history and heritage were regular in British bombing documents, so much so that it suggested an undeclared culture war. In the history of bombing, German heritage and culture was treated as collateral damage, but was often the targeting point. There were no instructions to avoid bombing historic buildings or places of culture. Too many prominent buildings or heritage sites were swallowed up in broad-brush targeting. The consequences of that kind of indiscriminate bombing policy emerged in the raid on Aachen's centre and marshalling yards on 5–6 October 1942. In foul weather and without Pathfinders, 257 bombers dropped their loads on Burtscheid (Aachen district), destroying churches, a hospital, housing and five industrial buildings. More bombs, intended for Aachen, were dropped on Lutterade (today part of Geleen) in Holland, destroying 800 houses, killing 83 people, leaving 22 injured and 3,000 homeless.[9]

RAF Bomber Command's raids on Aachen opened in 1943 with nuisance and decoy raids. These kinds of raids had more social impact than has been previously realised, because they caused the inconvenience without the destruction and extended the days of raiding. The raids began on 15 January, with nuisance raids when eight bombs were dropped in the Bergdreisch district between 11.40 and 0.05 hours—they killed three people and injured eleven. On 20 January, Göring announced: 'With immediate effect blackout will be enforced one hour after sunset until one half-hour before sunrise; to-day from 6.23pm until 8.28am tomorrow morning. I therefore request that action on these lines be taken in the future.'[10] Ten days later, the tenth anniversary of the Nazi Party coming to power (30 January)—three bombs landed in

Reumontstrasse, killing three people and injuring eight. The nuisance raids continued through February, starting on St Valentine's Day, in four minutes—20.23–20.27 hours—dropping 770 firebombs and 15 incendiaries, killing one and injuring another. A Bomber Command report from 1945 noted that on 25 February at 21.04–21.06 hours, a single aircraft dropped six bombs on Lütticher strasse, killing three and injuring nine. The following day, an aircraft dropped seven bombs at 21.04–21.06 hours, with one person was injured in Theresienstrasse. On 1 March, at 23.47 hours, a bomb landed in Krefelderstrasse without casualties. On 9 April at 23.45 hours, *Gelb Kaserne* (Yellow Barracks) was bombed, killing one and injuring three.[11] At 17.10 hours on 27 April, two parachute flares were dropped that stirred fears of a larger raid. A balloon with a fire-flash was dropped over Eupenerstrasse at 09.10 hours on 4 June, and on 19 June more balloons were released over the Lousberg (the hill overlooking the city).[12] Then on 28–9 June, a fast raid 02.00–02.10 hours dropped two mines, three HE bombs and 512 incendiaries on Kreuzerdriesch, killing four and injuring eight. This was possibly a navigational error or an aircraft jettisoning its bombs during a larger raid on Cologne. The next raid was the night of 13–14 July.

II. Reporting the air battle

At 16.30 hours on 14 July 1944, Bomber Command issued the first after-action report of the raid, issued to the Air Ministry. The report covered twenty-four hours, noon-to-noon from 13 July, and included a brief note about a daytime operation of ten Armstrong Whitleys from 91 Group on anti-submarine duties—'there were no sightings'. Night 13–14 July referred to 374 aircraft: 32 from No. 1 Group, 66 from No. 3 Group, 159 from No. 4 Group, 69 from No. 6 Group and 48 from No. 8 (PFF) Group—of which 327 claimed to have attacked the target. The PFF markers were 'punctual' but cloud obscured some of the ground markers. The earliest reports claimed the bombing was scattered but with some concentration observed in the western area of the town. Although the cloud closed in, aircrew reported 'many fires taking hold' and large explosions. There were additional reports of bombing to the north and north-west of the city; 'the glow of fires were reported as being visible up to 150 miles after leaving the target'. The opposition was regarded as slight from the ground defences, and few enemy aircraft interceptions. Elsewhere, leaflets were dropped across cities in France, an intruder raid by two Mosquitoes was abandoned due to technical failure and a Whitley crew were picked up from a dinghy. The attached target sheets confirmed the narrative, with lists of bomb loads, aircraft types and the missing aircraft—twenty reported missing at that time. From No. 3 Group (3 aircraft—a Short Stirling and two Avro Lancaster bombers), No. 4 Group (8 aircraft—7 Halifax and a Wellington), No. 6 Group (7 aircraft—6 Halifax and a Wellington) and No. 8 (PFF) Group (2 aircraft—both Halifax). The report concluded with a foreign broadcast from Berlin at 11.38 hours:

> British bombers made a heavy attack during the night 13/14 July on Aachen, the ancient coronation town and residence of Charlemagne. The population suffered casualties and numerous cultural monuments, public buildings and dwelling houses were destroyed. 21 enemy aircraft have so far been shot down.[13]

On return of the bombers to their squadron bases, the crews went through a debriefing by intelligence officers. Eventually, forty-one reports of aerial combats either with fighters, flak or friendly fire, and compiled for the tactical report of 20 July (six days after the raid). The collected data of 'raid plots' were sent by teleprinter to Bomber Command headquarters. No. 4 Group's return included: sightings (25), combats (10), flak (3), searchlights (2), activity at sea (3), flares (12), shot down (19), in flames (21) and others (4). The twenty-five sightings were all enemy night fighters' interceptions with map grid-references, along the designated flight path from Noordwijk in South Holland to Aachen to Cayeux in France and return. The crews observed ten 'combats' between fighters and bombers—aircraft were observed being shot down in flames. In regard to flak, the crews had different interpretations of its intensity. Above Aachen, at 01.40 hours an aircraft at 20,000ft was struck by 'a sudden burst of flak and go down in flames'. Three minutes later a bomber was observed at 18,000 feet hit by 'air tracer seen resulting in a ball of fire getting larger and disappearing into cloud—apparently hit ground and exploded'. Four minutes later, a bomber flying at 17,500 feet was observed with wings on fire, dived into clouds and exploded. At 01.53 hours a Stirling was hit by flak and began to burn, then it was attacked by an enemy fighter and crashed. At 02.03 hours, a Halifax was attacked by a fighter over Aachen; it burst into flames and began to descend when an engine on the port side caught fire. A parachute opened, believed to come from the doomed aircraft. On the return journey, a Halifax was observed firing its machine guns at another Halifax; they were approximately thirty miles south of Lille.[14]

The teleprint from No. 3 Group presented different interpretations—four sightings identified by place—The Hague (Holland) and Abbeville (France). There were seventeen 'combats', fourteen cases of flak incidents and twelve 'aircraft seen falling' all 'on fire', 'in flames' or mid-air 'explosions'. No. 1 Group appeared organised, structured and timed at 07.17 hours. There were seven 'encounters' with enemy aircraft and three 'combats'. In addition, three cases of flak but mostly 'inaccurate'. Under 'aircraft shot down' they observed seven bombers falling in flames, crashing or exploding on impact—but without aircraft types or mention of parachutes. No. 8 (PFF) Group issued the report at 16.00 hours and was well presented for analysis: sightings (7), combats (5), flak (1), references to weather (outbound and inbound), aircraft seen falling (11) and other content (5). They reported inaccurate flak activity over Aachen, with most shells bursting at 15,000 feet and virtually no searchlight cover. In an aerial combat above Aachen, a Pathfinder Halifax at 17,000 feet was intercepted by a Junkers 88 'with a red light in nose'. The Halifax crew saw the Junkers to port, at 600 yards, as it turned to attack. The Halifax pilot turned to port, towards the enemy. The Junkers broke to starboard before the Halifax could open fire. The 'enemy aircraft passed to starboard showing its belly on which the cross could be seen and our aircraft opened fire'. Tracer was seen going into the Junkers, which then dived and disappeared from sight.[15] In addition, another report from Pathfinder confirmed five additional sightings and over Charleroi a Halifax was attacked from below by a night fighter closing to 600 yards.[16]

The teleprint from No. 6 (RCAF) Group was a jumble, with navigation references scribbled out by Bomber Command headquarters' staff. The group reported: sightings (13), encounters (7), flak (7), searchlights (5), enemy airfields, decoys, lights and flares (15) and aircraft shot down (21). The crews observed an aircraft shot down over Aachen, with two parachutes opening at 10,000ft. Another bomber was seen to fall after flying through some heavy flak over the city. They also confirmed two bombers crashed in the vicinity of Rotterdam and over Amsterdam, a bomber was 'coned' by searchlights, was struck by three heavy flak explosions and burst into flames. The observing crew watched as the burning aircraft turned towards them but losing height, 'then broke into 3 burning pieces which disappeared through cloud and hit the ground with a violent explosion'.[17] Overall, twenty aircraft were shot down during the raid.

The final moments of some of the downed aircraft have been investigated by enthusiasts, archaeologists and local historians in Belgium, France and Holland. Their discoveries add to the story of the raid. Handley Page Halifax II (JD297) codename DY-Q (Queenie), from 102 (Ceylon) Squadron, based at RAF Pilkington in Yorkshire, took off for Aachen at 23.34 hours. Wing Commander Henry Reginald Coventry was a career officer and a highly experienced pilot, the commanding officer of 102 Squadron. Born in Canada in 1915, he came to Britain on 6 December 1932 to attend RAF College Cranwell and received a commission—Pilot Officer effective 15 December 1934. He was posted to 58 (B) Squadron at RAF Worthy Down and then to the Second Armoured Car Company in Palestine. Coventry was promoted to Flying Officer (1936) and transferred to Iraq; then Flight Lieutenant (1937), Squadron Leader (June 1940) and Wing Commander (1941). He received the Distinguished Flying Cross while with 102 Squadron; the citation stated he 'has proved himself to be an outstanding and skilful captain and an inspiring leader'. The crew included: Flight Lieutenant Frederick Edward King, also 'acting' squadron navigator, from Willesden in Middlesex, a 'VR', he was promoted Pilot Officer in January and Flying Officer in October 1942; Sergeant Geoffrey Tristran Pine-Coffin (Flight Engineer) was a twenty-four-year-old; Flying Officer Crosby Frank Read (bomb-aimer) a 'VR' from Clatford in Hampshire; he had been a Flying Officer since February 1943; Sergeant Walter Brown (radio) a 'VR' from Durham; Sergeant William Hardy (air gunner) a 'VR' air-gunner from Hucknall in Nottinghamshire, and the other was Flight Lieutenant George Frank Hogg, a 'VR' from Caernarvonshire. Hogg was commissioned in December 1939, and was the squadron gunnery leader.[18] They were intercepted by a night fighter at 02.19 hours above Maubeuge in northern France. The attack was observed by aircraft from No. 3 Group: at 02.35 hours, flying at 10,000ft five miles east of Maubeuge, the bomber received 'air-to-air tracer and aircraft seen going down in flames. Glow on the ground seen.' There was also a sighting of three small fires and lights like incendiaries within a minute of the same area at 02.34 hours.[19] They were shot down by Oberleutnant Rudolf Altendorf, flying a Messerschmidt ME110. He had been flying twin-engine fighters since 1940. In June 1941, Altendorf had served with NJG.3. On 1 October 1942, he was promoted to Oberleutnant and transferred to NJG.4 and serving with 2./NJG4 based at St Dizier in France, when he shot down Halifax JD297. By the war's end, Altendorf was credited with 22 'kills'. His personnel files record he was shot down, but also that he was relieved from commanding a fighter group; in October 1944, he was demoted and ordered to redeem himself in combat.[20]

At 22.33 hours, Handley Page Halifax II (JB801) from 78 Squadron took off from RAF Breighton in Yorkshire. The aircraft was captained by Warrant Officer Peter Horrocks and his crew Flying Officer Doug Hosken (navigator), Flight Engineer Wyndham Harries, Sergeant Arthur Jelfs (bomb-aimer), Sergeant Bill Rouse (air gunner), Sergeant Jack Chaplin (wireless operator) and Sergeant Geoffrey Bowden (air gunner). They were an experienced crew, having flown missions on 3, 9 and 13 July— Cologne, Gelsenkirchen and then Aachen. The 78 Squadron records noted: 'This aircraft took off at 23.33 hours and nothing further has been heard of the crew or aircraft since. It is therefore presumed missing.' It's not certain but the Halifax was probably 'bounced' inbound to Aachen and was attacked four kilometres south-east of Utrecht and shot down. The Halifax was intercepted by Luftwaffe Oberfeldwebel Karl-Heinz Scherfling fly a Messerschmitt Bf110-G4 from Leewarden airbase in northern Holland. The radar station 'Gorilla' operating the Würzburg-Riese system from nearby Leerdam in central Holland had guided Scherfling to the Halifax. The downed bomber spilled the crew across fields and ditches and was strewn across a field. The next morning, a local Dutch civilian retrieved a flare pistol before the Germans cordoned off the area. Scherfling was born in Gelsenkirchen, September 1918, and had served with 10/NJG 1 since September 1942. In April 1944, Scherfling was awarded the Knights' Cross, and credited with thirty-three 'kills' before being shot down and killed. Luftwaffe Oberleutnant Klaus Degler Scherfling's airbase commander was allegedly responsible for ordering the execution of fourteen civilians from Wamel on the suspicion of being in the anti-Nazi resistance.[21]

Flying Officer Rod Larson (RCAF), the pilot of Lancaster II (DS660), lifted off from RAF Wretham (Norfolk) at 00.24 hours. At 02.28 his aircraft was intercepted and shot down near Metz-en-Couture by Luftwaffe Hauptmann Hubert Rauth, an Austrian, from 3./NJG4 based in Florennes in Belgium. Larson was able to bail, becoming a PoW, but his crew were all killed. They were Sergeant Mervyn Jones (Flight Engineer), Pilot Officer Chester Armstrong (navigator), Flying Officer Frederick Leonard Yates (bomb aimer), Sergeant Peter Williams (wireless operator), Sergeant John Thomas Newton (air gunner) and Sergeant Derick Murphy (air gunner), all 'VRs' and buried together in the CWGC cemetery at Grévillers.[22] There were witnesses; two of the crew were seen to fall out of the aircraft, and their bodies were located next morning: one landed in a tree and the other in a field found by three girls. One local, Monsieur Lecap, attempted to pull the remaining four bodies out of the crash before the remains were consumed by fire. In the morning, German troops arrived and took the crew remains away. The Germans formed an honour guard and a firing party for a burial, and wreaths were laid on the graves.

WAR COMES TO AACHEN

III. Raining fire

There were two contemporary accounts, given by Nazi officials, of the events on the ground on 14 July. The first was a statement from an official in Josef Goebbels' propaganda ministry. Leonhard Ostniki, from the first propaganda company, made a recording of the destruction, assisted by a sound engineer, Herr Pappenbrunner, believed to be an NCO in the company. They were posted to Aachen in June 1943, to make 'victory' sound recordings with city officials and locals. Ostniki began, 'Sirens sounded, terror bombing of the old Kaiserstadt.' When they eventually arrived in the city centre there was 'impenetrable black clouds, and fires ... the air gangsters had given notice of new crimes of destruction of defenceless Aachen'. They were among a throng of aid workers, fire engines, ambulances and mobile kitchens, which suggests they had arrived after the raid was over. As they drove through the 'burning city', they were forced to navigate through fallen tram cables, 'rubble, glass, burning beams, burning churches and towers bending with the heat'. The heat burned eyes, and there were flying embers and sparks; everyone wore handkerchiefs over the nose and mouth. The fire fighters had to cope with the fires and collapsing buildings, warning people to stay away with loud hailers. The faces of people were terror stricken and ashen. Some people were clutching at children, or a household item. Ostniki claimed there was no overall command of the situation, which indicates the report was for Goebbels' attention. He claimed the cathedral was in flames, with Charlemagne's tower seriously damaged. Houses began collapsing like cards after the fires were extinguished. The Rathaus and coronation chamber was also on fire. People were crying, overwhelmed by the experience, beside the dead and the injured, wrapped with temporary bandages. Some people were helping others, comrades; ordinary people and auxiliaries were trying to do what they could. All attempts to stop the fires made them worse. There was a determination to prevent social breakdown and disorder: 'The hate for the criminals was unlimited. There will be revenge and even more terrible, making it easier to bear the suffering.'

FRYING ELVER

The second account from Eduard Schmeer, Aachen's Nazi *Kreisleiter*, was reputedly an interview with Ostniki, several hours later and recorded in the Rathaus. Schmeer was reading a report about how the enemy had focused on the heavily populated areas of the city, with high explosives and incendiaries. There were particularly painful cultural losses to be endured by the city, ones that would surprise the world. Both the Rathaus and the Granusturn had suffered from extensive fires, with their towers destroyed. The coronation chamber with its frescos were damaged. The destruction against other cultural places included Elisenbrunnen, the Vespian house, the theatre and five churches. Several hospitals and one for children had been seriously damaged. Ostniki added: 'the city was prepared, thoroughly planned, and these preparations were triggered when the attack started', including the firefighting, clearing rubble and supplying medical assistance to distressed persons. He continued, 'The preparations were tested and stood up well, all working according to plan.' The attitude of the people was regarded as exemplary.[23] There were, however, deep cultural connections destroyed by the raid: 'The bombing raids of the British and Americans have caused wounds that cannot heal. The people standing in the marketplace watching the flames engulf the Rathaus. Swirling flames, with sparks spraying out and the towers destroyed.' The cultural destruction became the conclusion of the report. The main hall was described as being in 'thick fumes'; the 'crime done to the sanctity of the German people', the 'history in the stones' and the 'great masters absorbed into the building' identified how far the Nazis were painting the allies as cultural destroyers. That the larger structure of the *Granusturm* was still standing retained the link with the ancient greatness of the German past. They discussed that the *Krönungssaal* (coronation room) was once the centre of an empire lined with coats of arms of the noble families and later with frescos by Alfred Rethel (1816–1859), the Romantic artist born in Aachen. That room was filled with smoke, while beams could be heard collapsing, stones crumbling and glass shattering.[24]

On 17 July 1943, Rudolf Storpil, a journalist from the *Aachener Anzeiger Politiches Tageblatt*, wrote *Deutsche Schicksalsstadt im Westen*

(Germany's fated city in the west), the headline news. He set the scene of entering the city after the air-raid sirens had sounded the all clear, which is paraphrased in translation. The British had bombed the city many times before, but in the morning afterwards, there was thick smoke, and a ghostly red glow broke through the dawn sky. Storpil followed the emergency services, and people everywhere wanted to help in those critical early hours. It was laborious walking through burning residential areas and climbing across heaps of rubble. Women, children, soldiers and fire fighters were trying to rescue possessions from burning homes, stacking the items in the streets. Everyone covered their mouths with handkerchiefs, or other material, to prevent inhaling the toxic hot fumes, and some wore their gas masks. There were awful scenes being witnessed in the old city.

Storpil made his way to the marketplace towards the town hall through tons of rubble. 'The heart aches' when he saw the ancient town hall in flames above the foundations of the old imperial palace. In the pathos of the moment, he conjured up images of the generations influenced by the building and the fateful events that had befallen the town hall. He described the figures on the walls as shattered or lying in the rubble, and the gothic towers had collapsed. Sparks were spraying out of the broken windows from the many burning artefacts. There were fires in the *Kaisersaal* (coronation room), and there was a bomb crater. The roof had cracked, and sparks from the fires were falling from the ceiling. There were streams of water running down the hallways caused by the fire brigade's hoses. The fire brigade struggled to save as much of the building as possible. The frescos by Alfred Reidel, a world-renowned artist, 'had been destroyed in an hour by this madness'. Arriving at the cathedral, he saw more damage: 'this new terror attack of British bomber forces reveals an attack on German high culture. Not an attack on arms but on our monuments and peaceful people … In spite of this horrible night, they are not broken but are hardy and experienced border people and know the meaning of fate because they remember the British of 1919–1923.'[25]

During the arson raid, two youths were killed and two more injured. A parachute mine landed on the Eilendorff battery, exploding between the command post and radio post. The blast destroyed the power supply and the radar-guided equipment ceased working. Two Luftwaffe gunners and the two youths were killed, and two youths wounded—all from the grammar school. The deaths of their comrades brought home the reality of the war, which was reinforced by the screams of the bereaved parents. The youths had started to hate the bombers, but the deaths deepened their anger. Several youths were awarded the flak badge. The older soldiers didn't want the medal, but the boys were proud to wear them. Others went home and used family silver to make copies, which they wore proudly. Initially, marking 'kills' on the gun barrels involved the single rings, but gradually as their successes increased, they adopted the ten aircraft rings. They also visited aircraft shot down to take photographs.[26]

In 1984, Hans Hoffmann collected oral testimonies for his book about the bombing of Aachen. A former air-raid warden, Peter Franzen, and Agnes Selvar recalled moments from the raid. Selvar remembered her husband wrapped a towel around her head because her teeth were chattering violently as the bombs landed. Franzen, from Bahnhofstrasse, kept a diary. In 1942, he became an air-raid warden. After the raid, he saved people in a burning house. The weight of bombs also caused buildings to collapse, killing people in the cellar-shelters. Since the beginning of the war, small numbers of aircraft (1, 3, 5, 11) had attempted to cause damage by dropping bombs on Aachen—'the horror was dripping'. The July 1943 raid destroyed all optimism about the future of the war and survival. At 01.00 hours, the sirens were sounded, and forty-five minutes later two hundred aircraft dropped bombs, lasting fifty-five minutes.

During the raid, Carl Peters managed to reach Martin Luther Strasse, struggling against burning streets and rubble. He saw the entire Theatrestrasse in flames. He met his father, who was holding two small cases. There were other people, all standing in shock watching as their homes burned. They wrapped wet clothes around their faces against the sparks and hot ash. Peters and his father went back to his home, which had survived. The shops in Lutticherstrasse were all in flames as was an office, with all its goods and equipment burning. They reached the family shop in Grosskölnstrasse; the entire street and houses were all burning. The marketplace, the Rathaus and its towers were all in flames. Their warehouse in Julicherstrasse was burned out. The city's municipal buildings were destroyed.

Curate Paul Wipperfürth first heard the railway flak guns open fire, followed by the heavy flak batteries, and then came the bombs. A 'concert of hell'—cellars shook, pipes whistled, the howling of falling bombs, the bursts of explosions, waves of air pressure and, after ten minutes, all the electricity was cut. The houses in Adalbertsteinweg by Kaiserplatz were all burning. The lack of air doused candles, and the bomb blasts became heavier as they crept into the very corners of their cellar. There were the sounds of collapsing houses, the crackling of fires, glass splinters and chips of mortar in the air, the smell of chalk, ears beginning to buzz, and time slowed. It was 02.00 hours and still going on, which meant they could not leave the cellar to check on the houses and church. At 02.20 hours, the bombing stopped and 'we thanked god'. The house was covered in rubble and detritus but was relatively safe. St Adalbert church was on fire—two canisters of phosphorous bombs were burning. Herr Jansen extinguished a bomb in the choir with water. Two houses (number 8 and 9) had survived, but the door of the first was on fire. Wipperfürth removed an incendiary bomb from the stairs of number 9. Sister Thaddäa and two senior churchmen worked on the Sacristy, which was damaged by a nearby bomb, and the curtains were burning. He then ran around the church warning people of the fire and for them to leave. The fire began to rage and was spreading to neighbouring houses. The house owners of Adalbertstift were virtually cut off for an hour as they worked to keep the fire from their homes.

The shock of the raid hit hardest at 05.00–06.00 hours, as dawn broke and daylight revealed the extent of the destruction. Wipperfürth was standing beside Curate Ingenkamp watching the church tower burn like a torch; the roof had burned out, but the houses in the Kaiserplatz were burning ferociously. The tower swayed and finally toppled into the church, causing them deep heartache. By 08.00 hours, the Sacristy had burned and caused fires in connecting rooms. They collected in a house in Adalberstift at 09.30 hours. They were all 'deathly tired', exhausted, with sore eyes and covered in black soot. Their hair was matted with grease and dust, there were blisters on the hands and their clothes were covered in holes. They all took a swig of Cognac. Accompanied with three others, Wipperfürth went to the first-aid centre at Milchhäuschen, in the Kaiserplatz, to receive eye drops and a short rest on an emergency cot. They returned to the church to see some of the beams still glowing and almost everything except the tabernacle destroyed. The marble panels had broken away from the walls, and the organ was in ashes. There was a pungent smell of fire, and Wipperfürth was shattered by the experience, but the priest had physically aged. Initially, Wipperfürth was flummoxed about the combustion of the church, which began forty minutes after the raid. In the streets, flames were reaching six metres in height. The firestorm caused burning paper and other items to swirl and carry combustible waste to the church. The fire started in the organ chamber, as music sheets began to burn from phosphorus particles. They later found that eight incendiary canisters had landed on the church. Wipperfürth had requested help from the fire service or emergency auxiliaries. He claimed to speak with firemen in the Kaiserplatz, who were sitting around, but they refused because they had not received orders to assist people. Many churches were destroyed, and one collapsed fourteen days later.

Fifteen-year-old Gisela was in the cellar of her house in Rethelstrasse in the Hühnermarkt. She recalled the tip of the *Granusturm* struck their house. Everyone struggled to cope with the incendiary bombs. A woman was crushed into the walls when a building collapsed. Hoffmann referred to an article in the *Westdeutscher Beobachter*, the fanatical Nazi newspaper, which asked: 'Was there need of more proof of the ruthlessness and barbarity of the English conduct of war or the people responsible and their shameful deeds against the the Reich'. This was regarded as evidence that Aachen, 'the cradle of medieval culture of the occident', was destroyed in a terror attack. The newspaper claimed Bomber Command had targeted the city's historic area and monuments, in an extreme case of culture war.[27]

WAR COMES TO AACHEN

Aachen's dead were buried in a solemn ceremony held in the Waldfriedhof on 21 July 1943. Rudolf Storpil was there to report the event for his lead article the next day. He set the scene: the ceremony took place in the chapel, before the old city walls; the dead of the British terror attack were buried under the forest's fir trees beside the fallen of the Great War. The local *SA-Standarte* draped the coffins with their banners, while the army band played Schubert's *Grablied* (1815), with services from both Catholic and Protestant priests, and finally laid to rest while the musicians played the *Trauermarche* (funeral march) from Beethoven's Third Symphony 'Eroica'. Eduard Schmeer gave the oration, in which he offered the Nazi ideology of social Darwinism as survival and said that victory would go to the mightiest. He claimed the home front to the fighting front:

> Death in a storm attack by the infantry or in the rubble of the cities, will always appear horrifying. Death in combat is elevating and the courageous overcome death by suffering it. Fateful death is accepted at the front. The real soldier is not defeated even after death; the fire of his belief will continue to burn! He hands over the flame of power to his comrades. This applies equally to the fallen in the homeland.

Schmeer railed against the bombers, who, he said, 'under the protection of darkness and following Jewish commands', dropped their bombs on women, children, the old and the sick. He added, 'whoever experienced this night knows that to murder the people is to break the people's morale, but they will not succeed'. The great effort to kill the people was compared with the still 'greater pain of the dead who were cherished who died in their homes as loyal Germans'. They were proud members of the national community, he claimed, as he ranted about the right of the German people to live forever. He called to the SA to lower their banners and for the congregation to sing the 'Gut Kammeraden'. A salute was given, an honour company fired a rifle volley, and the flags were then raised to the exclamation: 'life is eternal, the nation is the bearer'. The dignitaries—Gauleiter Grohe, President Vogelsang, army garrison commander Osterote, Oberburgermeister Jansen and Police President SS-Standartenführer Flasche—placed wreaths on the coffins as the national anthem was played. Storpil then concluded by claiming the nation was in mourning. Behind the mourning, however, 'the people are united in their hatred of the murderers of defenceless women and children'. The bearing of the Aachen people would become the guide for the future and the commitment to the war.[28] Not out of touch with the people and had to give meaning to the dead to sustain the war effort.

In summary, the arson raid struck Aachen at 01.45–02.42 hours. The German air-raid officials counted 200-plus aircraft delivering twenty-six mines, 489 bombs, 110,000 firebombs and 21,000 incendiaries. The total casualties: 294 killed outright, 745 injured, 3,600 with serious eye damage, 368 people buried alive, of which 147 were dead. Hoffmann claimed that 6,900 were rendered homeless, an unknown number were buried alive, and the full extent of those with eyesight damage remained never fully accounted. More than 28,500 people fled or were evacuated from the city (this based on uncollected ration cards). There are indications that in October 1944 they were settled in Saxony (14,196) and Lower Saxony (17,124). The dead were buried in the city's Waldfriedhof on 21 July. The city suffered extensive destruction, mostly in the cultural centre, with lasting damage to the medieval *Rathaus*, the theatre, the *Elisenbrunnen*, the Couven museum and the Marschiertor (one of the last surviving medieval-wall gatehouses). Hoffmann claimed the raid cost the city 44.3 per cent of its buildings and acreage: 2,631 buildings demolished, 435 severely damaged, 650 medium damaged and 3,274 slightly damaged. A subsequent survey of the *Rathaus* led to recommendations for reinforcement of the building to support the structure.

IV. *After arson*

On 14 July 1943, a photo reconnaissance aircraft from 542 Squadron took damage assessment photographs at 07.45 hours. A summary report stated, 'the whole of the Central and North-eastern part of the town is obscured by smoke or is in smoke cloud'. Eight hours after the raid, 'when great conflagrations were burning', there could be no assessment of the damage. A summary list of fourteen industries 'heavily damaged' during the raid included: Flamor-Gesellschaft Veltrup (claimed to be producing machine-guns for Junkers), Waggonfabrik Talbot, H. Krantz (textiles and weapons components) and C.H.R. Penners (foundry and armaments). In conclusion, the report added that 'a number of unidentified factories, many public buildings including the Cathedral and large areas of residential buildings are seen to be damaged or on fire'.[29] Bomber Command-Operation Research Section issued a final report on the July raid on 8 October 1943. The report summarised: 'Over half the town was devastated in a concentrated attack by 333 aircraft (out of a total force of 374).' Although obscured by cloud, the OBOE markers dropped their TIs accurately, enabling the bomber swarm to concentrate their bombing. The textile manufacturing and engineering firms, 'which constitute the industrial importance of Aachen', was very heavily damaged. The force lost twenty aircraft, with five shot down by fighters. Seventeen aircraft returned to their bases due to mechanical problems and one crew reported sick. The night photography equipment carried by the bombers to record bomb hits had failed due to the density of the clouds. Under the section 'narrative of attack', the report described the success of the Pathfinder operation, referred to as 'excellent'. The TIs had marked the target and 76 aircraft had bombed within four minutes, marking it as an attack with a build-up of 'unusual speed'. The report highlighted that 80 per cent of the attacking force had claimed to bomb on TIs—'a most satisfactory figure in view of the cloud conditions'.

Another daylight photo-reconnaissance flight brought back photographs that 'revealed severe damage to industrial bases and residential property'. The heavily damaged factories were believed to be in the north-east districts of the city, while in the centre of the town there were 'numerous textile works and small old fashioned firms stand in fully built up areas'. The report confirmed: 'Aachen contains no very large industries and few priority targets but is noted for a multitude of small textile and engineering firms, and others producing needles and spinning machinery.' Out of 140 small and medium firms, the report claimed 80 severely damaged and over half of them destroyed. The scale of economic destruction claims was extended to include 'electrical equipment and cable manufacture, bleaching and dyeing, boiler making, needle making, glass and mirror manufacture, and railway wagon construction'. The report also explained: 'Aachen is an important communications centre, and damage to railway property was serious.' The railway buildings were on the edge of the centre of the city, and the report included banks, the police headquarters and municipal buildings, a 'vast number of buildings wholly or virtually destroyed'. The report concluded up to half the total area of the city was 'devastated and 16,000 housing units were rendered uninhabitable'.

The report referred to the special equipment used in the raid, all navigational devices. OBOE received the most praise for ensuring the accuracy of the TIs. There were also 22 aircraft carrying H2S sets, 14 of which remained serviceable during the raid. GEE was also being used to send guidance signals to 14 aircraft with signal ranges between 210 and 300 miles, although one of the signals stations suffered sending problems due to the weather. The report noted the German defences were not particularly strong since the route was set to avoid main centres of flak. There was particular criticism of the target's defences: 'Aachen was poorly defended for a target so near the Ruhr, even allowing the cloud conditions hampered the defenders, especially in their use of searchlights.' The report added the defences were exclusively 'barrage' orientated, causing damage to 21 aircraft and destroying 2. The British had been listening to German night fighter wireless traffic. They had reported 15 interceptions and claimed 8 bombers shot down. The RAF aircrews had reported a total of 67 interceptions—'33 per cent outbound, 21 per cent over the target and 46 per cent homebound'. The known casualties were 20 aircraft missing (5.4 per cent), and 28 aircraft damaged due to flak (21), fighters (2), British incendiaries (3) and 2 others.[30]

Finally, a report on the Aachen arson mission was placed before Churchill's War Cabinet largely based upon the earliest analyses. Burning smoke still obscured a large part of the target but the scale of destruction was apparent from photographs taken on 14 July.

The reports claimed, 'Industrial damage is particularly severe, and among the more heavily damaged factories which have been identified are works engaged on Textile Machinery, Optical Glass, Electrical Equipment and probably on armaments ... and many public buildings have been damaged or destroyed, and there was large area of residential buildings which are still on fire.' Further photographs were taken on 15 July, leading to the estimate that more than 300 acres of residential and business property had been devastated. The centre of the city was destroyed by fire, with every house in some streets gutted by fire. The *Rathaus* had suffered considerable damage, but the cathedral appeared undamaged. Aachen was regarded as an important junction on the main railway line between Brussels and Cologne. The report accepted: 'although it does not compare in industrial output with the great Ruhr and Rhineland centres, the combined production of its numerous factories ... was far from negligible in total in view of the acute shortage of consumer goods and industrial components of all kinds from which Germany is suffering more and more acutely as the bomber offensive progresses. The elimination of this production is, therefore, a valuable contribution to the industrial paralysis which is being produced in the Ruhr and Rhineland as a whole.'

The selection of Aachen as a target 'had the advantage of involving a shorter penetration of the defence zone in the full moon period than the more important German targets'. A good concentration of fires was started, creating a 'vast pall of smoke from fires still burning'. The evidence shows that 'Aachen has been dealt with in a single attack almost as completely as were Krefeld, Barmen and Elberfeld.' Two thirds of the inner city was destroyed by fire and the 'number of persons who will need rehousing is probably from 30,000 to 50,000, out of a total population of 160,000 ... a substantial contribution to the "housing blockade of the Reich," which German propaganda admits is being imposed by persistent bombing'. The cathedral, the report continued, which naturally figured largely in German reports of the attack, appeared to be undamaged.[31]

On the fiftieth anniversary, 14 July 1993, *Aachen Nachrichten* ran a front-page article with photographs of the *Granusturm* on fire and of St Michael church gutted, without a roof and surrounded by destruction. The article referred to Will Hermanns (1885–1958), who claimed the raid had destroyed 'baroque Aachen'. It mentioned Dr Stephan Bruchkremer (then ninety years of age), who had organised the *Domwache* (cathedral watch) of youth persons who saved the cathedral from bombs and incendiaries. The article also referred to Storpil's article from 17 July 1943 under the caption '*Deutsche Schicksalsstadt*' but avoided Nazi phraseology.[32] The description of the raid has changed with time. Hubert Beckers, in *The Bomber Command Diaries* (1989), referred to the raid: 'Terrorangriff of the most severe scale was delivered.'[33] In 1965, Bernhard Poll had adopted *Grossangriff*.[34] Decades later, Jörg Friedrich controversially wrote: 'The atrocity was carried in the bomb bays of 214 Halifaxes, which appeared as harbingers of the imminent destruction on the clear summer night of 13 July 1943. Massive fires could be ignited right away, which destroyed three thousand structures, killed 294 people, and damaged a series of buildings important to the war effort: the cathedral, city hall, theatre, police headquarters, main post office, and prison.'[35] Memory of the arson raid on Aachen was soon surpassed by the Hamburg firestorm, but together they marked the opening of a bombing campaign that perpetrated war crimes against German civilians.

PART THREE

WAR OF DESTRUCTION

The administrative district of Aachen (Regierungsbezirk Aachen, extends northwards along the Belgian and Dutch frontiers from the central Eifel across the Hohe Venn to the western edge of the Kölner Tieflandsbucht, and occupies practically the whole area watered by the river Roer. The southern part, as for as the town of Aachen, is a thinly-populated, wooded and mountainous area, producing lead ore in the upper Urft valley. The Hohe Venn is covered by barren, desolate moors; hydro-electric power is provided by a system of dams, or which the Urft dam is the most important. The central area, apart from numerous thermal springs, is rich in minerals; iron, zinc, lead and the extensive hard coal deposits of the Inde, Wurm and Mulde valleys, which form the basis of the metal and textile industries of Aachen, Eschweiler and Düren, have resulted in a considerable increase in the population density. In the northern part of the administrative district, which is likewise densely populated, the fertile uplands of the lower Roer are given over to agriculture. The area is 1,740 square miles and the population is 753,800 SicS.

The cathedral city of Aachen (Aix-la-Chapelle) is on the Dutch, Belgian and German frontiers, and therefore, an important centre of railway communications. It lies in a furtile valley-basin surrounded by gently sloping wooded hills; to its north and cast aro the most westerly of the German coalfields, for which it is the administrative centre. It is 614 feet above sea level, its area (Stadtkreis Aachen) is 20 square miles, and the population is 163,000. Aachen is a former coronation city und the ancient capital of the Holy Roman Empire; its hot sulphur springs have been famous for centuries and it had a large tourist industry. The inner town, which is compact, closely built-up and densely populated, is circular, with a diameter of about 1 mile. The north-eastern half of the circle is bounded by broad avenues, formerly the sites of the city walls, of which only certain gates now remain. The curve of the railway line from the main railway station defines the south-western half of the circle. Outside the circle the town tapers gradually eastwards for about 1 mile to the Gelbe barracks; this area includes the law courts and certain industrial works but is mainly residential SicS.

TNA, W0 252 /252 The Town of Aachen, Inter-Service Topographical Department, September 1944.

6

THE PARALYSED CITY

Aachen is an important railway junction on one of the main routes from north-west Germany into Belgium and France. It is the centre of a large coal-mining area, and many companies exploiting these mines have administrative offices in the town. In peace-time textiles formed the main industry in Aachen proper. There are a large number of spinning and weaving mills, many of which were closed early in the war. The leading firms of Aachen's engineering and rubber are mentioned in the report. The town has been heavily damaged by bombing, and the production of several of these firms reduced, but much of the industrial damage, particularly to the main factories, has been repaired ... The central part of the town is closely built, and has largely preserved its mediaeval character.[1]

The RAF's devastating 'arson' raid on 13–14 July 1943 dealt a fatal blow to Aachen, leaving behind a scene of widespread destruction. Later in 1943, the Royal Air Force (RAF) introduced a groundbreaking innovation aimed at enhancing bombing precision: the 'master bomber'. This concept involved a Pathfinder aircraft equipped with high-frequency radio gear, enabling direct communication with other aircraft crews. Acting as a central command, the 'master bomber' relayed radio instructions to Pathfinder crews to mark the target accurately. However, this pivotal role was fraught with peril, as evidenced by the tragic loss in 1944 of Guy

Gibson, a revered figure among RAF aviators. Following Gibson's untimely demise, Air Commodore John H. Searby (1913–1986) assumed the mantle of 'master bomber', honing and refining the techniques pioneered by his predecessor.[2] Air Vice Marshal Don Bennett, the founding commander of the Pathfinder Force, delved into various methods of target marking to cloak the approach of the bomber formations. Employing tactics such as spoofs, dummies, dog-legs and decoys, Bennett sought to maximise the effectiveness of bombing missions. Yet his clashes with RAF high command, particularly over the selection of political targets like Berlin, underscored the contentious intersection between military strategy and political considerations. Bennett attributed the mounting losses among marker aircraft to what he deemed unsound political decisions rather than military necessity, fuelling his rivalry with Air Chief Marshal Ralph Cochrane within the context of target-marking methodologies.[3]

A subsequent heavy raid on Easter Tuesday, 11 April 1944, was a 'blitz' attack, which ran counter to the allied plan for destroying railway facilities in the preparation for D-Day.[4] The attack technique involved Oboe ground-marking, with Mosquitos tasked with marking the aiming point using red Target Indicators, while other aircraft aimed greens at the centre of the red markers. Scheduled to commence at 22.45 hours and expected to last twelve minutes, the raid involved 350 aircraft, including Lancasters and Mosquitos.[5] Despite being set for 'zero hour', the main body of bombers arrived five minutes early over the target. While ground-markers were well concentrated, resulting in some effective bombing, there was notable undershooting to the north-west and a dispersal of the attack. Although small fires erupted with explosions, reports of successful outcomes buoyed the morale of the returning crews. Moderate flak and ineffective searchlights were encountered, resulting in the loss of nine aircraft. An RAF intelligence report from May 1944 attributed the most significant damage to 60,000 four-pounder incendiary bombs.[6] Noble Frankland, reflecting on the raid fifty-four years later in his memoirs, recalled the navigational challenges faced during the mission, highlighting the risk of collision during manoeuvres to reposition for a successful bombing run. Despite the dangers, the second attempt proved successful, with the target hit at the correct time.[7]

On 4 July 1944, the BC-ORS compiled a comprehensive report on the 11 April raid, outlining the meticulous planning and execution involved. The primary target for the 350 Lancaster and Mosquitos was the marshalling yards. Despite the presence of thin cloud cover over the Ruhr, the Mosquitos adeptly ground-marked the yards, enabling highly concentrated bombing that inflicted significant damage. Notably, the distraction caused by fighters resulted in the loss of only nine aircraft—an impressive feat given the circumstances. Daylight aerial photographs revealed that the raid had effectively targeted the station and marshalling yards, extending damage to the southern and western suburbs of the town. The station itself suffered a staggering 75 per cent destruction, while locomotive sheds incurred 50 per cent damage and goods sheds endured 25 per cent destruction. Both marshalling yards bore the brunt of the attack, with tracks, rolling stock and even the bridge spanning the yards sustaining significant hits. Additionally, numerous textile factories and residential properties in the city suffered severe damage, underscoring the widespread impact of the bombing campaign.[8]

On the night of 24–5 May 1944, a formidable aerial assault unfolded as two waves, each comprising over 200 aircraft, converging to strike the two rail yards of Aachen West and Rothe Erde simultaneously. A staggering total of 432 aircraft soared over Aachen, with 409 unleashing their payloads on primary targets crucial to the flow of railways to France. The 'narrative of attack' provided detailed accounts for each target: at Rothe Erde, Mosquitos executed their mission with precision, their red markers backed by a robust concentration of greens, although some crews bombed late and undershot the target. Similarly, at Westbahnhof, markers were punctual and concentrated, yet most crews homed in on the red markers.[9] The aftermath revealed twenty-five aircraft reported as 'missing', accounting for 8.9 per cent and 2.8 per cent of the raids on Rothe Erde and Westbahnhof, respectively. German night fighters engaged the main force with forty-four interceptions, while moderate yet accurate flak posed a threat both over Aachen and the route to Gilze-Rijan. The toll on bomber crews was grim: casualties included those lost in combat, to fighters, flak and even a ship off the Dutch coastline. The local record documented 198 fatalities, 156 injuries and 14,800 displaced, with significant infrastructure damage including Monheim Industry, churches and the railway flak train.[10]

Rothe Erde faced another assault on 27–8 May, utilising OBOE ground-marking and H2S, with instructions for blind bombing if target indicators were obscured. Despite the loss of twelve aircraft, the raid proved effective, severely damaging railway lines and halting all through traffic. Local casualties numbered 167 dead and 164 injured, underscoring the human cost of the relentless aerial campaign.[11]

This chapter delves into the profound impact of the bombing campaign on Aachen and the resilience of its people amidst the devastation. It marks a pivotal juncture in the transition from strategic aerial bombardment to the gruelling warfare on the ground. Despite the passage of decades, Aachen's wartime narrative has been dominated by the siege and subsequent American conquest, often shrouded in myths and legends. Tales of a German general's attempted salvation of the city and local Nazi efforts to sabotage were ingrained in its historical fabric and are still open to interpretation. By weaving together the narratives of aerial bombardment and ground combat, this chapter aims to offer a nuanced perspective on the lead-up to the siege, shedding light on the complexities of war and its enduring impact on Aachen and its inhabitants.[12]

I. Aachen's War Cabinet

As the city trembled under the relentless barrage of bombings, the War Cabinet of Aachen found itself grappling with an impossible task: how to salvage what remained of their once-thriving community. At its helm stood Quirin Jansen, appointed by the infamous Hermann Göring himself, desperately striving to maintain order amidst the chaos. Alongside him, Hans Croon, a formidable figure in both industry and politics, manoeuvred to protect the city's interests, leveraging his influence within the city council and the Nazi economic chamber. Despite their efforts, the devastation wrought by the bombings paralysed Aachen, leaving its inhabitants to navigate a landscape of destruction and despair. Meanwhile, Eduard Schmeer and his brothers, Rudolf and Hugo, occupied positions of authority within the Nazi hierarchy, their actions shaping the city's fate in ways both profound and perilous. In the crucible of war, their stories intertwined, painting a vivid portrait of power, ambition and the struggle for survival in the final throes of Nazi rule.[13]

In the aftermath of the US army's occupation in November 1944, Aachen's municipal records were passed to the British Foreign Office translation service. The bulk of German documents covered the period 23 September 1943 to 7 April 1944, and included documents to the 13–14 July 1943 arson raid. Additional papers were located for the 11 April 1944 air raid and final raids in May 1944. Among the documents were the minutes and reports from council meetings held as recently as August 1944 but reaching as far back as 1940. A large number of the documents were about financial claims made by industrial concerns for damage following air raids. The translated documents were passed to the BC-ORS prior to a survey of Aachen. These records, tracing back to the raids of May 1940, provided crucial insights into the city's wartime experiences. From the urgent requests for aid after devastating raids in April 1941 to the meticulous assessments of damages by the *Reichskriegschadenamt*, each document revealed Aachen's resilience amidst the chaos of war. As directives and regulations emerged, such as Albert Speer's plans for post-raid reconstruction and the Chief of Police's classifications of bomb damage, the city's leadership navigated the challenges with determination. The Oberbürgermeister's call for a comprehensive survey of war damages administration exemplified this resolve, despite logistical struggles noted by Aachen's chief of buildings. These documents not only chronicle Aachen's wartime trials but also underscore its enduring spirit in the face of adversity.

On 13 February 1943, amidst the turmoil of wartime Aachen, the city's senior master craftsman, a stalwart figure in the Nazi association of craftsmen, delivered a stirring address. Gathered before representatives of the main construction firms and subsidiaries, he reflected on their collective response to the relentless air raids that had besieged the city. Casting his mind back to the harrowing events of 10 July 1941, he commended not only his skilled craftsmen but also the companies utilising PoW labour, whose swift and satisfactory work proved instrumental in the city's recovery. Despite the challenges of dwindling resources and manpower, exacerbated by the call-ups to various emergency services and the armed forces, the craftsmen persevered, stabilising the situation with unwavering dedication. In a poignant gesture, he acknowledged the resilience of the city's poorer inhabitants, who, in stark contrast to their wealthier counterparts, displayed remarkable patience and gratitude in the face of adversity, 'a testament to the indomitable spirit of the Aachen populace'.

By February 1943, the landscape for Aachen's craftsmen had undergone a dramatic transformation, ushering in a new era fraught with challenges and complexities. With all skilled building workers evacuated to emergency quarters and commuting daily to the city via trains, trams or bicycles, the situation presented a unique set of circumstances unparalleled elsewhere in Germany or even among the Nazi leadership. However, the mobilisation of labour faced fierce opposition from 'undisciplined managers of firms', officials, and even architects, who disrupted efforts to organise the reconstruction process. Criticisms also extended to the labour exchange for failing to redirect redundant workers towards reconstruction tasks, exacerbating tensions within the workforce. Amidst the chaos, the leader lamented a system where the mobilised workforce was constantly shuffled from one job to another after each successive raid, toiling on weekends and holidays, while others, including officials and architects, enjoyed substantial free time and engaged in private work. Demanding change, he insisted that firms and managers obtain approval from senior craftsmen before issuing work orders, urging municipal leaders to prioritise the interests of Aachen's public and air-raid victims. The plea for cooperation extended to labour exchanges, highlighting the urgent need for a coordinated approach. While acknowledging the concept of self-help, he cautioned against its misuse, emphasising the importance of confronting realities and preparing for the future. In a candid address, devoid of personal attacks but brimming with resolve, he called for collective action to navigate the challenges ahead.[14]

In the aftermath of the devastating arson raid on 13–14 July 1943, a pivotal meeting convened on 27 July between Freiherr von Schroeder, President of the Nazi Cologne-Aachen Gau-IHK, and Hans Croon, President of Aachen IHK. With bomb damage escalating and future repairs looming large, they issued a joint circular, signalling a united front against the destruction. Their mission was clear: to ensure the continuity of industrial production, regardless of the havoc wreaked by bombings. Aligned with Goebbels' wartime priorities, their directive emphasised the ethos of self-help within the framework of the 'national community' doctrine. Neighbouring firms were called upon to lend support by offering skilled workers to aid in the restoration efforts of their counterparts. However, as shortages of labour and materials mounted, what began as a doctrine swiftly morphed into dogma. Only in cases where the damage was deemed severe and the firm indispensable to the war effort did state intervention supersede self-help. Yet the escalating catastrophe necessitated a surge in Nazi bureaucracy, spawning new committees, sanctions, policies and procedures to manage the deluge of war damage claims. Priority was accorded to restoring transportation networks to full capacity, not only to bolster productivity but also to mitigate the growing concern of absenteeism among industrialists. Addressing the plight of workers displaced by bombings, factories were mandated to provide shelter and sustenance, underscoring the core tenets of self-help. To stem labour migration from bombed cities, factories were granted authority to reject resignations. Moreover, a contingency plan was devised for company managements displaced from their offices, with the IHK maintaining a list of vacant spaces for their accommodation.[15]

On 9 August 1943, against the backdrop of unprecedented destruction, Jansen convened a pivotal meeting of the city's architects. With a staggering 40 per cent of housing lost in the cataclysmic 13–14 July raid, the scale of devastation was daunting: 13–14,000 apartments lay in ruins, while an additional 4,000 stood badly damaged, earmarked for urgent repair. Tasked with mobilising the workforce for this Herculean endeavour, the handicraft-workers and labourers' association assumed the responsibility of sourcing labour for the repairs. Meanwhile, the formidable *Organisation Todt* was entrusted with the monumental task of restoring major firms to their war production capacities. Against this grim backdrop, the Aachen IHK undertook the arduous task of identifying priority projects to guide the reconstruction efforts. On 6 September 1943, thirty-five architects convened to receive directives from the city's chief architect regarding the priorities stemming from the 13–14 July raid. A stark definition was drawn: any building without a first floor was deemed beyond repair, while every effort was to be made to salvage residential apartments. However, the looming labour shortage posed a dire challenge. Construction battalions, including essential carpenters and glass workers, had departed after a brief two-month stint in the city, leaving a critical void. Bomb-damaged companies mobilised their workforce for salvage and clean-up operations, while fuel shortages hampered rubble removal efforts. In a gesture of solidarity, Gau Aachen-Cologne pledged assistance, and architects were authorised to seek aid from foreign firms, albeit under stringent conditions. Salvaging efforts amidst the rubble included collecting reusable wooden beams, while stockpiles of stones, bricks and rubble alleviated material shortages. To maintain a semblance of normalcy, temporary roofs fashioned from red materials were promptly camouflaged. Furthermore, the subsidisation of evacuation expenses underscored the city's commitment to aiding its displaced populace, drawing from a dedicated fund housed at the town hall.[16]

In August 1943, amidst the chaos following the air raids, the Nazi labour service issued directives to all managers overseeing foreign labour. The dispersal of foreign workers in the aftermath of bombings posed a significant challenge, hindering the operations of factories, even those with minor damage, due to labour shortages. With efficiency at stake, urgent measures were implemented to round up key workers and ensure their prompt return to their designated workplaces. These instructions, issued by none other than Heinrich Himmler, chief of the SS-Police, mandated the swift relocation of workers to alternative job sites if their primary place of employment was inaccessible. Moreover, workers faced with prolonged or permanent closures of their workplaces were to be reassigned based on their technical expertise. Local authorities and police were tasked with the responsibility of gathering these workers and transporting them to designated reception camps. Recognising the plight of workers affected by the raids, provisions were made for their care by German officials, including the provision of interpreters. Preference was accorded to workers fluent in German and deemed politically reliable, extending even to members of the 'French comradeship' and Dutch and Flemish volunteers serving in Germanic SS units. While some degree of consideration was extended to Slavic workers, the measures underscored the regime's prioritisation of efficiency and control in the face of wartime exigencies.[17]

On 4 October 1943, the architects reconvened for a second meeting primarily aimed at evaluating the efficacy of the new procedures introduced on 12 August. Among the key developments was the establishment of a 5,000RM ceiling from a self-help fund, with larger projects up to 30,000RM falling under the purview of building committees, and those exceeding 30,000RM subject to assessment by Speer's *Ruhrstabes*. This marked a concerted effort by the Nazis to impose limitations on repair costs, with officials from the building police and ARP services overseeing the process. Housing projects were deemed of paramount importance, with labour expected to remain on-site until completion. Architects were urged to prioritise salvage efforts and utilise materials salvaged from bomb sites. In a bid to expedite housing repairs, certain municipal buildings, like the labour office, temporarily suspended repairs to facilitate the transition of workers. Furthermore, emphasis was placed on the meticulous sifting of debris and the preservation of salvaged bricks.[18] However, the challenges persisted, exemplified by the devastating loss suffered by trade groups in Berlin on 24 November 1943, when their offices were destroyed in a raid, necessitating the resubmission of all claims for damages.[19] On 27 December 1943, Albert Speer issued a directive prioritising the repair of railway damage above all other local work, underscoring the strategic importance of transportation infrastructure in the midst of wartime exigencies.[20]

On 14 April, the *Wirtschaftkammer* Aachen convened to assess the aftermath of the 11 April air raid, noting damage was less severe than in the 14 July 1943 raid. Priority was given to repairing water and power supply, with a significant decrease in gas availability. Urgent provisions for workers' food, shelter and local transportation were highlighted. While initial food supplies were secured, rationing was implemented after three days. Large-scale civilian evacuations, especially of women and children, were deemed necessary, though capacity constraints in air-raid shelters posed challenges. Despite 40,000 people being displaced and 1,000 approved for evacuation, voluntary evacuations were ongoing, with 10,000 still absent from the 13–14 July raids. Some 60 per cent of labourers returned to work on the second day post-raid, with building temporary homes a priority. Factory food kitchens provided rations, and power supply from the Goebbelgasse station continued, though household power was not expected until autumn due to extensive tram infrastructure damage. Transportation was hampered, with tram service suspended for months, but 22 buses were arranged, albeit facing fuel and tyre supply challenges. Despite damaged businesses, repairs were underway, with priority given to reconstruction work. However, materials shortages, including bricks, nails and paper, hindered progress. Food supply remained a priority, with 40 of 100 bakeries damaged, and meat stocks requiring immediate consumption to prevent spoilage.[21]

On 31 May 1944, the board of the *Wirtschaftskammer Aachen* convened at the Hotel Quellenhof to discuss the air raids of 24–5 and 27–8 May 1944. Those present included: President Croon, secretary Goerres, three directors and army captain Neuhaus. The 11 April raid damage had been cleared quickly, but the debris of the later raids would take longer. The Aachen–Herbesthal railway line had remained operational, but the Aachen–Düsseldorf and Aachen–Cologne lines were seriously damaged. Bus replacement services were running from the Hauptbahnhof to Würselen, Stolberg and Kohlscheid. The tramway director claimed 97 per cent of rural area was working, and 12 kilometres of the city network. The cables were severely damaged in Westbahnhof and across the eastern quarter. There was no current for trams in those districts. Gas was in short supply, as three holders were hit by bombs, though some supply was coming from a smaller facility. There was no expectation for an improvement for several months. Only concerns working for the war effort were allocated gas. Water supplies were disrupted because pipes from Stolberg had been destroyed. The 27–8 raid destroyed the main pipes in Triererstrasse in twenty places, and there was water rationing. The labour office had reported there was no surplus labour since the raid on 11 April. Special directions had been imposed to conscript labour. A ministry had released 3,600 labourers and the army assigned 25,000 soldiers, but it was not enough to fill the demand. The German Labour Front reported a lack of willingness for work since the 27–8 raid. Only 35–70 per cent of workers had turned up for work, because of the need for repairs of homes. The army representative advised that totally destroyed concerns were no longer being repaired.[22]

On 6 June 1944, Aachen's officials again convened at the Hotel Quellenhof to address the aftermath of the air raids on 24–5 and 27–8 May. Described as worse than the previous 74 raids, with five classified as major raids, the destruction necessitated urgent action. Priorities were set to clear streets of rubble and remove unexploded bombs. With only one water supply line operational, providing 7,000 cubic metres per day, repairing broken pipelines became a pressing concern. Despite efforts to repair a small gasometer, production processes remained halted pending repairs to power sources. While railway lines were expected to reopen within days, the tram system operated at reduced capacity, with buses assisting main routes but unable to fully compensate. A return-to-work plan was drafted on 5 June, with 600 workers drafted into the city since 11 April, joined by 2,600 emergency service personnel and 900 army men. Voluntary work was scheduled for Sundays, with foreign workers assigned to bunkers in the *Westwall* defences and female workers prioritised for beds in the city's air-raid bunker.[23]

II. School's out

Hans-Detleff Heller recalled in 2006 being conscripted as a flak auxiliary, 'A Luftwaffe officer came into the classroom and said from 15 February, all the boys born in 1926 or 1927, would be called up as flax auxiliaries. There was an ear-splitting wall of joy, now we were part of it, now we were soldiers.'[24] Several former pupils recalled on 15 February 1944 that an entire school year of the KKG was declared fit for service. Their respective heights determined their posting: the 175–180cm range became gunners and were nicknamed the 'berserker'. Those in 170–150cm range were to operate the radar and the counter-measure devices and were known as the 'intelligentsia'. Those below 150cm were sent to the radios and signals, and were known as the 'reporters'. They thought school was out, but were horrified to learn their Latin and Greek classes were to continue. On 26 August 1944, the parents in St Vith (today Belgium) were placed under extraordinary pressure. One former pupil's father tried to convince him to remain behind but the youth was determined to go. His father walked him to the railway station and it was the last time they saw each other. A grand parade was held before the Elisenbrunnen for the *Luftwaffenhelfer* (LWH). They were joined by the Hitler Youth (HJ) and their leaders barked orders. The LWH contingent marched out of step to HJ instructions. Another recalled the fourth battery, all from the KKG, were required to attend a talk by a war hero held in the *Kurhaus*. The leaders referred to them as 'boys', so they continued 'bravo-ing and cat-calling' until the hero was drowned out by noise. During a speech by a Nazi *Alter Kämpfer*, on 8–9 November 1943, the young gunners were unruly in their applause and they were removed. One battery was transferred to Cologne during Christmas 1942, and several youths claimed they met members of the *Edelweiss Piraten*, a youth movement, male and female, that opposed the Nazis. Several wore the *Edelweiss* on their hats. Another detachment was sent to Augsberg and then returned to Aachen, and no one learned why.

During the 13–14 July 1943 raid, the young gunners had achieved some good shooting and believed they had shot down twenty-three planes. On 6 September 1944, a USAAF intelligence report advised that the flak in the Aachen area was 'intense, accurate'.[25] However, the 11 April 1944 raid was different, in part due to RAF's counter-measures and the attack. Wilfried Kohl was a gunner and vividly recalled that Easter Tuesday raid. The Nazi Party officially recorded the air raid at 22.40–23.01 hours, with 350 aircraft flying at heights between 1,000 and 8,000 metres. On the evening the warning alarm was received by all the batteries: 'Karl der Grosse—we are targeted'. There were momentary doubts, then the Christmas trees were observed in the direction of Beverau (south-east district). The 'Christmas tree' flares were dropped and the Hauptbahnhof heavily bombed, but the rail traffic was not destroyed. All communications were destroyed after five minutes and dispatch riders were employed to carry orders. The city was 'a wall of fire' and covered in smoke. Most accounts recalled the four 'Christmas trees' were dropped at the corners of the bombing area, then the main attack arrived. The weather was a clear evening, but once the bombing started the air was filled with smoke. Guns fired, shutting out the noise of the bombs. The mounds of earth protecting guns and instruments were shaking with the bombs and guns. The light flak kept firing throughout the raid. The electricity for the radar and other equipment was cut and the bombing intensified as it closed in on them. One boy recalled being crouched down with his steel helmet in shock as bombs created large craters and cascades of debris.

The raid left a deep scar on the memory of the youths; typical was the recollections of a 17-year-old gunner at the time. They were near the Hauptbahnhof when they saw the Christmas tree flares. The flak began to free fire, while the rest took cover in the dirt and some prayed. The bombs forced the air out of their lungs and they were unable to breathe. One saw a bomb come through the roof of a house and explode. The people in the cellar were trapped as walls collapsed. Local coal miners arrived with digging equipment to get people out. The sweet sickly smell of death began to putrefy the air and everyone was scared witless. When the first bombs dropped, all communication lines were cut. The battery had been hit, as the youths clambered out of shelters; someone was seen crawling, having been injured in the back. The youths applied bandages; there was blood everywhere. Another was badly hurt; in the agony of his death throes he kept ranting his name. Number 4 battery, with youths from Malmedy, was the major casualty, with six Luftwaffe soldiers and three Russian PoW/HIWIs killed. The main 88mm flak gun, *Frieda*, was damaged, and a youth from Monschau suffered ear damage. The casualties to the flak defences included two youths killed, and three out of eight radar sections were destroyed. The equipment was damaged and a Luftwaffe NCO sat down, grumbling that two 17-year-olds were dead alongside an Lw-NCO from Cologne.

All accounts agreed the attack lasted less than twenty minutes, but they all thought it felt like an eternity. Wilfred Kohl recalled the flak battery at Beverau (two miles south-east of the city centre) received a direct hit. The flak was overwhelmed, and only one plane was brought down over Aachen. The other flak positions were not attacked but they were unable to intervene. In Richterich, the battery reported the 'window' foil dropped first, then the TIs and then the bombs. Several accounts claimed the flak positions were deliberately attacked and others not. The Eilendorf Battery suffered casualties of two dead and two wounded, all from GLS.[26] A KKG pupil from the 1926 year recalled that the air mine hit the battery. The bomb landed between the headquarters and the radio room, ten metres away from the boys, but it was still within killing distance. The city was burning and everyone was shocked and fearful. Rumours reached the city and parents came looking for their boys. The battery commander met the parents and had to tell them the horrible news. A pupil from the 1927 year intake, from the first battery, was present when the mothers arrived and began wailing horribly, an unforgettable sound. The youths were at a loss when the parents of the dead boys arrived, so they departed the scene.

One 16-year-old gunner recalled he was about to go on leave when they heard a machine-gun-like noise in the direction of Maastricht. The radar began tracking the bomber swarm, but they kept flying towards Düren so they stopped tracking. The swarm then swung back towards them. The battery was furious because of the deception. The attack started at 23.40 hours and the Josef church's clock was stopped at that time and remained so for years afterwards. The intensity of the bombing was staggering and the noise deafening. The gunners struggled to target the bombers and began firing independently. The air was full of shrapnel and debris from the bomb explosions. The city was burning and the gunner, recalling his classical education, thought of Nero before Rome. Fires were everywhere and the third gun had been straddled by bombs; seven soldiers were dead. Some bombs had not exploded and others had missed the guns. A 17-year-old from the third battery in Richterich realised they were caught in the bombing pattern from Burtscheid. The radar-directed guns and searchlights were still operating and spotted an aircraft. It was a Pathfinder aircraft, shot down as a shell hit an incendiary in the bomb-bay. Bombs began spilling out over Röntgen and the flak battery was smashed. People were heard screaming in cellars. The light flak continued firing, hoping to keep up morale, but it was ineffectual above 2,000 metres and the bombers were flying at 6,000 metres. The barracks was on fire and there were dead and wounded. The youths defending Aachen had experienced the change in the intensity of the war. The flak gunners were shaken out of their childish fantasies of war in 1944 by the deaths of their comrades and by the response of the parents.

III. Terror

Between May and September 1944, the political violence in Aachen surged to its peak, catalysed in part by Oberst Claus Stauffenberg's failed attempt to assassinate Hitler on 20 July 1944. The repercussions of this failure reverberated deeply within Aachen, with consequences that remained largely obscured from the wider community for an extended period. This lack of understanding was compounded by the tumultuous events that followed: the successive evacuations of the city by the Nazis, the German army and, ultimately, the US army shattered the collective memory of the populace, driven both by fear and a reluctance to draw attention from British war crimes investigators, who arrived in the city after May 1945. In essence, comprehending the events of Aachen during the summer of 1944 necessitates looking beyond the wartime chaos to the post-war era for a comprehensive reconstruction. This chapter has so far re-examined the captured documents to reconstruct the Aachen War Cabinet and by redirecting the oral history of the flak auxiliaries towards the unfolding events within the city. In these final sections, we take post-war war crimes evidence and the myth of a 'great general' to reconstruct the final days of the old city.

On 22 July, a Nazi security organisation issued a 'Report on the terror raids on Cologne and Aachen and their impact on the public mood'. This was a sterile, impersonal format of reporting: 'the sorely tried population had put up with the raid with remarkable composure'. They acknowledged the 'complaints' from civilians, including that that Berlin had abandoned the Rhineland. Those Aacheners evacuated from the bombing were not well received. The civilians were 'offended' by military propaganda that claimed Cologne cathedral had suffered serious bomb damage, whereas Aachen cathedral had only suffered a 'scratch'. The populace were 'upset' by the regime's 'playing down' the destruction of dwellings and the casualties. There was despondency as to when the air raids would stop, and that retaliation would not come before the Rhineland was obliterated. Some homeless people believed the war could have 'a positive outcome'.[27] The harsh realities of life in Aachen were known to the authorities; as noted in the War Cabinet section of this chapter, security reports could not erase the actualities of existence in a paralysed city.

Those under the bombs were, like the bombers, following routines during raids. Rosemarie had two children. When the *Fliegeralarm* was sounded she grabbed a thick winter coat, woke the children, grabbed a small suitcase and went immediately to the shelter near the Pontstrasse. In the shelter the walls would shake from the percussion of explosions and guns firing. She later recalled people screaming and choking in the dust and shale splintering off the inside walls, a little boy in his Hitler Youth uniform praying, and the pungent odour from the phosphorus. The streets were strewn with dead women and children. People feared the loss of their homes and would stream out of the Monheimallee bunker to scenes of total devastation. The Nazis and Hitler promised revenge, with new weapons, but there was no reconciliation for the growing sense that the city was being dismantled by the bombing. Rosemarie and her children were eventually evacuated to Paderborn; others in her neighbourhood went to the Eifel.[28] In my discussions with locals, a former soldier recalled his wife was caught outside of a bunker during an air raid and was rendered speechless for many years. A woman recalled after the air raids the horrible conditions caused people to suffer from bronchitis or pneumonia. A doctor explained a large number of patients suffered psychological disorders from the air raids and were still being treated long after the war.

In the air war, German flyers were still scoring successes against the bombers. Heinz Rökker, a night fighter pilot, recalled flying unseen under the British bombers because they had no downward-looking capability.[29] In 1986, Johnny Johnston, a former RAF flight engineer, recalled his experience on 23 June 1943, during a mid-air collision over the target. His aircraft burst into flames and as it began to break up Johnston was thrown into the bomb-aimer cone. He tumbled out and began free falling among the aircraft's debris. His parachute opened and he could see the main force on its bomb run, while down below the fires were starting—the awful realisation that he was falling into the target area. He was captured by the Luftwaffe and taken by train to a PoW camp. The train stopped in Mühlheim railway station. On the opposite platform was a Red Cross train and he watched in horror as a line of children, with their eyes bandaged and holding hands, were being led into the train by nurses. His crew had bombed the city a few days before.[30]

The weather for August 1944 reached a maximum of 37mC. The heatwave added to the unbearable situation from water rationing and virtually no supply of basic amenities and public utilities. The month recorded the *Fliegeralarm* had sounded 779 times for a total length of 1,064 hours during the war. The Americans also joined in the bombing and escalating the destruction of the city. The USAAF 8th Air Force carried out a daylight nuisance raid on Aachen on 9 August. Sixteen B-17 Flying Fortresses of 3rd Bomb Division delivered thirty-eight tons of bombs.[31] There was a nuisance raid at midnight on 25 July. The city recorded that an allied bomber had crashed near Würselen with ten bombs and eight men taken prisoner.[32]

The crashed aircraft came from USAAF 524th Squadron, 379th Heavy Bombardment Group, based at RAF Kimbolten and had attacked Saarbrücken and Ulm. They were on their return trip. A subsequent British military occupation trial examined the story. The B-17G was hit by flak over Aachen and the eight crew bailed out. The crew two crew were: Engineer-gunner T/Sgt John C. Phillips, from Greenville, South Carolina, who was single and 24 years old; and tail-gunner S/Sgt Alvin Williams Brady, from Laurel in Maryland, 20 years old and married. They came down nearby Würselen, about five kilometres from Aachen centre. The other six crew disappeared from record. Phillips sprained his ankle on landing, but was helped by Brady. They were apprehended by German civilians and a Luftwaffe private, possibly a flak auxiliary, was out to 'claim' the bomber for his unit. Brady carried Phillips to a house, where a woman bathed his ankle. They were 'interrogated' by a civilian who spoke English. Then three German officials arrived, one dressed as a civilian but who was Aachen's chief of Gestapo, and all were wearing Nazi armbands. The Gestapo chief kicked Phillips' ankle and punched him in the face. Phillips's face began bleeding. They were taken to a wagon and told to take off their shoes, socks and field jackets. They were then taken to Aachen, where they were forced out of the wagon and made to walk barefoot for a mile through the town. Along the march, the officials encouraged civilians to stone, abuse and beat them. Phillips was knocked about and Brady was kicked and stoned until unconscious. Phillips, with an injured foot, was forced to carry Brady. A civilian knocked them down and others began kicking them. Brady returned to consciousness in the police presidium and the Gestapo chief continued to kick him in the groin. At around 17.30 hours, a Luftwaffe officer and guard arrived and took both men into custody. The train finally arrived in Cologne at 21.00 hours, and the men were taken to a Luftwaffe supply depot to receive medical attention.[33] They were lucky, because many captured allied airmen were lynched or beaten to death by enraged civilians. The war crimes case is discussed in chapter nine.

THE PARALYSED CITY

On 25 August 1944, the President of the Gauwirtschaftskammer Köln-Aachen confirmed, in writing to Croon, that total war had been declared on 16 August. In all practical purposes, the War Cabinet's days were over, as local party Kreisleiters were ordered to liaise with the Reich Defence Commissars in the final defence of Nazi Germany.[34] One consequence of the failed July plot was the further centralisation of the regime's power. Heinrich Himmler, the chief of the SS, became Reich Minister of the Interior. In that capacity, Himmler issued orders for the defence of Germany on 10 September 1944.[35] The party was responsible for ensuring the people were in the highest state of readiness and the state agencies were ordered to assist the party. The *Gau* level was ordered to work towards this initiative and the Reich Defence Commissioners were to ensure a uniform state of defence. In the event of constructing fortifications, the *Gau* authorities were to administer all activities not deemed military. State agencies had to supply workers to assist in the building of fortifications through emergency conscription. He added, 'The Party is responsible for the evacuation of the population. This also applies to the ethnic alien population. It should prevent the population from flooding back in an unregulated and precipitate fashion.'[36] On the same day, Himmler declared: 'Aachen will not be evacuated.'[37]

Since the beginning of September, Oberst Helmut Osterroth (the first Aachen commandant) had continually advised Eduard Schmeer that it was necessary to evacuate the women and children. Schmeer claimed that Hitler sat on the decision, but had visited Josef Grohé in Cologne to discuss the matter. Finally, on 11 September, Grohé, had received instructions from the general commanding Wehrkreis VI to evacuate, and in his capacity of Reich Defence Commissar he issued the declaration of a mass evacuation of Aachen. The specific groups to be evacuated included those unable to march, the sick, the frail and pregnant women, women with children and adolescents born after 30 June 1930, as well as women without children and males (but only after reconstruction work has been carried out on the *Westwall*). The local party officials received instructions in the evening and thirty special trains were arranged for the evacuation. During that time, the

Wehrmacht units in Aachen were also to be evacuated. The exceptions involved those in maintaining utilities, and those collecting food produce. The basis for evacuation was the rules governing air-raid victims. The announcement included the available allocations to other Nazi *Gau*—60,000 Weser-Ems, 80,000, Wesfalen-Nord and 100,000 Südhannover-Braunschweig.[38] This was not a scorched earth policy as the allies claimed at the time.

Previous mass evacuations were to Saxony and Lower Silesia. This time, the civilians were evacuated to Brunswick, Thüringia, Münster, Minden and Hannover. It was believed that 143,000 persons had been evacuated since the air raids started in 1940. The IHK transferred to Düren-Birkesdorf and later to Bonn. The next day, heavy fighting erupted in Eynatten-Köpfchen and Aachen forest (both to the south) against the Westwall defences. American shells began landing on the city, as the last of the evacuees departed. The city's administration officially transferred to Siegburg. Later, they moved to Wiedenbrück to form a settlement and counselling service. At 10.00 hours, the last air-raid warning was sounded, without an all clear. The ARP police fled the city on the roads to Duisburg and Cologne. At midnight, German railways stopped all traffic to Aachen. Museum director Dr Kütgens, with approval from Oberbürgermeister Jansen, was deputised to take responsibility for Aachen in his absence. Kütgens was to establish the emergency administration of the civilians who remained behind in the city. Patients in the hospitals had already been discharged and taken to other cities. The keys to the hospitals were given to the nuns, and the last convoy of wounded was moved to Cologne on 18 September.[39]

IV. The German Army occupation of Aachen

The final seven weeks of old Aachen's existence was a tragic comedy on a vast scale. What remained of the city's populace became pawns to rival ideologies. From the political-strategic perspective, Hitler hailed the final struggle to defend Nazi Germany's sacred frontiers would become the defining moment of National Socialism. For the local Nazis, the final weeks became a struggle

THE PARALYSED CITY

between personal survival and holding on to power. For the German army, under the spotlight since the July plot, was added the problems of contending with major defeats like the Battle of Falaise and reforming fresh defence lines to conduct coherent counter-offensives. This period in German military history revealed the sham politics of the generals and colonels. Like some banana republic, the colonels became politically more influential than the generals. The generals, never having a uniform mindset, were also in a state of political flux. Field Marshal von Rundstedt was cleverly weaving his survival while others literally committed suicide. Kluge shot himself and Rommel, judged guilty of treason by his peers, took poison to save his family from national disgrace. In that climate of lethal uncertainty, the German officers resorted to extreme violence instead of rational decisions, and traded integrity for duplicity.

Why Hitler decided to turn Aachen into a bastion of National Socialism is not altogether clear. During the pre-war years he snubbed the city but made flamboyant public gestures of visiting the nearby *Ordensburgen Vogelsang* Nazi political school in the Eifel. In the wake of 20 July and the collapse on both fronts, east and west, there was a period of shock inertia, which broke in September as the fronts stabilised. Also since Kovel in January–February 1944, Hitler had faith in using fortresses like anvils to hammer counter-attacks. Ideologically, Aachen represented the majesty of Germany combined with the symbolism of the body politic of National Socialism. There was a ritual solemnity to defend the city at all costs and by whatever means. On 3 September 1944, Hitler issued instructions for military operations in the west. In the absence of a determined line of defence, the confused situation made it difficult to bring forward reinfocements. German forces were ordered to hold up and stall the advancing allied armies through local counter-attacks. The aim was to hold up the advancing allied armies and stall them with local attacks. Therefore, Hitler issued orders for 'The right flank and centre of the army in the west (including 1st Army)' to put up stubborn resistance for every inch of ground. Hitler recognised penetrations of the German line could not be prevented but large Wehrmacht formations were ordered to avoid encirclement at all costs. Commander-in-Chief West was ordered to re-establish the front lines. The process of forming the Fifth Panzer Army was underway. Panzer brigades in reserve would be released for the west. Fortress troops on the Westwall would replace two grenadier divisions, which could be released to stiffen the front. Hitler acknowledged the lack of reserves advising four grenadier divisions would be released later in September to take up positions on the right flank. On 7 September, Hitler issued plenary powers to Field Marshal von Rundstedt as Commander-in-Chief West. Two days later, he issued instructions for the defence in the west. All departments and bureaus, including the *Wehrkreis* VI, XII and V (military districts) of the Wehrmacht, were placed under Rundstedt's command.[40]

The records for 13 September note that German Army General Gerhard Graf von Schwerin, commander of 116th Panzer Division, became commandant of Aachen. His first orders were to put a stop to the 'wild' evacuations of the population. The number of citizens remaining in the city were around 30,000, with many existing in the air-raid bunkers. The next day, Dr Kütgens informed the civilians of the emergency administration. The administration took up residence in the Hotel Quellenhof. On 15 September, a lawyer in the administration was arrested for voicing anti-Nazi comments and taken to a Cologne prison. At 14.00 hours, the power supplies shut down and the telephone line was cut. Schwerin was relieved from command and ordered to attend a court martial on 16 September, because of his differences with the party. Also on that day, the evacuation of the city was restarted and the German army occupied the city. From 25 September, the US forces began to encircle Aachen. On 30 September, Oberst Leyherr, commander of 689th Grenadier Regiment, set up his command in Rolandstrasse, in advance of the arrival of Oberst Gerhard Wilck as the new commander of Aachen.[41]

History records a far more brutal story. Peter Quadflieg has written that Eduard Schmeer, the police and other officials left the city by train at 21.00 hours. There was a general assumption that the Americans had broken the German lines and would be in the city within days. German panzer troops began assembling in the

THE PARALYSED CITY

Würselen area and a regiment arrived in Aachen at 23.00 hours on 12 September and set up a headquarters. The soldiers arrived in the city and saw utter chaos. Quadflieg thought 25,000 civilians were still in the city. On 13 September, Schwerin informed one of the last Nazi Party officials in the city that he didn't have the military strength to hold off the Americans and could not defend the city. He also ordered all civilians in the city to remain in the bunkers. Then Schwerin decided to write a letter to the Americans, informing them that he was turning Aachen into an 'open city'. He wrote, 'I stop this stupid evacuation.' Regardless of his intentions, Schwerin had no contact with the Americans, and had not made his intentions clear to them. Instead, he passed the letter to the trust of a postal official in Aachen.[42] He then returned to his comfortable headquarters in Schloss Rahe, two miles north of the city.

What happened next turned into a tragedy. Realising the Americans were not coming, Schwerin was in a predicament over his letter. On the afternoon of 13 September, Schwerin received word from a regimental commander that plundering in the city. He ordered a summary court martial, and two plunderers were found guilty and shot the next day. They were both boys, fourteen years of age—Johann Herren and Karl Schwartz. According to Heinz Günther Guderian, the evening passed peacefully, but on the morning of 14 September Schwerin rang the Chief of Staff of LXXXI Korps, complaining that Luftwaffe soldiers had fled and some impudent flak gunners had exclaimed that 'conditions in Aachen were devastating'.[43] That same day, Finni Kruth witnessed the execution of the boys:

> It spread like wildfire. Children are being shot back there. I was curious. Then suddenly they were dragging the children out of the door. I was very, very shocked as I knew both the boys. I couldn't believe it. They blindfolded the boys with men's handkerchiefs. Karl kept calling out 'Mum, mum, I don't want to die! I didn't do anything. I don't want to die.' Then someone called out 'fire' and the shooting started. Karl Schwartz did fall over but he got up again and walked off towards Feldmannplatz. And a young lieutenant walked behind him and said 'what? You don't want to die?' And finished him off.[44]

WAR COMES TO AACHEN

According to Guderian, Dr Kütgens visited all 22 air-raid shelters, holding 25,000 persons, and another 5,000 hiding in the ruins. At 11.00 hours, he held a meeting at the Quellenhof Hotel and they discussed calming the population. Then Kütgens met Schwerin and they discussed security and Schwerin agreed 'to establish a citizens' defense against looting'.[45] On 15 September, Schwerin submitted his report for the period 12–14 September to LXXXI Korps, explaining his actions. He then arrived at the Hotel Quellenhof to inform Kütgens he was moving the division out and the city was open to the Americans. Then later that day, Schmeer returned claiming there was an attempt to hand his city over to the enemy. Kütgens was arrested but then released and Schwerin was removed from his command but survived investigation. Both men escaped the Nazi terror, which was in stark contrast with how Rommel was not protected by senior officers or spared.

In a taped recording made in 1974, Schwerin explained why he had tried to save the city; having arrived to scenes of chaos in Aachen, he wrote a letter leaving the city 'open' to the advancing Americans. For decades, Germany and many scholars had assumed Schwerin had acted honourably to save Aachen from ruin in September 1944. A German scholar has argued that Schwerin was one of the first to refuse to implement Hitler's orders and survived.[46]

The decision to make Aachen an open city was, according to Quadflieg, based upon a sound military appraisal. This is difficult to judge even with hindsight. Hitler had declared 'Aachen was to be defended by all means to the last stone and to the last drop of blood. There is no retreat or surrender.' Others have argued that Schwerin's actions explain German army actions at that stage of the war.[47] If the army was sending a message to the people of Aachen, through extreme violence, why did it rest with the death of two boys? With virtually all the population gone, how was killing two boys going to change their behaviour? Perhaps a better interpretation of Schwerin's behaviour arises from including the actions of Kütgens and the flak gunners. Playing the humanitarian card with the Americans was Schwerin's way of dodging allied war crimes justice, which had been a concern for senior German officers since a BBC announcement, during the Warsaw Uprising, claimed war criminals would be prosecuted. Killing two boys in the name of civil-military order also appealed to Nazi terror. Schwerin was cautious as well of the men under his command who were strictly loyal to Hitler. As a precaution, he retained detachments of loyal troops at his headquarters and when travelling in Aachen. Was Schwerin playing a duplicitous hand—protecting himself, while trying to conform to Nazi policy and the high command, but setting in place an alibi with the Americans? He saved his life, but he was not the defender of Aachen or the protector of the people.

On 19 November 1957, Schwerin was honoured by the people of Aachen. Oberbürgermeister Hermann Heusch (1906–1981) awarded him with the equivalence of the freeman of the city and he was lauded as the saviour who tried to save the civilian population. Schwerin's story became central to Aachen's memory.[48] Later, in 1962, General Schack was requested by Bernhard Poll, the city archivist, for an opinion of Schwerin's claims for saving Aachen. He replied, 'The heroic deeds of Count von Schwerin, told by himself.' He was a a general 'known for his vanity and deep desire for recognition', and 'his claim that the fate of Aachen fell to the 116 Panzer Division was factually untrue and pompous'. Schack believed Schwerin became jittery when he realised he had misjudged the situation and that even the enemy were not acting in the way he expected. Schack asked what Aachen had seen in the merit of Schwerin. He believed the city had made some poor judgements over special honours but Schwerin was a better choice than honouring Churchill (reference to the Karlspreis in 1956—refer to Reflections). Yet Schwerin pandered to Hitler, what a poser he was.'[49]

On 25 September, Hitler issued the decree for the raising of the *Volksturm*, the last armed force of the Third Reich.[50] On 18 October, in a speech to the *Volksturm*, Heinrich Himmler drew on parallels with the Landsturm in 1813 and the Battle of Nations. He declared that, 'on the anniversary of the Battle of the Nations at Leipzig, our Father and Supreme War Lord Adolf Hitler, has called all German men between 16 and 60 years of age who are at home and capable of bearing arms to fight in the German Volksturm to defend the homeland'.[51] On the same day, Rundstedt gave the funeral oration for Erwin Rommel, who had committed suicide ten days earlier. He announced, 'Fate has taken the Field Marshal away from his place just as the struggle was reaching its zenith. He was a zealous soldier imbued with National Socialist spirit.' It is difficult to judge if the *Volksturm* played any part in the defence of Aachen, but these speeches were given as the battle in Aachen was coming to a final conclusion—hence the absence in propaganda of references to the city.

In the final days of the battle of Aachen, the city was isolated and eventually occupied. The authors of *Die Tragödie von Aachen* argued Hitler wanted to stage a 'German Stalingrad', with fanatical German resistance. They hypothesised that the Americans knew of German intentions and thus both sides used propaganda to break each other's fighting power. They also claimed the Americans played Schwerin and Wilck off against each other in their wartime propaganda leaflets, which cannot be confirmed in First US Army papers.[52] The evidence does highlight how far Schewerin misread the movements of the Americans but also his failure to properly address the conditions of the civilians. The final air raids had unhinged the people, causing them to disply demonic anger at one extreme and mass panic at the other. The incompetent handling of the first evacuation exacerbated an increasingly shambolic situation. In that context, Kütgens acted responsibly and with sound appreciation for the actual conditions in the city and among the populace. Whereas Schmeer's failure was a gross act of cowardice and political incompetence. As for Schwerin, the impudence of the teenage flak troops exposed a brutal and arrogant Nazi general.

7

THE STALINGRAD OF THE WEST

A team of battlefield investigators from the *After the Battle* magazine, during a visit to Aachen in 1983, observed:

> Within the city the most famous landmark of all still stands—an event which is remarkable given the German preoccupation with eliminating all traces of the war, both physically and mentally. Although its outline is softened by the post war growth of a line of poplars. Oberst Wilck's bunker headquarters still stands on Rütscher Strasse.[1]

In 2014, while the city commemorated Charlemagne's birthday, Wilck's bunker was quietly destroyed by pneumatic hammers. The contrast in the politics of culture could not be more palpable. The official bronze plaque, fixed to the entrance of the bunker that once claimed Aachen was the first city to be 'liberated' from Nazism, disappeared. The bunker as a symbol of defeat was erased, but it also served as a proud moment in post-war German history as the start point of democracy. In its destruction, Oppenhoff's state corporatism was triumphant. The 'new' apartments were not called 'Democracy Buildings' or 'Liberation Homes', and there is nothing to indicate the historic events that took place there eighty years before. During the destruction of the bunker, the first 'Surface Concrete Shelter' in Sandkaulstrasse was also demolished to make way for a new hotel. According to the RAF Bomber Command's survey report, from 1945, it was the first to be erected following local pressure on the Aachen municipality. Technically, it could have been reclassified as a symbol of the passive public resistance to the Nazi regime. The bunker and the air-raid shelter were arguably the most historically significant buildings in Aachen, if not Germany. Like many German cities, since the 60th anniversary of the end of the war, Aachen has been erasing the last traces of the Nazi past and the war. Urban battlefields decay faster than others and are deceptively difficult to preserve, but there is also the erasing of memory which, although it might appear noble at the time, might have consequences. A revitalised urban landscape erases memory. Erasing historic sites and hoping society will maintain the history from books, in the social media age, is wishful thinking. By 2044, the hundredth anniversary of Aachen's surrender, it's likely there will be few remaining landmarks of the battle or the Nazis.

In the cold light of history, the Battle of Aachen is an enigma. Simple questions—when did it begin and when did it end, or even how many battles of Aachen were there—have no simple answers. The US army has several lineages for the battle—it is written into the Rhineland Campaign or the Siegfried Line Campaign or identified as a stand-alone battle. Wikipedia compresses the battle into two weeks and five days (2–21 October 1944), but acknowledges the German interpretations of several battles, starting with the 'first battle', 10 September–2 October 1944.[2] If the RAF bombing campaign is included in the Battle of Aachen, then the start date would be 13 May 1940. We can also ask the significant social history question—was it an Aachen battle? The demographics at the time of the battle indicate the civilians numbered were less than 2.5 per cent of the 1939 population; the rest were evacuated from the bombing or deported in September 1944. The German military forces fighting for the city and the commanders were not from Aachen. Many of the German soldiers being ordered to fight to the death in the ruins were not Aacheners. There are also questions about Hitler's real interest in saving the city. The Aachen electorate had not voted for Hitler, and he'd repeatedly snubbed the city, refusing to grace it with an official visit. How can military history reflect these factors within the limits of a battle narrative? Military history and political nostalgia have become a potent cocktail in the age of social media. However, not all societies are fixated on war(s). Fewer Germans today care to know about Germany's wars of the twentieth century. The anniversaries of the war and the ceremonies of battles pass barely noticed by the younger generations. However, there are important issues over how the battle should be depicted in Aachen's future, if only as a reminder that democracy and national integrity come at a very heavy cost. This chapter deconstructs the battle's history into constituent parts, examines the discrepancies in combat reports, surveys the history makers and reflects on a future history.

I. The US Army Historical Branch

During and after the battle, the US Army Historical Branch collected combat reports from the fighting units and 'interesting' personnel. The decision to centralise historical activities was made by General George C. Marshall, chief of staff of the US army. In March 1942, the US army planned to place operations of the Historical Branch within the G-2 function of the general staff. The new office became operational on 20 July 1943, 'providing historical officers to supervise the accumulation of documents, and researching, and writing the operational histories of the ongoing war'.[3]

S.L.A. 'Slam' Marshall became chief of the Historical Branch, and he ordered his scribes to Aachen to record after-action reports.[4] Forrest Pogue made an interesting observation about Marshall: 'when he was writing an article or pushing some point of doctrine, he was capable of pulling a figure out of the air and suggesting that this was based on solid information gathered by 200 combat historians under his command'.[5]

By 3 January 1945, Marshall's scribes had compiled twenty-one army ground combat reports. This list increased to twenty-six reports with lectures from victorious battalion commanders or soldiers with distinguished service. The units that complied with the request included 16th, 18th, 39th, 115th, Infantry Regiments, the 1106th Combat Engineers and the tank battalions from the US 1st Infantry Division 30th Infantry Division. There were several USAAF IXth Tactical Airforce reports, which were issued later. The reports are an assortment of rough drafts, sometimes conveying a sense of pride in the participants; some are pre-citation reports for medals, some displayed the indifference of combat veterans for rear area soldiers. Immediately after the battle, First Lieutenant Harry D. Condron, 2nd Information and Historical Service of First US Army, issued a general summary of the battle. He began with the official statement: 'At 12.06 pm, on 21 October 1944 Colonel Wilks [sic] the commander of Aachen, surrendered the garrison and installations of the enemy pocket to Brigadier General George Taylor, assistant commander of US 1st Infantry Division.' George Taylor (1899–1969) had been made a colonel just four months before leading his men off the Omaha beaches, and his famous order, 'There are two kinds of people who are staying on this beach: those who are dead and those who are going to die. Now let's get the hell out of here.' He was awarded the Distinguished Service Order for extraordinary heroism.

Condron described the city—a population of 165,000, a railroad centre, in a valley surrounded by hills; there were numerous industries, including railway manufacturing, light engineering and aviation, textiles and one of the largest needle factories in the world. Many civilians had fled the city from the British bombing. Condron claimed the city was bombed for the first time on 11 April 1944, demolishing half the buildings, and the raids on 26–8 May completed the destruction. He had driven to the city on the day of the surrender and saw 'the complete gutting of buildings' and 'it was rare indeed when a building was found that was still usable'. By the time the Americans arrived there were fewer than 15,000 persons (in real terms 4,000), mostly women and children left in the city. Nonetheless, Condon claimed Aachen 'was not important to the German Army because it was neither a natural nor an artificial fortress'. The railways and factories had all been destroyed.

On 12–13 September, US VII Corps received army directives identifying the Siegfried Line and Aachen as the objectives for attack. Since Aachen had no value to the US Army, the plans were set 'to sweep around and envelop it'. Eschweiler, north-east of the city, became the designated meeting point for XIX Corps and VII Corps, in preparatory moves towards taking the advance to the Rhine River. VII Corps had three divisions (1st Infantry, 3rd Armoured, 9th Infantry) in the drive, while the prominent XIX Corps encircling force was 30th Infantry Division. From the outset, German resistance was stubborn—3rd Armoured was halted before Stolberg, 9th Infantry was held at Schevenhutte and 1st Infantry was beginning to face tough opposition after initial successes. The encirclement, however, was not complete, with a gap in the lines to the north-east, which the Germans used to feed supplies and reinforcements. Aachen was reassessed as a significant threat in the rear of the US advance, and 'it was decided to close the gap out of Aachen and clean out the city'. The Americans had offered the Germans a 24-hour ultimatum to surrender the city. No heavy bombardment was planned, because 'the city was already demolished', but selected dive bombing and shelling was to 'soften defences', inflict casualties, and to cover the US entrance into the city. The plan being to keep American casualties low. On 11–13 October, IXth Tactical Air Force conducted strikes on the city, with 367th, 404th, 368 and 370th (flying Lockheed P-38 Lightnings and Republic P-47 Thunderbolts) delivering 172.75 tons of bombs. Afterwards, aerial cover was only involved when directly called upon by the infantry.

On 10 October 1944, American assessments of German forces in Aachen ranged from three to four thousand troops. The Americans were uncertain but judged there were '52 company strength units', in Aachen area, with the 246th Volksgrenadier Division being the principal formation (352, 689 and 404 Grenadier-Regiments). There was a mixed collection of battalions, field artillery detachments, six self-propelled assault guns and two tanks. There was a police detachment of 125 men, operating in eight-man squads, with rifles and a machine gun and led by the chief of police, Major Zimmermann. The most aggressive German formation in the city was *Kampfgruppe Rink*, a Waffen-SS detachment from Hitler's Bodyguard division, variously designated a battalion or a regiment, and estimated at 200–300 men. On the night of 15–16 October, eighty policemen from Cologne broke through the lines to join the defence. The Americans believed the defenders were far from crack troops, with 50 per cent over 35 years of age, but they were well armed with 1944 equipment and were virtually all Germans bar fifteen Russians. The Germans continued to resupply the defenders by air during the last weeks of the siege. Condron barely referred to the fighting or the German counter on 15 October. Instead, he listed the daily surrenders of German soldiers from 11 to 21 October. Six officers and eighty-one ORs surrendered on the first day, two days later six officers and 307 ORs, and on the day of surrender forty-eight officers and 1,626 ORs—the overall tally being eighty-one officers and 3,391 ORs. There were 193 evacuated by medical services and 600 walking wounded, and they estimated one German dead to every wounded. The information for the report was supplied by US 26th Infantry Regiment.[6]

In contrast to the urban battle, 18th Infantry Regiment fought over the difficult terrain of the encirclement battle. The regiment filed several sets of after-action reports at battalion and company level. Company 'K', Third Battalion, compiled an after-action report on 24 October. This covered the struggle to control the Ravelsberg area (described as Ravels Hill). The high ground was a key to the battle, lying two miles north-east of the city centre, a road junction that converged with roads to Würselen, Eilendorf and Brand. The terrain was unsuited for armoured forces and required determined infantry combat, to take trenches and pillboxes, and hold them. The company accounted for more than two hundred enemy soldiers in 'two days of gruelling warfare'. Another Company 'K' report was about the Ravels Hill fighting in detail, covering the first German attack at 06.30 hours on 18 October. The weather was demanding, with high winds and heavy rain, common at that time of year. German infantry, supported with tanks, overran several American positions. Then about fifteen tanks and self-propelled guns began pounding the American positions. The firefight turned into a vicious struggle for the heights, as the German pressure overran several US platoons and held the position. Next day, Company 'B', in support of the displaced platoons, countered to retake the positions. Two tanks supported the attacks

Introduction: the Aachen City plaque commemorating the end of Nazism and the beginning democracy. Once fixed to the massive German Army bunker, it was removed and the bunker demolished in 2014. (Author collection)

The Great War: memorial to the fallen Jewish soldiers in the Synagogue; RWTH-Aachen University Aula auditorium with the doors framed by the roll of honour of names of students and faculty etched in marble; memorial to fallen German soldiers from Kelmis, a neighbouring community now in Belgium; Aachen war memorial erected on a turret of the old walls after the Great War. Destroyed in 1944, it was reconstructed sometime after 1946. (Author collection)

Letting Go of Democracy: Aachen Nazi Party and SA leader Eduard Schmeer. (NARA, Hoffmann Collection, courtesy Michael Miller); Ordensburg Vogelsang, the Nazi political school for future leaders, today a museum in the Eifel National Park. (Author collection)

In Defence of Aachen: Hochbunker, Sandkaulstrasse, the first bunker in 1941 and demolished in 2014. The demolition exposed the housing cells used into the 1950s; Hochbunker Kasinostrasse, in proximity to where two American airmen were beaten and stoned, encouraged by Aachen police officials. (Author collection)

Frying Elver: the area where the RAF's target indicator flares were dropped and the centre of Zone 1 fires; the 14th-century *Rathaus* (town hall) with its coronation hall was seriously damaged during the air raids and all the surrounding municipal buildings were destroyed. (Author Collection)

The Paralysed City: Aachen Burtscheid area after the heavy bombing raids against the railway lines; destruction to the *Hauptbahnhof* after the battle. (US Army Signals Corps, NARA); an image of Adalbertstrasse in October 1944, and in 2004, before the redevelopment. (Author collection)

The Stalingrad of the West: American Sherman tanks in Rolandstrasse after the firefight; American anti-tank gun team in the city centre; German soldiers surrendering; Captain Bobbie E. Brown, received the Medal of Honour for acts of bravery on 8 October 1944, during the encirclement battle. (US Army Signals Corps, NARA)

Restoring Democracy: civilians being evacuated after the battle; women and children being fed with US Army rations in Brand; Aachen's first post-Third Reich police force November 1944; Franz Oppenhoff, Aachen's first post-Third Reich Oberbürgermeister. (US Army, NARA)

Defiance and Disorder: soldier and smuggler, Heinrich Schreiber 1923–2020. (Author collection); Aachen city centre, believed to be 1954. (NARA)

Ordinary People: Aachen's ornate synagogue destroyed by arson in November 1938. (Aachen Stadtarchiv); former Gasborn police precinct designated as the collection point for the units and personnel assigned to the destruction of the synagogue on Kristallnacht; one of the Judenhaus in the university district that served in the ghettoisation of Aachen's Jews; memorial plaque decorated with candles and flowers during Kristallnacht memorial service in November 2023. (Author Collection)

Conclusion: the civilian dead air raid, 11 April 1944, buried in military style by the Nazis and under the watchful gaze of the Bismarck tower from 1905. (Author Collection)

but were knocked out, as the fighting increased in ferocity. In the afternoon, the Germans unleashed a heavy barrage on the hill lasting thirty minutes and, believed at the time, the heaviest intensity the Americans had experienced in Europe. Behind the bombardment, three rifle companies and five tanks advanced under a heavy smokescreen. Initial German success was countered by stiffening American resistance as platoons supported each other. The artillery was called to drop shells near US positions and knocked out several German tanks. The Germans were driven back as the artillery broke up their efforts to concentrate for a fresh attack.[7] On 31 October, Captain J.P. Gurka filed a summary of operations from 1 to 26 October for the journal of Third Battalion. The list of entries covered movements, places, actions, performance and casualties—26 killed, 180 wounded and 67 missing.[8]

Officers from the 26th Infantry Regiment, including both battalion commanders, were interviewed about the urban battle. The report was the most comprehensive about the urban fighting in Aachen. The regimental plan envisaged dividing the city between both battalions. The Second Battalion was tasked to clear the southern streets in the vicinity of the embankment from *Rothe Erde* railway station (that spans over Trierstrasse) towards the *Hauptbahnhof* (main railway station). Each company was operating with three tanks and a tank destroyer in support. One company came through the station, while another scaled the embankment but struggled to find a shallow drop-down on the other side but came under virtually no enemy fire. There was a hold-up from a German 75mm gun and machine guns, emplaced nearby *Rothe Erde*, held up their drive. There was an indication that a vicious breach battle had erupted but had not been reported to the historical branch. Tanks were brought up to clear the artillery and machine-gun positions. The battalion was to drive along Adelbertsteinweg, advancing in parallel with Third Battalion to the right. Third Battalion, commanded by John Thomas Corley (1914–1977), was assigned to clear the factory district, driving north-east through the city limits to capture the Lousberg. On 24 October, he issued field order No. 1 that was back-dated to read 18 October suggesting the order was issued before the end of the battle. At that time, Germans held the Kurhaus and the Quellenhof (Palace) Hotel, and the mission was to secure the buildings. There was hard fighting on that day, and it's unclear whether the orders were written after combat to avoid scrutiny from higher echelons.[9]

In an after-action report, Lieutenant Colonel Daniel (Second Battalion) claimed, 'the secret of street fighting is to search every building from cellar to attic' and clear them; and to keep all units in line without any getting ahead or left behind. It was slow teamwork but ponderous process that kept US casualties low. The tanks were firing fifty shells per day—direct fire at buildings to counter ambush or sniping. The mortar teams were firing more than two thousand bombs and smoke per day. A demolition team with a flamethrower and using Beehive demolition charges worked with each company. Supply troops kept moving rations and ammunition forwards. Unlike the Germans, the US troops received two hot meals per day, and were supplied with 'C' rations. The wounded were evacuated by the medical services. As the Americans advanced, they began to meet stiffer resistance. On 15 October, two German Mk. IV tanks loaded with infantry attacked the Third Battalion. The Americans on Observatory Hill (Lousberg) defended and halted the Germans, knocking out one of the tanks as the fighting spilled across Krefelderstrasse. The Germans continued to probe and attack. Second Battalion faced stiff resistance around Heinrichsallee and Hindenburgstrasse (Theaterstrasse today). German resistance briefly continued in Templargraben and from the Technical University, but after an hour the Germans surrendered. By 20 October, Third Battalion captured the Lousberg and US 155mm self-propelled guns fired several rounds directly at Wilck's bunker and the Germans began to surrender. The report ended noting that if more information was received the report would be rewritten.[10]

After the war, German generals and colonels in allied captivity were invited to write about the Aachen battle. While still chief of the US Army Historical Branch, 'Slam' Marshall looked to incorporate German interpretations for his study of the Ardennes battle and Bastogne.[11] The Germans were also encouraged to compile reports for the US Army Foreign Military Studies (FMS) programme. Throughout the 1950s, the former German officers contributed to

THE STALINGRAD OF THE WEST

a large body of writing, about 173 in total, covering the fighting in the area and the primary combat formations, and about twenty specifically about Aachen—not all were translated to English. The senior contributors to the Aachen FMS reports included: Friedrich Köchling (1893–1970), the corps commander of LXXXI *Armeekorps* commanding the Aachen sector; Gerhard von Schwerin (1899–1980), the commander of 116the Panzer Division; and Gerhard Wilck (1898–1985), divisional commander 246th Volksgrenadier Division and commandant of 'fortress' Aachen. Regardless of his post-war claims, Schwerin had no bearing on the battle. Köchling, however, wrote his observations for several reports. He claimed the Nazi regime was concerned with the psychological capture of Aachen, but the operational concern for the German army staff was the disorganised front. There was an imperative to restore the front lines, impose order, prevent collapse and prepare for a counter. Thus, the army demanded the soldiers fight to the last man, alongside Hitler's demands for national sacrifice and a fight to the death. Köchling's candid opinions extended to Aachen's history and culture being second to defending the Ruhr industrial heartland as a strategic imperative. According to Köchling, Wilck was ordered to swear an oath that he would not surrender the city. He also claimed Wilck was a political appointment because of his reputation for his 'aggressive firmness'. In addition, a large number of his officers were Nationalsozialistische Führungsoffiziere (known as NSFO, 'National Socialist Leadership Officers'), and they spurred the defenders to greater sacrifices. In August 1944, Wilck's last known personal assessment noted that he qualified as politically reliable for the command of a Volksgrenadier division.[12] It would be very difficult to prove Köchling's claims, this long after the war, but even if there was only a small number of ideological officers it might account for the cases of stubborn resistance during the battle.

After Wilck surrendered, he was taken to Britain and processed through the prisoner of war system. A British intelligence report assessed Wilck's behaviour in Aachen:

> (Wilck) admits that the defence of Aachen was purposeless from a military point of view but confirms that his orders did not allow for capitulation. Having disobeyed his orders, he fears reprisals on

his family, but still believes that what he did was for the best and in accordance with his conscience. He stated that he would feel relieved if his family fell under allied control after occupation of the sector where they live, south of Cologne.[13]

Decades later, in 1975, Wilck gave an audio recording in which he stated: 'of course I could have stopped earlier, perhaps, in order to stop the unnecessary bloodshed. But then I'd have been sentenced to death for breach of duty. There was a constant struggle going on inside me between obedience, duty, and honour.'[14] On the balance of evidence, if Wilck wasn't a Nazi, he was certainly fully committed to Hitler.

Wilck, in his FMS report, followed a typical military style, unemotional, and laced with pedantic details. The decision to assemble a Volkgrenadier Division was made by OKH and on 2 September 1944, Wehrkreis XIII (Nürnberg) sent orders to General Weisenberer at the military training depot Mylowitz, near Prague, to assemble the 565th Volksgrenadier Division. Wilck was selected because he had been a successful regimental commander and battle experienced on the eastern front. Elements for the new division included the shattered remnants from 246th Infantry Division which had been fighting in Vitebsk (Belarus), then in Soviet Russia, during the Red Army's Operation *Bagration*. The 565th was renamed in honour of the 'brave fighting men of the 246th'. Assembling the division involved bringing in officers from a wide range of services, including the Luftwaffe and Kriegsmarine. Most officers had received basic infantry training but that was all. Less than a third had front experience, but those officers could handle weapons and had combat leadership. The ordinary ranks were in a similar condition: the best-quality third were the sailors and marines. They were well trained and the fittest soldiers. The third from the Luftwaffe were mostly ground crew and were at best average. A final third were entirely untrained recruits, some within days of recruitment. There were few specialist personnel but with two to three weeks for training, Wilck could only cover some weapons training. There were some capable NCOs but too few to make a difference.

Divisional war material—artillery and trucks—arrived on schedule given allied bombing and the pressures on all fronts. An

THE STALINGRAD OF THE WEST

artillery battalion only received its guns on 27 September. There was new equipment, but the greater problems were the lack of anti-tank weapons, the severe shortage of shells and ammunition, and fuel was rationed. The ammunition shortages forced restrictions on training; the infantry had no dummy munitions, the artillery ammunition only allowed two practice barrages. There was also a restricted terrain limit for training with heavier weapons. The German high command pressed for the activation of the division. Finally, on 24–8 September, transport arrived, without warning, and the division began rolling west. The division command assumed they were going east, but instead arrived in Bedburg, a small town between Cologne and Jülich. The division's deployment roughly covered Aachen's southern city limits of Burtscheid to Würselen, and from Kohlsheid to Verlautenheide. On the right flank was 49th Infantry Division, and on the left 12th Infantry Division. The 246th covered Reichsstrasse 57, the Aachen–Jülich road. The American encirclement plan traced the same flanks, covering the entire area of the 246th.[15] Wilck placed himself inside Aachen, a standard military routine since Stalingrad if not before. If we assume Wilck was a political appointment, there were precedents for his behaviour. On 14 January 1944, Hitler had ordered Erich von dem Bach-Zelewski to defend Kovel, because of his political reliability and with a small mixed force of SS and army units. The successful defence of Kovel in January–March 1944 set the direction for Hitler's fortress battles—smaller forces inside cities, protected by large forces for counterattacks.[16] We can assume the decision to defend Aachen was made before Schwerin was dismissed or when Wilck was designated commandant.

In his FMS report, Wilck claimed the final phase of the fighting began at 18.55 hours on 14 October. The 116th Panzer Division assisted by 108th Panzer Brigade and 3rd Panzer Grenadier Division assisted by the 506th Heavy Panzer Battalion attempted to break the encirclement and relieve Aachen. This was a high-risk attack, being late in the afternoon, and without Luftwaffe support. The US army controlled the battle space and had massive artillery support. The Germans suffered heavy casualties, compounded by command confusion between 7th Army, 1st SS Panzerkorps and LXXXI Armeekorps. The failure sealed the encirclement and the

German fighting lines in Aachen were struggling as isolated pockets of defenders kept fighting until they ran out of ammunition. The anti-tank guns ran out of ammunition. There were only two supply deliveries by road transport on 10 and 14 October. The last supply attempt, led by Leutnant Wagner, was destroyed near Würselen.

On 15 October, Waffen SS-Obersturmfüher Rink, of the 1st SS Panzer Division, broke into the city with 150 men. His group and remnants of 404th Infantry Regiment (from the 246th) planned a counterattack against the US Third Battalion. According to Wilck, it had the limited aim of recapturing lines lost on 13 October. This counterattack caused bitter combat in Fawick Park, at the Kurhaus, at Kaiserplatz and across Hansemannplatz. Places changed sides several times as Rink's self-propelled assault guns joined the attack. There was good cooperation between the SS, the Grenadiers and the assault gunners. The Americans brought up fresh troops and assaulted the centre of the attack, bringing Rink's assault to an end. The fight for the city was decided, as the Americans reached six times force superiority against the Germans. The German reservists were put in the fight but folded under American firepower. The defenders were forced into a 'shoot n' scoot fight', which barely delayed the Americans. They kept pushing with artillery, which forced Wilck to transfer his command post to the Rütscher bunker. The German artillery on the Lousberg (Observatory Hill) continued to engage the Americans. On 17 October, the Americans secured Richterich. In Second Battalion area, the Americans were streaming through the streets unopposed; the Germans had no mines or obstacles. A few German soldiers with *Panzerfausts* attacked tanks, but the Americans had endless resupply. Wilck sent out one of his last messages: 'Aachen fights with its last strength and losses on both sides.'

By 18 October, the US controlled a third of the southern area. The Americans called the Germans to surrender. Wilck claimed some civilians still at large in the city were assisting the Americans through the cellars and behind German defences. He claimed Oberleutnant Gross was trapped and forced to surrender because of the civilians helping Americans. Wilck thought the people were exhausted from the war and the battle, and they knew the war was coming to an end. Some civilians began hiding young German soldiers. This was a sad moment for the German people, as the soldier did his duty, but the civilians wanted it to stop. The Germans tried to evacuate the wounded in half-track personnel carriers but were intercepted and captured. The wounded were well treated by the Americans. Wilck was still being promised that help and relief was coming. Heinrich Himmler announced by German radio the sacrifice of the troops in Aachen would turn around Germany's fate. Field Marshal Model ordered no surrender, and that the men must fight until churned into the rubble. German morale had virtually collapsed.

By 19 October, the German defenders were in a desperate condition; their rations were spent and there was no realistic escape. The Germans were down to a thousand men, two SP guns and two infantry guns, and controlled a few roads. There was still hard fighting in the encirclement battle around the Würselen area. The infantry detachments in the railway area surrendered. Hauptmann Neubert, commanding *MG-Bataillon 34*, led his troops to a cloister and continued the fighting to the last day. The German defence area was reduced to a square kilometre (Rütscherstrasse-Ponttor-Westbahnhof-Lousberg). The last remnants gradually stopped fighting. Wilck claimed he didn't know Rink's assignment and Rink had 'run his own war' from the Quellenhof Hotel and issuing signals messages contrary to Wilck. Rink disappeared on 19 October without informing anyone. By 20 October, it was clear to Wilck that it was over, although there were sporadic firefights across the city. He released seventy American PoWs and told them he wished to end the battle. At 09.00 hours on 21 October, three American soldiers returned and advised that a large attack was being prepared. At 11.30 hours, Wilck advised he was in German high command final battle. Eight minutes later Wilck accept unconditional surrender to the commander of the 26th Infantry Regiment and for his last 300 soldiers.

II. The politics of a battle

The writing of military history can be quite political, but few battles during the Second World War generated politics quite like

Aachen. The serious political squabbles among the allies erupted during the Normandy campaign and continued long after the war. The Falaise Pocket (12–21 August 1944), the allied encirclement of all the German armies fighting in the Normandy lodgement, was the strategic highpoint after the landings on 6 June. On 20 August, Eisenhower tried to soothe the deep Anglophobia stirring among the US generals, by taking direct command and resorting to a broad front strategy. The allied command coalition changed its operational dynamics at a critical moment. Eisenhower became a micro-manager of several senior commanders of very different calibre and character. Roger Cirillo has argued the allied command were 'no Band of Brothers', and that 'Eisenhower's idea of stretching the enemy assumed that the allies would not have the initiative, nor would they achieve a superiority of forces at the critical point, instead providing a defensive stance as they moved and fighting the enemy on near even terms ... an attrition strategy designed to kill the German army one unit at a time.'[17] Eisenhower had effectively redirected a winning strategy by fracturing operations into a series of senior commander-level initiatives. One of the first being the Mons Pocket (31 August–5 September), the consequence of US Twelfth Army Group striking out northeastwards towards Liège (Belgium) and Aachen (Nazi Germany). Troops from US 1st Infantry Division crossed the German frontier on 14 September at Roetgen, south of Aachen, and three days later infiltrated parts of the Siegfried Line (West Wall). The Battle of Arnhem (17–26 September) was unleashed by British Twenty-First Army Group, coordinated with the divisions from First Allied Airborne Army.

After the war, the politics of the allied campaigns continued to rage in the generals' memoirs. In 1948, Eisenhower's campaign book in particular reads vague about allied strategy in Autumn 1944. He wrote, 'The American First Army, at the end of its brilliant march from the Seine to the German border, almost immediately launched the operations that finally brought about the reduction of Aachen, one of the gateways into Germany.' Eisenhower claimed Lawton Collins and VII Corps had 'skilfully' surrounded the city and had reduced the stronghold 'by the simple expedient of dragging

THE STALINGRAD OF THE WEST

155mm "Long Tom" rifles up to point blank range—within 200 yards of the building—and methodically blowing the walls to bits'. He added the German commander's observation, 'When the Americans start using 155s as sniper weapon, it is time to give up.' Eisenhower seemed fixated by the terrain and the Rhine River in particular, as a means to isolate the German armies and expose them to a Cannae-like manoeuvre, recalling his fascination with the history of ancient battles. It is unclear from Eisenhower's rambling chapters how that could have been put into practice.[18]

In the art of military politics, General Omar Bradley (1893–1981) was a master. Reading his first memoirs, however, it's not altogether certain who was his greater enemy—the Germans, the British or those American generals not within his immediate clique. In 1951, Bradley's undisguised Anglophobia was directed at Field Marshal Montgomery. His entire argument about the failure of allied strategy was attributed to Arnhem, which was also indirectly blamed on Eisenhower. He claimed the British operation had forced the Americans in Aachen to straighten their lines. This was absurd, as the Americans had turned east to encircle Aachen and Hodges had reported reforming his lines to attack the city. On page 408, Bradley claimed, 'By the end of September, Hodges had exhausted his supply of motor fuel in First Army without having broken through the sturdily held Siegfried Line.' This was clearly not the case, as the combat reports revealed. On page 418, Bradley dramatically inflated Nazi Germany's refit and reorganisation: 'Meanwhile the German had not been idle. Between early September and mid-December, he tripled his forces on the Western front to 70 divisions. And of his 15 panzer divisions, eight were refitted with panther and tiger tanks.' He then stated, page 419, 'While caching supply for this November attack, Hodges was to exploit his penetration of the Siegfried Line and take the city of Aachen as a foothold inside the Reich. Thereafter when he had stocked his dumps with reserves, he would strike out for the gothic towers of Cologne on the Rhine.'[19] In 1981, Bradley's biography continued his political screed against Montgomery.[20]

'Slam' Marshall later argued that, under questioning, Eisenhower and Montgomery gave him different reasons for staging Operation

Market Garden. Consequently, with no records, 'memories had become befogged; the result was an irreconcilable conflict in their statements'. He then went on to discuss the relationship between Eisenhower and Bradley behaviour. They had been amicable before the Battle of the Bulge, but during the battle, after Eisenhower had passed command of US Ninth Army to Montgomery, Bradley became apoplectic with rage. Afterwards, the staffs of both generals used every opportunity to intensify the friction between the two generals. Marshall observed, 'The bickering was still going strong ... in 1950.'[21] This rivalry between the generals inevitably cost soldiers' lives by engaging in wasteful battles. Consequently, this general unreliability of the senior commander's memoirs partly explains why the immediate postwar histories are often buried in myths and dubious memories.

Chester Wilmot, the Australian war correspondent, published his groundbreaking study of the western theatre in 1952. He questioned Eisenhower's 20 August decision and believed Bradley had agreed with Montgomery's plan on 17 August, to push a single thrust via the Aachen corridor to the Ruhr. Two days later, Bradley had changed his mind. Eisenhower held a staff meeting on 20 August and announced the change of command system. He had decided to take personal command of all army groups on 1 September. US 12th Army Group was directed towards Metz and the Saar to link up with Dragoon force. Although not present at the staff meeting, Montgomery disagreed, and assumed because of his meeting with Bradley on 17 August he had his endorsement. Meeting with Bradley on 23 August, Montgomery learned he had been duped. Wilmot was critical of Bradley's claims of shortages by explaining how he kept Hodges and Patton supplied. He had observed that Collins had 'driven head on into the defences at Aachen'. Wilmot blamed the failing initiatives between Arnhem and Aachen on Eisenhower's broad front strategy. He saw the impact of Nazi Germany's recovery and failing to capture the Ruhr in 1944 as a serious failure—'The defensive victories which the Germans won at Arnhem, Aachen and Antwerp prolonged the war into the spring of 1945.'[22]

J. Lawton Collins (1896–1987), the outstanding US Corps commander, claimed he had read about Germany's 1914 campaign and the march from Aachen to Liège. The American command faced an 'intriguing tactical problem'—to take and clear Aachen before attacking the West Wall, or 'should we try for a quick, sharp break through the Stolberg corridor?' The map in his memoirs of the battles around Aachen illustrated the complex challenges the Americans confronted. Collins claimed that, in discussions with 1st Infantry Division commander, General Clarence R. Huebner (1888–1972), they were reluctant to get sucked into costly street fighting. Hoping to reach Düren, Collins claimed he'd sent a reconnaissance force, and his command post advanced to Kornelimünster. However, German resistance was stiffening daily. The German pressure and the broad front led First Army to reduce its fighting front, completed by 25 September. Collins argued for bypassing Aachen, because it no longer had any military value, but Hitler and the Nazi Party placed great political and psychological importance on the city. He continued: 'Hitler … fancied himself as a second Charlemagne … Hitler had ordered that Aachen hold out at all costs.'

Until the 1960s, the Battle of Aachen had all the appearances of a subject military historians and warriors wished to avoid. In May 1961, Charles B. MacDonald explained why he wrote the US official history of the Siegfried Line campaign, with a critical caveat in the preface: 'Some who have written of World War II in Europe have dismissed the period between 11 September and 16 December 1944 with a paragraph or two … The fighting during September, October, November and December belonged to the small units and individual soldiers'. He later claimed the city had great ideological importance to Hitler as the symbol of the Holy Roman Empire and the First Reich. This: 'To strike at Aachen was to strike at a symbol of Nazi faith.' MacDonald's narrative was a compromise between the grand sweep of history but referenced with individual acts of bravery in the footnotes. The story of Captain Bobbie Brown (discussed later) was reduced to a footnote on page 287. MacDonald's importance in this story was his calculation of casualties. Since the war, the generals and the US army had cautiously avoided the political downside of the cost of battle. MacDonald asserted Aachen had cost the US army an estimated

3,500 casualties. However, if Aachen was central to the Siegfried Line campaign, then the losses were very significant. First Army suffered 47,039 battle casualties (7,024 killed, 35,155 wounded and 4,860 missing). Ninth Army sustained 10,000 casualties and similar proportions. However, if the non-battle casualties are included, a further 51,000 casualties incurred by First Army and 21,000 by Ninth Army are added to the final totals. MacDonald concluded the Siegfried Line campaign cost America 140,000 casualties.[23] These numbers reflect the true cost of Eisenhower's broad front strategy.

A more unusual depiction of the battle was drawn by American historian Russell F. Weigley. His focal point was the encirclement battle, isolating XIX Corps under Charles Corlett with 30th Infantry Division under General Leland Hobbs and 2nd Armoured Division under General Ernest Harmon. He focused upon the rocky relationship between Corlett and Hodges, commander of First Army, and Weigley teased his readers with the ferocious battle between both men that continued throughout the encirclement battle. Harmon was not impressed with Hodges' plan, a professional armoured soldier, and was not on the best of terms with the army commander. Corlett, Hobbs and Harmon devised a plan for breaching the second line of West Wall defences, using the armour to shield the infantry assault. Weigley described the air strikes by IX tactical air force as abject failure. There was a calamity when a Belgium town, 45 kilometres away, was bombed by accident. Weigley's criticism was withering: 'When military operations are of such a nature that they are likely to kill or injure any civilians at all, they ought to receive hard moral scrutiny; when an operation produces so little of military value as this West Wall air strike, while exacting a grievous civilian toll in a not uncommon kind of miscalculation, the effort should cause a moral revulsion whose apparent absence in October 1944 is a testament to the deterioration of ethical values produced by the war so far.'[24]

Weigley claimed the ground forces' progress was more than acceptable by 4 October, and the US army was ready for the German counter. Meanwhile, Bradley and Hodges again visited XIX Corps command post, and the latter dressed down Corlett for using a large stock of artillery shells—another argument flared between both men. The ferocity of the fighting escalated in intensity when the German 12th Infantry Division attack was supported by the 108th Panzer Brigade. By that stage, Hodges was virtually pestering Corlett hourly on the telephone for updates and ordering him to move faster. Corlett realised the German forces were pitching powerful forces against him: 'If the 116 Panzer and the *Adolf Hitler* are in there, this is one of the decisive battles of the war.' Hodges threatened Corlett and Hobbs with new jobs if they didn't raise their game. Hobbs pushed the 119th Infantry Regiment forwards to reach the 18th Infantry Regiment—Aachen was encircled. Regardless of the success, on 18 October, Bradley relieved Corlett of his command. Bradley's only comment in his memoirs was that Corlett was relieved on grounds of ill health in December 1944.[25] Weigley's conclusion was deeply contemptuous: 'In the battle for Aachen, the first spasmodic effort of the once overwhelming Allied onslaught of July and August clutched at a local victory, and then died.'[26]

The Germans also faced political issues, shaped largely by postwar socio-cultural anti-war attitudes. To the English-language readership, Charles Whiting's *Bloody Aachen* was his own work. The book originated with Wolfgang Trees (1942–2009), an Aachen historian and journalist who wrote *Die Amis sind da!* Whiting's book was a cherry-picked manuscript drawn from that book; Trees was his close friend and partner across many books.[27] Whiting's book has 160 pages, maintains a fast pace, and has no index or bibliography. Trees was the local researcher conducting interviews with Gerhard Wilck and Graf von Schwerin, as well as locals and other soldiers, including Herbert Rink, who gave a vague synopsis of his part in the battle and detailed his escape route after the surrender. After having seen a picture of himself, for the first time since the surrender, Gerhard Wilck wrote to Trees, explaining that the photograph informed his siblings their brother had survived the war. In a 1984 version, Kurt Malangré, the Oberbürgermeister, wrote a foreword entitled *Nicht vergessen* (Not to forget). The theme was the cost of the fighting to Aachen and the people. He claimed there had been 75 air raids and two great battles in the autumn of 1944. After the forced evacuation of the city, six thousand people remained in a city where 42 per cent of the housing was destroyed and 40 per cent of all other facilities. There had been 2.7 million cubic metres of rubble at the end of the fighting—'a picture of desolation'.

There are two issues that arise from the reports that have been at the heart of the myths about the battle. In 1946, Lieutenant Colonel Derrill Daniel delivered a lecture for the School of Combined Arms Regular Course, at the Command and Staff College at Fort Leavenworth. The former Second Battalion commander discussed the urban battle and stated: 'We coined a slogan, Knock 'Em All Down', which became a battle cry because the soldiers were quick to realise that the defenders could hardly deliver accurate fire with buildings falling about their ears.'[28] Meanwhile, more studies followed about the battle after the war for the Advanced Infantry Officers Course, at the Infantry School in Fort Benning, Georgia. A study from 1948 to 1949 covered the entire battle and summarised Second Battalion actions. The report was a professional assessment of American methods and was strictly objective, without reference to individual performances, and made no reference to the *Knock 'Em All Down* slogan.[29] The historical branch after-action reports, compiled in 1944, also had no reference to the slogan, and with no reference to it in the regimental records.[30] Charles MacDonald and Lawton Collins also made no reference to the slogan. Then, in 1972, a US artillery officer conducted a survey report of Daniel's battle and avoided reference to the slogan.[31] Scrutiny of the reports suggests there is a case for Third Battalion, under Corley, which was supported by 155mm SP artillery and supported by regimental for claiming a knock them all down tactic.[32]

Interestingly, in the Foreign Military Study, Wilck made two observations. First, he completely refuted Eisenhower's claim that he surrendered because of American 155mm SP guns and rejected all his comments about the battle. In his opinion, none of Eisenhower's comments were true. Wilck concluded that, in the battle, 'The German soldiers in Aachen experienced the same merciless sacrifice as the fighters in Stalingrad.'[33]

THE STALINGRAD OF THE WEST

III. An SS officer's story

One mystery in the German account was the case of Herbert Rink. In the 1984 edition of *Die Amis sind da!*, Trees interviewed former Waffen SS Obersturmführer Herbert Rink about his part in the battle. Trees had previously relied on Waffen-SS man Peter Schaaf from Aachen to tell the tale of *Kampfgruppe Rink*. The encirclement battle around Würselen was threatening the last German supply route to Aachen. On 9 October, SS-Hauptsturmführer Diefenthal, the commander of *Kampfgruppe Diefenthal* from 1st SS Panzer Division, *Leibstandarte*, was ordered to move forward to Stadtkyll (Rhineland-Palatinate), subordinated to *LXXXI Armeekorps*, and placed in mobile reserve. Rink was a battalion commander under *Kampfgruppe Diefenthal*, which had been fighting micro-battles since Falaise in an effort to prevent a collapse of the front lines. Diefenthal and Rink were the last of those experienced Waffen-SS officers that turned the regiment into a fearsome fighting panzer division. Unlike in the earlier period of the war, when death in battle was hailed as a blood honour. The new orthodoxy was to prosecute the short-sharp-shock-attack against the enemy, but to withdraw when the advance stalled. This reflected the German resort to micro-battle within micro-operations, because German fighting power was depleted and in the spiral of decline[34] There were no longer the supplies of men and material to sustain big war. Until the end of the war, Diefenthal would be a political vanguard, on the battle front, leading the death throes of National Socialist warfare.[35]

Rink explained that, prior to breaking into Aachen, he and Diefenthal drew straws as to who would go—'Rink lost'. On the evening of 14 October, *Sturmgeschützabteilung 217* broke through to Monheimsallee, and the following morning Rink with his *Kampfgruppe I* drove in half-tracks, with fuel, ammunition and 128 men, and broke through the lines and reached the Hotel Quellenhof. At 08.00 hours on 15 October, Rink informed Diefenthal they had arrived and at 09.55 hours, the Kampfgruppe was moving into action. Rink reported to Wilck; they had met previously at an *LXXXI Armeekorps* pre-battle briefing. Wilck was relieved that they had arrived safely. The Americans were in control of the Kurhaus and had pushed forces into the city park. They were firing mortars at the Germans. Wilck had explained, the day before, 300 Americans and five Sherman tanks had pushed through from the Ostfriedhof into the park. With Wilck and a large map, he was advised about the resort area, and it was important to clear the enemy before the Quellenhof Hotel, and push the enemy back to Passstrasse running along the edge of the park area. They reconnoitred the area and climbed through a tunnel connecting the Quellenhof and the Kurhaus. The Americans were unaware of another tunnel, from the Kurhaus to the indoor swimming pool, which the Germans exploited to achieve surprise. Prior to Rink's attack, there was to be a ten-minute mortar bombardment, which succeeded in forcing the Americans to seek cover. One company pushed through the tunnel and caught the Americans by surprise. The second company went through the pool tunnel and reached the weather station. The Germans began to dig in, but they were unable to see Passstrasse, and the maze of housing around Rolandsplatz and towards Krefelderstrasse. The situation looked different upon reaching the ground, and in the mass, Rink loss sight of his eighty men. Dispersed over a large area, he was concerned to retain contact with all his attacking troops.

The Americans countered and, on 17 October, they were back in control of the Kurhaus and the Quellenhof. Wilck had retreated to the Rütscherstrasse bunker. Meanwhile, Rink prepared for a counterattack against the Americans in the northern part of Fawick Park. At 04.40 hours, they crept to their forward positions. Just before dawn, they attacked and drove the Americans from their positions in Fawick Park. The Americans responded with a blanket barrage of artillery fire. Rink recalled he had not experienced such firepower since Caen in Normandy. It was like a tornado ripping the park to pieces. The numbers of wounded mounted and were taken to the medical bunker in the Saarstrasse. The enemy lost perhaps 25 men and Rink took 13 PoWs, but the Germans had more casualties—perhaps 10 dead and 20 wounded, an entire platoon. The Americans had broken under the attack from infantry and assault guns, but it was a pyrrhic victory. At 17.00 hours, the attack was promptly stopped by American artillery. On 18 October, the last German troops were ordered to defend Quellenhof, Soers, Richterich, Laurensberg, Westbahnhof, Boxgraben and the main railway station. The fighting turned into close combat in Rolandstrasse and spilled into a contest for Krefelderstrasse. Americans broke into the Hansemannplatz area and houses along Monheimsallee. Rink was forced to pull back to the defensive line on the Salvatorberg area. Wilck requested to break out due to declining numbers, 1,200 fighting troops, and rapidly diminishing ammunition. The Americans continued to advance. Rink turned a cellar in a house in Weyhestrasse as his last command post and was still in contact with Wilck. Rink led a counterattack towards the Quellenhof, on 19 October, but the Americans moved towards threatening his command post. Realising the half-tracks were under threat, he decided to load them with wounded and get them out of the city. They were disarmed of mortars and machine guns and the Germans painted red crosses on them.

The German 7th Army headquarters issued the order: 'In keeping with the significance of the city of Aachen as the seat of the Kaiser and the crown, it is to be defended to the last man and the last bullet. If necessary, the combat Kommandant at Aachen must let himself be buried in the rubble.' Wilck issued his own message:

> The Kampfgruppe at Aachen is now arming for the final battle. Pressed into a tiny area, it is to follow the Führer's orders and defend the city to the last man, the last grenade, the last bullet. I expect from each of you, the defenders of the venerable imperial city of Aachen, devotion to the end. True to your oath, I expect valour, resolve and perseverance. Long live the Führer and our beloved Fatherland.

Friedrich Köchling issued the following: 'The LXXXI Armeekorps gives the highest respect to the defenders of Aachen, fighting to the end for the Führer and the People.' Neither Wilck nor Köchling recalled their supra-patriotic messages after the war.[36]

On 20 October, the Americans forced Rink away from the centre of the battle and Wilck's command. That day, the Americans kept pressing and forced the last resistance out of the TU main buildings. Corley's Third Battalion pressed towards the bunker at

Rütscherstrasse—this was the final act in the tragedy. According to Rink, at 05.00 hours on 21 October, Wilck arrived at his command post in Nizzaallee, and asked the men to fight to the last bullet. Rink had explained a pile of rubble was not worth the sacrifice, but he would break out to continue the fight. Rink recommended Wilck surrender. They shook hands in parting and Rink mentioned his respect for Wilck as a soldier. Meanwhile Corley's troops had temporarily ceased firing. Two hours later, at 08.00 hours, two American soldiers under a flag of truce came forward to negotiate with Wilck. He requested two hours, and when they returned at 10.00 hours, Wilck came out of the bunker and surrendered. There was still sporadic fighting, but Rink refused to surrender. When Wilck had departed, Rink distributed the last ammunition and divided his troops into small squads. He sent a message to 1st SS Panzerkorps that he was going to break out, and each man was to make the best way possible. Rink received the go-ahead. His account became an escape and evasion story, and he finally arrived at German lines three days later, on 24 October.[37]

IV. The all-American hero

In a history of the American soldier, Peter Kindsvatter has written, 'The leader not only had to order the men he cared for into harm's way, but he also had to be willing to take same risks himself. The men did not respect a leader who would not share their dangers and hardships.'[38] US Army Captain Bobbie E. Brown (1903–1971), commanding officer of Company C, 18th Infantry Regiment (1st Infantry Division), was an outstanding combat officer. In 1946–7, he gave a lecture at the Infantry School at Fort Benning, Georgia. The subject was 'Company in the attack on Fortified Position'. This was an account of the events on Crucifix Hill (8–9 October) during the encirclement battle. The lecture set the scene by describing 1st Infantry Division operations from D-Day via Falaise Pocket to the Mons Pocket—the division participated in heavy fighting against those Germans attempting to escape Belgium— they killed 5,000 and took 17,000 PoWs. Afterwards, the division advanced on Aachen. The terrain was described as rolling hills, with woods and high ridges. Towns were in the low ground and heavily concentrated; there was extensive bomb damage and heaps of rubble, often causing obstacles for tanks. The state forest south of Aachen was thickly wooded and lying on steep slopes.

Brown described the Siegfried Line and Crucifix Hill's strongpoints in some detail. Crucifix Hill (Haarberg Hill 239) was a hill lying between Haaren and Verlautenheide, with a strongpoint of connected pillboxes and emplaced bunkers, and a large crucifix monument on the hilltop. The defences were reinforced with anti-tank ditches, minefields, obstacles, dug-in tanks and tank turrets, trenches, foxholes, slit trenches and large emplacements for machine guns, 88mm guns, automatic weapons and field artillery. The first barriers were the ditches, twelve feet deep and four feet wide, placed seventy yards from dragon's-teeth tank obstacles, usually fifty feet wide. Brown later recalled that from his approach the defences were about three feet high, but four feet when facing the enemy. Behind them and covering the entire area were concrete installations, about eighty-seven feet in circumference and camouflaged. Among these were smaller bunkers, with reinforced steel doors, ventilators and stockpiles of ammunition. The rotary fields of fire ranged from 250 to 500 yards. Behind the strongpoints were heavy artillery set to fire on the positions.

On 7 October, the regiment's three battalions were assigned continuing attack missions. The Second was to take Verlautenheide, the First to assault Crucifix Hill and Third to remain in reserve. This leapfrog manoeuvre was intended to close the German supply route to Aachen. The Second was expected to hold Verlautenheide and block the area. The First was expected to capture the hill and close the Haaren-Zuiweden with fire and mines. The Third was to capture the hill north-west of Eilendorf. 'C' Company was to seize the hill, 'A' Company was to attack on the left and 'B' was held in reserve. The battalion support included a battalion of light artillery, four 155mm field guns, a platoon of tank destroyers (634th TD Battalion) and a platoon of tanks (745th Tank Battalion), and a battalion of mortars were also meant to move forward with the assault. For the assault, Brown's company was assigned a Ranger platoon with the mission of flank security. The Second Platoon, the company's base platoon, was to assault the trail that led west from

Verlautenheide. First platoon was to assault from the right, using the same trail as a guide. Third Platoon was the designated support platoon, situated in a cemetery near Verlautenheide and ready to advance when called. The squads had been prepared in advance for specific missions and were informed on how they fitted the overall company mission.

Detailed observations were made by all of the officers of the assault companies conducting reconnaissance missions, along with squad leaders and NCOs. On 7 October, Brown and Captain Edward McGregor (Battalion S-3) spent the day studying the objective from forward observation posts of 'K' Company of 16th Infantry Regiment. They returned to the battalion command post at 18.00 hours and were informed of the attack the next day, with 'H' hour set at 04.00 hours. The motor transport officer arranged for trucks and the battalion was taken to the bivouac area in the darkness, arriving at 00.45 hours in Brand. They then marched to Eilendorf and moved into cellars. At 04.00 hours, the artillery barrage started. Second Battalion took its primary objective by 07.00 hours, and at 08.00 hours the First Battalion set off, arriving at the assembly area by 10.00 hours. Brown arrived later and reported his company's situation; they had been shelled and had taken casualties. The battalion commander wanted the attack immediately, but McGregor intervened, clarifying that it would take them time to reach the jumping-off point. Meanwhile, Brown's executive officer, Lieutenant Van Wagnor, had advanced with the company command group and two platoons. The Germans were shelling the town, making it difficult to reach the cellars. Brown got the company 'rolling' and they reached the cellars. The fire support teams were placed on roofs and sent his platoon leaders back to their units to carry out one last reconnaissance. His movement attracted the attention of the Germans and received small arms fire and from mortars. He reached the covering force and one of them opened fire; immediately three Germans surrendered. Brown took the PoWs back to the command post, where the Rangers had brought twenty-two PoWs, taken by Sergeant David Cooper, who later received a battlefield commission. Brown informed the battalion commander of his observations and attack plan, but the commander said nothing.

THE STALINGRAD OF THE WEST

Finally, Brown's attack was set for 13.30 hours, the final checks were made, the radio operators checked their 300 sets and then the company moved to the jump-off positions. There was constant shelling from the Germans, and as they reached the base of the hill the assault platoons came under heavy machine-gun fire. He received a radio message that the Rangers' commander was wounded, but they were still assaulting. Brown scaled the embankment but discovered that both assault platoons were pinned down and not moving. He ordered Lieutenant Marvain, 2nd platoon leader, to throw him some pole and satchel charges. Brown wrote:

> I picked the charge up and crawled to the pillbox and ran up to the aperture ... an enemy rifleman opened the door and started out. However, when he saw me he dashed back into the fortification ... I jumped at the door and tried to slam it shut; however, the excited enemy left his rifle in the doorway. I opened the door and at the same time I pulled the fuse on my charge and tossed it inside the bunker, slammed the door, and jumped back over the embankment as the pillbox and its occupants were blown up.

Brown received another radio message that the Rangers' leader was wounded a second time, but they had destroyed the pillbox. The assault platoons were still pinned down under artillery and mortar fire. Brown and his runners grabbed more satchel charges and attacked another pillbox. He fired a yellow flare to indicate to the 155mm artillery to lift their barrage. He began the assault of the last pillbox. The pillbox required a pole charge and a satchel charge until it was destroyed. The fire on second platoon lifted, then Brown was wounded in the knee and his runner advised that the leader of the Rangers was killed by a third hit. A sergeant had taken over, but the platoon was stalled by enemy small arms and artillery fire. The second platoon had moved from its position but was again stalled again and its leader wounded. A flamethrower and a skilled rifleman were sent to clear another bunker. This lifted pressure off the platoon, but Brown was wounded again, in the chin and wrist; he wasn't sure how it happened. With five bunkers destroyed, the assault troops were no longer receiving 'grazing small arms fire'. He sent his runner back to bring up the rest of the company and inform the battalion commander of the situation.

WAR COMES TO AACHEN

Forty minutes of fighting had passed when, at 14.10 hours, he contacted the battalion. The crucifix had been shot down, the leader of first platoon was wounded and he had joined Lieutenant Marvain. They rushed another bunker, unmanned, with nine enemy dead lying around it. They had taken the hill, which was then communicated to the battalion commander. The Germans were beginning to form up south of the hill, and Brown ordered artillery to fire on them. Brown then prepared the company for the customary German counterattack. Mortars and machine guns were placed in positions and the wounded were evacuated. It was 15.30 hours when he started to prepare fire protection points with the artillery. At 17.30 hours, the Germans began to place artillery and machine-gun fire on the American positions. While out reconnoitring the immediate area, Brown was shot in the shoulder and his sergeant shot in the stomach. Brown received medical aid and the sergeant was evacuated and then he moved to his company command post. He met with Captain McGregor, and they prepared the defence measures with listening posts.

At 04.00 hours on 9 October, the Germans finally counterattacked, with three waves of infantry and combat engineers. The defenders held their fire until the last moment, and then unleashed ferocious 'grazing fire'. The heavy machine gunners were 'swinging their guns with free traverse, blazed away at every enemy in sight'. The Germans 'withdrew as suddenly as they attacked, leaving behind forty-one dead within our "bloody rock" throwing distance; also leaving thirty-five prisoners'. More than a hundred dead could be counted from the artillery fire. The Americans suffered sixty officers and ORs killed. 'A' Company had failed to gain its objectives, leaving 'C' Company exposed on the hill. The battalion assigned more support for 'C' Company to help assist 'A' Company achieve its mission. That finalised the mission.

Brown added some thought on how, if 'B' Company had been committed, the mission could have been over earlier. He concluded, 'This completed one of the most difficult and important missions assigned the 1st Battalion, 18th Infantry of the 1st Infantry Division.' 'C' Company casualties included five enlisted men killed, two officers and thirty-three enlisted men wounded; Ranger casualties were one officer and three men killed and six men wounded. The Germans suffered 150 killed in action, 21 wounded and 76 PoWs. Brown later thought the deciding moment in the battle was in the first five minutes. The enemy had put their fire on the Ranger platoon, allowing the assault platoons to get in the enemy rear. The enemy failed to fire from Crucifix Hill. Although the platoons were pinned down, Brown was mobile, and that made the difference—'think fast and act correctly'.

Captain McGregor, in the monthly battalion report, was more eloquent in his after-action report than Brown and gave a slightly more positive spin on 'A' Company's performance. On page three of his report, he commended Brown for his bravery, being wounded three times and yet keeping the fight going. There was no indication of favouritism for Brown being recommended for medals. On 24 October, 18th Infantry Regiment received a citation 'For extraordinary heroism in action. Brown was later wounded during street fighting in Aachen, a shell landed almost beside him. He spent several months in hospital and ended the war with 'C' Company in Czechoslovakia in 1945; Brown became the 74th recipient of the Medal of Honor on 23 August 1945, for his actions on Crucifix Hill on 8 October, and received the medal from President Harry Truman on 1 September.[39]

In November 1971, the *New York Times* announced the passing of Bobbie E. Brown. It was not front-page headlines, but appeared on page 51 alongside adverts for a stereo music system and a language course for children.[40] He was described as a 'rough-hewn Southerner born in poverty and was an enlisted soldier with more than 20 years' service when he received a battlefield commission. Brown's former regimental commander, Lieutenant General Robert H. York recalled, "I finally made one of the toughest decisions of my life. I decided to give the company in spite of his limitations... He was absolutely fearless."' Brown's army personnel report classified him as having the 'educational equivalent of a 12-year-old'. He had never completed a full year of schooling but was offered a football scholarship at several universities. The offers were withdrawn, however, when it was discovered that he'd only completed the seventh grade. Brown was a platoon sergeant before he received the commission and was promoted to captain. After 28 years' service, he retired from the army with the rank of captain. He found work as a waiter at West Point mess hall and later as foreman-janitor in the custodial department of the academy. Brown had struggled with his war wounds, and it is believed he gave up the struggle by committing suicide at his home, a self-inflicted gunshot wound to the chest. Brown was 68 years old and in 'failing health', and he was buried at Arlington National Cemetery.

The collection of after-action reports for the Battle of Aachen represents an important resource for historians. Especially since many US Army records were lost during the postwar archival process. Aachen was a busy battle, and many questions remain unanswered. For instance, why did Brown's company remain motionless throughout the action and receive no criticism or comment? The battle for the military history of the war was being waged by historians on all sides, while the war progressed. After the war, Slam Marshall would extend historical analysis into the controversial themes of 'firing and fatigue'. In time, the critical scrutiny of Marshall would outweigh the scholarly examination of the historical reports of the battle. Military history has failed to reconcile the contents within the reports and Marshall's findings. Eighty years later and a remarkable number of questions still remain unanswered about the Battle of Aachen.

8

RESTORING DEMOCRACY

I solemnly swear to perform the duties of *Bürgomeister* of the Stadtkreis Aachen conscientiously; to obey all orders of the Military Government and not to act in any manner to the prejudice of the military government.[1]

On Sunday evening, 25 March 1945, Franz Oppenhoff, the first post-Nazi *Oberbürgermeister* (chief-mayor) of Aachen, was murdered by an SS assassination squad. They were operating under special orders from SS chief Heinrich Himmler.[2] The ensuing scandal was investigated and later the Adjutant Generals Office of the US army reported how the murder was carried out. The killers, feigning to be Luftwaffe personnel, broke into Oppenhoff's house and questioned the maid about his whereabouts. He was in a nearby house, and the assassins forced the maid out of her bed to fetch him. The mayor returned with a colleague. Upon entering the house, Oppenhoff was accosted by three men in German paratrooper smocks speaking in German. They claimed they were trying to reach German lines and required a safe place and food. According to his colleague, Oppenhoff refused assistance on the grounds that it would jeopardise his position with the Military Government. Then an argument ensued and after he'd gone to get help, Oppenhoff was shot through the head, and the body found in the hallway next morning. The Adjutant General's report added that a tank destroyer unit located nearby discovered their telephone line was cut in a way so as not to rouse suspicion. When two men were sent to repair the line, they heard at least three men in the darkness, but when called the men fled. Investigations of the area discovered an odd collection of German accoutrements. The German civilian administrators in Aachen were initially agitated by the assassination, but the intensity of the US counter-intelligence investigation had restored confidence in the Aachen community.³ The US army had drawn a line under the Oppenhoff case, a story that started in scandal and ended in death.

The story began at 16.00 hours, on 30 October 1944, when Oppenhoff was formerly sworn in as chief mayor by the commanding officer of the US Civil Affairs Detachment in Aachen. He was allocated three offices at 14, 16 and 25 Wilhelmstrasse in the centre of the city. A subsequent US MGO report, although incorrectly spelling his name as 'Oberhoff', drew a neutral political profile for the first mayor of a large German city to be appointed mayor by the Military Government. Born in Aachen in 1902, he was a 'prominent Catholic', married and had three daughters. He came from generations of judges and lawyers and began as a barrister in Aachen in 1933. In 1935, Oppenhoff became the legal representative for the Bishop of Aachen, Johannes Joseph van der Velden (also misspelled as 'Welden'). Oppenhoff had allegedly defended civil and political cases against Nazi state prosecutions. In commercial law, Oppenhoff had defended some major concerns as well as some Jewish firms. Oppenhoff had a reputation for being an expert of Nazi law, being an astute lawyer, and with a fine reputation among 'churchmen, lawyers and businessmen'. The report's clinching personal assessment: 'he is not reported to have had any Nazi connections'. During the war, he was initially employed in the legal department of *Veltrup Werke*, the manufacturer of aircraft parts for Junkers, but later became an assistant production manager. It was alleged the Gestapo had unsuccessfully tried several times to force him into the army, and in September 1944 he had gone into hiding in nearby Eupen (then part of Aachen). When questioned for the position of mayor, Oppenhoff gave several reasons why he wanted the job. Oppenhoff believed he was the best qualified of the people remaining in Aachen. He also argued that the people in Aachen 'have degenerated physically and morally and are greatly in need of adequate direction and guidance'. Oppenhoff claimed he was disgusted with Nazism, and it was his duty to establish 'a good city administration'. He also believed a well-functioning city would support the allied war effort.[4]

This chapter reconsiders the Oppenhoff story from the records of US Military Government's mission to impose democracy by force—a battle over who would control the civilians. This chapter loosely follows chapter two, which discussed how Aachen 'Let go of democracy'. The US Military Government tried to apply a simple benchmark that cities, communities and people could be classified as 'Nazi' or 'non-Nazi'. The multiple representations of Nazism, how it advanced through German society, and why strains continued long after the allied takeover, challenged the allies' comprehension of Hitler or the Nazis. The fundamental question in chapter two was how a city that had not supported Nazism at the ballot box before 1933 was, by 1939, showing all the signs of becoming a complicit accomplice in Hitler's war. The road to complicity with Hitler began with the city's rapid Aryanisation of institutions, professions and elites, and was completed in 1938 with active participation in the nationwide *Kristallnacht* action against the city's Jewish community. In 1944, the US army's Civil Affairs officers did not question Oppenhoff about the Nazi crimes or the atrocities. Instead, the investigators judged Oppenhoff's moral compass through comprehensive political questioning. Consequently, Aachen turned into a hard test of American faith in democracy, and what democracy meant in practice. A second aspect of the Oppenhoff case concerned the conditions in Aachen, and how American perceptions of the 'dead city' was draining to their efforts to promote allied success to the world. Doubts about the efficacy of the Aachen-MGO's performance were already circulating in the allied corridors of power before the year end. The Oppenhoff scandal became a direct challenge to the performance of the MGO system, and Anglo-American relations. There were already signs, before Oppenhoff's assassination, that the allies were prepared to wash their hands of Aachen. The Oppenhoff story was about the people of Aachen and how they would be governed after the war. A silent struggle emerged between American idealism and the determination to impose democracy: the Germans wanted the end of the war and self-determination. The war remained the hurdle dividing Americans and Germans—in an endless argument over authoritarianism or democracy.

I. MGO Aachen and the German civilians

In the fighting for Aachen, during October 1944, the senior officers of US 26th Infantry Regiment confronted a humanitarian crisis. The commanders realised there were civilians in the city, existing in the ruins or housed in air-raid bunkers. Surveying the city, the Americans discovered not only large bunkers but medium-sized bunkers and cellars converted as air-raid shelters. At the same time, the commanders were concerned about rear area security; they could not take the risk of allowing the civilians to remain at large if they were German saboteurs in disguise. When the battle started, the civilians had moved to the shelters, and in one large bunker, the Americans found 600 persons. They reported that in large air raids in April–May 1944, several bunkers were 'covered in debris that those inside never did get out'. That contention was never confirmed, but the Americans found a PoW who knew the bunkers and shelters in the city, and they could estimate how many civilians were in the city. The infantry, sweeping the ruins, captured civilians and led them to the rear and handed to the Military Government officers and Military Police. Some had a few belongings and sometimes the army transported them in vehicles returning to the rear. During 12–13 October, the army rounded up 609 civilians, including 200 Polish and Russian persons, some in German uniforms. They were taken to a 'cage' in Homburg, in the vicinity of Plombières, in Belgium. After processing, they were segregated, and the non-Germans were interrogated by Polish and Russian officials. The German civilians were warned that, if any German soldiers were discovered, they would be shot as spies if they did not give themselves up. Seven stepped forward.

The Military Government officers devised a plan for a larger occupancy because they secured the German Army barracks in

RESTORING DEMOCRACY

Brand. On 14 October, the daily counts were 1,600 on 15 October 275, 300 on 16 October and 400 on 17 October; afterwards, the daily count ended, but a final total was counted of 3,742 on 28 October 1944. The majority were old men (1,300), women (1800) and children (400). The report observed: 'Some of the women were dressed in furs while others were in rags, which was a rather good indication of the closeness of their connection with the Nazi Party.' The civilians were assigned rooms, keeping families together in seven barracks. Any building with war damage was repaired by civilians under Military Government supervision. A barrack leader was appointed, and the Americans issued them daily instructions. A German committee took over the billeting of civilians. From 31 October, there was no central heating and civilians brought in stoves, for which they gathered wood. The women were assigned to work in the kitchens and men to work on nearby farms. Each person was issued an identity card but restricted to the barracks. Some received permission to go to their homes in Aachen to collect possessions but had to return before night. The garrison site was guarded by MPs but gradually the German civilian police took over policing. There were only two cases of ill-discipline, caught signalling at night, and the offenders were taken into custody. Medical services were handled by German doctors and nurses, under US army medical supervision. Medicines were collected from Aachen and strenuous efforts were made to prevent epidemics. The civilians brought what little they had; thirty tons of German army rations were brought from Liège (Belgium) and other captured supplies from France, Belgium and Germany, or from local farm produce. Food was prepared in two messes and served in two sittings—the first for 2,000 and the balance for the second—receiving 1,700–1,800 calories per day. The civilians received bread and coffee in the morning and soup with bread in the evening. The food was issued to their individual containers and consumed in their rooms. Ration cards were stamped, and when meat was consumed it was requisitioned and an IOU or bill of exchange to be paid by the city of Aachen once it was functioning again. The civilians were issued with German army warm-weather clothing captured in the barracks.

The Americans planned to release the civilians back into Aachen on a priority basis. At that stage, doctors, nurses and farmers were the priority group. The rest would 'be released to return to Aachen when the tactical situation permits'. The Germans had been propagandised into believing they would face 'harsh and cruel treatment', placed in 'barbed wire enclosures with no shelter', and families broken up. They had been re-socialised in American captivity, which wasn't perfect but was the basis for reconstructing a 'new' Aachen. The Americans believed: 'Most of them are very glad to get out of Aachen, and are resigned to the fact that Germany has lost the war. They want the war to end so that they can start life over again.'[5]

On 21 October 1944, the same day Aachen surrendered, Colonel Damon Gunn (assistant chief of staff, G-5 Civil Affairs Division, US First Army) issued his first Intelligence Bulletin. Gunn set directions to all staff officers, G-5 personnel and Military Government (MG) Detachments.[6] He opened by drawing attention to an annex in the Civilian Affairs handbook—'The Occupation of the Rhineland 1918–1930'. The previous occupation had failed and Gunn, in a warning from history, advised there were four key reasons for failure. First, there was a lack of distinction between the allied government's executive powers and the supervisory control over the administration of Germans. Second was the determination to establish 'normalcy' during an emergency. Third was the fatal decision of taking over the German bureaucracy, thereby preserving the old regime. Fourth, that by siding with the nationalist and reactionary higher civil service, the allies had stifled the emergence of republicanism. He also noted that an 'English observer' had criticised the British occupation for restoring the mayors who enabled the preservation of the old regime. Gunn was adamant that 'normalcy' would not happen until the Germans learned to live in a state of lawfulness, which had been absent from everyday life since Hitler came to power.

Gunn also raised the issue of mass psychology: 'Weariness and exhaustion, and the over-whelming pre-occupation with the elementary necessities of life are likely to be predominant in the minds of the great majority of the German people.' The removal of 'Gestapo spying' and the absence of terror was believed to benefit the process of change that would lead Germans 'to take civic and political responsibility'. Responsibility would be granted to anti-Nazi elements on the political left but only cautiously to the anti-Nazi elements of the right, who went along with Hitler after 1933. Political responsibility could only be offered after the Germans had shown they were 'prepared to make … the reconstitution of public life on a democratic basis'. Gunn was adamant that all known Nazis must be excluded from public life and prevented from behaving divisively against allied authority. The general public health was also in a parlous condition given that 'the entire population is undernourished'. There was almost an epidemic of heart and lung (TB) troubles, and children were particularly exposed to diseases. The average German received rations of 250 grams of meat per week, 350 grams of bread daily, 1,000 grams of fat per month, and a family of four received 100lbs of potatoes for the winter. Milk was given to children but not to adults, men received 1.5 cigarettes per day, and women over 23 received a similar cigarette ration. A black market was thriving and all banks, near the frontlines, had transferred their financial assets to Berlin. Escaped foreign labourers and PoWs were drifting towards Holland in ever increasing numbers. The Nazis had also released refugees to impede the advance of the allied armies.

Gunn summarised the situation within Nazi Germany. Heinrich Himmler, as chief of the SS and Minister of the Interior, had sent fanatical young Nazis into the Rhineland, initially to dig anti-tank ditches, but since the siege were 'submerging' as a fifth column. Although many Nazis had fled from Aachen, they remained dangerous, and their wives classified as Nazi fanatics. He noted that 'all mayors in Germany are embittered Nazis'. By contrast, cooperation was expected from the railway workers, known to be democratic and openly anti-Nazi. Captured railway workers, serving in the Wehrmacht, had proven to be staunchly anti-Nazi. However, German agriculture was still organised on Nazi grounds. Industry and the workers were separated between either direct importance to the Nazi war effort or left redundant. In an appendix, a list of German 'personalities' from Aachen (or within Aachen regional administration) were identified by categories: 'A'—Black List identified for immediate arrest, approximately and included 110, mostly men; 'B'—21 individuals known to be at large in occupied areas but location unknown; and category 'C'—a White List of 27 persons believed to be trustworthy.[7] This essay continues the examination of thread about the politics of violence that emerged in the first essay and has continued through several essays and emerged in the US occupation of Aachen.

In November 1944, the US MGO Lt Col Carmicheal filed a report giving his explanation for the selection of Oppenhoff:

> There is no royal road leading to the appointment of a burgermeister. It appears to me that in most cases, under the present conditions, the route will be difficult and tedious. The 'spade work' in this matter is going to devolve upon the detachments. The Detachments will probably play the most important role in the selection of most of the officials in Germany. The selection should be made as properly as is consistent with the selection of the proper man ... It appears that the Catholic Church will play an important part in the matter of selecting officials in Germany. While the Catholic Church in Germany does not have a perfect record, it is unquestionably true that it has provided real opposition to the Hitler theory of government in most parts of Germany. The Catholic church is particularly strong in the Rhineland Province. This does not mean that the Catholic Church should play any part other than that requested by Military Government ... A burgermeister should be allowed to assume the duties of his office in a quiet way, without ceremony of any kind.[8]

On 21 November 1944, Robert Daniel Murphy (1894–1978), while serving as Eisenhower's political advisor, arrived in Aachen to assess the progress of the occupation. Murphy met the bishop and Oppenhof. He was informed by the bishop that the civilians left behind by the Nazis were all 'good Catholics'. He also claimed that in normal times there were a thousand priests and 500 parishes. The bishop generously described his flock as *Friedhofgemüse* (graveyard vegetables), while many Aachen families had fled to Eupen or Malmedy. Oppenhof explained that the greatest needs were in food and transportation. Industries and manufacturers had distributed materials and stocks to avoid war damage. The transport was required to supply stocks to factories. The bishop added that there were plenty of coal supplies but they were out of reach in neighbouring districts. Both men complained about the red tape of allied bureaucracy, and the long waits of standing in line to fill in questionnaires. The Aachen roads were designated military highways, and closed to civilian traffic, and Oppenhof recommended clearing secondary roads. Civilian work had seen the opening of forty bakeries and forty butchers, The city administration had employed a hundred public servants. There was a plan to open a savings bank. The working relationship between German civilians and US military government was excellent and morale would increase with more food.[9]

On 11 December, Second Lieutenant William Ballou (Public Safety officer) issued a report, having taken command of the detachment. His main task was to clean up the prison, using German civilians to carry out the work. There were ovens and coal to return the kitchens to working order. They extracted two tons of German army food stocks to supply rations to prisoners. He had integrated the German police detachment in his public safety operations but had sacked thirteen police officers due to their political unreliability, but increases had raised the numbers to 176. He employed Wilhelm Seeger, an anti-Nazi, as a personal assistant. They had been compiling a list of unreliable and suspicious persons. Six Nazis had managed to take positions in various municipal posts—they were sacked on 21 November. A few days later, he sacked seven more officers, several of whom had been members of the SS. Since then, the city had been divided into six precincts to raise the effectiveness of policing. The US Military Police battalion was the most powerful security force in the city, controlling traffic. A small volunteer fire brigade was being raised. There was no functioning civil defence service, but, in general, state services were working well though none of the German staff were from Aachen.[10]

II. Aachengate

In early December 1944, a small team of US Psychological Warfare officers were granted permission to enter Aachen by First Army

Headquarters. They drove to the city via Henri-Chapelle, where a US military cemetery was being filled by GIs digging graves; there were long rows of dead waiting to be buried. There was a sombreness and the team travelled on in silence, and 'seeing the first big city that seemed totally dead ... there was no sign of life ... imposing stone buildings were gutted and burned ... It must have been a beautiful city, I thought, judging by the spaciousness and the massiveness of the buildings.'[11] In 1946, Saul Padover (1905–1981) published his experiences as an American intelligence officer in Germany during 1944–5. He provided little insight into his motivations or background. Born in the Austro-Hungarian Empire, Padover migrated to America in 1920, earning BA, MA and PhD degrees. He served in various public roles and as an OSS officer, alongside scholarly pursuits. President Truman awarded him the Bronze Star in 1945. However, Padover's account of his military intelligence service soon vanished into obscurity, with scarce copies resurfacing only in select second-hand bookstores. Titled 'Experiment in Germany' in the United States and published in New York in 1946, the book took on a different guise across the Atlantic, where it was released as 'Psychologist in Germany' in London that same year. The divergence in titles—'psychologist' and 'experiment'—hints at underlying messages or perhaps even coded narratives within its pages. The real enigma lies in Padover's archival reports, which present an alternate perspective not articulated in his published work. Within these reports lie commentaries that diverge significantly from the narrative portrayed in his intelligence dispatches, two of which merit particular scrutiny.

During Hitler's Ardennes Offensive (16 December 1944– 3 January 1945), American commanders sensed a disturbance in Aachen, prompting investigations by the US Ninth Army after Eisenhower divided the command with Montgomery. Saul Padover took charge of interrogating the leading figures—Oppenhoff, deputy mayors, locals and the Bishop of Aachen—throughout January, issuing reports thereafter. In his 3 February 1945 report titled 'The Political Situation in Aachen', Padover meticulously dissected his findings. He began by highlighting the emergence of a new ruling group in Aachen over the past three months, with

Franz Oppenhoff and Bishop Johannes Joseph Van der Velde his persons of interest. Padover asserted that their anti-Nazi stance served as their strongest bargaining chip with the Americans, their sole proof being their non-membership in the party. Regarding their *Weltanschauung* and ideas, Padover observed their youthfulness (aged 33–50), upper-middle-class backgrounds and lucrative gains under the Nazis, indicating their prosperity under Hitler's regime. Consequently, Padover concluded that Oppenhoff's circle harboured deeply undemocratic sentiments, vehemently opposed to Weimar republicanism and the notion of multiple political parties. Their exclusivity extended to their work, where they marginalised outsiders, particularly from the working class and their representatives.

When Padover asked 'What does this group have in mind?', he unearthed a dream-like fantasy. 'Politically, it is perceived as small state clericalism, and socially it is based on owners and managers of small and medium-sized enterprises, with the support of the skilled "labour aristocracy"—foremen, Meister, Obermeister, artisans.' Their agenda included staunch resistance against elections, mass-based political parties and trade unions, instead promoting a culture centred around 'work' and 'pride in one's work'. They held disdain for politicised workers, advocating for a simplistic solution encapsulated by one mayor's remark as relayed by Padover: 'Give the worker a glass of beer and a loaf of bread, and he is satisfied.' Padover interpreted their stance as an endorsement of the 'Christian Staendestaat' or corporatist state idea from the depression years in Austria.[12] Accordingly, Oppenhoff's reconstruction plan was envisaged as 'non-political (non-democratic), authoritarian, paternalistic', reflecting a dearth of political education and evolution since Hitler's ascent to power in 1933. Oppenhoff was building an authoritarian, highly bureaucratic state, with paternalistic small-scale industry based on a hierarchical labour system of skills and handicrafts.

Turning to a pressing concern at the time—why Nazi Party members still held positions in the administration—Padover revealed that out of 72 positions, at least 22 were occupied by former Nazi Party members. Additionally, 35 business licenses had been granted to Nazi Party affiliates. Oppenhoff's strategy involved purging the 'small fry' while safeguarding 10 key individuals, one of whom held authority over food store permits. Oppenhoff was willing to defend the employment of Nazis, citing two categories: those who joined before 1933 but renounced their beliefs, and those who joined for career advancement. Regarding the complexities of removing Nazi members and others, Padover cautioned against bureaucratic entanglements, noting that Oppenhoff retained legal rights based on the original agreement with the US Military Government (MGO). Padover referenced the case of 'Bolognini', an Italian fascist and war contractor notorious for mistreating foreign slave labour and local workers, who was initially dismissed by the MGO only to be reinstated by Oppenhoff as the city's building contractor. Padover criticised the MGO for its handling of Dr Goerres, an influential Nazi Party member in the IHK, who was dismissed only to be employed in the MGO's legal department. He also highlighted Dr Gerhard Heusch, a former Wehrmacht Major implicated in crimes in Soviet Russia, who was initially hired by Talbot and later appointed by Oppenhoff as Mayor of Labour before his dismissal. Padover cautioned that such revelations would be damaging if US newspapers caught wind of the story.

In the second part of his report on 'The Position of the Military Government', Padover outlined several issues. Firstly, there was a concerning turnover of MGOs, with three changes since October 1944, each interpreting their roles differently. The efficiency and performance of MG teams were evaluated based on how quickly a town could resume functioning, a challenging task when team members lacked proficiency in German. Consequently, MG teams recruited anyone capable of facilitating town operations, leading to political apathy despite the reliance on Nazis to achieve objectives. Padover recalled warning his Aachen team in October 1944 about the significance of *Veltrupwerke*, where many key individuals associated with Oppenhoff congregated or worked, but his concerns went unheeded. Despite efforts to address the issue, no one had considered whether the Oppenhoff group posed a threat to allied interests. The plan remained to remove forty-five known Nazis from the fifty-five key positions in the city. As for the absence of Social Democrats in representation, only one SPD member had been approached, but he declined Oppenhoff's offer, believing it aimed to exploit workers while favouring the affluent. Thus, the primary obstacle to Aachen's reconstruction lay in Oppenhoff's plan and recruitment strategy.

In deconstructing 'How the Oppenhoff Group came into the Administration', Padover pondered why this particular upper-class circle was selected among the thousands left behind. It had all the appearance of being rehearsed, as if the group was prepared and made themselves available. Following the failed plot on Hitler in September 1944, Veltrup had advised Oppenhoff to flee to Eupen. Their plan was to await the Americans. When an American MG officer encountered the Oppenhoff circle, negotiations ensued— but who approached whom? The MG officer, Swoboda, said: 'In the latter part of October, Lt Col Carmichael', the commanding officer of Aachen MG team, 'finding Aachen a dead and depopulated city, asked him to find a Mayor'. However, Padover observed that Swoboda spoke no German and Oppenhoff spoke no English, causing the negotiations to be filtered via individuals with poor translation skills. In this regard, Swoboda relied on the bishop's influence and recommendations. Oppenhoff's side of the story was different. He claimed Swoboda arrived in Eupen with the bishop, engaged with him, and subsequently met with Carmichael for an extensive 8.5-hour conference. Oppenhoff rejected Carmichael's proposed candidates, instead advocating for his own selections, and declined to work for the envisioned 'republican, democratic Germany'. His focus was on securing specialists rather than administrators, with a willingness to employ Nazis and to also exclude the church from all involvement. Ultimately, Swoboda and Carmichael extended the job offer to Oppenhoff, which he accepted.

The role of the bishop, however, proved more significant than any of the men involved wished to admit. Despite the bombing and shelling since 1942, the bishop remained in Aachen, discovered by a US patrol in the cathedral on 18 October and subsequently taken to the evacuation centre. Swoboda met the bishop every day and arranged special privileges including transportation, one one witness wryly observed, 'Swoboda, guards the bishop like a mother hen'. The bishop expressed his confidence in Oppenhoff and his deputy mayors to Padover. However, Swoboda's protective stance extended to obstructing investigative officers' attempts to meet with the Oberbürgermeister and his mayors. Swoboda's departure from Aachen, having been promoted to colonel and reassigned to another team, left the bishop somewhat distanced from politics. The MGO's treatment of him remained cautious, dating back to Swoboda's view of the bishop as 'the voice, the conscience, and the Parliament of the people of Aachen'. Despite this reverence, the bishop's use of the term *Friedhofgemüse* to describe the Aachen population did not endear him to Padover. Aacheners interviewed expressed little interest in the bishop or were absolutely opposed to his interference.

The population in February 1945 was estimated at 11,000, and their primary interests were repairing their homes or scrounging food. There was little contact between Oppenhoff and the ordinary people because there were no means of communication. No electricity, no radios, and the bishop remained aloof. There had been circulars criticising the Oppenhoff clique. Several people claimed 'It is the same old racketeers'. Why did a city of 11,000 need nine mayors and an Oberbürgermeister? Oppenhoff and the others were aware of the discontent. They were called 'lefties', 'communists' or 'dangerous reds', although they remained in 'low profile'. The deepest sense of discontent lay with the lack of labour or work, which meant minimum rations and income. The upper class wanted the working class to do the hard labour. The small business owners were also criticised for avoiding reconstruction so they could open their businesses. These issues were extended to the influence of Nazi Party members and the emerging rift between social classes. Someone recommended all Nazis should wear armbands like the Jews were made to wear stars. One man's son suffered TB, yet the labour office assigned him to collecting and burning bodies. He added that they assumed things would be different and believed the BBC that all Nazis would be wiped out, 'now you see them everywhere in fine jobs and opening stores'.

Padover concluded his report: 'It must be pointed out as a warning that the discontent will become more serious when the true facts of the civil regime is made known'—once the working class discover the plan for them, in other words, there will be trouble. He warned of the absence of democracy and how the working class would challenge this power grab by Oppenhoff. On 21 February 1945, Robert Murphy wrote to General F.J. McSherry after reading Padover's report. Both men were unaware of the report's progress and first learned of its existence through the public press, in particular, Dorothy Thompson's article in the *New York Post* on 1 February, believed to have originated from a leak to the press by Padover. Murphy recommended that, as more territory was overrun, 'a more effective liaison must exist between your office and the agencies operating in the field'.[13] The impact of the Padover report among the MGOs was recorded by Arthur Kahn: 'they produced a scathing exposé of rampant Nazi influence in the city administration'. In response to the report, Eisenhower ordered the 'shake-up in the Aachen MG and a purge of Nazis from the city administration. He continued, 'But in April 1945 my colleagues and I did not appreciate how ominous a precedent this first military government experiment would prove to be.' Kahn later revealed how anti-Nazi or antifa (anti-fascist resistance) movements were quashed by the US army in contravention of SHAEF orders.[14] This policy duplicity was a red thread of US civil-military relations in occupied Germany.

III. The holy hand grenade

Culture war was waged by all sides in the Second World War, but the 'Monuments Men' movement was a political culture initiative. The allied bombing had de-housed and killed civilians, but also shattered German cultural artefacts and sites with callous haphazardness. The allies confronted the political conundrum of rescuing culture after destroying culture. For two weeks, two American Monuments Men waited patiently as Aachen burned—glowing at night and trailing long columns of smoke by day. Finally, their time came to enter the city, by-passing anti-tank obstacles and navigating roads coiled by collapsed tramway cables. They approached an abandoned tram car and frightened civilians clambered out in fear of being attacked. All the houses, large and small, had few windows, and closer to the centre all were roofless and many with collapsed walls. Those houses with gardens were littered with household items. In some streets, the rows of buildings disguised an 'emptiness' behind them; the 'city was utterly abandoned ... a skeleton city is more terrible than one that the bombs have flattened'. Germans had daubed defiant messages of resistance and victory on several walls. The 'desolation' stretched far into the commercial district. In the midst of all this chaos, an American soldier 'wearing the complete regalia of an Indian chieftain galloped past on a horse'. A number of soldiers were wearing odd clothes, having ransacked the shops. The two men decided to take different paths to the town centre. One recalled picking his way through 'heaps of evil-smelling rubble that blocked narrow streets' and only encountered a 'band of Belgian marauders in uniform'.

The two men: US Army Intelligence Captain Walker Hancock (1901–1998), a well-known sculptor, and US Navy reservist Georg L. Stout (1897–1978), an art conservator and museum director. They were Art Commandos, or Monuments Men, specialists in fine arts and antiquities, two of the 400 men and women tasked with rescuing the antiquities and fine arts of war-torn Europe.[15] The Fine Arts Program (MFAA) was raised in 1943 by the Civil Affairs and Military Government branches under the command of US Army Major L. Bancel LaFarge (1900–1989), an architect by profession. His mission was later explained as 'locating, and protecting the numerous repositories, many of them in mines or castles, to which the Germans had removed both of their own moveable art treasures and those systematically looted from the countries they had occupied'.[16] Hancock remained in Germany until early 1946 and his accounts have become most well known in Aachen's story. He wrote an article for the College of Art in 1946. Then, in 1977, he gave an oral account of his work in the MFAA for the Smithsonian Institute. Later, in 1991, Hancock gave a televised interview for the BBC *Timewatch* series.[17] They contain subtle differences, reflecting how memory alters over the decades.

Hancock received his commission in the Intelligence Branch and began service in the Pentagon, but after arriving in England he was assigned to the US First Army, specialising in German and Belgian art. About Aachen, Hancock told BBC: 'The moment the city had been cleared of the population, all evacuated to a camp just outside the city, George Stout and I went in together. George stayed in the Suermondt Museum, which was his first interest, and I went on to the Cathedral, which was the only building still standing that I saw anywhere in the city.' In 1946, he described the day as dark, with the odd shell whistling overhead, followed by total silence. He noticed the 'steel frame of the Rathaus tower drooped limply into the square'. He told *Timewatch*, 'When I went into this wonderful octagon, which had been Charlemagne's court chapel, I was aware of clothes, unfinished meals, plates, toys, all over the floor'.

In 1946, he recalled, 'the place must have been uncomfortably crowded until the sudden evacuation'. Hancock assessed the damage caused to the vaults of the apse and the demolished high altar caused by an unexploded bomb. Then he was interrupted by the 'vicar', who beckoned with 'Hier' and led him to a 'little den'. In 1946, he was 'Vicar Stephany' and was trembling because of the bombardments. The 'vicar' was actually Dr Stephan Buchkremer, the son of the cathedral's building-master and the organiser of the fire-watch.[18] Buchkremer urged Hancock to bring the boys of the fire-watch back to the cathedral. The fire-watch had saved the building five times during the war and, although they wore Hitler Youth uniforms, they were not Nazis—'all German boys loved to wear uniforms'—and had been taken to the Brand internment camp. Hancock promised to get them released but later claimed Stout was less enthusiastic. Stout didn't want to make exceptions in the treatment of German civilians because it would antagonise First Army officials: 'the cathedral will just have to take its chances for a few days'. Both men went to MGO Major Lancer, the G-5 of 1st Infantry Division, for a decision to release the fire-watch to guard the cathedral. Lancer agreed and ordered an intelligence officer to get the German youths released. The nominal leader of the fire-watch was Helmut Hansen, an 18-year-old. Upon being informed he was returning to the cathedral, Hansen called to 'Hans, Georg, Willi, Carl, and Niklaus', all flushed with excitement. The fire-watch cellar in the cathedral was re-stocked with

213

food, the US army issued passes, and his mother was released, and she received a pass to cook their meals.[19]

Hancock and Stout located a list of Aachen's art and antiquities in the Seurmondt Museum. Discarded files littered the floors but a list and a museum catalogue were found, with items marked in blue and red pencil—those items taken to the Siegen mines. A further problem they faced was to find local museum staff or experts. The Seurmondt Museum director, Dr Kütgens, 'had been a good Nazi and fled east of the Rhine' with all his colleagues. US Army Captain Thornton scrutinised Aachen's Labour Exchange records to locate persons connected with the cultural or arts buildings in the city. By chance, an elderly woman claimed Professor August von Brandis (1859–1947), an artist and teacher from the Reiff Museum, was in the Brand internment camp. The Brand camp was a barracks turned into a holding camp for the remaining population. The rooms and corridors were crammed with civilians. They finally located Brandis, an 86-year-old, being assisted by the Reiff Museum's caretaker, Herr Jansen. Franz Reiff (1835–1902) had bequeathed a collection of his art and copies to the Technical University and a museum was opened in 1908. In 1944, the building was smashed in bitter fighting, and abandoned weapons from both sides littered the corridors and stairways. Many paintings and pictures survived the damage, including paintings from the baroque Couven House, in Aachen, which had been flattened and turned to rubble.[20] Meanwhile, a local architect was made responsible for supervising the protection of the remaining monuments. Jansen and the fire-watch were assigned to repairing roofs and walls. When Aachen later came under control of the Ninth Army, US Army Captain Walter Huchthausen, an architect by profession, restored the *Bauamt*—the organisation for the protection of buildings. He was an enthusiastic preservationist, but during an inspection trip accidently drove within the range of German machine-gun fire and was killed.

In his Smithsonian recordings, Hancock recalled the Janus face of the US armed forces in their treatment of art works—'the army was wonderful, and it was awful'. The army issued Brandis with passes for him and his wife to remain in their Aachen apartment.

However, he became frail and was increasingly exhausted by the work. Hancock therefore decided Jansen should be granted a military pass to help save the university's scientific equipment and preserve the museum artefacts. Hancock tried to explain to the major commanding Brand camp of the arrangements made for Brandis and Jansen. The major wasn't interested: 'I don't care who he is ... He's just one more Kraut to me. Bring him back, and I'll let him go tomorrow morning. You [meaning Hancock] signed for two Krauts.' Hancock claimed the common soldiery saved most of the artwork, and their antics to save the antiquities 'amused' him. Some officers took great care of art works and others were callous to the point of committing vandalism.[21]

During his *Timewatch* interviews, Hancock referred to the conundrum of understanding the soldiers' behaviour:

> People, I think, have very poor ideas of what the psychology of troops who have been fighting and seeing their comrades killed on all sides can be. They aren't careful of anything they see. I had one student from Philadelphia, a sculptor, very sensitive artist, and a good musician. He had been an infantryman in the First Army, my army, and after the war it was all over, and he had coped to a degree. He said, 'you know when you've been in a battle like that and lost what you lost. If they put you in a fancy chateau you had to shoot the chandelier.

Hancock's account(s) of recovering Aachen's treasures differed over the years. In order to protect the artefacts from the air raids, the treasures had been boxed and taken to a mine in Siegen. American soldiers had found the treasures. Stefan Buchkrammer (vicar) was deeply apologetic because he'd known all along their location and was surprised the Americans had discovered them. They didn't realise the 'vicar' was under strict orders from the bishop to identify the conditions of the treasures and report only to him. Hancock claimed it was about April 1945; they faced travel difficulties and were forced to avoid the bitter fighting and shelling, even though allied armies had driven deep into Germany. Hancock remembered when they first entered the Siegen tunnels, they were met with the sickening smell of masses of terrified civilians. The vicar said the people were frightened that the Americans would shoot them.²² In his account for *Timewatch*, Hancock wrote: 'One little boy rushed out from the crowd, there were 5,000 people in there, and took hold of George Stout's hand and stayed with us as we went on past the shelters to the gallery that had been locked off, which not only contained the cathedral treasures of Cologne, Aachen and Essen, but the best of all the great Rhineland museums.'²³

There was a guardian of the tunnel, Herr Etzkorn, and he informed Hancock that the former Aachen Oberbürgermeister, Quirin Jansen, had tried to acquire the treasures. Etzkorn led Jansen and his cronies along a different tunnel, passing the long galleries used for storage of paintings and sculpture. The cathedral treasures, in great chest, were at the far end of the gallery and the seals unbroken. The Aachen treasures included a silver bust of Charlemagne that contained his skull, 'a robe of the Virgin', Lothar's processional cross, and a cameo of Augustus. Hancock received nineteen trucks with French drivers to transfer the treasures back to Aachen. The drivers asked about the load; when told it was Charlemagne and the bones of saints, the drivers responded with great care in driving the treasures. Once in Aachen, the treasures were taken to the Hubertus chapel.²⁴

There is an alternative account of Aachen's antiquities and monuments. Among the US army's G-5 returns to SHAEF, US First Army reports provide a more complete survey of the situation. The monthly reports from 1 November 1944 indicate a general inspection of artefacts was conducted on 22–6 October, a day after the surrender. The report confirmed the decision to organise and appoint a competent German civilian agency with responsibility to protect the city's monuments and to organise a central depository office for the protection and cataloguing of items. There was to be continuing inspection and supervision of repairs to priority monuments. The selection of German civilian appointment began on 15 November 1944, with: Professor Theodor Rehman 'canon of the Münster'; Erich Stephany, 'vicar of the Münster'; Herr Heinrich Jansen, 'superintendent of the Reiff Museum' at the Technical University; and Professor August von Brandis from the Technical University. Rehman and Stephany had been in the same positions throughout the war, but their religious duties reduced their time in repairs and technical assistance for the military government. Jansen was given residence in the Reiff Museum to extend his authority. Brandis was 'anxious to cooperate with the military and civilian authorities' but was physically incapable of arduous work. The report's summary observed: 'the great destruction to the city, the wide dispersion of its collections ... the relatively complete evacuation of the population, and the difficulties attendant on the supervision'. On 13 December 1944, Major Jack Bradford (DMGO Detachment FIC2 VII Corps) held a conference with Dr Schwippert, 'the Burgermeister responsible for all buildings, architectural construction, and subsidiary matters', to discuss the transfer of authority from the 'Art Commando' to German civilian control. Professor Menicken and two civilians from the faculty of the Technical University were allocated positions. There was no positive vetting of the Germans at that stage.

The Suermondt Museum, in Wilhelmstrasse, was occupied by the US Military Police and other local buildings were identified as possible alternatives for MGO activities. The museum was cleared of artefacts by the Nazis in December 1943. The building suffered minor damages, but several rooms could be used to lock and guard items. Remains of the collection including framed paintings, maps and charts, sculptures in wood, plaster and metal, books from the museum library, and two cabinets of coins and medals were discovered in the basement. There was evidence of pilfering and vandalism. The cathedral was inspected on 11–13 December 1944: 'no artillery fire; fire hazard continues moderate because of disruption of contiguous mains. Streets surrounding edifice largely cleared.' Wooden scaffoldings were placed around the Hungarian chapel and the Anna-Kapelle, which allowed access to the Octagon roof. The roof was patched with lathe and tarpaper. The two fractured vaults of the choir and a shattered buttress on the outside to the south could not be repaired due to shortages of labour and materials. The *Rathaus* was inspected on 13 December, and both towers remained standing unsupported after the nineteenth-century buildings had been cleared. The building was identified as damaged but not beyond repair. Four pieces of art by Alfred Rethel remained intact.

The old Stadtarchiv was inspected on 11–13 December. The surrounding area was cleared of debris and crates of stored items taken into secure rooms. The inspections raised the general agreement for emergency repairs, and the supply of building materials. However, the civilian authorities were constrained by the lack of labourers, considered as an important lesson for the military occupation.[25]

In December 1944, a G-5 report issued by US First Army explained:

> Preliminary surveys of Aachen, including photographing of the destruction done to historic buildings and monuments in the city, was completed by 1 November and emergency repairs were commenced to prevent further damage by the weather ... Later in the month, the archivist of the cathedral archives in Aachen was given charge of the preservation of all archives in the city.[26]

On 3 February 1945, SHAEF's G-5 assistant chief of staff issued a report on 'Art Commando' operations in December 1944. There were confirmations that more German documents had been located, identifying storage depots. They were copied and sent to London for further analysis. George Stout had filed a report that was incorporated into civil affairs' procedures, but thus far the report has not been located and was not cited by Hancock. It appears Stout was placed in an important position to coordinate matters more efficiently, which Hancock did not approve. The Aachen reports confirmed the 'improvised machinery that was set up to care for monuments' and this was the beginning of the preservation procedures. However, less well appreciated by the civil affairs officers was the ideological sympathies of the Germans they were employing.

IV. Democratic assassination

Franz Oppenhoff's interrogation by Saul Padover and Lewis Gittler, on 2 February 1945, could never be a comfortable experience. A self-made intellectual, Padover's history and politics were defined by Jeffersonian democracy and American constitutionalism. In contrast, Oppenhoff was an upper-middle-class lawyer who profited from defending church clients accused of immoral practices by the Nazis, and not only surviving but also profiting through the Veltrup concern. He was as profoundly anti-democratic and anti-liberal as he was anti-Nazi and anti-Hitler, and had stifled any popular movement among the people. Oppenhoff had been briefly conscripted by the Wehrmacht, but on 12 September, during the evacuations and chaos, he trashed his uniform and fled to Eupen. When the war started, he joined *Veltrupwerke*, which had been benefiting from Junkers contracts since Hugo Junkers was relieved from control of the company. There is a conspiracy theory lingering that involved Hugo Junkers' demise and how Hermann Göring, Veltrup, Oppenhoff and a host of others profited afterwards—but that's way beyond the confines of this book. However, Padover observed, 'Oppenhoff is the leading spirit of the Aachen city administration and has positive social and economic ideas, which he expressed with blunt candidness.' He accepted his regime was under pressure to remove the former Nazis. This he believed unjust and he would not commit to such injustice. For Oppenhoff, there were only two kinds of Germans—those with *Kadavorgehorsam* (an extreme form of blind obedience to orders) and those who give the orders. Hence why democracy was unsuitable for the future Germany. Oppenhoff actually believed the US MGO system would prevent the rise of democracy and political parties.

Padover was not surprised by Oppenhoff's ideas of world politics and the rise of Hitler. He saw little irony in complaining how big business had fuelled Hitler's success, when he himself had profited from the system. Similarly, he blamed the Treaty of Versailles for giving Hitler the grounds for a political platform, because it had taken Germany's 'honour' away. In his opinion, 'frontiers were a joke', preferring a unified economic area, a unified Europe. Oppenhoff's Europe excluded Russia, referring to the Russians as 'Asiatics' and people he despised. Germany should join the west in a common front against Russia. He claimed that, if America didn't join the Germans, everywhere east of the Rhine would be 'Asiatic'. Padover concluded, 'Oppenhoff spoke as if he were a citizen of a victorious nation. Neither his plans nor his ideas reveal any awareness that he is a member of a defeated country and an official of an occupied city.'²⁷ After Padover was gone, First Army filed a report in March 1945, 'To assist MG officers in their selection of men to serve as public officials, a First US Army letter dated 7 March was dispatched to Corps, Division and separate unit commanders setting forth the requirements to be met in the process of selection' (p. 5). 'Stress was placed upon removing active Nazis or sympathisers as retention of such persons would encourage possible enemy resistance groups and discourage groups otherwise inclined to cooperate in ferreting out Nazi sympathisers and in operating Military Government.'²⁸

Earl Ziemke reflected on the Oppenhoff case in the official US army history of the occupation of Germany. He wrote, 'His was the most important appointment yet made in Germany and one that was certain to attract attention on both sides of the front.' Oppenhoff was commended for his bravery because Himmler, the chief of the SS, had recently announced, through *Das Schwarze Korps*, that any collaboration with the allies in administering Germany would warrant an automatic death sentence. Ziemke noted that F1G2 was a *Regierungsbezerke* or provincial-level organisation (as designated by the 'F' in its designation), with 35 officers and 48 ORs, but the entire Aachen region had yet to be occupied. This meant that Aachen was under far greater scrutiny than would have been usual. He acknowledged that Oppenhoff had remained in Aachen during Hitler's Ardennes Offensive, which had granted him praise from the community. This did not count for long because the fundamental doubts had grown within the MGO since his appointment. Oppenhoff's recommendation by the bishop had been agreeable when the Americans assumed the church was hostile to Nazism and resisted. Subsequent occupations and captured records, informed the MGO network that the church was strictly neutral under Nazism. Three months of the MGO had seen the church adopt a neutral stance. Concern began to grow among the Americans that a political continuity with the Nazi past had taken hold in Aachen.²⁹

There are questions about the Oppenhoff saga that reframes his story. Several concern Padover and the comments from his book. For instance his thoughts about the character of the people: 'the connection between "good" Germans and "gas houses"' (p. 27), was that a preconceived opinion or acquired from his experience as an occupier? He also had favourites like Heinrich Hollands, Aachen's first post-war newspaper proprietor, or Professor Peter Mennicken, a cultural historian with a dubious associations with the Nazi occupation in Brussels, which Padover chose to ignore or was unaware.[30] A pertinent question, given the centrality of democracy: why did the MGO not re-educate Oppenhoff and his group? It seems odd until one considers salient facts that have remained dormant in the interrogations—why were the Americans failing? The little things like the continuing lack of electricity and the unburied dead indicate that, although the MGO was looking to raise the functionality of destroyed cities quickly, they were not engaged in the minutiae of everyday life. Given the dangers Oppenhoff was living under, was his employment of Nazis a means of protection against Nazis retribution? Perhaps political naivety, but Oppenhoff was operating under a pseudonym—'Mr Selwyn'. This disguise was necessary while the war was in progress, and recklessly exposed by Padover. Interestingly, upon requesting the file, marked 'Mr Sellwyn', the archive insisted access was only available in a private room, illustrating its continuing sensitivity.[31] After the American press published Oppenhoff's name, he was a dead man walking. He was assassinated by an SS team of killers operating under the name *Unternehmen Karneval* (Operation Carnival). In March 1970, Kaiserallee was renamed Oppenhoffallee and a memorial unveiled by Oberbürgermeister Hermann Heusch.[32]

After the war, Eisenhower was one of the few to refer to the Military Governments in post-war memoirs and histories:

> Our first military government experience was gained at Aachen before the crossing of the Rhine ... the situation was new and difficult and became more acute because of our policy of non-employment of Nazis for any governmental work. In much of our necessary public utility work it was only the local Nazis who had sufficient knowledge to be of assistance. The question at once arose as to whether we should use them or non-Nazis, who knew little or nothing about the particular facility. It was difficult, but as quickly as possible we got rid of party members and trained others

for necessary operation of public works, public utilities, sanitary services, posts, telegraph, and telephones.[33]

Subsequently, Kahn observed that McSherry announced in 1946: 'The new Germany would have to be built around the working class because virtually all German industrialists have been imbued with the twin philosophies of superiority and aggression. Even the most liberal-minded among them scarcely knew the meaning of the term democracy in the American sense.'[34] Oppenhoff doesn't fit Eisenhower's tale or deserve Padover's betrayal, but in the end became another victim of the war. Whether Oppenhoff was a flawed or tragic hero, he was a family man with children, who risked everything for a 'new' future and was a victim of that cause.

PART FOUR

POSTMODERN WAR AND SOCIETY

When Germany has been beaten we shall find there a surprising chaos of ideas and beliefs, of political and personal aims. National faith will be dormant; the idea of the Reich will seem dead. Germans will express, and even feel, the wish that their country, or their part of it, should become a British Dominion or a Republic of the Soviet Union. Bavarians will denounce Prussians, Saxons, Silesians, Rhinelanders the rest. Few Germans, indeed, will profess any loyalty to Hitler or the Nazi faith; and, indeed few at that time will have any. No nation in the world will have better cause to revile Hitler than the Germans; for of all the nations he will have laid low, he will have laid the German nation lowest ... There will probably be a strong religious revival; and there will be devotees too, for creeds that never were German, like pacifism, or that have long ceased to have any real meaning in Germany, like Monarchy.

(TNA, CAB 193/2, German Reactions to Defeat,
2 January 1945)

The control machinery in the British Zone has evolved in two different ways: (a) the Military Government staff of 21 Army Group (the British element of the Allied Expeditionary force which was responsible for the short term problems of civil administration in the wake of the advancing Allied armies during the operational period; a (b) the long term Control Commission for Germany (British element); this had been built up in London prior to the defeat of Germany on the lines of the European Advisory Commission Agreement on Control Machinery, with twelve Divisions similar to the twelve Directorates of the Allied Control Authority.

(TNA, AIR 55/252 German Occupation, Memorandum on the Occupation of Germany, Main Headquarters Air Division, 26 April 1946)

9

BRITISH MILITARY OCCUPATION

The American control of Aachen came to an end in May–June 1945, with the handover to the British Military Government. According to Giles MacDonagh, 'The Rhineland was the first part of Germany to be liberated from the west, and the first city was Aachen. ... The American installed administration estimated that they could make the damaged properties habitable within a year, but to rebuild the city would take twenty.'[1] The British army arrived remarkably ill-prepared for occupation given that the Foreign Office, the Ministry of Economic Warfare, the Ministry of Home Security and RAF Bomber Command had spent so long studying the results of the bombing. In his memoirs, Air Chief Marshal Arthur Harris wrote: 'Aachen surrendered on October 21st and gave the Allied armies their first sight of a German town destroyed by fire bombs.'[2] After four years of seeking accurate results of the bombing of Germany, the RAF were gifted with evidence from Aachen. In chapter six, we saw how the captured documents were sent to UK for translation, from November 1944 to January 1945, to the Foreign Office and the Ministry of Economic Warfare. In March 1945, Bomber Command's Operational Research Section (BC-ORS) surveyed Aachen.

In their subsequent report of the survey the BC-ORS identified five objectives: '(i) To obtain a broad picture of the effects of bombing on the town as a domestic and commercial centre; (ii) To discover the effects on the industrial capacity of the town both as regards direct damage and also through damage to town as a housing and commercial centre and to the morale of the workers; (iii) To discover the effect on the town as a centre of railway communication; (iv) To explore the possibility of obtaining information which may be of value in the interpretation of aerial photographs; nanda (v) To explore the possibility of obtaining information on the relative effectiveness of different weapons.' Their comprehensive set of questions came with a caveat in the final report: 'little concrete evidence was discovered.' The report noted there had been 121 raids after the city was 'first visited' on 13–14 May 1940. The raids continued until July 1944 (no record) and, overall, 1,932 aircraft dropped 6,750 tons of bombs. The mission: 'The purpose of the majority of these attacks was to reduce the town's industrial potential by direct damage to plant, damage to housing and utilities, and destruction of the morale of the workers.' The report observed that, after the 'Bomber Command offensive the town was subjected to tactical bombing and shelling during the Battle of Aachen.'[3] They had no scientific evidence or critical analysis to make any judgement that morale had been broken because there were no German locals to interview.

The report was later included in the British Bomber Research Mission, part of a series of bombing studies initiated by Bomber Command under Harris's command.[4] Less well known was that, in October 1945, Harris published through the government stationery office a record of Bomber Command operations. In the introduction, he explained that 'the main task' of Bomber Command was 'to focus on the morale of the enemy civil population, and, in particular, of the industrial workers'. He added that his 'primary authorised task' was 'to inflict the most severe material damage on German cities'.[5] Churchill's early faith in bombing began to wane. After the bombing of Dresden, he penned a minute of 28 March 1945 critical of the bombing, which was later withdrawn, but his relationship had cooled. Part of the reason, according to Overy, was because Churchill had seen the extent of the damage to the cities during a visit to Germany on 3 March 1945.[6] Alanbrooke gave a different impression: 'Aachen was very badly damaged and it was a relief to see at last German houses demolished instead of French, Italian, Belgian and British! There were a few Germans in the town but not many.'⁷

On 7 April, minutes passed between Churchill and the Chancellor of the Exchequer, arranging for a committee to investigate the bombing. Professor Solly Zuckerman had been working to establish a study of British bombing in line with the USAAF survey. The situation was further advanced on 21 May 1945, when, over dinner at Chequers, Churchill invited Harold Macmillan to take over the Air Ministry as Secretary of State for War.⁸ The meetings of the planning committee for the Bomber Research Mission was formalised on 18 July 1945, chaired by Geoffrey Vickers, representatives from the War Office and Admiralty with Zuckerman.⁹ Vickers had previously been deputy director at the Ministry of Economic Warfare and a member of JIC, and had seen the evidence collected and the reports during 1942 as discussed in chapter four.

On 20 April 1946, Harris received a letter from the Air Ministry confirming that he was denied publication of his 'Despatch'. The reasons for denying publication being 'insuperable security objections to the publication of the appendices'. More significantly, Harris's comments and statements were challenged on the grounds that, in 1945, when 'Despatch' was drafted, there was little evidence to support the statements, since then the British Bombing Survey Unit's Report had analysed Bomber Command's, 'which does not confirm certain of the C-in-C's conclusions, and places a different complexion upon others'. The reviewer referred to Harris's statement on the tasks of Bomber Command and his primary tasks. He countered, this 'tends to obscure the fact that the Air Staff intention was always to return to the bombing of precise targets as quickly as the tactical capabilities of the bomber force, and the improvement of night bombing technique, would permit'. In 1941, the Air Staff was pressing Bomber Command to improve effectiveness of night bombing. The development of tactical ability in 1942 was conveyed in the bombing directive that preceded Harris' arrival. The reviewer reiterated that 'the Air Staff had accepted, temporarily, the need to concentrate effort on area targets ... and revert to the attack of precise targets'. Harris' description of the formation of Pathfinder Force was entirely rejected.

Also, the claim that the enemy's sinews were confined to the cities was also rejected; instead, oil and communications were identified as Germany's weaknesses, but they were not targeted by Harris. The final criticism concerned Harris's claims of target interference by government departments, and the selection of primary targets were not resolved. The reviewer's reply was damning:

> The work of selection must always depend heavily on intelligence sources, and it cannot be denied that there was, in Bomber Command, a reluctance to attack specific targets, born partly of operational inability and partly of an underestimate on their part of their own ability. This made it difficult to advocate for them any real target system other than industrial areas—which, as is demonstrated throughout the despatch, they wanted most to attack.[10]

When confronted by the evidence of the bombing, since the first examination of the results from Aachen, in March 1945, which had revealed the shortcomings, Harris continued to disregard the obvious. In trying to publish his 'Despatch' report he finally confronted organised opposition and serious critical analysis of his wartime leadership and performance. If 'Despatch' was intended to be his legacy project, it had become his indictment.

The management and administration of Aachen was passed to the British army. Their task proved to be a humanitarian challenge. This chapter examines the arrival of the British and their methods of occupation by imposing law and order. They also carried out an examination of the conditions in the city in May–June 1945, which was the most comprehensive assessment since the RAF had studied the extent of the damage. During a visit in 1947 they met Victor Gollancz, a German railwayman, who was: 'one of the very few working-class people I met in Germany who were still, in the positive sense, pro-British'. His observation of the British military occupation: 'there are two worlds in Germany today, the world of the conquered and the world of the conquerors'.[11]

I. Enter the British

In Lille (France) on 27 April 1945, the British 227 Civil Affairs Detachment (CAD) received its movement orders—Aachen. At

BRITISH MILITARY OCCUPATION

09.00 hours on 1 May, the detachment set off for Schooten, near Helmond, in Holland, 71 miles north of Aachen. On the same day in Le Touquet (France), 07.30 hours, 311 CAD with four officers and ten ORs climbed aboard their vehicles and departed for Gravelhazel. Both detachments came under the command of Lieutenant Colonel R.C. Matthews. On 2 May, in Schooten, the commanders of 227, 311, 316 and 627 CADs were redesignated Military Government Detachments (MGD). Two days later, a British major set to locate the headquarters of the US army, MGD F1G2, in Aachen to begin the handover on 6 May. The British column was led by two motorcycle outriders, jeeps, a 3-tonner truck with the officers' luggage, a second 3-tonner truck carrying the MGD's stores and equipment, a third carrying officers and several ORs, and two 15-cwt trucks assigned to carry ten officers—six majors, three captains and a lieutenant. The column set off after breakfast at 07.00 hours and the route took them via Maastricht to Aachen, with a ten-minute break and lunch at noon—a journey time of five hours. The officers were ordered to wear battle dress, web belts, anklets, revolver and pouches, and the ORs the same except skeleton equipment, steel helmets and their packs and rifles. Another smaller convoy of two 3-tonners, two 15-Cwts and three motorcycles arrived at 16.45 hours.[12] There were more officers and troops set to arrive over the following days. The war diary for 8 May noted 'Victory in Europe Day'.

Upon arrival, the British received their first mission; they were to 'Understudy to American Military Government Detachment'. Colonel Matthews issued orders for the final handover to take place at 23.59 hours on 21 May, but was extended until 25 May. In Aachen, it was agreed a US army unit would remain in operational command, adding duplication to the workload. The US army's communication and courier systems were also retained. Colonel Matthews was limited to disciplinary matters under King's Regulations. On the same day, Matthews sent a report to his command that the first phase of handover had been planned and preparations made. He again requested more personnel and also more transport to the amount of five jeeps and two drivers.[13] The 311 MGD finally transferred back to RB Aachen on 26 May.[14] They were assigned a large property at No. 18 Kaiser Friedrich Allee. On 28 May 1945, the 311 Det took control of Aachen from 227 Det and was billeted in Lohmühlenstrasse, in the residential suburbs to the south-west of the city (near the Kaiser Friedrich Park).[15] In 1966, F.S.V. Donnison recalled:

> Although distribution of resources was very uneven, rural areas were naturally better off than Aachen. This city of 165,000 was practically deserted on occupation by the allies. If this city was to fill up again imports of relief supplies would soon become necessary not withstanding the allied policy of not helping the Germans.[16]

The 227 MGD was continuing to prepare for the takeover. To confirm US authority, he reminded all troops that the US flag took precedent and 'if the Union Jack is flown, the US flag will have the commanding place on the right or above'. Units without a US flag were authorised to requisition one. Preparations were being made for handling civilians by formulating a salary payment system for civil engineers.[17] The handover was still not completed by 1 June. However, on 5 June, Colonel Matthews received a visit from the commanding officer of 6th Guards Brigade finally replacing the US military command. There was a general holiday to mark 'the commemoration of "D-Day 6 Jun 44"'—ordered by General Eisenhower.

II. Management accounting

The first period of the MGO's operations in May–June 1945 was chaotic because of the turnover of manpower due to demobilisation. On 25 May, Colonel Matthews issued a final update report, which explained that no additional personnel, across all ranks, would be forthcoming until the handover had been completed. Typically, the first comprehensive monthly report came from the legal officer, Major Hirst of the Royal Artillery, on 30 June 1945, but he was then released from the army on 7 July. Three days later, Colonel R.C. Matthews was 'demobbed'; eventually they were replaced Major J.H. Smith and Colonel J.T. Leslie MC, on 12 July. However, before he departed, Matthews had pressed the importance of government finance for Aachen's communications network, which had been destroyed and pillaged, but not restored by the Americans. The British made efforts to acquire coal, timber and food. He claimed the progress made could not be sustained unless an officer with a technical background was assigned to the detachment. Matthews also thought there were grounds for employing more locals with a technical background to make up the shortfall.[18]

The second phase of British MGO control of Aachen began on 3 July 1945, recorded in the first 'RB Aachen' situation report issued by the new British MGO Colonel Leslie. It covered the handover from the US army and provided a summary of conditions the British had found, and in some cases reflected against the American record. The fighting had raged in the region from September 1944 to March 1945, 'no town or village and a few outbuildings undamaged by shell or bomb'. It was estimated that 10 per cent of the land and forests were littered with unexploded mines. In appendix A of the report, the population situation was summarised. Aachen's total populace was reported at 40,000, down from 165,000 in 1944 and with 60 per cent of housing destroyed. Landkreis Aachen was reported at 90,000, down from 190,000 in 1944 and with 50 per cent of housing destroyed. Jülich's population was reported at 20,000, down from 51,000 in 1944 and with a loss of 70 per cent of housing. Landkreis Düren was reported to be 23,600, down from 119,000 in 1944 and with 80 per cent loss of housing. Düren town was 3,600, down from 50,000 and also with 80 per cent of housing destroyed.[19]

Leslie recognised that the rate of return was uncontrollable, since even the Germans had no idea where Aachen locals were held as refugees, but steady streams were returning from the Rhine areas and Belgium. This had placed pressure on housing, food and health, especially in towns, and the clock was ticking towards the onset of winter, which all parties feared. Leslie had fixed the limit for Aachen at 50,000 and 5,000 for Düren, with the German civilian authorities told to house them in the villages with adequate water supplies. It was hoped Aachen would gradually increase its capacity, but Düren's damage level was too high to sustain such growth. The food prospects would not improve, and the difficult period was set to arrive sometime between July and 1 November

1945. It was believed that the Aachen area had never been self-supporting, and Leslie expected to call on 'supplements from other areas'.

In regard to officials and administration, Colonel Leslie referred to continuing shortages, partly due to the policy of not employing former Nazi members, and partly due to the 'shortage of efficient inhabitants'. The policy over former Nazis was being relaxed to allow 'non-ardent Nazis' to take up less responsible positions. He noted that there had been little 'control and direction' from the RB Aachen level, a direct criticism of US army methods. There was, for example, no coordination between the town and the provinces. The morale of the people varied. On the land it was 'good', as the workers in agriculture and reconstruction was progressing, but in the towns, 'Labour organisation is not satisfactory especially at Aachen'. There had been a significant increase in food queues. Crimes of assault with robbery by Russian DPs included cattle and agricultural produce, with similar complaints against Italian DPs but to a lessor extent. Leslie recommended the swift removal of DPs out of the sector. Their removal would provide 10,000 homes in Aachen and the release of 1,500 homes in the mining area of Alsdorf.

The public safety system was not working, since the German police lacked training and leadership, while Leslie judged the 'material is unsuitable ... inevitable in an area depleted of its population'. A scheme was introduced to raise a police school from police officers in the area. The legal system was 'satisfactory', with the civil court in Aachen 'functioning'. There would be a new court set up in Monschau. The problem, however, was the system could not function without the return of former Nazis, even though limited to junior positions. The fire brigade still suffered from missing equipment and the system was deemed inefficient. The medical and health systems were functioning, but they had taken in former Nazis to maintain their efficiency. The banking system was working, and at least one bank had opened in each community. The return of people had caused pressure on employment, with some idleness because of limited job openings. However, there was a high demand for architects, builders and agricultural labour.

BRITISH MILITARY OCCUPATION

The housing for miners in Alsdorf was a serious problem. Some former Nazis were 'shirking work', but Leslie intended to put a stop to the situation.

There was a high demand for coal and supplements requested called for brown coal in Cologne to be supplied to households. There was a plan for substitutes to coal, and wood was being collected for the winter. There was adequate clothing, but the reserves were small. The local textile factories were destroyed and could not meet the demands. The tramways and railways covering the localities were still far from being restored and repaired in time for winter. A motor pool was organised at the Kreis level to support primary transportation needs, but the problems of collection and distribution in all areas was under pressure. To sustain the existing pool of vehicles, workshops and maintenance teams were set up in the city. An application was being made to return the Englebert tyre factory back into operation for repairing tyres. In July 1945, there were still no brickworks, tile factories or cement suppliers in operation anywhere in the RB Aachen. Consequently, housing programmes were suffering from the lack of building materials and the stores of materials had been exhausted. Huts were being raised to fill the gap. Monschau was being organised to cut 'pit-wood' for pits in Alsdorf. The utilities were still a problem, with the water system in Düren totally destroyed, but elsewhere there were some wells. There had been some cases of typhoid. Sewerage was a major problem and was the main reason why population numbers were being controlled in Aachen, but this was improving, and Düren required an entire new system. The roads were in generally poor condition due to the war damage and lack of maintenance. The clearance of debris continued in Aachen. In rural communities, potholes in roads were being filled in. Electricity was a work in progress, with repairs to the transmission lines to Cologne; the shortage of electricity had affected food production.

Regarding food, Leslie reiterated the point that the area had never been self-sufficient. He estimated no more than 50 per cent of the existing agricultural land would contribute to the 1945 harvest. Cattle were reduced by 65 per cent, there was an acute shortage of horses and there were no food reserves. There were plans being drawn to take supplies for other sectors. This also meant there was an urgent call for agricultural labour. Ration cards had been issued throughout RB Aachen, with a lowering scale of calorie counts across the area. The US army had trained labour for the mines, but they were inefficient and being removed. The mines needed to be cleared to help collect the harvest. Leslie concluded that the Aachen area was destroyed and could not support more than 50 per cent of its original population before April 1946. He also added that it was inadvisable to house people in areas that had not hitherto had inhabitants.[20]

Leslie included a report from 30 June 1945 by Lieutenant Colonel O.M. McConkey on food, agriculture and forestry as an appendix D. He began with food shortages, with a tabulation of the daily rations' calorie deficiencies: Monschau was the highest at 1,168, Aachen was 1,005 calories, but in Aldenhoven village it was down to 570 calories per day. He referred to a assessment by Colonel Wood, who had estimated that rations in the region were 70 per cent deficient. This had led them to make large indents to 21 Army Group for food supplies. The situation had been improving, as food trains began to arrive in the city. On the day of the report, train number 15/TC/018 had arrived, with fifty wagons carrying 657 tons of potatoes, while similar-sized train loads had carried 650 tons of flour to Stolberg and 600 tons of flour to Alsdorf. In a note of hopeful desperation, McConkey wrote of waiting two months for the start of the harvest. Herr Gaul of the German food association was meeting directors of the mines to decide how best to feed coal miners. Plans had been instigated with kitchens and canteens, and stock with food stores. The miners were to receive a minimum ration of 1,150 calories and the 'father breadwinner' an extra allowance of 1,500 calories. Extras were to be provided in the form of canteen meals and sandwiches. There was a common purpose to make the ration scheme work.

Aachen's department of agriculture got some of its records and office equipment back, in some cases from the other side of the Rhine River. The former Nazi leader and his deputies had embezzled or stolen office funds and sold evacuated cattle for over two million Reichsmarks. There was an on-going criminal investigation. There was a desperate need to remove unexploded mines laid in farming areas, and I Corps had requested 100 German soldiers per district to clear mines. Because the region came within the Westwall defence area, the need for soldiers was great and urgent. Local arrangements involved raising mine disposal squads and training farmers. Each Landrat had organised a mine removal committee and, because of the urgency over food, a crop planning committee. The mission was to grow food on every available hectare. A survey of farming and interviews of everyone involved in food production in the entire Aachen area was a work in progress, and the results were expected to help form a coherent food strategy. In regard to forestry, it was recognised that a forestry commission was required. A meeting had been held with Herr Van der Heyden, the acting chief of forestry, and a few remaining officials. The overall mission for food, agriculture and forestry was to identify competent people administered by 'encouragement and giving clear objectives and requiring strict discipline'.[21]

III. De-Nazification

Among the more difficult tasks carried out by the British was the de-Nazification programme. The least satisfactory case concerned Josef Leopold Julius Hirtz, known as *Bubi*, the first post-war Burgermeister of Food, Commerce and Agriculture, under Oppenhoff. There are three studies of Hirtz, two by allied intelligence officers and one recent study of the Aryanisation of the textile industries in Aachen. Two correspond, and the third takes a sympathetic viewpoint. This section provides some insight into the challenges of conducting de-Nazification in Aachen.

In February 1945, Saul Padover interrogated Hirtz, 'a rich, sporty 33-year-old textile manufacture ... with an involved story'. Hirtz's reputation was in question because, though there was little evidence to confirm it, 'he claims to be half-Jew, raised by Jewish step-parents, married to a Catholic woman'. The details Padover received from Hirtz framed his interrogation. Hirtz's step-father was dead, and his step-mother was deported to Poland in 1942.

WAR COMES TO AACHEN

Padover described him as 'a big stocky man who wears ski shoes, loud woollen stockings and knickers, impressed us as being a weak-willed spoiled (step) son of a rich and indulgent (textile) manufacturer'. Padover noticed that Hirtz's default position was, 'I am completely unpolitical, I am a sportsman', and a tennis champion for Aachen. In 1936, his step-parents handed the textile business to him when he was 26 years old—three factories, 450 workers and earnings upwards of 200,000RM annually. There were rumours that he then became an anti-Semite, but Padover could not find evidence to substantiate the claim. Hirtz negotiated large clothing contracts with the army for winter uniforms. Padover emphasised the long-standing friendship with Oppenhoff and Faust, which Hirtz said was not a clique but were his old friends. According to Padover, Hirtz was living with three of his mayor 'pals' in a plush villa, with steam heating and two married women. They had a car and a ration of 18 gallons of fuel per month.

Padover reported his observations on Hirtz's mannerisms and the constant comments that he thought would deflect the Americans. For instance, Hirtz denounced the Versailles myth and Germany being stabbed in the back. Padover wasn't convinced and decided Hirtz, like Oppenhoff, was vehemently anti-labour and pro-capitalist. Hirtz blamed the working class for voting for Hitler. Yet Padover noticed he was challenged by the presence of Nazis in his department. Hirtz responded, 'why, if I had not been a half-Jew, I don't see how it would have been possible for me to stay out of the party'. Padover knew that Hirtz had tried very hard to join the Nazi Party. Hirtz also claimed all his appointments were approved by the US MGO. Hirtz was asked to comment about Dr Heusch, a former *Feldkommandantur* in Russia, who was then facing war crimes charges. Hirtz claimed he was his lawyer and friend and harmless, having been captured by the Americans. Hirtz's plan for the future was to restore the textile industry because people would need warm clothing, which also fitted with Oppenhoff's 'plans for an undemocratic paternalistic industry'. Padover concluded that was he was 'a weak and fawning person' who obeyed Oppenhoff to the letter.[22] Interestingly, Padover did not include all of his criticisms of Hirtz in his book, but it is possible that copies of his reports were passed to the British.

BRITISH MILITARY OCCUPATION

Hirtz either resigned or was dismissed from his mayoral position by the British. He was subject to the denazification process, but his case file remains closed to the public. Andreas Lorenz has described Hirtz sympathetically, a person who suffered at the hands of the Nazis. However, his known record pointed to war profiteering and being a member of the Veltrup clique.[23] While the Americans failed to comprehend the consequences of the clique, the British later confronted other cliques that emerged after its demise. Gitta Sereny has written, 'The recovery of real political and psychological independence and civic responsibility was slow. One must not forget that every aspect of German life had been controlled by the party, and every civic function, whether administration of the Länder (federal states) or of the schools, universities and courts was held by those who could be trusted by the regime.'[24] 'Trusted', in this context, being the pertinent word.

IV. War crimes prosecution

One of the least known and appreciated aspects of British post-war policy has concerned the prosecution and administration of war crimes. The roller-coaster period of British trials began in 1945 and closed in 1949, with exceptions. The total figure included 1,783 individual cases, 1,403 convictions and punishments with 372 executions. Britain employed Albert Pierrepoint, the public executioner, to conduct the executions efficiently and economically. One of the first legal instrument was the War Office's 'Special Army Order' introduced on 18 June 1945. This set the 'Regulations for The Trial of War Criminals' in thirteen points. The warrant defined its working parts in simple and suitably broad terms, leaving the widest possible scope of interpretation:

> 'War Crime' means a violation of the laws and usages of war committed during any war in which His Majesty has been or may be engaged at any time since the 2nd September 1939.
>
> 'Military Court' means a Military Court constituted and held under these Regulations.

The trials of war criminals held under the British jurisdiction followed the court's martial system of military justice. The convening officers of the Military Court were granted the powers of arrest over any person who it 'appears ... committed a war crime'. Point four also ruled that such a person was to be incarcerated pending trial without time limit. The Military Court was constituted of a minimum of two officers, neither of which had to be serving officers in the armed forces. The president of the court was expected to hold the appropriate legal qualifications or at least to be assisted from a Judge Advocate. The courts were open to the public, limited to the capacity of accommodation. The punishments available to the court included fines, confiscation, imprisonment (up to and including life) and death. In the event of a case involving the 'taking, distribution or destruction of money or other property', the court could rule a restitution award or equivalent penalty. In the event of a death penalty, most of the court officials had to concur. Thus, in a court of three, at least a two-thirds majority, and in the case of a larger number, then the decision must include the president. The accused was granted fourteen days to petition the 'Confirming Officer' of the court over the judgement, as long as this was decided within 48 hours of the judgement. The petition and the proceedings were then passed to the Judge Advocate General (or deputy) for 'advice and report'. Once confirmed, the judgement was deemed valid. The Secretary of State for War, or any officer of Major-General rank authorised by the secretary of state, was granted the authority to 'mitigate or remit the punishment thereby awarded or to commute such punishment' within the limits of the original sentencing.

The court could withhold the publication of all or part of the proceedings on the grounds of national interest. Guilt or innocence was to be announced in open court, although acquittal did not entitle the defendant to be immediately released. The final point summarised the intention of this order: 'in these Regulations such course will be adopted as appears best calculated to do justice'. Allied war crimes regulations required the local occupying power to conduct investigations and to prosecute cases, regardless of nationality. From April 1945, Aachen came under British control, and it was the British army that prosecuted the Brady-Phillips case. The first presiding authority was 2nd Army, under the command of General Dempsay; officers were released to conduct investigations and later to form the courts martial. The German defendants and witnesses were initially handled with procedures from British military jurisdiction, but later the courts martial followed the benchmark set by the Nuremberg war crimes tribunal.

Today Heimbach is a small town (approx. pop. 4,000) on the Rur River, a major tributary to the River Meuse. The town is in the Eifel national park but falls within the district of Düren. The town's webpage claims that 80 per cent of the city was destroyed by 1945. The only reference to the Nazi period was the completion of a reservoir that draws water from the Rur and was completed in 1938. On 31 May 1946, the Department of the Judge-Advocate (DJAG) of the British Army of the Rhine (BAOR) in Bad Oeyenhausen issued briefs for a war crimes investigation into the 'Murder of Allied Airmen at Heimbach November or December 1944'. The brief's papers were arranged by an unnamed RAF Group Captain and Lieutenant Colonel J. Leicester Warren. The allegation's covering 'narrative' stated:

> Information has been received from Alex Niessen, a senior police officer in Heimbach (Kreis Schleiden) that an allied airmen who crashed in or near Heimbach in Nov or Dec 44 was murdered by Rademacher who was assisted by Loehrer. Radermacher was the burgomaster of Heimbach and is said to be a fugitive now. Loehrer is an alleged accessory and also comes from Heimbach. Andreas Kuepper is said to be a witness. It is alleged that the body was buried in a bomb crater together with 18 or 20 horses near the Ruhr Bridge at Heimbach.

The instructions with the brief were: to locate and interrogate Radermacher, Loehrer and Küpper; obtain the names of other witnesses; to make the necessary arrests; to locate the airman's bodies, exhume them and await a report from the pathologist on the cause of death; and to obtain any documents to identify the airman.[25] The police officer, Alex Niessen, gave a short summary statement on 11 April 1946, in German, which was then translated by W.G. Bowen SQMS Interpreter, War Crimes Investigation Unit, some weeks later. On 20 June, an arrest warrant was issued for Rademacher, 'former Burgomaster of Heimbach, married; has two children'. Persons known to be of assistance were his father-in-law, Herr Maus, and Frau Zenz, who were both known to live in Düren. On 6 July, Josef Radermacher was arrested in Detmold and placed in custody in No. 5 camp Paderborn. He was not immediately interrogated by 'Haystack', the code name for War Crimes Investigation Unit under Captain B.D. Bone.[26]

Between June and July 1946, British officers from Bad Oeyenhausen descended on Heimbach to investigate the allegations. Heimbach is about 43 miles from Aachen and like Monschau was regarded as integral to the city's affairs. On 10 June, Captain Stephen Beer of the Highland Light Infantry took a sworn statement from Police Officer Niessen (born 1903), originally from Menerath and transferred to Heimbach in September 1944. He claimed he first gave details of the incident to the 'American Commission for the Care of Graves' and was told they would investigate but never returned to Heimbach. On the same day, Beer took a sworn statement from Elisabeth Küpper (born 1920), who claimed to have been told by Andreas Küpper that Rademacher had shot someone. She hadn't heard a shot 'but since the village was under enemy fire, it is possible that shots in the village itself could remain unheard'.

On 11 July, a brief was written for the pathologist. The 'narrative' confirmed that a wounded allied airman was discovered on the farm of Ignaz Juelich in Heimbach on 8 November 1944. The airman was escorted away by a Wehrmacht NCO and Radermacher but to an unknown location. Later, local rumours began to circulate that Radermacher had shot someone, also unknown. Three juveniles witnessed a body floating in water in a bomb crater near the village. They described a man with black wavy hair, wearing a blue suit, with work boots and a haversack (a map was attached but no longer in the file). Later Loehrer, the Burgermeister's clerk, was seen throwing wood into the crater. In December, the carcasses of 18–20 dead horses were also dumped into the crater. The report added, 'it has been suggested that the body may be that of a German deserter'. The pathologist was told to proceed to Heimbach and conduct an exhumation and an examination of the contents in the crater. Details were expected in the event of a human body being discovered.²⁷

On 20 July, Captain R.B. Aptaker of the BAOR-WCIU visited No. 5 Civilian Internment Camp in Paderborn to take a 'statement voluntarily and without coercion' of Josef Rademacher. He was born in Buir in Kreis Bergheim, in November 1902, married in 1924 and was a member of the Nazi Party from December 1930. Rademacher became Heimbach's Bürgermeister when he was 'called to office' in June 1933 and was also made an honorary local judge. He recalled Juelich's daughter arriving at his office because an English or American airman was in their loft. Rademacher told her to return to the farm and he would follow behind; he then went to an NCO stationed in his town and then to get his rifle. They drove to the farm and met Ignaz Juelich, who told them the airman was an English Flight Lieutenant. Rademacher entered the loft to conduct a search when an army car arrived with a colonel who took the airman away; the NCO told him it was his commanding officer, and he had no choice but allow the airman to be taken away. The NCO and Rademacher then drove back to Heimbach. That evening at 21.00 hours, a detachment of fifteen SA troopers arrived in Düren (Lucherberg) and requested accommodation for the night. He gave them the skittle alley in the 'Zur Krone' hotel (Heimbach Eifel Hotel zur Krone was still in existence in the 1950s).

Rademacher told the SA troop leader that 'west workers (slave workers)' might also be accommodated in the hotel but there were no other rooms in the town. Then the troop leader told Rademacher that the prisoners were in his office and the airman was with them. The troop leader objected to the presence of the airman and asked if he should no longer be treated as a prisoner. Rademacher claimed he cut him short and told him it was a Wehrmacht matter. The leader again requested Rademacher should join them in the hotel, but he said it was not necessary; meanwhile, the rest of the SA detachment had followed them and had lined up by the Inn Schifmann. In the office, Rademacher found five prisoners and the airman. He recalled they were being guarded by an SA man. A senior NCO then arrived with a lorry and said he needed to collect the prisoners but asked whether the SA could supply a guard for the journey. The SA were reluctant to assist, and the local Nazi leader's office didn't offer their assistance. Rademacher claimed he went for a meal and found the NCO had collected all the prisoners (50) in the Fraikin Hall. Then a military truck arrived with a lieutenant and soldiers and searched the prisoners; most had frozen feet. Then Rademacher left and that was the last they saw of the airman, who was supposedly taken to the field dressing station at Mariawald. According to Rademacher, several days later the senior NCO told him that a rumour was circulating that he had shot a British lieutenant. Later, his wife informed him that a body had been seen in the bomb crater. He asked Loehrer to fill the crater with wood before the crater was to be filled by the Volksturm. Rademacher then pondered whether the pilot was wounded. He recalled a bomber had crashed in the district of Vlatten and four or five dead bodies had been recovered. The bodies were left lying at the site for two weeks. He had received orders to cordon off crash sites and leave the Wehrmacht to conduct their investigations. He pressed the civilian authorities to resolve the issue by getting the bodies buried in a local cemetery. They took the identities of the aircrew from their documents before they were buried. As to dead horses, Rademacher did recall six dead horses near the crater and the police recommended they be buried in the crater. The horses were buried by Josef Schiffmann, the innkeeper, and Josef Nase, another local. There were other craters, mostly caused by the carpet-bombing on the town.[28]

Captain R.B. Aptaker of the BAOR-WCIU took sworn depositions on 26 July. On the same day, Apatker took a deposition from Andreas Küpper (born 1915) from Heimbach and a 'commercial employee'. He walked past the crater and met Elisabeth Küpper from Heimbach. She told him that there had been something going on and that someone had been finished off (shot) near the crater. He returned to the crater to find Herr Loehrer throwing rubbish and wood into the hole. Loehrer allegedly told Küpper that if he didn't throw the stuff into the crater that 'he might come up again'. Juepper looked around the crater but could not see any bodies, so he walked away. He was evacuated from the town in December

BRITISH MILITARY OCCUPATION

1944. Josef Schiffmann (born 1896), from Hetzingerhof, claimed he was informed by the Bürgermeister's office to bury dead horses in a bomb crater by the Rur. The carcasses were lying across the road to Mariawald. Fladt Willi, Josef Naas and Josef Kruff, all from Heimbach, had been working on anti-tank obstacles and they helped bury the horses. After he came back from evacuation in the summer of 1945, he was told the rumour that the airman was in the crater. Josef Naas (born 1910) from Heimbach confirmed much of Schiffmann's account, except he was told by Rademacher and Dohmann to throw the horses into the crater. He heard the rumour of the body with the black hair: 'I intended to make sure myself, but I was afraid because I might have been put against the wall.' Matthias Bongard (born 1896), from Heimbach, claimed that on 22 or 23 November 1944 he asked several coachmen to bury 18 dead horses. Several times, horse carcasses were taken to the crater and thrown in. As a police official he was responsible for such jobs, and it was only after his return from evacuation that he heard the stories of the corpse.

Wilhelm Blankenheim (born 1904), from Kirchheim, had been assigned to work duties on fortifications but in his spare time assisted Ignaz Juelich, a farm owner. One day in autumn 1944 he had gone to the loft to collect hay for the cattle and found a wounded airman asleep. He woke the airman and searched him for weapons and because of the wounds helped him with his boots. He called for Herr Jülich and they carried the airman out of the loft and took him to the kitchen. Frau Juelich gave him a cup of coffee with milk, but he refused food. A daughter fetched Rademacher, who wanted to know if there were others, and the loft was searched. An NCO then took the airman to a car and eventually together with Rademacher they drove away. The airman was described as 1.70 metres tall, blonde, between 22 and 24 years of age, wearing a grey-brown flying suit and 'long shafted yellow shoes', and under search he placed a large silver ring on the kitchen table. Then Apatker took a deposition from Ignaz Juelich (born 1897) from Vlatten, a local district of Heimbach. He recalled that the incident took place on 8 November 1944 at about 16.00. The airman said he was an American, flying a P38 Lightning, and was shot down over Zuelpich. He had been in the loft for days, living off water and fruit. Rademacher had arrived with an NCO but also a senior German officer, who had remained in the car. They took the airman to the Cremers' house, where he was fed and then later taken to the hospital in Mariawald. Susanne Cremer (born 1924), from Heimbach, confirmed she came home to find the wounded airman drinking coffee and eating bread. German soldiers were billeted in the house, and they took him to sit on the balcony. Later, a colonel took him to the hospital in Mariawald. She added that it had nothing to do with the Nazi Party and was handled as a Wehrmacht matter. Cremer confirmed the airman was blonde and tall, and added that his eyes were bloodshot, he had a wristwatch on his left hand and wore a ring and was limping with one leg.[29]

In his report of the investigations, Aptkar accepted that an airman had been captured, taken away by a Wehrmacht colonel, and then taken to a field dressing station. Three children did see a body in the crater and had a reasonable description of what they had seen. The horses were buried in the crater, and this was based on three witnesses. Aptkar awaited the pathologist report. There was little information on the Gestapo in Heimbach and the details of the airman remained obscure. There was no similarity between the body in the crater and the airman. A final report was written on 21 September 1946 by an unnamed lieutenant colonel, who recommended the release of Rademacher. He explained that rumours had spread in the village of Heimbach/Aachen that an allied airman had been shot. There was little doubt the airman had been taken to a hospital in Mariawald. However, Rademacher went to his office at 21.00 hours and the airman was there but all the prisoners were taken away; 'no evidence in support of, or to disprove, this story has been found, Rademacher being the only one to state he saw the airman again'. The crater was opened under the orders of Major Mant, Royal Army Medical Corps, and the remains of eighteen horses were found but no trace of a corpse. Thus: 'no one has proof that the airman, or any other person, was shot; the descriptions of the airman and the crater body do not match, and there were no traces in the crater other than horses'. The colonel concluded that 'in the absence of evidence to the contrary one must believe Rademacher's statement'.[30]

BRITISH MILITARY OCCUPATION

V. *The Aachen case*

The defendants—August Flasche, Johann Bergmann, Johannes Konstantin Schwenke, Johann Wink, Jacob Kappes and Gottfried Fiesler—were read the offence charged:

> Commiting a War Crime in that they At AACHEN on or about 9 August 1944 in violation of the laws and usages of war, were concerned in the ill-treatment of two unidentified Allied Airmen, prisoners of war.

A file was compiled of prosecution documents. The facts of the case corrected, there were no Pathfinder aircraft involved and other minor details. The investigating officers had drawn a map of the incident over a 1:13,000 street map of Aachen. There were defendants' letters, lists of the seventeen witnesses and their witness statements, and notes for the US War Crimes Liaison Detachment attached to the BAOR, as the British army of occupation was being dubbed. The case had been investigated by the British army, an American officer and the German police. The entire Aachen police force was identified, listed and set against the charges where appropriate. During those investigations, a witness made a statement about former SS-Brigadefüher and Police President Carl Zenner and his murderous behaviour in Soviet Russia, in one of those moments, as so often happened in war crime investigations, which unearthed the details of Holocaust crimes. Pages were duplicated, triplicated and rubber stamped umpteen times.[31]

On 26 July 1946, the instructions for the case were issued. It would be heard in Bochum in a courtroom organised by the Military Court system of 320 MGD. The Permanent President of War Crimes Trials was Lieutenant Colonel Stanton of the King's Own Scottish Borderers. The court martial board included: Major W.G. Lowther (8th Hussars), Major P.A.L. Vaux (5th Royal Tanks), Major R.E. Worsley (Rifle Brigade) and Captain R.F. Lether MC (5th Dragoon Guards) as well as the 'waiting member', Captain J.E. Deighton (1st Royal Tanks). The accused were held on remand at Recklinghausen Camp and were again informed of the charges.

WAR COMES TO AACHEN

The 53rd (W) Infantry Division ensured the accused were seen by a medical officer before the trial, and to arrange the courtroom. The German lawyers for the defendants (Flasche, Bergmann and Wink) were Heinrich Kutsch, Gerhard Heusch and Dr Herbert Wallichs. The lawyers Dr Ernst Nellen, Dr Heinz Beginnen and Dr Steenhauer, all from Düsseldorf, defended Kappes, Fiesler and Schwenke.[32]

The investigation file, as so often, includes the grim mugshots of the perpetrators, the defendants and a few witnesses, as well as more maps, detailing the progress from the crash of the aircraft to their arrival at the police headquarters. The photographs along the route, where people were standing and a drawing of the room where they were received add to the grimness of the case. Finally, after investigations and interrogations, there is the testimony of the flyers. On 31 August 1945, when Technical Sargeant John Cecil Phillips was interviewed by Special Argent Willian A. Allen of the Security Intelligence Corps, he was living in Greenville, South Carolina. He lived with his parents, was born in 1920, graduated from high school and started life as a carpenter and painter before entering the army. After his release, he had returned to the USA on 17 July 1945. He was placed in Stalag Luft 6, but was then transferred to Stalag Luft 4 in East Prussia, then transferred to Stalag Luft 357 at Fallingbostel. He confirmed the events of being with Sergeant Brady when they were attacked and stoned by civilians. He confirmed the details of the mission discussed in chapter six. He recalled how well the Luftwaffe soldiers looked after them. His memory of the perpetrators was a little more vague. Former Staff Sergeant Alvin William Brady was already back living as a civilian when he was interviewed on 2 February 1946, in Worcester, Virginia, by Walter G. Abromovich, a Special Agent of the SIS. He was born in Maryland in 1924, had been married since 1942 and had recently qualified for college entrance under the government test. His job before the army was as a clerk in the time-keeping office of the Glenn L. Martin Company (the aircraft manufacturer). He had arrived back in the USA in May 1945, and he had a vague recollection of PoW camps before finally arriving in Stalag Luft 1 in Berlin. Brady confirmed Phillips's account, but there were detailed differences of recollections. He

BRITISH MILITARY OCCUPATION

believed he could identify the main perpetrator, the Gestapo chief. Unusually in the file, there is a photograph of an unnamed Luftwaffe soldier.

In Phillips's written statement, he recalled they were on a mission to Munich when their aircraft was forced to turn back and hit by flak at around 10.00 hours. He recalled they were driven to a cemetery (*Ehrenfriedhof*) and the Germans pointed and shouted but they were unable to understand them. They were taken to the centre of Aachen to be exhibited; the crowds were sullen at first. Then the Gestapo chief whipped up the crowd. They began to hurl bricks and rubble. Brady was hit on the left rear side of his head with a brick, thrown with some force, causing a two-inch gash as blood spurted. This caused long-term concussion and he continued to complain of headaches through their captivity until release at the end of the war. Phillips was told to 'pick up the filthy swine' and carry him to the police presidium. They arrived at the building at about 02.00 hours. Brady lay on the floor bleeding and receiving random kicks, as the Germans interrogated Phillips. At around 17.30 hours, a Luftwaffe officer and guard arrived and took both men into custody. They located a pushcart for Brady and wheeled him to the main railway station. They were put in a normal compartment beside regular passengers. At the first stop, 20 minutes later, the officer found bandages and a canteen of beer. The train arrived in Cologne at 21.00 hours, and the men were taken to a Luftwaffe supply depot to receive medical attention.[33]

A remarkable feature of the Brady-Phillips case is how the story continually changed, and the social demography. When Captain H.P. Kinsleigh, Cheshire Regiment, issued a JAG case for the British court in Bochum on 30 January 1946, he had different details. His case report stated that a 'twin-engined Pathfinder aircraft with a crew of nine crashed near Schmidhof water works after striking high tension cables'. One body was found dead in the aircraft, the others parachuted and one believed to have escaped through Holland. Brady and Phillips landed near the Kerres' house, who took them into custody with a local police officer called Bock. Brady was wounded and taken into the house to bathe his ankle. Bock telephoned his headquarters to report the incident. At midday, four members of Aachen *Kripo* (criminal police)—Bergmann, Wink, Stoeber and Muss—arrived by car. Wink struck Brady in the face and reprimanded the police officer for giving aid to the enemy. The two were then driven to the outskirts of Aachen and made to walk through the streets to the police headquarters, barefoot with their arms raised. They were attacked and stoned by the civilian population on the encouragement of the Kripo officers. The men were beaten in the police headquarters and then were collected by Lw-Senior Sergeant Kremer from a flak detachment, who took the men to *Fliegerhorst Butweilerhof* in Cologne. After that, there had been no trace of the men.

Kinsleigh had already identified the perpetrators. Flasche had 'instructed the Jagdkommando to the airmen, to march them through the town in order to give the civilian population an opportunity to lynch them'. Schwenke ordered the police not to interfere if the civilians tried to lynch them. Bergmann was the senior office of the Jagdkommando. Wink 'probably' struck one of the victims in the house. The civilians cited in the case included Beus, who threw stones and potatoes at the men; Fiesler, who threw cobblestones at the men; Jacobs, who incited the crowd to violence; Kappes, who threw cobblestones and roof tiles and caused a head wound; and Kremer, who was charged with negligence.

One of the first witnesses was Ewald Weber, born in 1907 and the Kriminalsekretär of Aachen, on 21 March 1946. He gave details of how the Kripo operated and explained that Himmler's RSHA had instructed the police to raise Jagdkommandos to hunt down enemy airmen, including in Aachen, in 1943. Weber could recall that Bock was the first arresting officer. He also claimed the chief of the ARP Hauptmann Zimmermann requested to collect the men but was refused. Several Kriminalsekretär witnesses, including Rudolf Stieler (born 1904) and Erich W. Buechner (born 1903), were serving in Aachen during the summer of 1944, but could only recall Dr Schwenke instructing that all enemy aircrew must be protected from civilians mistreating them. Anneliese Huerten (born 1922) was a telephonist in the ARP command post when the incident happened, and she recalled police president Flasche saying that 'the people shall judge the fate of these enemy airmen'. August

BRITISH MILITARY OCCUPATION

K.H. Zernikow (born 1888) was a retired police officer on duty when Bock's call was received and recalled passing on the call to Heimich. Leonhard Josef Heimich (born 1890) gave his witness statement confirming the reporting of the arrest of two airmen.

Anton Henkel (born 1912) was a uniformed police warrant officer. He was on leave in May and June because his mother was killed in an air raid. He heard that Lieutenant Muss was the leader of the Jagdkommando and ordered to collect the airmen. Muss had lost his wife and three or four children during an air raid. It was at the time when Goebbels was rabble rousing over the treatment of enemy aircrew. Henkel volunteered to be the driver because he was concerned and wanted to drive the men to the Luftwaffe command post. Muss refused and when he returned mentioned he had struck both airmen. Henkel claimed that, despite Muss and Goebbels' propaganda, the people were more hateful towards the Nazis.

Leo Kerres (born 1902) was the house owner but also the local Ortsbauernführer (district farmer leader). He was being visited by uniformed police officer Bock in normal duties when the aircraft crashed. Two other farmers had also been involved in arresting the airmen: Leo Ahn and Josef Rademacher. Then a stranger arrived wearing SS trousers and a pullover, carrying a pistol and threatening to shoot the airmen. Then another person arrived called Fuerst, who spoke English and translated for Bock. The crewmen told Bock that they were Pathfinders and had not carried bombs. After Bock called, a police car arrived. Kerres heard the wash basin roll across the floor and thought, 'what our prisoners being made guests and being bathed here?' Then the airman was struck and bleeding from his mouth. The men were kicked as they were put in the car. Bock and Kerres were then interrogated by a Gestapo officer called Hansen.

Josef Bock (1893) was a retired police officer from Aachen. During 1944, he was the police officer responsible for the Aachen-Lichtenbusch district. He believed he saw the aircraft break away from the squadron and begin circling downwards and crashed 100 metres from the waterworks. He recalled twenty or thirty people milling around, but could not remember who they were. They secured the airmen, one he believed had a dislocated leg, and he

251

gathered their parachutes. He could remember the uninjured airman was Phillips. Someone in the crowd could speak English and he translated the details about the Pathfinders. The men were given water and they bathed the foot of the injured man. A further squadron of aircraft flew over and they dropped ten bombs—there were fatal casualties—and he was required to assist. Concerned about the growing ill-feeling, he left a member of the Wehrmacht called Haupts, from Trierstrasse and living with widow Struwe, who was on leave, and Bock left the men in his protection and returned forty-five minutes later. The airmen still had not been collected. He informed his headquarters and reported the air raid. Then Kriminal-Kommissar Bergamnn and Obersekretär Wink arrived and told the men to stand. One didn't move fast enough and was struck. The bowl was kicked away and Bock was accused of giving them water and a foot bath and Wink said 'this might be a convalescent home'. The men were made to take their shoes off and then led to the car. He travelled with them in the car to Eupenerstrasse, where he got on his tram. The last thing he saw was the men being made to walk before the car in the streets. Two days later, he and Kerres were forced to attend the Gestapo and were threatened with concentration camps and death penalties. Julius Schorn said in his deposition: 'A crowd of about 50–80 people followed ... I saw several children throwing stones inside the Police headquarters.'

Josef Haller (born 1896) witnessed the start of the mistreatment in Kasinostrasse by the air-raid shelter as a Gestapo agent incited the crowd. Gottfried Fiesler (1928) threw cobblestones, and his sister Helene Beus joined in. Paul Kappers (1926), the son of former political chief Peter Kappers, threw cobblestones and bricks. They progressed from Kasinostrasse, Schleife, Normaluhr, Hindenburgstrasse and Bahhofstrasse. Men of a *Wehrkommando* shouted 'shame' at the crowd, but were powerless with the Gestapo presence. Hermann Lenz (born 1899), a worker, witnessed all of the same as Josef Haller, but added that a labourer called Jakobs was inciting the crowd. At the officers' mess at Bahnhofstrasse, two officers tried to stop the mistreatment. He saw Muss push the two men to the ground and stamp on them.

BRITISH MILITARY OCCUPATION

Hubertine Rodenbusch (1921), a housewife, came out of the Kasinostrasse bunker when the all-clear sounded. The men were walking past barefooted. She claimed to show her disgust at their behaviour. Later, Beus reported her to the Gestapo. Wihelm Dressen (born 1903), a Kriminalbeamter, was a Kriminalsekretär with the Aachen Kripo. He thought the date was 9 July but remembered all the details and the names of the people involved. He was in room 440 in the police headquarters and heard a piercing scream. He was warned by his senior officer Eickhoff not to interfere. There was a crowd of people and the two airmen. He recalled the mistreatment and the arrival of the Luftwaffe soldier. Max Leo Julius Jantz (born 1884) was a retired Kripo secretary. In the summer of 1944, he was in the Kripo in Aachen. He recalled it was a hot summer's day and his window was open and he heard screams. The Kripo officers Bergmann and Wink were leading the two airmen being stoned. Being on the second floor, he could not recognise anybody. Ernst Mechelke (born 1885) was a Kripo officer. He was ill and not on duty. He knew of the Jagdkommando and the men involved. He accused Muss of the mistreatment. He attended a conference where Dr Schwenke was believed to have said it was a regret the airmen were brought to the police station alive and should have been lynched by the public.

Hermann Nickel (1886) was a retired Kripo officer. He was the adjutant to Kriminaldirektor Dr Schwenke. Secret orders arrived from Berlin for the treatment of enemy flyers. He claimed the order stated that, where civilians attacked enemy airment, the police officials were not to interfere. He went into room 437 and saw the two airmen lying on the floor: one had no shoes and his feet were bleeding. When he asked who did this, Wink shrugged his shoulders. Wilhelm Josef Tings (born 1897) was a Catholic and a uniformed police officer. In the summer of 1944, he was the chief transport officer at the Aachen police station. He allocated a driver and a vehicle for the job, but Muss had taken over himself. He added 'Muss was very much of a man who went on his own, and rather a stong egotist'. He also managed to avoid service at the front. Gertrud Hammers (1899) was a Catholic housewife. She was an attendant in the police building and recalled the two airmen arriving: 'We were inquisitive to see them but were forbidden from entering the room.' She recalled the Lw NCO from the flak came and collected them. Peter Klinkenberg (born 1907) was a tailor. In the summer of 1944 before the evacuation, on the day he was in the transport office, he claimed he spoke to Muss, who told him about mistreating the airmen. Theo Schweden (born 1907) was a Catholic businessman. He claimed that he had made a report of the incident to the Americans on 18 May 1945. He didn't know who was involved, but he saw the men being beaten and also getting on the train. The injured man was taken in a wheelbarrow to the Hauptbahnhof.

Magdalene Maria Beus, a Roman Catholic born on 12 January 1929 in Aachen, was 15 when the incident took place:

> In summer 1944 two enemy airmen who had landed by parachute were led to the Kasinostrasse. I was in the vicinity of the air-raid shelter. The officials of the Gestapo who were accompanying the prisoners encouraged us to throw stones at the airmen. I too, was asked to do this, and picked up a potato which I threw, though I hit nothing.

On 6 September 1946, Major Hodgkinson, the prosecuting officer, filed a report of the case—it opened on 13 August and terminated on 5 September 1946. The accused had all pleaded 'not guilty'. The case against Kappes was stopped because at the time of the incident he was 13 years old by reasons of *doli incapx* (deemed incapable of forming the intent to commit a crime by reason of age), but his case was retained for a further higher command decision. Fiesler was found not guilty but held in camp for confirmation of the finding. The rest were all found guilty.

10

IMPOSING THE RAJ

In September 1944, the War Office in London opened a topographical file on Aachen. The file includes an interesting mix of documents, such as a 1930s Pharus Plan of Aachen streets, and the report shows which German handbooks were scrutinised. Aachen's geography, political, economic and cultural, were integrated into the report and illustrated a degree of naïveté. The report referred to the photographs from the post-air raid reconnaissance flights from 12–13 July 1943 and 11 April 1944 and added:

> Aachen is a former coronation city and the ancient capital of the Holy Roman Empire; its hot sulphur springs have been famous for centuries and it had a large tourist industry.
>
> The inner town, which is compact, closely built-up and densely populated, is circular, with a diameter of about 1 mile. The north-eastern half of the circle is bounded by broad avenues, formerly the sites of the city walls, of which only certain gates now remain.[1]

That cultural centre had been largely destroyed in the air raids. The densely populated streets were flattened. The three railway stations and railways were mentioned but not the Vennbahn. The fourteen German army buildings and the seven Nazi Party offices, including the SA's offices in Nizzallee near the Rütscher Strasse bunker, were neatly identified, as were all the banks, hotels, Nazi agencies, schools, municipal departments and places of interest. The appendix to the report included twenty-six photographs from pre-war Aachen. It was a study of a soon-to-be-dead city.

The only official British engagement with Aachen on the record concerned a strange incident on the frontier. In March 1939, Sir William Lawther (1889–1976), a British trade unionist, was strip searched by Aachen border guards. The incident took place at the former Herbestahl railway station on the German-Belgian frontier. The station was levelled and replaced by Welkanraedt on the Belgian railway network. At the time, Lawther was acting president of the Miner's Federation of Great Britain and an agent for the Durham Miners' Association. He was homeward bound from attending a conference of the Miners' International in Cracow (Poland). Lawther was indignant at his treatment and had told the *Sunday Times*: 'On leaving Poland he made the usual customs declaration, but at Aachen he was taken to a room on the station platform, detained for an hour, and ordered to strip. All his belongings were examined, including the handle of his shaving brush and the rubber pads on his shoes. The result was the train left without him.'[2] On 14 March, John Evan, the General Secretary of the Executive Committee of the Durham Miners' Association, wrote to Foreign Secretary Lord Halifax to 'lodge our most vigorous protest against German officers for the unwarrantable treatment meted out to Mr. W. Lawther'. The committee made a request to Halifax to make enquiries and to stop this kind of treatment against trade unions transacting their official business and travelling through Germany.[3] On 15 March, William Whiteley (1882–1955), Labour MP for Durham, questioned Prime Minister Neville Chamberlain in Parliament over whether he would 'protest against this action and thus prevent similar treatment'. R.A.B. Butler replied on the prime minister's behalf, and parliamentary discussion followed among several MPs, but was concluded with a call for more information.

The Foreign Office replied to Evan on 20 March that Halifax was prepared to act once he received full details of the incident.[4] The next day, Lord Halifax issued a request for a report on the incident, with Evan's letter enclosed, to the Consul-General in

Cologne and sent a copy to the embassy in Berlin.[5] On 23 March, the Consul-General wrote to the *Zollfahndungsstelle*, in Aachen, requesting an explanation of why Lawther was strip-searched. Before receiving a reply, he wrote to Lord Halifax explaining that the 'Customs authorities possess the right of search according to German law.'[6] Meanwhile, the *Zollfahndungsstelle* in Aachen confirmed it had received the request and passed it on to the Hauptzollamt Bahnofsplatz, also in Aachen, to reply, as they were responsible for the incident.[7] There was another comment raised in Parliament and Butler confirmed that inquiries were in progress.[8] On 31 March, the Hauptzollamt Bahnofsplatz wrote to the Consul-General confirming an earlier telephone conversation in which *Oberzollinspektor* Katzenberger explained it was a 'customary sample search as laid down by German Exchange regulations'. The letter included a mild rebuke of the *Sunday Times* for its entirely misleading story. The reason why Lawther missed his train was not the border guards' search but the railway authorities, after being made aware of the search, deciding they could no longer hold up the train and departed. The German officials were regretful that Lawther had missed his train.[9] R.A.B. Butler wrote to Lawther on 8 April 1939, and reiterated his reply made in the Commons and went on to explain that the British government had no grounds to issue a complaint against the German government. He wrote: 'I am afraid, however, that this sort of inconvenience is being caused to travellers at many frontiers throughout the world today.'[10]

Frontiers have gradually disappeared from geopolitical discourse with the rise of the European Union, and Aachen became part of the Meuse-Rhine Euroregion in 1976. The centrality of this region is highlighted by a total population of four million people, which formulates a common regional concept between Aachen, Liège, Maastricht and surrounding territories—about 4,200 square miles. From 1945, the British military occupation attempted to police this zone, not only for law-and-order purposes, but also against smuggling and black market offenses. The policing of Aachen and surrounding territories forced the British to make compromises on its determination to 'educate' the Germans to be 'better people'. In this chapter, the focus lies on law and order, and education—the struggle to bring a shattered community to some form of acceptable level of socialisation and the failure of the British to break a long-standing Aachen tradition.

I. Social crime

In appendix B of Colonel Leslie's report (refer to chapter nine), Major Hirst summarised the legal situation. The military court in Aachen had, since 15 June, handled the following cases (totals): curfew cases (3), border crossing (2), unlawful possession (2), false statements (3), brawling (1), travel without a pass (1), theft and supplying troops with liquor (1) and looting (24). It was noted that prosecutors received inadequate arrest reports from frontier and security guards. The German courts were working properly, with theft, the illegal slaughter of animals and selling food above the regulated prices being the main cases. The worst feature was the backlog, with 131 cases still outstanding. These had been moved to increase the capacity of the court. The prison was monitored regularly, with counts of inmates. There had been 25 released under US board review; they received long sentences for harbouring in the city during the fighting in the rural areas to the east. The British took over the review process. There had been 12 political arrests but received no charges and 9 were released on the orders of the Oberburgermeister. The Field Security officers were awaited because 40 persons were detained in the prison on orders from US CIC, and some were alleged to be war criminals. German lawyers had been requesting permission to work and Nazi Party membership was no longer a reason to be denied a permit. Hirst concluded with some trace of empathy:

> In my view, considering the shortage of food and bad housing conditions of the people, both conditions being aggravated by thousands returning from across the Rhine, I do not think the incidence of crime is at present high. Looting remains the most common crime.[11]

The MGO court in Aachen officially began work under British judges at 10.00 on 31 May 1945. The sitting president of the court was Colonel H. Brown OBE, with Lieutenant Colonel

F.D. Richardson and Major C.H.R.B. Sommerville serving as members of the court. The court came within Corps District. Corps headquarters issued the orders for the court to stand, and two registers of cases were maintained through the occupation. British registers were organised differently from the US army and included all cases heard by the court with dismissals and referrals. There is evidence that small cases or misdemeanours were conducted in bulk form and were not registered. The court registers are not complete, with the entire month of August missing (possibly because the court didn't sit); not all the ages, sex and nationality of defendants are entered, and some cases were referred but never closed. The ages of juveniles were initially posted in the register, which possibly meant the rest were simply regarded as adults. However, trends such as growing juvenile delinquency led to the general input of all ages, sex and nationality by December 1945. The serious crimes were mostly firearms related, with the 'unlawful possession of arms' and the use of weapons being the most common. The sentences reflected the seriousness of offences in the mindset of the military occupiers. This has to be set against the background of caution since Oppenhof's assassination, the general allied contempt held for Germans since Belsen was liberated and the demands to maintain security partly explain some of the sentencing.

In one register, there were more than 95 serious sentences issued by the British MGO central court from 31 May 1945 to December 1946. The first case was heard and judged on 31 May 1945, when Heinrich Schifenhövel was given a one-year prison sentence with fourth months suspended for the 'unlawful possession of arms'. Eleven days later, Josef Schon received a three-year prison sentence for 'assisting' and 'failing to report' members of the German armed forces. The average age of the 83 persons' known ages was 30. The only female was Käthe Forster, represented by Dr Heusch, who received a three-month prison sentence for being in the 'unlawful poseession of arms'. The youngest were both 15 year-olds. Peter Dederichs was found guilty of being in the 'unlawful possession of a firearm', but his father was found guilty, fined 600RM and bound over as guarantor of the boy's good behaviour for two years. The other was also German, Erich Laossat at

15, and was found guilty on 27 August 1946 of being involved in smuggling with an armed gang. (In all, eleven men, probably all from the same gang, were found guilty.) He was found guilty of possessing weapons, as was G.G. Petrick, aged 16. Both were given three-year prison sentences in juvenile detention. The oldest was Wilhelm Frohn, a 70-year-old German, charged with being in the 'unlawful possession of a firearm' and given a one-year prison sentence or a 500RM fine, which was paid on 4 December 1946.[12] The noticeable change in the sentencing concerned how juveniles were initially bound over into their parents' care, but by the end of the year sentences involved juvenile detention.

In the second register of all cases from May to December 1945, there are some indicative trends: May–June—93 cases, July—73, September—114 (possibly including a spill-over from August's unheard cases), October—115, November—134 and December 146. In June, there were 24 women, all adults; in July, there were 24 women (two aged 14 and 15); but in September, the number of female cases increased to 38, with the age range 15–62. From October, it is possible to look at some specific trends. In October, there were 115 cases including: 40 women, four Poles, eleven Dutch, three Belgians, two Luxembourgers, four stateless and a French person. By November, the cases had increased to 134, of crimes such as border offences, curfew offences, fraudulent identity papers, being in possession of allied forces materials and likely to prejudice good order. There were 52 women, three Belgians, fourteen Dutch, one Pole, a Hungarian and two listed as 'stateless'. In December 1945, the numbers increased again to 146, including 51 women and several non-German nationals. The average age was 30, with fifteen teenagers in the 15–19 age range, and the eldest was 58.[13] The scale of this activity when compared against the overall average population in RB Aachen, in 1945, of 675 cases within a population of 40,000 reveals how social crimes had become a major headache for the British.

II. Regulating a European frontier

Seven years after the Lawther incident, the British arranged the administration of border controls on the frontier with Belgium and Holland.[14] On 18 January 1946, Major G.B.W. Woodroffe (responsible for finance and administration) in 227 Detachment (Aachen Regierungsbezirk) replied to a questionnaire issued by Headquarters Mil. Gov. North Rhine Region to evaluate their overall situation regarding border controls (*Zollgrenzschutz*). The questions asked ranged from number of staff to quarters and equipment. They had thirty fully trained staff to guard five road crossings. There was no training for German staff because they had yet to be employed. The former German border staffs were no longer capable of employment, and it was expected to circulate at least 700 job questionnaires (*Frageboden*) if they were going to employ 344 Germans. They were not hopeful of positive results, as screening had identified how acute the staffing problem would be. There was an acute shortage of living quarters, and where there were border posts, many Germans were using them for shelter and sleep. In regard to equipment, they had a few telephones and bicycles but no cars or binoculars.[15] The reason for this interest in border controls was explained in a survey report of the Aachen frontier: 'The Approximate mileage of the RB Aachen frontier is given as 120; this figure is incorrect and should read 150. It is further noticed that although RB Aachen is the longest of all, it has the lowest allocation of Customs personnel.' The report argued for a threefold increase of staff in comparison with Münster, which was smaller, less complex, more wooded and with a greater population in the frontier areas. The report noted that in 1932 there had been 500–600 frontier guards, which had increased to 1,200 in 1934.[16] The record of the British frontier controls and regulations in Aachen, during the period 1946 to 1950, is virtually complete and represents the largest surviving collection of documents from Aachen.

By the beginning of 1946, the British were experienced enough to categorise those persons most likely to conduct smuggling. The first group was 'Frontaliers': persons in receipt of permits to regularly cross the border in their work. There had been 350 Frontaliers issued and more than 200 had gone to German railway personnel, mostly working coal trains into Belgium. Another 1,200 Frontaliers had been issued to Dutch forestry workers. Both groups of workers were crossing the border and British guards were 'thin on the ground' and there was known to be smuggling but it was deemed harmless. Belgian troops were the next category. There were two battalions of Belgian Fusiliers on the Belgium side of the border assisting the Gendarmerie and customs officials. On the German side, there was another battalion based in Monschau that carried out border patrols under the supervision of the 4th battalion Coldstream Guards—'it is considered these troops indulge in smuggling and black-market activity on a very large scale'. It was claimed that the Belgian soldiers visited towns in Belgium selling goods and earning a lot more money than their military pay. The problem was made more difficult because looting in Germany was regarded as a form of returning property taken by the Nazis during the occupation. The British military were also concerned that the presence of the Belgian troops was worsened because German border guards had no jurisdiction to arrest them. Belgian civilians 'are the main offenders and are definitely organised in bands'. Their main contraband was coffee. Dutch civilians had shown little interest in working in the German black market. US army personnel were handled by US army MPs posted on the frontier to assist in maintaining good relations after a previous incident involving British border guards. The US MPs in Verviers and Liège, however, were only checking tickets and ignoring loot coming into Belgium. British military personnel, 'a minor element is doubtlessly smuggling goods over the border in very small quantities'. This had reduced further during the imposition of travel restrictions. German civilians were generally not smuggling; they knew the 'the severe penalties for this activity and are scared'.[17]

By 24 June 1946, the German customs posts had arrested 276 persons for illegally attempting to cross the Prohibited Frontier Zone, which had been in place since 1945. The cause of the illegal activity was the worsening food situation and the problems over falling rations. The first monthly report in June 1946 was quite detailed. There had been a drop in smuggling activities from the Belgian border but an increase along the Dutch border. Officers of the FCS had conducted wide-ranging patrols and had caught or arrested several people, including a 'most interesting case of tungsten smuggling'. There were an increasing number of juveniles smuggling (430 for the period); parents were held responsible for their children and given criminal sentences. The old German border railway station at Herbesthal had since been annexed by Belgium, but an agreement was made that it would be employed by Belgian customs officials to control Belgian army trains. Five German officials had been dismissed, one for lying, another 'for having carnal knowledge with a young girl' and would receive 'ten years penal servitude' and the other three for 'normal' disciplinary offences. Along the Dutch border, there had been two violent incidents where civilians had tried to wrestle the guns out of German customs officials' hands. In one case, an official was stabbed in the leg and his rifle stolen. There was concern over whether to allow the Germans to use their weapons, albeit recognising it was 'an extremely delicate matter' so close to the end of the war.[18]

The first full report of the FCS in RB Aachen was issued on 28 June 1946. There was a sense of success after a draft of a hundred German officials had been assigned to the area, leading to an immediate reduction in smuggling. British guards had gone out on patrol. In December 1946, a major concern of the FCP was the tensions caused by customs controls of US military personnel. The reluctance of Belgian and Dutch officials to examine US personnel before crossing into Germany meant subsequent examinations by British-German was greeted with little enthusiasm by the Americans. On 30 December, an American officer driving a ten-ton truck approached frontier post Book on the Aachen-Liège Road. Upon being ask if he had 'anything to declare', he told the officials he was carrying rifles and rye whiskey for his unit. When asked to open up the back for inspection, the officer refused and began hurling expletives and insults at the border guards. Only when a guard threatened to bring in the US military police in Liège was the officer prepared to calm down. The truck was inspected but nothing illegal was found. The Dog School brought some welcome news to the FCS in the 1947 New Year. In January 1947, *Asta*, 'a brood-bitch', was recovered by the border services in Halen in Belgium three months after the dog had been stolen. The dog *Kuno* had been helpful in locating a stolen pig, and the use of dogs had left a favourable impression on the local community.[19]

In January 1947, the train control branch processed 191 trains, a total of 5,500 military personnel and 1,100 civilians. The Field Security personnel from the army had been working the system but were about to be withdrawn, in February 1947. The 'Rhine Army Special' was controlled from Dalheim but the report noted that the 'odd gentleman of Polish origin' would still conceal themselves on the train. The 'BAOR Leave Train' was also controlled for import and export customs. The list of confiscated 'export' items in January 1947 included: typewriters (4), binoculars (2), cameras (8), radio bulb valves, ladies' stockings (16), razor blades (400), cigarettes (2,600), German books, miscellaneous silverware, cooking pots, accordions (2), coffee (40 kilo) and a 16-bore shotgun with 42 rounds. In addition, there were: 6,000 RM, 250 cartons of aspirin, 250 kilo of ground coffee, 1,350 Belgian Francs, and 45 pounds and 10 shillings sterling. This contrasted with the Belgian army leave trains that departed from Aachen-Süd twice a day. There were two Belgian border officers based at the station and worked with Mr P.J. Poole in charge of the British FCS post. They had examined 67 trains with 3,500 military passengers. Their collection of confiscated 'export' goods included: radios (6), razor blades (3,250), accordions (3), gramophone needles (1,000), cutlery (220), cutthroat razors (258), sets of car tools (49), immersion heaters (13), cameras (4) and electric drills (14).[20]

In one case, on 17 January 1947, Sergeant W.T. Williams of the US army, accompanied by two females—a German and a Belgian—arrived at the FCP post 'whip' in the Vaalsquarter. He told the customs officials they were secretaries from his unit. They had travel papers for Brussels to procure supplies. Williams returned minus one female on 23 January. He explained that an unnamed US army officer had transported her back to their base. Investigations led to the discovery that Williams's travel documents were not in order. They had also returned in a Chevrolet car with a Belgian licence plate at the front and a US army plate on the rear. The car was impounded, the US army arrested the sergeant, and the German female was handed over to the civilian authorities. In the same month, a British Field Security sergeant and a Belgian gendarme were arrested for trying to drive an army 15cwt lorry into Belgium at an unauthorised crossing point loaded with 30,000 steel measuring tapes intended to sell on the black market. The sergeant had previously worked in the FCP post in Aachen-Bildchen. In another case, Staff Sergeant Millar was arrested for smuggling Dutch nationals across the border but had been intercepted by Major Colvin of DAC Ratheim. There were other internal disciplinary issues among the 551 frontier personnel. Four officers were dismissed in January 1947: one for unstipulated political reasons, one for holding too many ration cards, one for theft and another for brawling. They were judged: 'morale general is good' but there was a caution that the men required proper equipment and uniforms.[21]

III. Education, education, education

Aachen Technical University has outgrown the city. Founded in 1870 but with older polytechnic roots, the university's student intake before 1914 was less than two thousand in a couple of faculties; in 2017 it had grown to 44,517, with ten faculties. The total area of the university is 620 acres and it has important buildings in the city centre, in the suburbs and at off-campus sites in Jülich. The story of the university after 1933 was yet another example of early compliance with Nazism that escalated into a more leading and pace-setting position. Like all technical universities, Aachen had a larger complement of Nazi supporters among both the student body and in the faculties.

The British military occupation plans for schools and universities fell into two phases. In the immediate period of occupation there was a rigid de-Nazification process. Lists—black, white and grey—were drawn up, with those of impeccable character on the whitelist, while those on the blacklist were initially prohibited from teaching. After categorising all teaching staff, the next task was to 'cleanse' all reading material of Nazi influence. SHAEF's categories of unsafe reading material was anything that glorified the military, promoted war, military geography, science and industry associated with war, discriminatory against race or religion and everything that lauded the Nazis or Nazism. The second phase was administered by the Control Commission, which instructed the military government to restore German education to its former level of respect and to broaden the fields of study. German education was to generate an interest in 'popular democracy', 'freedom of opinion' and the value of the 'press and religion'.[22]

The question of education was assumed to be working by the end of 1945. In January 1946, the Technical University was reopened. But, on 15 February 1946, the *Kolnischer Kurier* included an item on 'A demand for the closing of the Technical College'. The article claimed that, during the first sitting of the Aachen Municipal Council, on 11 February, representatives of the Social Democrats, Communist Party and the Free Trade Union had demanded the closure of the Technical College. The reason: the students had been asked by a member of the Military Government 'to give their impressions of the Nuremburg proceedings [International War Crimes Tribunal] in order to obtain a survey of the attitudes of the academic youth of Germany'. The majority of the students had refused, explaining it was 'beneath their dignity', or 'the laughing conquerors sat in judgement on our former leaders', the proceedings had no legal foundations and that it was a propaganda show. The municipal representatives claimed it was not: 'the will of the population of Aachen to tolerate a fascist stronghold within the walls of Aachen, the students of which still look upon those who destroyed Europe as their heroes and to whom they still believe they must give moral support'. The representatives demanded a 'reinvestigation of the moral attitude of the professors and students'. The college was to only be reopened after it could be guaranteed that the students would be taught 'in the spirit of truth and justice'.[23]

A.V. Askwith, CSI, Chief Inspector of Education and controller of Internal Affairs and Communications in Headquarters Military Government, had read the article, and on 18 February wrote to the 'Co-ordinating Office' to explain the situation. He'd spoken with Senior Commander Abbott, who was entirely unaware of the situation until it was published in the *Kurier*. He was concerned that a letter to Aachen Mil Gov was sent immediately (which he'd drafted and attached) and raised a question over censorship rules before publication in German newspapers. Askwith's letter was to Colonel F.H.S. Pownall, Commander RB Aachen, on 19 February, informing him that he planned an investigation. His concerns were: who was the representative of the MG who requested the information from the students, was an MG officer responsible for education present and were German faculty involved. He also wanted to know if there were reports on the incident, whether the faculty members agreed with the students, what the German principal made of the incident, which departments fund the college, how far the Aachen municipality was prepared to go and how did the Cologne newspaper get the story? On 20 February, a second staff officer from the Intelligence section, an RAF squadron leader, visited I Corps to collect details about the incident. He discovered that Sergeant H. Young visited Aachen to request the opinions of the students; the MG was fully aware of his mission. In an arrangement with a professor, he'd addressed the students once, and the other times the subject was presented by German teaching staff. In the opinion of the report's 'compiler', the students were unrepentant and 'looked back with respect to their past leaders'. The reasons why the students refused to participate was: 'the trial was without legal foundation', the Russians should not be included, the German legal system could have dealt with the cases, German prosecutors and journalists should have been invited to attend and the 'Allied war criminals should have been tried'.[24]

Matters then spiralled as a full report was made on the university students and faculty. On 20 February, FS (Field Security) issued a report on the university written by a major from I Corps. The report confirmed that 5 per cent of the students had responded to the request but among the other 95 per cent the opinion was: 'Our leaders are sitting in Nuremberg in the prisoners' dock, whilst the war criminals of the victorious states are sitting in judgement on our poor leaders.' The replies, which included responses from the Journalism School, were collected and sent to I Corps headquarters. The British then received a barrage of complaints from the Communists, the SPD, the Rhineland Separatist Movement, the

Free Trade Union, and even the CDU, but less forceful. The weight of the complaints focused on 'the school as a hotbed of Nazism' and a venue for illicit meetings. There was also concern over the influence of the *Eschweiler Bergwerks Verein* (a mining company) due to the amount of funding it received. There was also a direct charge against Professor Rontgen, the rector, because of the content of his speech on the tenth anniversary of the death of Leo Schlageter (killed while blowing up a bridge during the French occupation in 1923). The reviewing officer felt that though Rontegen's speech had expressed nationalistic and anti-community sentiments, there was no references to Hitler, and at the time most people thought Schlageter was a national hero. Among its teaching fields the university trained mining engineers and architects, and had been considered one of the best in Germany before 1939. The university was 'controlled by a Board of Professors' called the Senate, and they also took an active part in the classes alongside the teachers. They had worked hard in conjunction with the MG to re-open the university; however there were concerns because two former Senate members were Professor Ehrenberg and Oberinspector Schumacher—both SS officers and SD agents.

This was not the only Nazi membership: 'it may be useful to point out that 22 per cent were Nazi Party members before 1937, that 59 per cent have been members at one time or another and that no less than 27 per cent had held membership of the SA'. The students were nearly all former Wehrmacht and 48 per cent were officers: 'many of them led a life of comfort in occupied territory'. Subsequently, they were living 'in ruin, acute food shortage and overall discomfort. They are bitter and extremely dissatisfied men, and they are also Nationalists.' Their teachers regarded them as 'discontented patriots, and possibly militarists but not necessarily Nazis'. An informant, however, claimed that they were 'more than militarists, they are pro-fascist', it was also known that few of the students were anti-fascist, and 'it is in the ex-Officers that the greatest danger lies'. There were 213 students: 204 ex-Wehrmacht servicemen (103 officers, 12 captains the rest below and 101 ORs); 38 former Nazi Party members, 14 former SA members, 61 former Hitler Youth leaders and, among the 25 female students, there were 5 with Nazi associations. In the opinion of the officer examining the records, the numbers with former Nazi associations were not remarkable for their age or education. Teachers with 'bad backgrounds' had been employed by Rector Rontgen in 'odd jobs' but he'd been ordered to dismiss them. The reviewing officer, although critical of the Nazi content, was prepared to accept that the time since January was too short to make harsh judgements.

There was a sense of British opinions changing after the bitterness generated by the discoveries of Belsen and other camps less than a year before. It looked the same, but it concerned the treatment of German youth:

> There is however, no doubt that although the teachers may be fully qualified technically, they are not suitable persons to maintain control of such a school. Feeling runs extremely high in the area, not only in political circles but also among the majority of the civil population as well. It will therefore be detrimental to British prestige if quick action is not taken in suppressing what is obviously a centre of unrepentant Nazism and a possible source of future trouble.
>
> It would be unjust to focus undue attention on this particular school. It is natural that intelligent soldiers returning to defeat and ruin after six years of bitter war should have a rebellious spirit. It is an unpleasant but unavoidable conclusion that the whole of German Youth between the age of 16 and 35 is permeated by Nazi ideology. This, of course, is the result of the intensified training which they have received in Nazi schools. There is no reason to believe that the Technische Hochshule is worse than similar institutions elsewhere in Germany.
>
> What, however, is excusable in Youth cannot be condoned in Age.

The remainder of the teachers, even though they had been favourably vetted by British authorities, were 'individually sound', but in a group and with the students it was a cocktail for potential disaster; there was also criticism of the political group that had formed to demand the closure of the university—all from the left. There had already been a previous altercation between Rector Rontgen and a local SPD official who wanted a say in the selection of staff. In conclusion, the report recommended the university's closure but accepted that was a Control Commission decision, which would have a knock-on effect throughout the British zone. In the event of not closing, it was recommended that a member of the MG was assigned to oversee the running of classes on a full-time basis.[25]

Askwith then met with Lieutenant Colonel K.R.F. Black at 227 Det, RB Aachen on 23 February. After the meeting, Black wrote to Askwith answering the questions he'd raised in his letter to Pownall, who was on leave. Sergeant Young was from 1 Corps District and was not part of the MG staff. Young had only discovered the problem two days after delivering the questions to the university staff and upon returning to collect the student's replies. Young had said there would be repercussions because the teachers had read the students' confidential replies. He also explained that, on 19 February, the municipal representatives had formed a committee headed by the Oberburgermeister to scrutinise the teachers. Black was confident they could only make recommendations. Black did not recommend closing the school, believing it would turn the students into future troublemakers. He recommended assigning an education officer on a permanent basis to the university, that the curriculum should be more balanced with political and cultural content, and that the teachers should be re-screened and the students re-screened. He was concerned that closing the university would mean closing all the other universities in the British zone. He added: 'I suggest the situation would never have arisen had the survey not taken place. This delicate subject should, in my opinion, never have been entrusted to an F.S.S. Sergeant, who seems hardly a suitable person to interview intelligent thinking students.' He enclosed a copy of a resolution that had arrived from the students.[26]

The students held a meeting (Fakultät für Bauwesen) on 20 February and passed a resolution as a defence against the accusations made against them. They were living in conditions that made it impossible for them to know clearly what was happening in Nuremberg; there were few newspapers available for them to read. Only a few answered anonymously, and they were not representative of all the opinions. The resolution added: 'About 40 students live in bunkers, the rest in unheated and only scantily patched up digs. <u>How can a student living under such conditions come to a clear understanding of the facts spread before the public in Nuremberg!</u>' The students went on to add 'that the Nazi-criminals must be punished exactly as a criminal'. They requested the protection of the MG and to ignore the 'calumnies' of a few reckless individuals who would be debarred by the student body. The students of Aix-la-Chapelle, as they called themselves, had confirmed to the British that they were playing their part in the 'remodelling of a true democratic world'.[27] The response was positive; Askwith wrote to Black to confirm he had decided against closure, but an Education Officer would be assigned to the university, who would also change the curriculum. The MG planned to re-screen the entire staff and students.[28]

On 21 February, the Education Branch of the Control Commission for Germany in Bunde wrote to the MGO personnel involved in the university case. The commission regarded the incident as orchestrated from an unnamed political party that had been trying to undermine the progress of universities within the British zone. The commission's investigation found that the incident had happened in January, when a member of I Corps had carried out the test, but it was only applied to a small number of students. The situation was raised at the municipal level by Frau Maria Pascher, a Communist Party member and responsible for the Journalism School. The Oberburgermeister refused to act until he had spoken with Rector Rontgen. A deputation of Communists then 'waited on the 277 Detachment commander' and repeated their demands for the university to be closed. The commission saw this as a propaganda campaign waged against the universities in the British zone. This could not be prevented but institutions were to be allowed to defend themselves. The letter concluded: 'Inevitably almost all of these will be ex-soldiers, more than usually sensitive to ill-founded criticism and always inclined to believe that such criticism is approved if not inspired by the British authorities. The most likely effect will be to increase their felling of resentment and their resistance to any measures of political re-education which are undertaken.'[29]

The Oberpräsident of North Rhine Province, Dr Lehr, wrote to the Headquarters MG North Rhine Region on 26 February, in support of the students and Rector Rontgen. He relayed Rector Rontgen's fears that the students were in 'a difficult mental situation and that hardly any generation lived through more hardship'. Those admitted to the university represented the opportunity to escape the conditions and offered a new hope to the students. To achieve the eventual benefits from this future, they expected it would take a lot of pain to eradicate all the baggage collected in the years under Nazism. He hoped the MG in Aachen would bring all the parties together and discuss openly the problems raised by this incident.[30] Lerner, however, included another student document: 'A Proclamation To Reason!' The proclamation revealed how far the students were handicapped with a vocabulary of Nazism and the kind of hostile attitude that defined life in the Third Reich. The proclamation opened with an attack on Frau Pascher:

> At the first sitting of the Aachen Town Council a hysterical old woman—from the Bachmann ranks, which are composed of a morally and spiritually degenerate class—in polyphrased outbursts demanded the mass expulsion of the so-called Nazi and militarist students of the Aachen Hochschule.
>
> ... point out to German intelligence the dangers of these nihilistic endeavours of illiterate and diabolical oligarchs ... we are not afraid of the provocations of these stupid sub-humans and pathological oddities.
>
> Communism is the most lost form of egoism! With it there is no sanctity through ardour!
>
> German Students: Unite Against this Clique of Criminals, Lunatics and Anarchistic Sub-Humans.[31]

The chief of Internal Affairs in Düsseldorf had not missed this content when he wrote to Askwith explaining what was in the document. Dr Lerner had not had it translated, 'it is truly a remarkable document, in the best Goebbels style'. He added that the translation was mild and may even carry worse comments. Although Askwith was not taking the case further, the Internal Affairs officer recommended Public Safety investigate the authors of the proclamation, 'as the person who drafted this appears to be too thorough a student of National Socialist propaganda technique to remain at large'.[32] The paper trail ends there. In the original—*Anarchistischen Untermenschen* (Anarchistic sub-humans), *geistlosen Untermenschen* (stupid sub-humans)—was the legacy of Nazi racist language and was still exacting a powerful hold over some of the students. This is a small indication of how large the task was in re-educating early post-war German youth.

The Technical University survived the scandal. In the summer of 1948, the Foreign Office sponsored British academics, scholarly experts and students to attend summer courses in German universities. Although strictly following on from the Aachen Technical University case of 1946, the file does provide an interesting impression of the progress in German academic life. Two official reports were compiled: the first was a general survey about the courses, the content and the success; the second was a compilation from the post-course reports submitted by the UK lecturers. There had been summer courses the previous year and the scheme was regarded as a success. The planning for 1948 had begun almost immediately but the introduction of currency reform just prior to the start dates almost derailed the plans. Control Commission Germany raised 75,000RM but courses in Kiel, Düsseldorf and Berlin were cancelled. There had been other effects; travel became expensive, and some students were forced to work in the summer, reducing the numbers even after the CCG stipend. Seven courses took place, in Aachen, Bonn, Brunswick, Cologne, Göttingen, Hamburg and Münster. The courses were two to three weeks long and held between 20 July and 12 September. The general themes for each course ranged from 'Modern European Thought and Culture' (Hamburg) to 'Recent Trends in Educational Theory and Practice' (Göttingen), but only Aachen offered a technical theme. The total students: 663 (German), 175 (UK) and over 130 from other countries. Aachen students were mostly scientists and engineers, with an average age of 24 and seven months; there were 102 tutors, with 46 from Germany and 35 from the UK. The courses had their plaudits; lecturers and students wrote letters to the

Foreign Office to thank all those behind the organisation. 'I was struck by the friendly attitude and by the politeness of the German student' was a typical comment. There was also a strong element of teaching the Germans lessons: 'If the discussions at those Courses can teach the Germans the spirit of civilised and tolerant debate, they will be worthwhile for that alone.' The UK students conducted a mock debate to show their German counterparts 'how it was done in UK universities'. The German students expressed their keenness to make the courses successful. Most UK lecturers complained that they had not been advised 'beforehand of the nature of their audience'. Briefings were not consistent and consequently some papers were wide of the mark. There was some weakness in the planning of travel and the organisation of information packs—two students plodded around Germany without any information of where their course was being held.[33]

The summer course in Aachen ran from 2 to 18 August; the theme was 'Science and Engineering, the Cultural Heritage of Mankind'. The student mix was 86 German, 3 UK, 3 Holland, the average age of the students was 25, and they were taught by 9 German and 3 UK lecturers. Dr A.C. Crombie was an Australian but listed from UK because he was teaching at the University of London; his lecture subject was 'The Philosophy of Science'. The Aachen lecturers represented an interesting mix. From those involved in the 1946 scandal, Professor Otto Gruber was the only one allowed to carry on working without full re-screening; his subject was 'Foreign Influences in German Architecture'. Dr Benno Schachner had been a professor in 1946 but had been recommended for removal; he was demoted; his subject was 'Technology and the Soul'. Professor Dr Mennicken had survived interrogation by Saul Padover in 1944 and a Special Branch re-screening in 1946, and his topic was 'The Eifel'. Professor Dr Wilhelm Several professors were screened by Special Branch in 1946, regardless of teaching on the course. Professor Dr Doris Schachner had been recommended to continue at the university following a re-screening by Mr Askwith and was also not teaching on the course. The rest of the papers were presented by professorial staff that had joined the university after the scandal.[34] The report by Dr Crombie for the UK lecturers attending the Aachen course combined a description of the university facilities with an assessment of the people. The report drew attention to some 'German problems': the first concerned the 'practical ineffectiveness of the good-willed intellects. This manifested itself in the intellectualism that avoided all forms of local and national politics', whereas the 'go-getting type ... on the whole more clever than honest ... was hand in glove with all sources of money in the district'. In effect, the devious, with their industrial monetary sources, played an undue influence on German society, which was believed required further research. Crombie continued, 'The other great moral problem always just below the surface is the problem of saving the Germans from their most dangerous temptation, the temptation to dissolve into self-pity.' Aside from his astute observations of Aachen academe, Crombie went on to recommend a list of British universities and departments where introductions might benefit future courses.[35]

There were undercurrents of criticism and a wide range of observations. Somerville Hastings noted that his lectures were badly attended but thought the German students had little interest in what any British lecturer said. In his opinion, the value of the course lay in the informal international discussions that continued through the night. One lecturer, M.R.D. Foot, the famous British historian and former SOE veteran tortured by the Germans during the war, wrote a letter to *The Times* in September 1948, with his opinions of German universities. He began with criticism of the lack of control the UK government administered over the universities, especially given their prestigious status in Germany. He claimed it was 'curious that some of the professorial staffs are politically so far to the right. Denazification cannot now be described as anything better than a farce; but the trouble does not come from Nazi professors alone.' Foot questioned whether it was a good decision to allow Germany's future leaders to be educated by 'vehemently nationalistic and vehemently conservative' professors. He also described how students look up to their professors and venerate them without criticism of their ideas. He also complained about the German students' inability to connect ideas; he suggested the British student would pounce on an idea and worry it, but the German students showed no sign of such attitudes. Consequently, Foot believed the German students needed 'reasoning ability'. Foot offered an example from a Rhineland newspaper, in which an article had argued that Hitler was not to blame for the war, because the armed forces had him in check in 1938, but 'the tragic pacifist Chamberlain, whose blundering interventions made it impossible to hold Hitler in check'. He concluded his polemic by recommending that German students should be soaked in the experience of studying in foreign universities.[36] F.T. Calvert of the German Education Department (Foreign Office) wrote to Foot. He thought Foot was wrong to judge on one visit to Bonn University; he also claimed the government was fully aware of the 'autocratic and conservative tradition of the German professorial system' but it was not 'our policy to force such reforms directly but advise and persuade the German education authorities'. He explained a commission had been working with the Germans on this subject and was chaired by the master of Balliol. There had also been exchange schemes for staff and lecturers. He also accepted that lecturers from the UK had not been briefed adequately prior to attending courses and this had been an error on the part of the organisers.[37] The consolidated report of the lecturers' reports was yet another example of how the Foreign Office used opinions to form policy criteria. The criticisms of the lecturers were included where they contained a general but positive viewpoint. The question of Nazi ideas prevalent among German staff and students was addressed:

> Several reports stress that the selection of German students might also be more judicious. Mr. Green considers it dangerous to admit to the course students and lecturers of near-Nazi or reactionary inclinations who are free to infiltrate their propaganda. To exclude them would, however, defeat the primary aim of the course which is to wean such doubtful characters away from their inclinations and there is no danger in their infiltrating their propaganda provided the remaining members of the course are competent to counter it.[38]

IMPOSING THE RAJ

Navigating the Nazi past was challenging. The university's uncomfortable past resurfaced in the 1990s, when the rector confessed to his Nazi life. The status of rector is an important social position in Germany. The case of Schneider-Schwerte was not just a social calamity for Aachen and the university; the disgraced rector had been a highly influential academic, shaping the minds of decades of students and was a leading scholar in his field. Ten years later, Günter Grass confessed about his service in the Waffen-SS. Schneider-Schwerte was, however, the more serious case, but Grass had spent decades castigating his fellow authors for their Nazi past or for not confronting the past. The scandals in both cases were soon forgotten as both passed away a short time afterwards.[39]

IV. Smuggling, gang warfare and social order

Heinrich Schreiber, one of the last of Hitler's *Landser* still residing in Aachen, quietly departed on 19 March 2020. His final battles were against aging in an indifferent society. Crippled with rheumatism and virtually blind beyond two feet, he navigated life on a small state pension. Living alone in his first-floor apartment after the passing of his wife years before, his home was spotless but furnished simply, it beamed with working-class pride. He was the last of his generation, the last of his peers and loneliness was his only companion. Every day for ten years, after his wife passed, he visited a city bistro for a mid-morning beer (*Früschoppen*), a Schnapps and a coffee. He had returned to a social routine once a tradition among the working class. Heinrich's adult life commenced at 15, first as an apprentice weaver, but the war prematurely ended that chapter. In 1946, he returned from war, and was directed to the building reconstruction of the city, and eventually transitioned into a stonemason. Despite his lapsed Catholicism, he took pride in his contribution to rebuilding the city's churches. In later years, *Caritas*, a Catholic charitable organisation, supplied his daily meals, empowering him to uphold his social independence. Following his bistro visits, Heinrich's afternoons were dedicated to carving intricate wooden ornaments at his dining table. These pieces were sold on Christmas markets. Heinrich Schreiber's life story was about resilience, community and purpose.

The war changed Heinrich's life, and there was a historical coincidence in his passing; almost seventy-five years to the day, he was captured by the US army in Cologne. Born in 1924, in the small town of Monschau within Aachen's wider county borders, Heinrich's roots were tied to his father, a tenant farmer on church lands. In the 1930s, rising rents imposed by the Church forced many farmers like his father to abandon their farms and seek work in Aachen. In 1943, Heinrich received orders from the Wehrmacht's Monschau recruitment office, and he was sent to the army to serve as an infantryman. His initiation to war was on the eastern front. While serving in the Smolensk area, he was wounded in the stomach. Following a prolonged stay in a military hospital, he was transferred to Cologne for recovery, but also received the *Infantriesturmabzeichen*—the ordinary soldier's badge of bravery. This military award, for hand-to-hand combat, remained one of his cherished accomplishments. Later in life, this badge served as a testament to his courage and his identity as a German—a common trait across nationaliites of working-class men who had served at the sharp end of war. Despite partial recuperation, he was reassigned to a light anti-aircraft detachment, operating 20mm flak guns, based in Cologne. He experienced several heavy air raids. During that time, Heinrich recalled visiting Aachen. The city buildings were strewn with Swastika flags and Nazi banners, and people greeted each other with the *Hitlergruss* (Nazi salute). He felt there was an artifical atmosphere of allegiance to Nazism. The city's landscape was one of widespread devastation. Heinrich's first wife was caught outside a protective bunker during an air raid. She was rendered speechless for months and suffered a life-long psychosis until her passing in 1989.

Heinrich was captured in Cologne (March 1945) by the US army and was badly beaten by combat-enraged American soldiers. He was sent to Herbesthal (Aachen's former frontier town) and incarcerated in a mud-ridden holding camp administered by American soldiers, assisted by displaced persons (DPs), mostly Poles serving as guards. The camp had no toilet facilities and no disposal of excreta, which added to the miserable conditions. He was then sent to France, first to Rheims and then Biarritz, where he remained for a year. The German PoWs were transported on trains, in open wagons, and French farmers and children threw stones. The American guards sometimes fired warning shots at the French. Once in France there was no contact with families, no cigarette rations and a constant shortage of food, with sickness being a major problem. Heinrich had told the Americans he was a weaver, but he was made to break rocks for roads. The poor rations and the hard labour caused him to suffer serious back problems. Then he was sent to Biarritz to clear the beaches of German mines, with a bayonet, working beside Spaniards imprisoned since the civil war. The Aachen that he came home to in 1946 had changed in more ways than just the bombing and capitulation.

Beyond his military experiences, Heinrich's recollections disclosed a rich tapestry of working-class culture in post-war Germany. Released from a PoW camp, he returned to Aachen in 1946. Assigned by the British to a team of laborers, which included Dutch workers, he embarked on the repairs to cloisters and churches. Among these projects, the restoration of St Peter's Church on Couvenstrasse held a special place in his heart, and evoked feelings of pride. The people of Aachen shared a powerful determination to salvage the ancient structures, sacred artefacts and their homes from the ruins of war. Amidst the rationing and meagre lifestyles, Heinrich became involved in smuggling coffee. Aachen had a longstanding tradition of smuggling, deeply ingrained in the local culture. With the transition from British to Belgian occupation, Heinrich's role shifted to timberwork during the day and smuggling by night. He was a 'storm group' member in the 'Monschau convoy' system, those small, fast-moving groups essential in a large-scale operation. His storm group served as a decoy, carrying smaller loads but trying to divert police and frontier guards away from the larger shipments. The convoy worked the border area between Eupen and Lammersdorf. Smuggling alongside his brother, Heinrich recalled the dangers he faced, including being shot at by frontier guards. There was satisfaction in his accomplishments, claiming to have smuggled significant amounts of coffee during each raid. Heinrich earned a reputation for smuggling and recognition among the 'kings of smuggling' from Monschau and Eupen. However, he was caught and arrested while in Cologne and served a two-week prison sentence. By 1947, smuggling had become all pervasive among his social circle, extending to many segments of society, including the police, state officials, British army personnel, the elderly, children, women and members of the clergy. This organised network was highly skilled, employing scouts, load-bearers, distribution networks and hard trading on the black market. Around 1950, coffee smuggling ended, marking another turning point in Heinrich's journey. He continued with stonemasonry until his retirement in 1990. Heinrich's life story was a testament to resilience, the intricate interplay of societal dynamics and the deep connection between historical circumstances and personal choices.

On 16 November 1948, a British Frontier Control service report claimed there had been a rise in gang smuggling. 'The gangs are well organised and frequently armed' in a specific comment about the RB Aachen frontier. In that month alone, there had been 3,655 arrests for frontier violations, which compared with 954 in Aurich (Lower Saxony), 287 in Hamburg and 307 in Schleswig-Holstein, and yet the report claimed the arrests were down. It was assumed that the 'casual frontier violator and the petty smuggler are going out of business'. The reduction in the coffee tax on 1 November 1948 had reduced the black-market value; however, the smugglers had swapped products, focusing instead on bars of chocolate and cigarettes. The trade with Belgium was for the new Deutsch Mark, which could be swapped for three or four Belgian Francs, the official rate being 13.25 Francs. The elaborate efforts by the smugglers and violators were matched step by step by the British determination to interdict the black market. The report contained the description of a typical incident. In September, a motorised border guard unit monitored a gang of seventy, all aged 17–35, intending to cross the Belgian frontier. The unit called out all available men with the aim of cutting off the gang, while Belgian gendarmes had forced several gang members back across the German frontier. Thirty men were arrested and being escorted when the remaining gang members had formed up and attacked the border guards. A vicious skirmish ensued as the guards defended themselves with rifle butts and truncheons. The gang members, including those arrested, were fought off and escaped, except one man, who 'was brought down and mauled by a customs dog'. The report explained that the guards showed 'remarkable coolness and forbearance' for not firing their weapons.[40] By 1948, the gangs were made up of war criminals, displaced persons (DPs), juveniles, the young and old, the elderly, the disabled and customs officials. But members of the allied forces were also involved in some form of illegal trade—in 1948 this was the everyday commerce in RB Aachen.

In December 1948, another report referred to 'the annual Christmas pilgrimage into Belgium'. The inability of the frontier guards to 'stem the tide' had seen three shooting incidents, two fatalities and the confiscation of six million cigarettes. The report reflected on developments in gang behaviour since the beginning of the year. Before the currency reform, petty smugglers crossed into Belgium to 'beg, buy or steal food, coffee and cigarettes'. The British and German officials struggled to cope with the problem because: 'The humanitarian view conflicted with the moral and criminal issues, and frequently both British and German officials were criticised for unduly harsh methods.' The currency reform eradicated the petty smuggler but led to 'a new and more dangerous type of smuggler ... the well-organised gang of anything up to fifty strong which operated with scouts and flank guards protecting the main body'. The members were regarded as tough and frequently armed, and it was assumed their tactics had been profitable because the gang culture had multiplied. The scale of smuggling had also multiplied—in one case three million kilos of coffee consigned to the Jewish Welfare Organisations had entered the 'Bizone' through RB Aachen, and in another case, it was claimed that a 'paltry' twenty-five million cigarettes had been confiscated of an estimated two hundred million that had reached the black market. On Aachen main railway station, an auxiliary shed was constructed on platform 3 for the control of international express trains. There was an informal agreement to hand over greater discrepancy powers to Belgian guards, which had succeeded in reducing frictions between officials.[41]

V. Juvenile delinquency

There is a myth that resides just below the surface in Aachen society—the story of juvenile smuggling. People will reveal in casual conversation that their parents were smugglers 'back in the day'. The picture presented of the young smuggler was more akin to a bit of poaching, a community tradition of communal smuggling. Former smugglers refer to the 'young ones' as decoys carrying only a pound of coffee or a carton of cigarettes. There are some local accounts of the smuggling in the central Aachen bookshop, but the stories are often drawn from memory or a newspaper article. A history of the smuggling devoted a large part to the juvenile smugglers.[42] The museum to smuggling and the customs frontier in Vaals also panders to the myths of juvenile smuggling. In 1951, Dieter Olof made the film *Sundige Grenze*. The director followed a popular style in German film of the 'wonderful homeland'. The narrative dabbled with an imaginative interpretation of youth and childhood dragged into smuggling. When the film was first aired in Aachen, long after social smuggling had ended, there is a story that former smugglers and customs officials sat side by side and had a 'jolly good time'. Did the film invent the myth or was it formed by the community? After all, it was based on actual events, but the nature of the actual smuggling life was more to do with a culture of violent criminality that neither film nor community allude to. In 2017, Phoenix Television used its expertise in documentary filmmaking to make a study of the post-war smuggling across the Aachen-Belgium border.[43]

By December 1946, British officials from RB Aachen through to the Military Government Headquarters in Bad Oeyenhausen were of one opinion—juvenile smuggling was a major crisis threatening British occupation policy. A comment about the problem in a report explained the growing concern of the authorities:

> The ever-increasing arrest figures for juveniles are causing considerable concern, not only to this service, but also to the Legal and

Education Branches. Legal Branch complain that they are quite unable to cope with the work of prosecuting the parents either by fine or prison sentences is having little, if any deterrent effect on the children. In actual fact it's probably having the opposite effect since the children have even more liberty while their parents are serving their term of imprisonment.

The Frontier Service solution was legislation to implement a juvenile legal process similar to 'the reformatory system in England', whereby the juveniles could be prosecuted for their offences, but they also argued that this might be difficult to implement. In January 1947, there were 1,386 arrests, with 193 juveniles arrested with goods and 662 arrested without goods.[44] Once the control of frontier regulations and duties was passed to the new West German federal government, in 1949, RB Aachen and British security controls ceased operations, and the smuggling ended.

11

ORDINARY PEOPLE

We have started to remove the Jews from the best houses. Our people lost their houses during the air raids. Jews caused the war, England bombs the houses, so who is more important? The Jew is a spy in our country. If they caused war again it will be their end. They succeeded again so now they have to leave Europe. We have to find a place to concentrate them if Roosevelt and Churchill won't open their arms. There are 6,000 Jews in Cologne and they eat our rations. Because they wear the star, our people can see how many they are.[1]

Reema S* was born in Wilna, Lithuania, in December 1953. Despite aspiring to be a journalist, she found herself studying Russian literature and medicine from 1971 to 1976, later serving as a combat nurse in the Soviet Red Army. Raised in Wilna, she knew little of the Holocaust, shielded from its horrors. In 1993, she clandestinely made her way to Germany, settling in Erfurt before finding a home in Aachen in 1995. There, she joined the Jewish diaspora, becoming one of 1,434 Jews from the former Soviet Union to call Aachen home. Despite the growing discourse on the Holocaust in 1996, Reema remained unaware of Aachen's pre-war Jewish community. She recalled reading short accounts in local newspapers about Jewish families and the Holocaust. She thought there were no discussions over Aachen's perpetrators or bystanders. Her friend recalled witnessing the old synagogue burning in 1938. Reema stands as a member of the third post-1945 Jewish diaspora in a world scarred by history and the rise of anti-Semitism.

Wally, born in Edenfeld in Würzburg in 1878, tied the knot with Otto Hirtz (1869–1939), scion of a venerable textile dynasty hailing from Aachen's oldest lineage. The roots of Jakob and Rachel Hirtz extend back to the late 1700s, intertwining with Aachen's burgeoning industrial epoch. August Hirtz (1837–1911) weathered the storms of economic downturns, spearheading textile manufacturing in the 1870s. His son Hugo, retiring in the 1930s, found himself ensnared by the Nazi regime's grip, forced into the confines of the overcrowded Judenhaus in Eupenerstrasse 249. Transported to Theresienstadt on 25 July 1942, he met his tragic end at 60 years old. Julius Hirtz, August's brother, and his daughter Mathilda, wedded Carl Heinemann, represented the scion of another textile dynasty, while Selli Heinemann, a legal luminary in Essen, cast a tragic shadow over their lineage. The night of 10 November 1938 witnessed the desecration of their home by SA henchmen, incinerating art valued at 40,000RM. Selli and his wife succumbed to despair soon after. Otto, Wally's husband, commanded formidable influence as a textile magnate and chaired the Oecher Platt association (the local dialect), fostering camaraderie among his Ripuarian-speaking workforce.[2] When Wally's sister died, they adopted her son '*Bubi*', mentioned in chapter nine, and gifted him a luxurious lifestyle. In 1936, Otto relinquished all his businesses to Bubi. In 1938, Otto became ill, and died in 1939. Wally was alone to confront the Nazi terror as it systematically dismantled and destroyed Aachen's Jewish community.[3]

In 2019, the *Aachener Nachrichten* shed light on Aachen's postwar synagogue trial conducted by the British military occupation on 28 May 1947. Helmut Irmen, a lawyer and human rights scholar, penned an article discussing the trial and featuring in an exhibition handbook about the war's end, showcased at Aachen's Charlemagne Centre.[4] Irmen highlighted the trial as the first in post-war Aachen and Germany to prosecute crimes linked to *Kristallnacht* and the first against Nazis in Aachen. He criticised the

British for lenient sentences and early releases, asserting that the trials were poorly investigated and lacked sound judicial processes and appropriate punishments. Irmen's analysis, however, lacks credible depth beyond a legal survey of a few files, leaving room for a more in-depth analysis of the case.

Investigating the story of Aachen's Jews and the Holocaust poses a significant challenge, with numerous reports but scant evidence to construct a compelling human-interest narrative of the victims. Post-war investigations, initiated in November 1944 by US army public safety officers, led to prosecutions. The British inherited war crimes and crimes against humanity cases, along with the daunting task of de-Nazification. From the early days of Hitler's regime, Aachen's Jews had faced institutional persecution. Jewish symbols became targets in Hitler's campaign against all religiosity and in particular Catholicism. The destruction of the synagogue also served as a warning to Aachen's Catholic diocese and terrorised the Jewish community, severing deep cultural ties rooted in Charlemagne's era and solidified during resistance to Bismarck's *Kulturkampf*. The trial of May 1947, like others, lacks city records. Trials in Aachen were not publicly documented or recorded in the *Poll-Chronicle*, revealing a city unwilling to pursue justice or confront the past. Aachen's Holocaust journey reflects a shift from passive racism to genocide—an institutional narrative beginning with benign prejudices and culminating in unspeakable atrocities. The events in Aachen serve as a sombre reminder and a cautionary tale for generations to come.

I. Nazi terror and Aachen

There is division among scholars about the nature of the Nazi dictatorship. One school argues that coercion was pivotal, while another promotes the notions of public voluntarism and widespread consent.[5] Setting a context is fundamental in any examination of Nazism, but it's reasonable to accept that the dictatorship did not remain constant throughout its existence. The patterns of violence fluctuated and in parallel public consent fluctuated. The findings from the research I have conducted tend to highlight extensive periods of coercion and violence. The violence was greater in the eastern borders to Poland than in the west against Belgium and Holland.[6] The central institutions of the Nazi terror were the party, the police and the Gestapo. However, the Aachen story should begin with the ideological confrontation between Nazism and Catholicism. The founding of the *Ordensburg Vogelsang* in Eifel—a Nazi university for ideological learning and development of political leaders—set the regime on a path of hostility with Aachen. The foundation stone of the complex was laid on 22 September 1934. The site was selected to showcase Hitler's political architecture and radiate Nazi dogma in the heartland of western European Catholicism. The struggle between Nazism and Catholicism has been an important topic for historians and does not need to be amplified here. The Vogelsang symbolised and solidified this ideological conflict. Hitler dedicated the site on 20 November 1936. His visit was a major event for a rural community and thousands crossed the country just to see him. A significant aspect of Hitler's visit was his outright refusal to visit Aachen. In July 1937, the Aachen diocese hosted almost a million people on pilgrimage. This was in spite of severe warnings not to attend by Nazi officials. The conflict between Nazism and Catholicism had reached a peak in 1938, with direct attacks on Aachen's Ultramontanism.

For a long time, the story of the *Vogelsang* was treated as a compound for Nazi cranks and shaman. Then a collection of photographs that once belonged to a former SS leader was published. Johann Niemann (1913–1943) was a junior officer of the SS and deputy commander of Sobidor extermination camp when an inmate killed him. He joined the Nazi Party in 1931 and in 1934 volunteered to serve in Esterwagen concentration camp. Niemann joined the SS in 1934 and in 1936 he was posted to Sachsenhausen concentration camp near Berlin. He became a member of the *SS-Totenkofverbande Ostfriesland*, a unit that specialised as guards for concentration camps. In 1936–7, Niemann was assigned to the *Vogelsang* and was present when Hitler arrived, taking photographs of the euphoria among the crowd. After his time in the *Vogelsang*, he went on to lead an integral part of the Nazi extermination system.[7]

The first case of political murder in Aachen involved Arthur May. He was the editor of the *Aachener Arbeiter Zeitung*, a Communist daily newspaper, which had opened in 1924. While conducting police duties, SS-Sturmbannführer Erwin Rösener (1902–1946) arrested May on 16 June 1933. In the middle of the night on 21–2 June, May was transported to Jülich for incarceration in the town fortress. May was placed under guard with two SS men but was shot; they adopted *auf der Flucht* (trying to escape), a common Nazi term to cover up political murder.[8] In January 1933, the SS and SA began para-policing patrols in all German cities. The Nazis formed a volunteer umbrella organisation, the *Hilfspolizei* (volunteer police), to bridge political volunteerism and professional policing. The primary objective was to break the left/socialist hold in Germany by inserting a Nazi loyal hierarchy into the regular police force; the second objective was to enforce anti-Semitism as a socio-cultural policy. Analysis of the *Hilfspolizei* in Aachen pinpoints the ease with which the Nazis were able to raise volunteers nationwide.

The initial order to raise the *Hilfspolizei* was issued by Hermann Göring on 23 February 1933 and was introduced by regional and state authorities. The order was also announced in the German newspapers.[9] The *Hilfspolizei* was portrayed as symbolic of the patriotic volunteerism that had raised the *Freikorps*. They were described as a short-term force and an armed response to potential armed opposition to the Nazis. Their duties were to defend the home and workplace, creating a *Wach- und Schliessgesllschaften* (a community of guardianship).[10] The Aachen *Hilfspolizei* was composed of thirty-two SS men, forty-six SA men and twenty-two men from the right-wing *Stahlheim*. Depending on the strength of local SS or SA membership decided which dominated the local *Hilfspolizei* units. In Aachen, there was a compromise in a disorganised unit of volunteers. The balance between SA and SS varied with the day of the week, and changes fluctuated between weekdays or weekends, when more SS men were available for duty. There was evidence of a power struggle over local authority and control. The 25th *SA Standarte* made a pitch on 1 March 1933 to control the *Hilfspolizei*, however, senior officers of the *SS-Sturmbann* IV/5 were the senior policemen of Aachen. They took the initiative and promoted themselves to overall authority exemplifying the practice of *Führerprinzip*.[11]

The *Hilfspolizei* received wider support from other organisations, like the *Stahlheim* (veteran soldiers' association). In Aachen, the significant non-Nazi group were the *Deutschnationalen Kampfringes*, a mixed group of war veterans, patriots, foresters and influential businessmen. Dr Schuler (a Great War veteran) raised a medical team with five assistants, which was propagandised as a mobile medical task force prepared for all eventualities.[12] The *Hilfspolizei* were expected to issue armbands and papers to their troopers, although most men were affiliated to a uniformed organisation, which meant they could wear their uniforms on duty.[13] The issue of weapons was also turned into an expression of volunteerism. In Aachen, they collected ten pistols, five rifles and a carbine, all government issue, and this was increased by another fifty-one privately owned Dreyse hunting rifles.[14] To raise their professionalism, the *Hilfspolizei* began a programme of intensive training from March 1933. This was divided into two parts, the *Praktische Ausbildung* (practical training), intended to provide formal training in weapons handling and working co-ordination with regular police forces, and the *Theoretische Ausbildung* (theoretical training), which provided a rudimentary introduction to German law and legal procedures.[15]

Heinrich Himmler's SS became the central institution for all racial security in Nazi Germany. In the Rhineland, the SS was a constantly evolving clique of highly motivated zealots. In 1929, the SS detachments in the Rhineland were centralised under the regional district *SS-Oberabschnitt West*. This office set up a headquarters in Düsseldorf and gradually turned into a formidable and effective security organisation. In 1936, the SS took control of all the German police, including the uniformed branches. The consequences of the SS-Police amalgamation had a profound ideological impact on policing and security. In terms of manpower, some police officers, troopers and officials had voluntarily joined the Nazi Party before 1936, but after 1936, suitable candidates for the SS were required to go through a strict selection process with positive vetting of racial profiles. The complexion of the uniform police was also changed through a planned process of militarisation. The consequences were that the German police before 1933 had been a typical civilian organisation, and between 1933 and 1936 it retained much of its older ideological past, but after 1936 the SS-Police became the pulse of the Nazi dictatorship. The SS supplied the guards for the *Vogelsang*, and several carried their experience into their Holocaust careers, revealing how critical the site was in its training.

The senior SS leader at the regional level in the Rhineland was Fritz Weitzel. He was born in Frankfurt-am-Main in 1904, a mechanic by trade, and joined the SA in 1924, the Nazi Party in 1925 and the SS in 1927. He remained the senior SS leader in this region until April 1940. In 1937, there was a major SS reorganisation of its regional level command system. The introduction of the position of *HSSPF* (meaning Higher SS and Police Chief) would turn out to be a critical decision for Himmler. In geographical terms, the HSSPF office holder was granted SS powers in parallel with the Wehrmacht's system of regional districts. However, the power invested in each HSSPF came from answering directly to Himmler and Hitler. These chosen men were the hatchet men of Nazi crime. In June 1938, Weitzel became *HSSPF West*; his headquarters remained in Düsseldorf, but his geographical authority extended across the Rhineland-Ruhr area (including Cologne-Aachen) and in parallel with the Wehrmacht's *Wehrkreis VI* (military administrative district). In effect, all the industrial cities, including Aachen, Cologne and Essen, came under this SS authority, which remained unchanged until the end of the war. The senior SS leader in Aachen, critical to the period 1937–42, was Carl Zenner. Born in Oberlimburg in the Saarlouis area in 1899, some accounts claim he served in the Great War and was awarded the Iron Cross, but he was also involved in the *Freikorps* movement in the Baltic region. Zenner was radicalised through his *Freikorps* experience, where he participated in para-militarism and the propagation of right-wing nationalist extremist ideologies. Zenner was married and in 1922 studied for a diploma in commerce in Cologne. His first job after qualifying was in a stone factory in Burgbrohl (today, in the Rhineland-Palatinate). He joined the Nazi Party in 1925 and the SS in 1926; he received some rapid promotions and raised SS units in Aachen, Koblenz and Trier. He was selected to join the RSHA, the secret state security bureau under Reinhard Heydrich and became Aachen's police president in January 1937 (with the rank of SS-Oberführer, equivalent to a British army brigadier).[16]

On 24 September 1944, Captain Kettler, a British army intelligence officer, interrogated Karl Happel in the London District Cage. Happel was treated as an influential Nazi operative; after he was captured, the British immediately isolated him from other German PoWs. He was an Oberleutnant der Polizei in the Order Police but later served in an army grenadier regiment when he was captured in Holland. He joined the Nazi Party in February and the SS in May 1933. In March 1938, Happel was assigned to the *Grenzpolizei* (border police) in Aachen, and under interrogation explained how they worked alongside and reported to the Gestapo. The border police also worked with officers from the *Reichsfinanzverwaltung*, or customs officials. He explained that co-operation existed between the *Bezirkzollkommissariaten* and the nearest *Grenzpolizeikommissariat* of the Gestapo. In the event of arrests of people wanted by the Gestapo, the *Grenzschutzpolizei* arrested them on the frontiers while trying to escape to Holland and Belgium. Regierungsrat SS-Standartenführer Seetzen was chief of the Aachen Gestapo and his deputy was Dr Puetz, a *Regierungs Assessor*. The Aachen detachment was originally 160 strong but was increased in May 1938 by a further 100 officers to cover construction on the Westwall. From November 1938, the *Leitstelle* in Düsseldorf controlled all Gestapo branches in Aachen-Cologne, Trier, Wupperthal and Koblenz, among others. The Aachen office had sub-offices in Monschau, Herzogenrath, Vaals border, main railway station, Westbahnhof, Lichtenbusch, Eupen, Kohlscheid, Bildchen and Simpelveld, with each office assigned two or three officers. The Aachen Gestapo was in direct telephone connection with Berlin and had another direct line with the Regierungspresident Dr Vogelsgang in the city's municipal offices, and a direct line to the central Police Presidium. All the offices were in daily contact, and lists of criminals were also issued daily. Arrested persons from Aachen were usually sent to the concentration camps at either Buchenwald or Sachsenhausen. There were two border police offices—Monheimsallee 5 (within 300 yards of the Synagogue) and Försterstrasse, with a Gestapo employee in the latter. The Kripo, the criminal police, technically came under the direct control of Zenner but actually took their orders from the Gestapo. In 1938, they had a total strength of 120 and they were quite adept at murder, house breaking and arson.[17] The pogrom led to the gradual ghettoisation of the Jews, which was completed with the onset of war. Victory in 1940 rendered the Westwall redundant and all construction ceased. The reduced workload barely touched the Aachen-Gestapo, and in a perfect example of Parkinson's law of making work, the officials smoothly took up the handling of PoWs, opposition and resistance movements in nearby occupied territories, and the administration of foreign workers.

In July 1945, US Third Army conducted an interrogation of Kriminalrat Richard Bach (formerly Chief of Gestapo Aussenstelle Aachen). Until 1942, it was a Gestapo Stelle under *SS-Sturmbannführer* and *Oberregierungarat* Noske. In 1942, it was reduced to an Aussenstelle under *SS-Sturmbannführer* and Kriminalrat Dirks. Later, Kriminalrat Bach took over the Aussenstelle. There were fifty-five Gestapo officials, including eighteen women, but this was gradually reduced to five or six very able individuals, as most staff transferred to Köln. A dual leadership system covering Aachen and Köln was inefficient and eventually the entire command was centralised in Cologne in 1943. There were three important officials: Kriminalkommissar Bechtel, a specialist of foreigners; Lange specialised in Jews and Churches; and Schmidt specialised in border and frontier matters. The frontier control (*Grenzreferat*) employed 120 officers, with offices in Heinsberg, Herzogenrath, Aachen, Eupen and Malmedy. Foreign workers presented a separate problem. Because of the proximity of the border, foreign workers trying to escape were frequently picked up in the Aachen sector. Eight to ten men were assigned to working on border problems. When the allies arrived before Eupen, prisoners and their documents were taken to Cologne. Thereafter, the problems involving foreigners fell into the sphere of the Landrät. Later, Bach did much of the work, reducing the efficiency of the office (i.e. no cover to prevent post-air-raid looting, search for new agents or dealing with beggars). All Gestapo officials and their administration finally deserted Aachen for Cologne on 14 September 1944, destroying their archives before leaving.[18]

II. Aryanisation: racial exclusion in Aachen

According to most leading accounts, there were Jews in Aachen at the time of the Romans. Charlemagne allowed Jews within his palace grounds. A man called Isaac accompanied Charlemagne's ambassador on a diplomatic mission in 802 AD. The Jews continued to thrive throughout the fourteenth and fifteenth centuries, although some converted to Christianity. In 1629, both Jews and Protestants were expelled from the city, but forty years later the Jews were allowed to return. In May 1815, the Jewish community paid homage to the Prussian monarch. The community began to thrive and in 1860–2 a beautifully ornate synagogue was constructed in the city centre near Kaiserplatz. In 1900, the rabbi was Dr Jaulus. The Jewish demographics are not entirely accurate: in 1900 there was a community of 2,100, but by 1905 there were already indications of decline, with a fall to 1,665. This trend continued, with a reduction to 1,348 by 1933 and by 1939 it had reduced to 780.[20] There are various accounts that claim upwards of 1,500 Jews were still struggling to exist on meagre rations in Aachen in September 1941. Whether these numbers were inflated by Nazi concentrations and deportations cannot be accurately ascertained.

On 16 June 1933, there were 3,482 Jews registered in the Regierungsbezirk Aachen (the city's legislative limits), of which 1,345 Jewish persons were living in Aachen. They were: Landkreis Aachen (445), Eschweiler (107), Stolberg (40), Würselen (20), Alsdorf (39), Eilendorf (23), Kohlscheid (6) and 210 elsewhere; in Kreis Düren (726) and in the town of Düren (358) with another 368 in the area; Kreis Erkelenz (117), Geilenkirchen-Heinsberg (280), Jülich (320) inner Jülich (120), rest (200), Monschau (3) and Schleiden (246); and finally Hohenzollerische Lande: Kreis Hechlingen (292) and Sigmaringen (9). There were 1,666 men and 1,816 women.[19]

In 1935, the Nazis introduced the Nuremberg Race Laws. They were two sets of legal codes: the first addressing citizenship and the second to protect German blood and German honour. Hans Globke (1898–1973), a leading civil servant and lawyer, examined the laws and accepted them into the Nazi codex, in effect enabling the legalisation and legitimisation of racism. As a senior Weimar official, he had introduced anti-Semitic rules before Hitler came to power. Globke had moved to Aachen as a child and became a pupil of the elite Kaiser Karl Gymnasium.

The Jewish community had made a strong contribution to Aachen's nineteenth-century economy and had maintained a significant role in the IHK. Jews served the city during Bismarck's *Kulturkampf*, acting as a go-between with the church and officials in exile in neighbouring Vaals. Nevertheless, Aryanisation, the Nazi programme of anti-Semitic exclusion, and the expropriation of Jewish property were well received by Aachen's political and business elites. The IHK, at the heartbeat of the economy, became fully Aryanised by the end of 1934. Thirty cloth manufacturers were closed or forced to change ownership under the Nazi code. They included: Hugo Hirtz, founded in 1861; Marx & Auerbach, founded in 1828; Julius Katz, founded in 1882; and B.Th. Vonachten, founded in 1843—several of these manufacturers continued into the 1960s with their German owners. Aryanisation extended Nazi persecution into the Technical University. Many students were fanatical Nazis and were quick to insult Jewish professors. This was followed by the removal of Jews from the university. Students also exposed those professors who supported the communists. To avoid the violence, those professors who could became Nazi party members; in the end, two-thirds of the professors became Nazis. From 12 professors, eleven Jews were removed from faculty, including Otto Blumenthal, a leading mathematician. He was a German soldier, a Great War hero, and died in a concentration camp. There were successive waves of Nazification in education through institutes and schools, and the civil servants led the way with their service maxim: 'doing something before being ordered to do it'.[21]

If there was a connection between the academic and the business antisemitism, it can only be rationalised in materialistic terms such as careerism, kleptomania and financial greed. The market mechanism at the heart of capitalism was manipulated to serve Germany's new masters. While at the same time the powerful anti-capitalist streak running through the Nazi movement promoted another virulent antisemitism. These two social forces within Nazi Germany sealed the fate of Aachen's Jews.

There was a gradual trajectory toward extermination. According to Götz Aly, in the summer of 1941, containers of furniture and belongings of Jews deported to the east were being auctioned off and some goods given to persons de-housed from bombing. In Belgium, furniture plundered from 4,000 Jewish homes and apartments was given to people de-housed in Cologne and Aachen.[22] The Nazi deportation of Aachen's Jews began in 1942, from 25 March, and concluded in September. There was a further deportation in December 1943 and the final deportation in September 1944. The deportations were to the 'east', Izbica (eastern Poland) and directly to Theresienstadt. The deportations marked the final phase of a race policy that began in 1933. There was Jewish emigration to Britain and America, but also desperate flights across the Belgium and Dutch borders.

The most famous of Aachen's Jewish refugees was Anne Frank's mother. Edith Abel Holländer was born in Aachen on 16 January 1900. She was the youngest of four children, Julius, Walter and Bettina (Betti), who died from an appendicitis operation in September 1916. Her father was Abraham Holländer (1860–1927), a successful businessman in the field of industrial machinery; her mother was Rosa Stern (1866–1942), buried in Aachen's Jüdische Friedhof. Like many Jewish families, the Holländers were integrated in Imperial German society but maintained a respectful regard for their religious culture. Edith attended the Victoriaschule in Aachen, a private Christian school for girls, and completed her final exams in 1916. On 12 May 1925, Edith married in Aachen's synagogue, and then lived in Frankfurt-am-Main, where she had two daughters. Anne Frank was born in Frankfurt in June 1929. Edith, Anne and her siblings moved to Aachen to live with Rosa. In 1934, the Frank family were reunited with Otto in Amsterdam and, in 1939, Rosa joined them. In 1940, Otto tried to take his family to the USA, but the papers were not processed, especially after the US

Consulate closed in Rotterdam. Ten days before her forty-fourth birthday, Edith died of starvation in Auschwitz extermination camp, on 6 January 1945. Anne, and her sister Margot, died in Belsen in March 1945 (weeks before the liberation by the British).[23]

A small number of Aachen's Jews escaped to Britain before 1940; their sad story is pieced together from a small collection of immigration index cards. The index card for Sophie Haymann (neé Aron) was typical of the basic details. She was born in Aachen in 1862 and died in England on 26 January 1942; she is remembered on a gravestone in the Jüdische Friedhof, but there are no details of when she emigrated. We know more about Hildegard Broda, who was born in Aachen in 1911, had become Austrian possibly by marriage and held a degree in medicine. She had become an assistant of Dr D.S. Barber in Chiddingfold, Surrey. She attended a tribunal at Guildford No. 4 office and was registered: 'Refugee, anti-Nazi—vouched for by reliable people. Restrictions would interfere with her occupation which is of value to the country.' However, exemption from internment was not always straightforward due to ethnicity. Grete Neckarsulmer was brought before the tribunal of No. 2 region, where, it was recorded, she was brought to Britain by the Jewish Refugee Committee in September 1938. She went to Bradford Grammar School, with the fees paid by the committee. She was designated exempt from internment, but, it was noted, 'Brother has been interned—parents still in Germany.' Her brother, Carl Israel Neckarsulmer, was 18 when he arrived in the UK in October 1939, classified 'B', and was immediately interned. He was later reclassified category 'C' as a student on 24 November 1941.

Irmgard Helga Tisch arrived in Britain on 22 January 1939. During her tribunal hearing on 5 December 1942, she was classified 'Jewish—Father was a worsted manufacturer—business closed under Nazi decree. Parents now residing in Harrogate.' Her mother, Lille Tisch, arrived in Britain on 26 October 1939 and was categorised a 'housewife', exempt from internment. The Heinemanns were one of the few refugee families to travel as a group. Herbert, the son, received a tribunal hearing on 9 December 1941, where it was recorded: 'Came to UK with parents on

21 December 1939. Jewish. Parents and brother in London—category "C". Father was a cloth manufacturer—lost business—under Nazi decree against Jews.' His father, Hermann, faced a tribunal in Cambridgeshire, which noted: 'Very little is known of this man who has a brother—a chemist—in Germany. He is also a skilled photographer. Has tickets for USA.' He had been interned but: 'After re-consideration exemptions seems justified by his intention to break off from Germany indicated by (1) presence at school here of twins of 11½; (2) Jewish race and religion; (3) USA tickets; and (4) no trace at MI5.' His brother was designated exempt at a London tribunal, and the Home Office sent letters regarding his classification. The brother, Otto Israel Heinemann, had arrived in Britain on 24 November 1939 but interned on 21 June 1940, at the time of the invasion scares, but was released on 29 September 1940. On 22 April 1941, Freidmann Schonbrunn was designated exempt on the explicit grounds of being a 'Jewish refugee' and having enlisted into the armed services under Home Office guidelines. Sibilla Buehler, a teacher, and Helma Sara Dietze, domestic, were both designated a 'refugee from Nazi oppression', further indicating a shift in official mindset about Jewish refugees. Elsa Levy attended the Nottingham tribunal and was declared: 'Genuine refugee from Nazi oppression. Opposed to German government and desire to return to Germany. No to this country.'[24]

The case of Lotte Herzberg, however, caused a stir among the British security services, which, given her profession as a cook and domestic servant, provides an insight of the security mindset in wartime. On 25 May 1940, she received a tribunal hearing before Richard O'Sullivan of No. 7 Bristol district. Her index card noted:

> The alien is a Jewess and unmarried. She was employed in the kitchen of her aunt's hotel at Aachen but had to leave for racial reasons. Her father is dead, but her mother and her brother live at Aachen. The alien desires to emigrate to America if possible.
>
> She came to England on the 1st March 1939, and has been in domestic service at Plymouth ever since. Her fiancé is in America. Mrs. Northcott her employer, attended and vouched for the alien.

ORDINARY PEOPLE

The Advisory Committee retained the alien in Category C, but recommended that she be required to leave the Protected Area by the 30th June 1940. They had regard to the fact that she arrived in this country only a few months before war broke out and her residence is one of the most important places in the Protected area.

This case was submitted by the Police as a 'Protected Area Case'.

Flora Sara Reis had only a short bio on her index card. She came to Britain to attend the wedding of her son but her relative refused to allow her to return to Germany. Her son was a teacher, living in Baghdad and 'married to an English girl'. In the British report, Frau Reis 'states Nazis burned her house in 1938 because of her being Jewish'. Her husband died in 1936 and she had another son living in Palestine. Henning Nuttgens was born in 1856 and had lived in Britain for sixty-eight years when he was brought before the tribunal on 11 December 1939. A brief note on his index card referred to two sons who served in the British army and he was employed in an arms factory. The tribunal agreed, 'can be safely regarded as a friendly alien'. Therese Rageb (née Hermanns) was a 'German subject married to an Egyptian subject'. She had lost her German nationality but was uncertain whether she gained Egyptian nationality, rendering her 'stateless' in British officialdom. Walter Kaufmann had been interned and ordered released only in Australia. He was shipped out of Britain aboard the SS *Dunera* on 10 July 1940 and was released nine days later when the ship reached Australia. He remained a category 2 refugee. He was joined, on board the SS *Dunera*, by Willi Israel Kaufmann, but it's not clear why both men were shipped out.

Among the refugees from Aachen to Britain was a Catholic sister, pointing to the Nazi terror's attacks on the Church. Sister Ruberta Michalek (born 1875) was a Roman Catholic residing in Roehampton when called before the tribunal on 13 November 1939. Michalek was representative of the breadth of German domestic opposition to the Nazis. By December 1941, there were 113 Aachen persons under arrest by the Gestapo or police. Their crimes included: 14 Communists, 9 opposition supporters, 13 economic and the rest (including 62 non-Germans) for refusing to work.²⁵ In the area of Aachen, between 1940 and 1944, there were 36 concentration camps of different sizes divided into three categories: slave labour, PoWs and punishment camps. Almost all of Aachen's industries had access to slave labour in the broadest category, with some also allocated to private homes, hospitals and clinics. The camps were dispersed within the municipal area of Aachen, making it unlikely for residents to ignore their appearance. Several camps had more than 500 prisoners, who were daily marched through the streets to and from work, also ensuring the locals saw these people.²⁶

There were serious tensions between the Nazis and the Bishop of Münster—von Gehlen. In 1943, Gehlen accused the Nazis of committing euthanasia. Aachen priests in camps included Joseph Buchkremer (Dachau, 1942–5), Nicolaus Jansen (Dachau, 1941–5) and Heinrich Selhorst (1942–5); Hans Rindermann (Dachau—1941–1945) was a critic of euthanasia. A clerical conference was held in Düren (14 September 1942), concerned with addressing the issue that a Bolshevik (Soviet) victory would spell the end for the Church. The British Foreign Office had received evidence from a Swedish medical director that 'lunatic asylums are being cleared of their patients by euthanasia to make room for the wounded from the Eastern front. He spoke of one asylum where 1,200 people had been removed by poison.'²⁷

III. Prosecuting crimes against humanity

At 10.00 hours on Wednesday 28 May 1947, the Military Government Court in Aachen opened the Juden-Pogrom-Strafsache (Jewish Pogrom Prosecution). The defendants were: Quirin Jansen (former Oberbürgermeister), Hubert Graf (Fire Brigade officer); Karl Zenner (former SSPF and Chief of Police), Paul Christgau (Senior policeman, Gasborn Police Station); Eduard Schmeer (local Nazi Party Kreisleiter), Franz Durbaum, Anton Dreuw, Alexander Hammers (Fire Brigade officer), Karl Heinrich Wilhelm Klarmann (Oberleutnant of the Order Police) and Kaspar Becks (Air Raid Police). The accused faced two charges with the Control Council Law No. 10: 'crimes against humanity and arises out of persecution against persons who were of a different race or religion'. The British tribunal prosecuted the culprits under the Control Council Law No. 10, 'crimes against humanity', and the investigators tried to piece together the events to reconstruct an account of what actually happened. Almost ten years after the crime, many perpetrators were dead or missing and recollections were inconsistent. Several months before the trial, the witnesses and defendants submitted written statements. These followed similar patterns: the defendants could recall in sharp detail where they were, what they wore, how drunk they were and even their movements. Their recollections of command, control or the communications of the crime were vague and inconsistent. For example, Fritz Weitzel was killed in an RAF bombing raid during a home visit to Düsseldorf on 19 June 1940. Weitzel was instrumental in alerting the SS-Police and Gestapo chains of command.

Regardless of their intelligence resources and the authority over the city, the British were unable to break the refusal of the defendants to confess to the crimes. The British prosecution was hamstrung from the outset. This is obvious from the prosecutor's opening general statement that Zenner, Jansen and Schmeer 'proceeded to hatch a plot for the burning down of the synagogue'. There were known details, pertinent to the case. The choice for instance the selection of Gasborn Police Station, as the command-and-control point, about eighty yards from the synagogue. They were less precise over the timing of the crimes by the perpetrators, especially those responsible for smashing furniture, looting valuables or burning the building. The synagogue's construction, being an elaborate oriental design in stone, posed a challenge and pointed to a significant degree of premeditation. The British understood the basic details of the crime and that it took place sometime between midnight and 09.00 on 9–10 November 1938. The perpetrators were known to include the Fire Brigade and SS-Police, with suspicions about the instrumental role of the Gestapo. They were also aware that instructions to burn the synagogue had been received at the Gasborn police precinct.

Given the general lack of details, the reason why the British decided to prosecute the crime appears uncertain. If the British hoped to flush out Nazis, or other perpetrators, or encourage witnesses to step forward, it was probably too late, being three years into the allied occupation. If the case was political, in parallel with the on-going de-Nazification process, its influence was marginal at best. If the British hoped they had deposited an archive of historical evidence, to educate the community of Nazi crimes, then the plan failed, because essentially few in Aachen knew of the case before 2019.

The prosecution opened with a summary from 7 November 1938, when a German diplomat was killed in Paris: 'allegedly by a Polish Jew, and this incident was made an excuse by the Nazi Party to instigate a whole series of persecutions against the Jewish race'. Documentary evidence was presented to prove how the Nazis issued instructions for local actions to be stirred against the Jews. According to the prosecutor, Zenner, Jansen and Schmeer 'proceeded to hatch a plot for the burning down of the synagogue'. Zenner selected the Gasborn Police Station as their meeting place, eighty yards from the synagogue. Between midnight and 13.00, members of the Fire Brigade and police arrived to receive their instructions to burn down the synagogue.

In the early hours, the building caretaker was woken and made to open the synagogue, whereupon furniture was smashed, valuable carpets and other property was taken, and the building was set on fire. The prosecutor explained: 'At first the fire did not go very well in a stone building, and a hole was smashed in the roof, windows opened, and petrol obtained and poured on the building in order to burn it down immediately.' There were already people in the streets, fully clothed, and not hastily dressed, as would usually occur with a fire. Zenner, Jansen and Schmeer were in attendance during the fire and were all guilty of actively participating in the fire. It was a breach of the duties of the fire officials and the other officials not to attempt to put the fire out. In effect, they contributed to the destruction by ensuring the building burned down. The fire service was deployed and an engine with its crew stood ready but only to prevent the fire from spreading to surrounding buildings. Under normal circumstances, this kind of arson case would have fallen under section 306, subsection 1 of the German criminal code. There was no defence of 'superior orders', which was denied under both the Control Council law and the German criminal code. Under the charges, any person was guilty whether they had planned or 'took a consenting part in the crime'. An onlooker who witnesses a crime against humanity and does nothing is not guilty of taking a consenting part: this did not apply to a fire officer who stood by and did nothing before a fire. This was the golden thread of the British case: the legal duty of the state-employed officials.

The first witness was Otto Garbe, described as the technical town inspector in the city administration, and he confirmed the accuracy of the synagogue's location on a city map. The second witness was Walter Gahen (born 1911 in Aachen); at the time of the trial he was chief of the Kreiswirtschaftsamt Aachen. In 1938, he was a member of the Jewish community in Aachen. He was asked about the most highly religious items in the synagogue, and replied: 'The five books of Moses, and the Ark of the Covenant.' Gahen then went on to describe a religious service. Herr Bergs, representing Schmeer, questioned Gahen on why the duplicates of the books of Moses and the Ark of the Covenant were particularly holy. Gahen replied that the books were written by hand, but Bergs asked why did that make them more holy? Eventually, the court intervened; the judge advised he would accept Bergs' line of questioning over the 'value' of religious objects and would grant him ample time. But, he warned, 'this case is really concerned with freedom of thought'; Bergs elected to withdraw. Herr Crott, representing Zenner, asked if Gahen knew of a small shrine of about 25 centimetres in length; Gahen replied that he did not. Brandeth, the prosecutor, stepped in and asked if he knew of a gold emblem or ornament that was a representation of Moses, but Gahen did not.

The third witness was Michael Schuld. In 1938, he was a senior order police NCO in Aachen, but since July 1946 had been the town secretary of Düsseldorf. He was asked about the evening of 9–10 November. He recalled being on duty on the 8th but attended the oath-taking ceremony for SS recruits, held annually since 1933 at the *Katschhof*, on 9 November. There were speeches, and Schmeer presented awards and gave a speech about the murder of the diplomat in Paris. The ceremony finished in the evening and then he went straight home. He recalled reporting for duty at 07.45 on 10 November at Gasborn Police Station. On his way to the station, he smelled smoke, and saw a large mushroom of dark smoke in the air. On entering the police station, he went to the guardroom, where Police President Zenner was sitting at the table. On the table there was a strong box of about 30 centimetres long and about 15 centimetres in depth. Zenner wanted to be connected by telephone to his police headquarters or to the Security Battalion, but the switchboard was unable to meet his wishes. When he departed, Zenner tucked the box under his arm and was heard to say, 'well now we can tear down the synagogue'. After Zenner's departure, Schuld observed a small yellow figure of 30 centimetres high, which was described as a 'golden Moses'. When he entered the main room it was disorderly with picks and shovels. There was a group of persons, partly in uniforms, but he didn't know them. He was asked to confirm whether Zenner was his superior office, which Schuld accepted.

Zenner's lawyer then questioned Schuld. He was asked if it was a valuable box but he could not state whether it was or not. He was also asked if the men in plain clothes were from the Gestapo, but Schuld didn't know. Lawyer Herr Bergs, representing Schmeer, asked if Schuld could be certain it was his client who gave the speech. Schuld recalled Schmeer stood at the fountain when he gave the speech. Bergs pressed on, with questions about whether Schmeer was at the SS ceremony. He claimed there were newspapers from the time which listed those in attendance, but Schuld stood his ground, claiming certainty that Schmeer gave a speech. Lawyer Dr Soninini, representing Klarmann and Becks, questioned as to whether Schuld knew if there was a party after the SS ceremony with the consumption of alcoholic beverage. Schuld claimed this had been the subject of talk afterwards. The judge interrupted and asked Schuld if he recalled the question over Schmeer's attendance at the SS ceremony and his written claim that he wasn't there. Schuld replied that he did recall the question but was unable to fully remember since it was eight years before. Since making his statement he had time to think about the question and had changed his mind. Bergs vouched that Schuld's testimony was not true.

ORDINARY PEOPLE

The fourth witness was Alexander Aretz, an Order Police Obermeister and the deputy chief of Gasborn Police Station, and presently unemployed. Aretz was not present at the start of the fire but was 'fetched' at 02.30. He recognised most of the defendants as present at the scene when he arrived, and added there were about thirty others in the vicinity of the fire and the police station. Some men were in uniform, and several had removed their tunics. There were picks and shovels in the precinct courtroom. He overheard a man called *Michlisch* (later killed during the air raid of 11 April 1944) loudly claim 'we have broken up everything' and heard the defendants speaking with him discussing the damage they had caused. Aretz said Christgau, Klarmann and Becks were tipsy from the consumption of alcohol. Zenner ordered him to seal off the vicinity of the synagogue and he took six men at about 02.45 to set up barricades. They walked to Judenplatz and, looking through the doors of the synagogue, he observed a number of small fires. There was no one around when he posted his officers to form a cordon around the building. Then Christgau came to ask if he knew where he could get more petrol, but Aretz ignored him. Christgau walked away but came back with petrol and told Aretz that he got it without his help and 'you can lick my back' was incorrectly translated into the court record.[28] He then watched as men made a hole in the roof, which encouraged the flames to surge.

Aretz didn't recognise the men but when he returned to the police station at about 04.30–05.00, he saw Schmeer and Zenner. Schmeer was on the telephone talking to Gauleiter Grohe, in Cologne, and afterwards he told Zenner, 'the synagogues at Düren, Düsseldorf and Bonn are burning'. Schmeer said there must be no looting, but Zenner replied, 'that's alright, we are going to do it as we like it'. Zenner then ordered his SS men to go into town and smash Jewish properties. By then, the synagogue was burning furiously. Aretz claimed he ordered his police officers to guard Jewish shops against the SS, but Zenner warned him not to interfere. At 06.00, Jansen arrived to join Zenner and Schmeer; they were standing together in Judenplatz. The fire by then had almost burned out but he stood there for around thirty minutes.

WAR COMES TO AACHEN

The Fire Brigade was spraying water on neighbouring houses as a precaution. There were two fire engines, one at the police station and the other near the synagogue. Aretz took over fire duties, attached hoses to fire hydrants and began spraying water at a house where petrol had been stockpiled. He then turned the hoses on the synagogue. The fire was brought under control by 08.30. Aretz was uncertain when Dr Oster, the Aachen fire chief, arrived at the scene. When Aretz departed at 10.00, all that remained of the synagogue was four walls, as the roof had fallen in.

The defence case opened with questions of the accused. Dr Heusch, representing Jansen, began by questioning his client. Jansen became Oberbürgermeister in 1933. On the day of the pogrom, Jansen departed Berlin at 14.00 and arrived in Aachen at 00.30. He was collected at the station by a driver from the *Rathaus* and taken straight to his home, outside the city centre, where he had food and went to bed. He received two telephone calls from the *Rathaus*, and another from Schmeer. In the first call, the telephonist told Jansen the shop windows owned by a man named Schurbaum had been smashed (page 143). He asked the telephonist to pass an order to a night-watchman to observe what was going on. Then he called SA-Brigadeführer Lampe, who was Director of Aachen Hospital in November 1938, and asked if the SA were behind the violence. Lampe was in bed but knew what was going on. Jansen then called his son-in-law to ask him if there were incidents in the centre of Aachen, but his son had heard nothing. Jansen received another call from the *Rathaus*; he was told there were no demonstrations, but Jewish shops had had their windows and shutters smashed; but police were preventing further damage. Jansen attempted to call Zenner, but he was not at the *Polizeipresidium*. He recalled the call was received but 'hung up' when they tried to connect him.

At 05.00 or 06.00, Jensen received a call from Schmeer and was told the synagogue was on fire and the Fire Brigade nearby. Schmeer told Jansen he was unaware who was responsible for the fire. Jansen asked if the fire was large and endangering the built-up area and Schmeer replied there was no danger as 'the Fire Brigade had mastered the situation'. Jansen asked Schmeer if the SA was responsible but was told by Schmeer he didn't know. Jansen remained at his house after the call. At 07.00 or 08.00, Jansen drove to the Rathaus, where he met with *Stadtverwaltungsdirektor* Schoneberg and *Verwaltungsoberinspektor* Wollweber, described as his 'close associates'. Jensen felt it was important to describe their usual working hours: Monday to Friday 07.30 to noon, then 14.00 to 18.00 and on Saturdays from 07.30 to 13.00—a 48-hour week. They had a meeting to discuss arson as a criminal act against the synagogue. Zenner then arrived and asked if they wanted to look over the town, but Jansen refused. Jansen blamed Goebbels' propaganda for the crime. He recalled Zenner thought the incidents were 'a piggery' but 'an order is an order'; they then drove to the synagogue, which was still burning.[29]

Bergs was first to cross-examine Jansen on behalf of Schmeer. Bergs' questions elicited that Jansen discussed the fire with Schmeer at lunchtime on 10 November, and the latter told him he knew nothing about the incident or being in the vicinity of the fire. Schmeer claimed surprise about the incident. Jansen claimed several officials were present at the Schmeer-Jansen meeting; one was later killed, and the other was not invited to the court. The judge ruled against Jansen's claim because it constituted hearsay. In the discussions, it was claimed Zenner had ordered Schneider (later killed) to burn down the synagogue. The prosecution quizzed Jansen about his trip to Berlin since it had not been included in his written statement. Jansen reiterated his denial at attending the ceremonies on 9 November. He also denied discussing the assassination in Paris while he was in Berlin. Jansen also claimed there were no anti-Semitic demonstrations in Aachen. Although he heard of the attacks on Jewish shops, Jansen had later claimed they were criminal but did nothing in 1938. Jansen said the attacks were spontaneous and he agreed with the prosecution that they were criminal and political. Jansen tried to clarify his position by alleging he was informed the SA were responsible, but he also denied responsibility, which he laid on Zenner. The judge again intervened to try to tidy up his account. Jansen had denied contact with Dr Oster (Fire Brigade chief) and appeared confused over talking with Schneider, an SS officer under Zenner. Upon being asked why

Schmeer might call the Oberbürgermeister, Jansen replied (page 156), 'the three persons mainly responsible for the town wanted to inform each other'.

Jansen denied having the authority to do anything about the fire. The prosecutor pressed Jansen over why officials would call him at 05.00 if nothing could be done. The prosecutor backed him into a corner with questions over why he had not prevented the looting. Jansen asserted Aachen was not an anti-Jewish city. The prosecutor countered by asking why he hadn't rounded up a few 'worthy citizens' and attempted to protect them. Jansen replied that by staying away he was offering more protection. Jansen denied watching the synagogue burn but then changed his answer to say he did but only from 08.00. The cross-examinations focused on what he knew of the fire, whether it was under control or not, and why he had not attended the scene. He was asked if his absence and lack of action constituted taking 'a consenting part in that crime'. Jansen's excuse for not attending the synagogue was that he wished to demonstrate to the citizens of Aachen that he had nothing to do with the crime. He was challenged if his attendance at other fires had made him responsible for them. Jansen said he attended every fire up to 1941. An interjection asked what the point of his presence was if he had no responsibility for the police or Fire Brigade, but Jansen was unconvincing and evaded the questioning. When probed as to why he bothered going to the synagogue, Jansen claimed Zenner had fetched him. He also added that 99 per cent of the Aachen citizens didn't know Zenner was responsible for the fire.

The prosecution then raised the question of crowd spontaneity. A reference was made to the AAPT of 10 November 1938, which had attributed responsibility for the fire and looting to the spontaneous actions of the citizenry. Jansen replied the article was nonsense, but the prosecution countered by asking why he hadn't issued a counter statement in the newspaper. He declined that this was his responsibility, and that the newspaper would not be published. He was shown the newspaper and asked if he had read the article on 10 November; Jansen could not say but added that by 1938 he was already opposed to the newspaper. He claimed to know the editor of the newspaper only 'by sight'. Jansen was then asked what Schmeer had discussed with him about the cause of the fire. Schmeer reported the synagogue had burned and claimed he had asked (page 166): 'What is that for a piggery, first the shops and now the synagogue, who did it?' Schmeer replied, 'I do not know who did it, maybe the little angels.' Jansen believed Schmeer knew those responsible for starting the fire. He accepted he had not asked if the fire was out or how the Fire Brigade was coping. Schmeer and Jansen were personal friends and had become the city's leaders in 1933. The prosecutor summarised his opinion of Jansen's answers: the telephone call took place at 05.30, Schmeer said the synagogue was in flames in an anti-Jewish protest, and by doing nothing Jansen had taken a consenting part in the action.

The judge questioned Jansen about his standing in the Nazi Party. Jansen claimed he was not a member of the SS, the SA or a party leader. He conceded the party leadership thought highly enough of him to give him the 'big job' as Oberbürgermeister. The discussion revolved around 9 November, being the sacred day commemorating the Nazi dead from the Munich Putsch (1923) and the ritual laying of wreaths. Until 1937, Jansen said he laid the wreaths every year in the city's Tomb of the Unknown Soldier. Absence from that event was significant but Jensen could still not explain what he was doing in Berlin. The judge noted that, while he was in Berlin, the city was buzzing about the assassination and letters were sent to city officials across Germany ordering revenge actions against Jewish businesses. Jansen claimed that in his cell overnight he had thought about the events on that day, but still claimed he was unaware of what was going on across Germany. The prosecutor then probed the statement that Jansen had called Lampe, his son-in-law, adding that it was strange the Oberbürgermeister should call them on the telephone and not the police. They claimed his testimony of innocence was not only inconceivable but also not truthful. In response to being told there were witnesses of him attending the fire and his name circulated, Jansen replied there were many thousands of Jansens living in Aachen, but he was not at the scene. Jansen told the prosecution he was a long-term Nazi Party member and partly believed in its philosophy. He was asked about Alfred Rosenberg's visit to Aachen in 1939 and was asked if he had given the welcoming address. Jansen responded by claiming he didn't believe in Rosenberg's ideas. Then the case closed with several of defendants having refused to give evidence.

The court judgement began: 'In 1938 Aachen was one of the many beautiful cities in Germany ... Sitting in this trial in this inadequate Court amid ruins of this once beautiful city, one can feel that the Immortal Gods up above must have said ironically: "Gentlemen, you wish to destroy your city. We will assist you" ... from the evidence that has been given in this court that the destruction of the Aachen synagogue was one of the manifestations of the effort of destruction by the German government, and as a result of that destructive power great parts of Europe are in misery and suffering, and in particular Germany itself' (page 418). The judge noted there was a trial of ten days, eight defendants, thirteen prosecution witnesses, thirteen defence witnesses and two charges. He explained his decision: 'I am concerned with evidence of fact only, and it is quite immaterial to me whether a man is said to be a Nazi, an SA, Communist, a socialist, or any other party or no part at all, or whether he was a Christian or a Jew' (page 419). In the judge's opinion, membership to the Nazi Party or SA was immaterial in the destruction of the synagogue, because the destruction of a Christian church would have also been a 'crime against humanity'. He dismissed Dr Heusch's defence that the Control Commission law did not exist in 1938 with an explanation about the commission's mission. The judge also referred to the generic duties of the persons on trial—*Quis custodiet ipsos custodies*—'who will guard the guards themselves?'

The judge was scathing about the behaviour of Jansen, Zenner and Schmeer. Jansen was compared unfavourably against the mayors in the occupied countries that had resisted. He noted Schmeer's refusal to give testimony to the court regardless of his repeated references to the Gestapo. The judge observed: 'there are frequent references to the Gestapo and that in addition to the Aachen police and other Aachen people, strangers presumed to be Gestapo were taking part in the destruction. No one has named in this court any member of the Gestapo.' The judge explained that Zenner and

Schmeer had denied knowledge of the Chief of Gestapo as a means to avoiding a full explanation being presented to the court. The judge referred to Christgau, Klarmann and Becks as being identified with the 'actual operation' of burning the synagogue. These refused to given evidence or receive cross-examination. The judge accepted that Christgau had carried petrol into the building but claimed there was no evidence that the police officers were drunk or tipsy. The firemen, Hammers and Graf, also declined cross-examination, were treated as difficult cases. Hammers had climbed to the roof, while Graf was described as a 'dangerous and astute man trying to cover up his activities'.

The sentencing was carried out on 12 June 1947: Quirin Jansen, Alexander Hammers and Hubert Graf were found not guilty on both counts. Carl Zenner was found guilty and sentenced to five years imprisonment and a 5,000RM fine (paid in full on 28 August 1947). He was incarcerated in Anrath prison, but on 3 June 1950 he received clemency from the UK High Commissioner and was released. During his time as Police President of Aachen, Zenner had led clandestine 'Jew-hunts' across the Holland and Belgium frontiers. After leaving Aachen in the summer of 1942, he served as the SS-Police Chief of Minsk, in the Soviet Union. In 1961, he was found guilty of the mass murder of 6,000 Jews in November 1941.[30] Eduard Schmeer received a five-year prison sentence and also received clemency like Zenner. Kaspar Becks was found guilty and received a prison sentence of two years with effect from 1 March 1947 (time served). The High Commissioner suspended his sentence on 31 August 1948. Karl Klarmann was found guilty and received a two-year sentence with effect from 15 October 1946 (time served) and was incarcerated in Anrath prison; his sentence was suspended on 14 April 1948. Paul Christgau was found guilty and received a two-year prison sentence, with effect from 12 September 1946, and suspended on 11 March 1948.

IV. Kristallnacht—a reconstruction from the intelligence report

The task of reconstructing the events of 9–10 November 1938 began with filtering the evidence from the 1947 court case with allied intelligence reports (Britain, America and Belgium). The known sources, pertinent to the Aachen pogrom, were gathered in national and state archives: Berlin, Düsseldorf, London, Washington DC and Carlisle Barracks (Pennsylvania). Not all the records are freely accessible and in regard to the fragmentary Gestapo records lodged in Düsseldorf's Hauptarchiv (HstD), have limited access under Germany's privacy laws. The primary sources with free access are in Britain and America, in particular the National Archives (NARA), the United States Holocaust Memorial Museum (USHMM) and the US army's archive in Carlisle Barracks. Local literature is less helpful. Herbert Lepper (1935–2014), Aachen's state archive director, published a book about the synagogue prior to 1942.[31] There is a short account of the pogrom in Hans Siemons' *Kriegsalltag in Aachen* (1998), mostly following Lepper, but with no reference to post-war trials. In Ulrich Kalkmann's study of the Technical University there are fleeting references to faculty and student membership to Nazi organisations and associations but less analysis of participation in acts of criminality.[32]

Guilt by association can often be the means to implicating persons without breaching the privacy laws. However, Aachen is a particularly complex case to examine because in 1938 there were three levels of state bureaucracy. The first level was *Regierungsbezirk* and the *Regierungspräsident* was a local government administrative structure imposed in 1816 under Prussian rule and acted like a county council over the city. The second level was municipal and involved the Oberbürgermeister, the senior mayor, who administered the city with a council made up of Bürgermeister responsible for specific tasks such as finance and public utilities. The third level of authority came from the frontier or border administration, which was concerned with controlling customs tolls, foreigners and taxes through working with the finance ministry. To understand the scale of local authorities helps to explain the levels of participation in the pogrom, which indirectly explains the reluctance behind the defendants in the court case to face cross-examination.

The general narrative of the 1938 pogrom is established. Herschel Feibel Grynszpan, a Polish-Jewish refugee from Germany, shot

ORDINARY PEOPLE

Ernst von Rath, a German diplomat, on 7 November 1938. Grynszpan's family had recently been expelled from Germany, having settled in Hannover in 1911. There have been claims that the act was the consequence of a homosexual relationship that had broken down, and that Von Rath was under suspicion by the Nazis as an opponent. Irrespective of the causes surrounding the assassination, Von Rath died of his wounds, and Nazi Germany used the incident as a pretext for instigating a pogrom against the Jewish communities. Von Rath died on 9 November, which happened to coincide with the sacred day of Nazism, the anniversary of the Beer Hall Putsch of 1923, as well as the end of the Great War. That evening, Josef Goebbels, the Nazi Minister of Propaganda, looking to ingratiate himself with Hitler, delivered a speech claiming there was to be no officially sanctioned retaliation against the Jews, but if the masses acted spontaneously, they were not to be prevented from taking matters into their own hands.[33] The speech galvanised the Nazi Party organisations into readiness for action. This focused minds to concentrate on 9–10 November as the designated period. From a theoretical standpoint, the Gestapo and SD were responsible for matters to do with religions and sects, which included the Catholics and the Jews.

From his headquarters in Munich, Reinhard Heydrich, SS chief of security police, issued orders via telegram and telephone to all SS and Gestapo offices across Germany at 01.20 on 10 November. Since 1936, after a political-organisational merger, all branches of the SS and police were centralised under Heinrich Himmler, Chief of the SS. Once Heydrich issued his orders, the entire SS-Police machinery, including the Fire Brigade, was placed on alert and ready to commit to the action. Heydrich's instructions were precise—the local Gestapo chiefs were to contact party leaders and leaders of the police. The orders called for controlled destruction—burning synagogues only so long as there was no threat to other buildings, and shops and residences were to be destroyed but not looted. Demonstrations were not to be hindered. All archival material in synagogues was to be turned over to the security police. The SD and Gestapo were in charge of all actions, but members of the SS paramilitary wings could also act in accordance with Gestapo instructions.[34]

313

WAR COMES TO AACHEN

The order quickly filtered to regional offices, local bureaus and police stations in German cities and towns. In regard to Aachen, all three levels of state authority and all offices were placed on alert. The *Regierungsbezirk* was located in Theaterplatz (the building still stands opposite the city theatre and about a mile from the synagogue); Eggers was the president and there was also the Gestapo and a *Kreisleitung* representative of the Nazi Party. The Gestapo in the border police station in Monheimsallee 5 (within 300 yards of the synagogue) was situated almost in front of the Hannsemann statue but was destroyed during the war. The offices of the Oberbürgermeister were in the municipal buildings and the *Rathaus* (about half a mile from the synagogue); they included Ortsgruppe representatives (local groups) of the Nazi Party. Regardless of whether Jansen was on a train or not, all of his authorities were mobilised for action. They were in contact with the local groups and Nazi organisations like the SA and other bureaus (discussed later). The Polizei-Presidium (today a hotel) in Kasernenstrasse was in the south, within proximity of the main railway station and customs office about 1.4 miles from the synagogue. The Presidium was in telephone contact with the Gasborn beat police precinct (75 yards from the synagogue). The Nazi motor corps leadership were located in Kaiserplatz (115 yards from the synagogue). The Fire Brigade had two stations, in Vinzenstrasse (north) and Bendstrasse (south, a mile from the synagogue); we know from his witness statement that Alexander Hammers was serving in Vinzenstrasse, which was four miles from the city centre.

The operation had two parts—first to steal the valuables and second to destroy the buildings. This was coordinated and planned, and not a spontaneous act of violence by outraged ordinary Germans. There was time to plan and prepare assets to conduct the action. From an organisational perspective, there were two priorities. Foremost was passed to the Gestapo, SD and border police, tasked with the 'smash and grab' of the synagogue's artefacts and valuables before its destruction. The beat police and fire officers were assigned the task of destroying the building. The police precinct on the corner of Gasborn and Promenadenstrasse was the local command, communication and control point. It became the collecting/gathering point for the perpetrators and for officers/officials to receive final instructions and specific tasks—to tunics for civilian clothing, and to maintain communications with senior authorities such as the Gauleiter in Cologne. The Gestapo officials, the beat police officers, the Kripo (criminal police) and the Fire Brigade, including Zenner and Schmeer, were all witnessed and reported within the proximity of this precinct. There is some doubt over which authority was responsible for supplying the trucks to remove the artefacts, but it was certainly under Gestapo control.

The demographics underpinning Aachen's perpetrators reveal a complex level of participation. At the basic organisational level, the most numerically significant (60 per cent) came from members of the Aachen Nazi Party and the SA. In 1939, the Nazi Party membership in Aachen was 9,605, and 59 per cent came from the 1891–1910 age groups, the majority age range of all participants in the pogrom. The Nazi Party administration of the city started with Eduard Schmeer with three important groups—the Kreisleitung, the Ortsgruppe and the SA—but due to the Nazi's passion for authority there was duplication of representation. From Schmeer's inner circle of full-time Kreisleitung (16 per cent of the total), several were representatives from hand working, business, teachers and architecture. The Nazis divided the city into twenty political districts (*Ortsgruppe*) and they contributed at least an 8 per cent participation level. Local Ortsgruppe representation came from Blücherplatz, Marschiertor and Frankenbergviertel. The leading Ortsgruppe directors represented hand workers and handicrafts, prison officers, business, criminal police and teachers. The SA represented 32 per cent of the participants in the pogrom; all were Nazi Party members. They came from a broad range of occupations: office workers, qualified engineers, gardeners, doctors, businessmen, locksmiths, tailors and labourers. The SS organisation represented 34 per cent of the total participants, but only 13 per cent of the total had been Nazi Party members before 1933. Their known occupations were beat police officers (mostly Polizeihauptmann), party financiers, lawyers and locksmiths. Six notable participants in the pogrom were only registered as members of the Nazi Party, and all joined before 1930. Their occupations were restaurateur, official of the IHK, merchant banker, Aachen court physician, salesman (a close associate of Schmeer) and an architect. In addition, eight senior officials of the *Kreisbauernschaft*, the Nazi's farming organisation, were also in attendance.[35]

The least known organisation involved in Aachen's November pogrom was the Gestapo and the security police. Based upon Karl Happel's interrogation to British intelligence from September 1944 (mentioned previously), the senior Gestapo chief in 1935–9 was Regierungsrat SS-Standartenführer Heinz Seetzen (1906–1945), and his deputy was Dr Puetz, a Regierungs Assessor. Seetzen was born in an area that falls within Wilhelmshaven today, and he studied jurisprudence before joining the Nazi Party and SA in May 1933. In 1935, he entered the SS and Gestapo, and was assigned to Aachen.[36] Conditions in Aachen represented a challenge for Gestapo authority because, according to Robert Gellately, the Aachen-Gestapo reported in September 1935 that the wholly Catholic community judged the Jews to be 'human beings' before recognising them as racial-political objects.[37] However, Gellately also noted that a member of the Catholic priesthood was identified as a strong candidate to become a Gestapo agent.[38] Happel had explained to the British how Gestapo officers were assigned to *Grenzpolizei* (border police) duties in Aachen. The border police also worked closely with officers from the *Reichsfinanzverwaltung* or customs officials. The Aachen-Gestapo detachment before 1938 was 160 but was increased in May 1938 by a further 100 officers to cover construction on the Westwall. There were at least nine Gestapo officials on duty during the Aachen pogrom. They were all born 1905–1915; four had joined the Nazi Party 1930 or before and all were resident in Aachen, working in a range of occupations including architect, teacher and locksmith. Critical to the pogrom was the involvement of the *Nationalsozialistisches Kraftfahrkorps*, the National Socialist Motor Corps (NSKK). This was a paramilitary organisation founded in 1931. The primary mission of the NSKK was to teach Nazis to drive—creating a pool of drivers, to supply vehicles to mobilise SA troops to actions, and carry supporters to rallies. The construction of the Westwall, from August 1938, required the NSKK to mobilise 15,000 trucks and 5,000 buses to service 22,000 construction sites—in Aachen, there were at least 120 fortification construction sites within the city and neighbourhood.[39] The headquarters of the NSKK was in Kaiserplatz in 1938 and the Aachen NSKK leader was Ernst Markow. Four senior NSKK officials were prominent in the pogrom, three born in Aachen (1914–16 age range) and the other from Eupen (born 1890). Three were locksmiths by occupation and one was also an SS officer, and two were SS men.

Orders are orders, except when the Nazis were involved. Within barely ninety minutes from receipt of the telegram, synagogues were burning and the Nazi hordes were in the streets. An American diplomat in Leipzig witnessed: 'At 3.a.m. on 10 November 1938 was unleashed a barrage of Nazi ferocity as had had no equal hitherto in Germany, or very likely anywhere else in the world since savagery began.'[40] Hans Siemons claims hordes of SA and SS men, under the direction of Zenner and Gestapo officials, moved through the streets using detailed lists of targets. Over 70 Jews were arrested and held in the central court's prison, but due to over-crowding many were temporarily held in a school gymnasium. The Jews were then deported to Nazi camps, 60 to Buchenwald and 10 to Sachsenhausen.[41] Accurate weather conditions were supplied by Dr Carl Appelrath, from the Meteorological Institute in Aachen, having made readings on 9–10 November. The night was overcast with 88–90 per cent humidity, poor visibility and twilight from 19.10. Visibility was three quarters of a kilometre. From his roof at 21.15 on 10 November, he saw 'very white smoke' drifting from the direction of the synagogue. The high level of humidity meant the Fire Brigade became central perpetrators in the destruction. The British trial revealed how the Fire Brigade fanned the flames by smashing the windows and roof, opening the doors, and thereby causing the destructive backdraft. During the US army occupation of Aachen (October 1944 to June 1945), American intelligence officers were able to identify 23 persons who were marked as being more than just 'active' in the pogrom. These particular men were described in the intelligence reports as 'brutal', 'mistreated', 'fanatical', 'killed' and 'stolen

Jewish property'. Three men deserve particular attention. Quirin Jansen, who was supposed to be on a train from Berlin, 'as an SA leader he was actively engaged in the Jewish pogrom of November 1938'. The intelligence report also noted he 'Stole Jewish property and lowered the rations for Jewish citizens.' Hans Guenther was born in Aachen in 1905 and was a resident of Alexanderstrasse. He joined the Party/SA in 1930. The intelligence report notes he 'actively and brutally engaged in Jewish pogrom in November 1938 ... and particularly active in the destruction of the synagogue in Aachen'. The third was Polizeihauptmann Romer, born in Aachen, an SS officer, and regarded as a leading participant in the Jewish pogrom of 1938. The intelligence report noted he was the 'leader of the mob which burned the Aachen synagogue. After the building had been destroyed by fire, Jews were driven into the remains and dynamited.' He was instrumental in the deportation of Jews during the war.

The scale of looting will never be fully known, but three culprits illustrate the people who participated. Polizeihauptmann Mohlert, born in Aachen in 1910 and a resident of Sedanstrasse, was also an SS officer. The US army noted that Mohlert 'mistreated Jews, destroyed their homes and stole their belongings during the pogrom in November 1938'. It was also known that he was in charge of Jewish deportations during the war. A salesman called Sauer, born in Aachen in 1890 and resident of Ehlisenbrunnen, joined the Nazi Party in 1927. He was known to be a close associate of Schmeer, a leading participant in the 1938 pogrom, representative of the IHK in sale of Jewish property to Nazis and profiteered from proceedings. Gerhard Scholl, a tailor by trade, was born in Aachen 1905, and resident of Franzstrasse 105. He joined the Nazi Party in 1930 and the SA in 1934. He was a leather and material cutter in Aachener Kleiderfabrik, known to be a Jewish firm. In the Aryanisation of the firm that followed the 1938 pogrom, he became its business manager. After the pogrom, the Nazis virtually curtailed Jewish public life and subjected those who remained to substandard lifestyles. A local demolition firm, Gerhard Vanhauten, charged 6,500RM to destroy the remains of the synagogue, and Rabbi Schönberger was forced to negotiate the details with A. Konigs, a city architect. The Nazis' sequestration of finances, both private and business, continued impoverishing those who remained. This reconstruction of events does not confirm or deny whether there was as a city-wide sporadic uprising by the German people against Jewry. Rather, it reveals a highly planned, coordinated and well-resourced action to cause maximum destruction for maximum looting. By 1939, there were believed to be about 1,800 Jews still residing in the city, but numbers in this narrative are woefully inaccurate.

The deportations of Aachen's Jews to the east for ghettoisation and extermination began on 25 March 1942. One train took 1,000 Jews from different communites on a three-day journey to the ghetto in Izbica, a village in eastern Poland. As they arrived, Jews were being sent to Bełżec extermination camp—the camp was in operation from 17 March 1942 to June 1943, killing upwards of 500,000 people. In April 1942, another transport carried 1,051 Jews to Izbica, including Jews from Aachen. Eight days later, another transport carried an unknown number of Jews from Aachen and Koblenz to a ghetto in Kraśniczyn, a small village in eastern Poland. On 15 June 1942, a transport with stops in Koblenz/Cologne/Düsseldorf carrying 1,003 Jews, arrived in Sobidor. There were four trains to Theresienstadt between 21 July and December 1943, transporting more than 1,000 Jews.

Wally Hirtz had escaped *Kristallnacht* largely unscathed. A year later, her husband, having relinquished control of his massive textile factory, died and was buried in the city's East Cemetery. The family was denied burial in the Jewish cemetery by the Nazis. She was forced to wear the 'yellow star', but would walk to Sandkaulstrasse every day to continue her volunteer work. Her stepson later wrote that he tried to get her out of Germany and into Belgium but he failed. On 10 April 1942, she was forced out of her home to register at the camp at Grünerweg. There she was ordered to live in a *Judenhaus*, one which had been the former Jewish old people's home. She surrendered her house and home to her daughter-in-law, because she was an 'Aryan'. On 15 June, Wally was placed on a transport east, a deportation train for Sobibor, the record listed as 'emigrated to the unknown'. She was killed in Sobibor, joining at least nine other persons of her extended family who were killed during the Holocaust. Years later, her stepson claimed he tried to bribe officials to switch her trains at Cologne but the attempt failed.[42] The final transport of Aachen Jews, to an unknown destination, took two or three persons away in September 1944. The lists of deportations cannot reflect the scale of misery the Nazi terror caused to the Jewish community. Barely 30 of the deported, missing and dead are named on gravestones in Aachen's Jewish cemetery. The new synagogue retains a memorial of all 779 murdered during the Holocaust.

REFLECTIONS

The resuscitation of the Roman Empire under Charles the Great on that Christmas day at the turn of the eighth century was welcomed by almost all with a sigh of relief in the hope that it heralded a return to the peace and prosperity and to the larger unity which had once existed ... Unity was preserved for less than 50 years. Wars rent Europe for more than a thousand years ... eleven hundred years after Charlemagne's, that in 1914 a war fiercer and more devastating than any which had gone before ... and flickering hopes which came to an end in 1939. Nor is it necessary today further to lament the six years that followed. You in this city know them well ...[1]

On 3 March 1945, amidst a whirlwind tour of the rear areas reclaimed by the allied forces, Winston Churchill, in a moment of impulsive defiance, relieved himself on the once formidable Siegfried Line. Field Marshal Alanbrooke vividly recalled the scene, describing Churchill's face aglow with a childlike grin of satisfaction at the audacious act. Pressing onward, they traversed the war-torn landscape, where the sight of Aachen's devastation offered a stark contrast to the familiar ruins of French, Italian, Belgian and British towns.[2] Churchill's encounter with the Military Government Officers team in Aachen remains unrecorded, overshadowed by the urgency to proceed to Jülich. Among the witnesses, American war correspondent Ralph G. Martin observed as Churchill, alongside the assembled generals, marked his territory on this symbol of Nazi fortification.[3] In the ensuing decade,

Churchill chronicled his wartime experiences, ultimately reclaiming the premiership with resounding success.

On 10 May 1956, the anniversary of Hitler's invasion of France and the Low Countries, Churchill was honoured with the *Karlspreis* by Aachen. Seven days before the ceremony, Churchill's physician, Lord Moran, found his patient excited because 'the chief architect of Germany's downfall' was Aachen's guest. Churchill said: 'Charlemagne worked for the unity of Europe, and that is the purpose of this award. The Nazis set out to rule the world and something went wrong.' Moran, in reference to the 'Nazis', replied, 'They are not all dead. You will find some of them in your travels.'[4] The *Manchester Guardian* had reported possible German hostility against the decision. The newspaper *Deutsche Zukunft* had published an article with a headline that caused concern: 'The Misdeeds of Sir Winston'. The main points of the article were summarised by Moran, like a doctor recording the patient's symptoms. Churchill had fought Hitler not for freedom but to maintain the balance of power in a divided Europe; he was a signatory to the Morgenthau Plan that called for the systematic destruction of German industry; he 'had introduced illegal partisan warfare' into Nazi-occupied territories (to which the Nazis responded with *Bandenbekämpfung* doctrine);[5] and he 'was responsible for the systematic bombing of undefended German cities'. The article claimed that, 'in his "blind hatred" of Germany [Churchill] had gambled away the British Empire and driven the devil, Hitler, with the aid of Beelzebub, Stalin'.[6]

The award marked Churchill's first trip to Germany since the Potsdam conference in July 1945. His nomination for the *Karlspreis* several months prior underscored his status as a pivotal figure in the post-war European movement. A Northern Irish newspaper, in highlighting Churchill as 'a great European', captured the political significance of the occasion.[7] Yet this alignment with European ideals did not mark a departure from his imperial power politics. Churchill's advocacy for a United States of Europe dated back to 1930, gaining momentum during his years in opposition following the 1945 general election defeat. While his Fulton 'Iron Curtain' speech of 1946 has dominated historical narratives of his opposition years, it was his fervent campaigning for European unity that arguably served as a more prominent platform for his charismatic politicking. His three successive trips to Holland in 1946, 1948 and 1949 underscore this commitment, culminating in his bold declaration in May 1948: 'I am a European.' In The Hague, he extolled the virtues of Benelux development and championed the idea of a community founded on mutual cooperation. Throughout 1949, Churchill's schedule brimmed with speeches, from the Palais des Académies in Brussels to the opening of the Council of Europe in Strasbourg and engagements in Paris. His efforts to cultivate Anglo–West German relations were further evident in Chancellor Konrad Adenauer's 1953 visit to negotiate NATO membership and German rearmament during Churchill's premiership. Adenauer, reciprocating Churchill's efforts, proposed him for the *Karlspreis* in 1955, a symbolic gesture coinciding with Germany's emergence as a founding partner in the European community.

Expectations dwarfed substance. The Foreign Office sent Churchill guidelines, but he dismissed them as typical ministerial protocols. Ten years on from his Fulton speech, this speech was crafted to stir up Cold War passions once again. He was determined to attend the *Karlspreis* ceremony, after a long bout of illness that had forced his retirement, and to give the speech personally. He spoke of the reunification of Germany but argued that in a divided Europe it was unachievable in the short term. *The Spectator* reported that Churchill had 'dismissed the European movement with a few polite words'. He proposed that Soviet Russia should be welcomed into a post-Stalin grand alliance of Europe and NATO. *The Spectator* commented on Churchill's ability to 'induce trains of thought ... without falling suspect of treachery to his country or his allies. His words were not just mischievous; they were also meant.'[8] Adenauer, after a translation of the speech, immediately distanced himself from the content, and told his advisors to ignore it. Adenauer's political opponents in Germany thought it was a 'statesmanlike' speech, but an East German spokesperson claimed the proposal had followed their ideas for the future. Churchill's call for the reintegration of the Soviet Union into western affairs was never likely to receive many plaudits, especially in the USA. Ten years on from Fulton, Churchill in Aachen was a pale shadow of his bulldog spirit. He suffered from ill health and age-related frailty. The *New York Times* ran a headline that Churchill had to be carried into the town hall by four sturdy Germans. A photograph of Churchill sitting beside Adenauer shows he was struggling with his hearing. The world leaders were no longer listening to Churchill with the same attention, especially when he banged the drum for a rapprochement with Soviet Russia.[9]

Churchill fought a moral war by immoral means. In the age of social media, with instant texts, we can adopt the *1066 and all that* benchmark. Churchill had stood up to Hitler, when many failed, which was a 'good thing'; but in defeating Hitler, Churchill adopted culture war and criminal means, which was a 'bad thing'. His actions reflected a belief in the concept of total war, born from the crucible of the Great War. In a sense, there were parallels when his war started with biplanes over Narvik but ended with the atomic bomb at Nagasaki. Indirectly, Churchill was an engine in that process of escalation. Despite warnings and evidence that bombing campaigns were ineffective, he persisted in mass destruction. To uphold Britain's moral standing, it's imperative to acknowledge that the embrace of extreme warfare was a grave error of judgement amid the fervour of total war.

Churchill's War

Richard Breitman has written of Churchill's wartime confidence in deciphered German police signals, which he called the 'Boniface' documents.[10] The accuracy of the police signals helped track the movements of the SS leaders during the period known as the 'Holocaust by Bullets' in 1941–2.[11] Although Breitman emphasised the knowledge of the Holocaust within Churchill's circle, there was police signals traffic about the air raids. The 'Summary' sheets of deciphered signals were distributed in report form with a section covering all theatres of the war against Germany and were distributed to the Air Ministry. In one 'summary' from 1943, there were police reports of damage in Berlin, Nürnberg, Bochum, Köln-Höhenhaus, Essen, München-Gladbach and Stuttgart.[12] After the war, some of the signals' content appeared in books, leaving an odd patchwork of evidence. A raid on Kassel, 8–9 September 1941 with ninety-five aircraft, caused the death of fifteen people and thirty-five injured. The Red Palace art gallery was gutted and four paintings by Adriaen van der Werff (1659–1722) were lost. These details were included in Martin Middlebrook's diary entry for the raid.[13] On 15 October 1941, the police advised of the escape of two RAF officers—John Richard Denny (born 9 May 1913) and Roger Joyce Bushell (born 30 August 1910). They were on a transport from Lübeck to a PoW camp. Bushell had been shot down on 23 May 1940 and escaped on 8–9 October 1941 but was arrested in May 1942. In March 1944, Bushell was murdered by the Gestapo for being the leading organiser of the 'great escape' from Stalag Luft III POW camp in Żagań.[14]

After the war, Churchill penned his war diaries, framed in a narrow political-military account which largely excluded his intelligence-bombing-driven strategy that defined his war. For readers in the age of social media, where politicians project self as a means of power, it might be difficult to grasp why Churchill omitted his doctrine from his histories. This was also coupled with the absolute secrecy he imposed over the Ultra story, which remained in force long after the war. In the 1950s, there were two cases where the impact of intelligence became entangled in official secrets controversy. During the war, Colonel Alexander Scotland was commanding officer of the British Army's Prisoner of War Interrogations Section (PWIS). In 1954, he tried to publish *The London Cage*; the first draft was seized by the police, and he was required to rewrite the book.[15] Perhaps of greater concern for historians were the efforts of Churchill's civil servants to prevent the publication of a famous book: *The Scourge of the Swastika* (1954). Lord Russell of Liverpool was a civil servant and senior officer of the Judge Advocate's department and was believed to be revealing secrets and breaking protocol. An investigation began and on 30 July 1954, Hubert Boggis-Rolfe passed his impressions to Gavin Simons, the Lord Chancellor. He was hostile to the book but not because of the official secrets act: 'This is, as you say a nasty book'. He continued, 'This book is a macabre and dreary account of endless atrocities ... No doubt this is largely true, and what Russell says ... about what the German people knew of the atrocities is probably a fair comment, but *there is no doubt that many Germans would now be frightfully hurt by this book.*' He believed that 'without reference to any other nations [this book] will do harm to international relations if it is read by Germans'. He recommended the Lord Chancellor should not intervene in the publication of the book, but the tensions continued to rise, as seen in a file note from 1958:

> Owing to Russell's arrogance and impertinent behaviour everyone's back has been put up and a fair muddle has resulted. Russell will be bringing out a book shortly (I think about Japanese war crimes trials) in which he will, we expect, indicate that he has been hampered in his preparations by the wilfully obstructive attitude of the War Office and the J.A.G.'s office. *Tant pis—no-one will rid us of this turbulent Peer!*[16]

Six months later, cabinet opinions were drawn to questions over Field Marshal Montgomery's memoirs. The memoirs were published by Collins & Co. without having been reviewed and vetted for approval by the Ministry of War. Montgomery had criticised Field Marshal Auchinleck, the NATO organisation and the American command during the war and matters concerning the allied occupation of Germany. In October 1958, Sir Norman Brook, the head of the civil service, attached an opinion of the memoirs which included the following observation:

> My impression was that, if the Field Marshal continues to make outrageous statements in public, the Prime Minister will not be reluctant to dissociate himself publicly from them.[17]

After three years of discussions and opinions the cabinet file was closed and Montgomery's memoirs remained unaltered and in print. However, the political ramifications spilled overseas. Montgomery's criticism of the Dieppe Raid (1942) led to the Canadian official history being adopted as the government's rebuttal, and Eisenhower's refusal to acknowledge 'Monty's' Christmas greeting was a sign of his disapproval of the memoirs.[18] The questions arisng from Montgomery's memoirs partly explained why ex-senior officers could publish but officers of lower ranks were prohibited. In a 1958 summary of the memoirs, it was observed that 'a commander in the field is governed by a special dispensation given to commanders' and that, 'In view of Lord Alanbrooke's book, I do not see how we could object to any of the contents covering that period.'[19]

Eventually, all the stories would break, as happened in 1974 when F.W. Winterbottom published *The Ultra Secret* about the Government Code and Cypher School at Bletchley Park, exposing the story for the first time. Subsequently, an official history by Sir Harry Hinsley (1918–1998) added yet another dimension to the intelligence history, although with hindsight he attributed greater importance to its value than was the case.[20] Churchill's 'secret service' has also collected growing attention over the years, with the study of secrecy and intelligence adding more myths to the literature.[21] The role of intelligence in the course of war was undeniable, but the history of British intelligence often gets entwined within the shadowy realm of the Secret Service.[22] The cabinet's papers about Montgomery would not be released until 1990, under the thirty-year rule. They have not attracted the attention they deserve largely because the British establishment has tried to diminish Montgomery, not because of his outstanding battlefield command but because of his blunt opinions and rudeness toward the Americans. In conclusion, there are indications of change as David Reynolds has since argued that Churchill's memoirs fell short of capturing the wider historical narrative.[23]

* * *

Aachen in 1900 was a major German city on the crest of a golden age. It was a *railopolis* with a modern industrial belt of textiles, needles and engineering, around a remarkable cultural centre, which traced its origins to the dawn of European civilisation. Within forty-four years, Aachen was in ruins, emptied of people and pronounced 'dead'. The age of total war in Europe had unleashed a tidal wave of extreme violence, cultural destruction and genocide beyond imagination. Aachen, because of its geopolitical position, ideology, strategy, military and culture, was in the vortex of the violence. From the kaiser's imperial time in 1900, through Belgian occupation, through Weimar, then Nazi Germany, the US army occupation, British military occupation, Belgian occupation and finally West Germany—Aacheners born and raised between 1900 and 1960 never experienced more than fourteen years of political stability. These were forty-four years of brutal violence fuelled by extreme ideologies and culture wars.

When Wolfgang Trees set out to research his book, he noticed a common theme written or said about Aachen in the final battle of October 1944: 'it was the shining example of German heroism'. When he announced his project in 1974, he started a series in a newspaper and received hundreds of letters and offers of interviews. The work on the book led to a collection of documents and photographs. There was a sense of being the last chance to document the story. Trees was born in Koblenz in 1942 and died in Aachen in 2009, but left a considerable legacy of local history. Charles Whiting (1926–2007) came from Yorkshire and served in the British army during the war. Later, he became a prolific writer under many pseudonyms, having studied in British and German universities. In May 2005, the *Aachener Nachrichten*, founded under the US Military Government, issued a magazine supplement, *Mein Kriegsende*, comprising individual memories on the sixtieth anniversary of the end of the war. Of the nine locals, only Waltraud Barth-Sayehli was in Aachen on the day. In May 1945, she was a 14-year-old, caring for the toddlers in a kindergarten in Kleverstrasse, near her home in Klara-Fey-Strasse (south side). She could no longer recall her emotions, but her father, an escapee from a US PoW camp, was in hiding behind the chimney in their home. Her 48-year-old father was a crippled veteran from the Great War and he gave himself up to the Americans. After some time under interrogation he was sent home, and that was her recollection of the end of the war. The wartime generation in my locality began to disappear from about 2010. One of the last, Heinrich Schreiber, passed in March 2020. They all shared different stories about the war, but held to the common opinion that they had survived a catastrophe.

REFLECTIONS

Today, Aachen is a city dominated by the Technical University. The age of total war is being erased, leaving a few scars and plaques. The railways remain important in the European network, and the street plan changes with every local election—between Green and other policies. The needle and textile factories have gone and some light engineering remains. The wartime population have all but gone; their offspring recall fathers and grandfathers having been soldiers. Few have happy memories, and the wars are not a talking point. Many of the places once prominent in the wars have been erased by jack-hammers, and the bombsites filled with concrete buildings. The city-centre car park that once stood where the target indicators landed during the arson raid of July 1943 was pulled down in 2022. The Hauptbahnhof railway station was rebuilt, but not Westbahnhof, which has been turned into a single platform with a bus shelter. The railway marshalling yards still work the massive freight trains that once made it a strategic target. The freight yards in Roth Erde are much reduced and there is little evidence of the US army's breach battle in October 1944. About six large air-raid bunker/shelters remain, and out of town there are traces of the Westwall. In the crossroads of Hansemannplatz, the statue is a reminder of Aachen's industrial past; buses pass every few minutes. A decade ago, someone would dress the statue with items of fancy clothing. Fifty metres across the road is a plaque in the ground marking the site of Anne Frank's grandmother's home. Few today realise that an innocuous-looking building on the opposite corner was once the site of the Nazi frontier police precinct, where the Gestapo snatch team stored the stolen property from the synagogue during *Kristallnacht*. The four rails of the now long-gone tramway, emerging from the tarmac road, symbolises a memory of Aachen in the age of total war, while the story on Wally Hirtz being sent away to Sobibor was a small tale in a global humanitarian tragedy. In Aachen in the summer of 2001, elderly neighbours in a local café were chatting. When *Lufthansa*'s preserved Junkers 52 was heard flying overhead, an elderly lady shouted: 'Der Führer kommt!' Everyone laughed.

329

NOTES

INTRODUCTION

1. NARA, RG407–427, Box 24012, records of 2 Information and Historical Service, 3 January 1945. Digest of Oberst Wilck's speech to the German soldiers on the surrender of Aachen on 21 October 1944, attached to Colonel Corley's final battalion combat report.
2. W.C. Sellar and R.J. Yeatman, *1066 and All That: A Memorable History of England* (London, 1999), p. 124.
3. Peter Calvocoressi, Guy Wint and John Pritchard, *Total War: the Causes and Courses of The Second World War* (Middlesex, 1972, second edition 1989), p. 3.
4. Richard Overy, 'Total War', in Charles Townshend, *The Oxford History of Modern War* (Oxford, 2000), p. 138.
5. Ian F. Beckett, 'Total War', in Marwick, Emsley and Simpson, *Total War and Historical Change: Europe 1914–1955* (Buckingham, 2001), p. 29.
6. Roger Chickering and Stig Förster, *The Shadows of Total War: Europe, East Asia and the United States, 1919–1939* (Cambridge, 2003), p. 1.
7. Roger Chickering and Stig Förster, *Great War, Total War: Combat and Mobilization on the Western Front, 1914–1918* (Cambridge, 2000), p.IX, p. 1.
8. Hugh Bicheno, 'Total War', Richard Holmes, *The Oxford Companion to Military History* (Oxford, 2001) p. 915.
9. Roger Chickering and Stig Förster, *A World at Total War: Global Conflict and the politics of destruction, 1937–1945* (Cambridge, 2005), p. 2.
10. Ian Garner, 'The Unbreakable City', *History Today*, August 2022, pp. 28–43.
11. Philip W Blood (ed), *Putin's War, Russian Genocide*, (Ibidem, 2023).

1. METROPOLIS

1. Viktor Gielen, *Es stand im Echo: Aachen 1914–1932* (Eupen, 1986), pp. 11–12.
2. Reichsarchivs (Martin Lezius), *Ruhmeshalle Unserer Alten Armee* (Leipzig: Militär-Verlag, 1927).

3. Adolf Hüttmann, Friedrich Wilhelm Krüger, *Das Infanterie Regiment von Lützow (1.Rhein.) Nr.25 im Weltkrieg 1914–1918* (Berlin, 1929).
4. Hans Ehlert, Michael Epkenhans and Gerhard P. Gross, *The Schlieffen Plan: International Perspectives on the German Strategy for World War I* (Kentucky, 2014).
5. Achim Konejung, *Das Rheinland und der Erste Weltkrieg: Aufmarschgebiet—Heimatfront—Besatzungszone* (Rheinbach: Regionalia Verlag, 2013).
6. A.J.P. Taylor, *War by Timetable: How the First World War Began* (London, 1969).
7. Andreas Knipping, *Eisenbahnen im Ersten Weltkrieg* (Freiburg: EK-Verlag, 2004).
8. https://www.rathausverein-aachen.de/das-goldene-buch The Golden Book opened in 1902 following the grand state visit of Kaiser Wilhelm II and and has continued.
9. The leading local authority is Herbert Ruhland, *Der Erste Weltkrieg und die Menschen im Vierländerland: Leben und Leiden der Bevölkerung vor und nach dem Krieg* (Eupen, 2018). See also Klaus Schulte, Peter Sardoč, *Eiserne Zeiten: Aachen—eine Stadt im Ersten Weltkrieg* (Aachen, 2014).
10. Annika Mombauer, 'The Moltke Plan: A Modified Schlieffen Plan with Identical Aims', in Hans Ehlert, Micheal Epkenhans and Gerhard Gross, *The Schlieffen Plan: International Perspectives on the German Strategy for World War I* (Lexington, 2014), p. 49.
11. Holger Afflerbach, *On a Knife Edge: How Germany Lost the First World War* (Cambridge, 2022), p. 15.
12. Mombauer, p. 53.
13. Afflerbach, p. 46.
14. Alexander Watson, *Ring of Steel: Germany and Austria Hungary at War, 1914–1918* (London, 2014), p. 121.
15. Bieberstein, *Lüttich-Namur.* (Oldenburg, 1918), pp. 13–15; part of the *Der grosse Krieg in Einzeldarstellungen* series published in the post-war years by the German general staff.
16. Martin Lezius, *Ruhmshalle Unserer Alten Armee* (Leipzig, 1920), p. 12, p. 65 and p. 112.
17. Philip W. Blood, *Hitler's Bandit Hunters* (Virginia, 2006).
18. Horne and Kramer, German Atrocities 1914, p. 123, p. 263, p. 252.
19. Ibid, pp. 10–17.
20. The frontier has changed four times since 1814: in 1914, 1918, 1940 and 1945. Before 1945, the German-Belgium frontier once ran between Welkenraedt (15 miles from Aachen centre) and Herbestal, where the main German frontier customs post was established.
21. Jeffrey Verhey, *The Spirit of 1914: Militarism, Myth and Mobilization in Germany* (Cambridge, 2000).
22. Jürgen Bertram, 'Perter Wamich', in A.K.V. Sammlung Crous, *Weststadt Statt Weltstadt: Aachens Grenzerlebnisse 1914–1929* (Aachen, 2014), pp. 86–99.
23. Jürgen Bertram, 'Perter Wamich', in AKV Sammlung Crous, *Weststadt Statt Weltstadt: Aachens Grenzerlebnisse 1914–1929* (Aachen, 2014), pp. 86–99.

24. Horne and Kramer, *German Atrocities 1914*, p. 130.
25. Diana Preston, *A Higher Form of Killing* (London, 2015).
26. John Horne and Alan Kramer, *German Atrocities 1914: A History of Denial* (Yale, 2001).
27. http://www.Denkmalproject.org/2008/vl_ir_luetzow_1_rhein_25_wk1_5.komp.htm
28. Martin Herzog/Marko Rösseler, 'Der grosse Zaun', *Die Zeit*, 16 April 1998.
29. Ruhland, op cit.
30. Gross et al., *Schlieffen Plan*, MGFA.
31. Gerald D. Feldman, *Army, Industry and Labor in Germany 1914–1918* (Princeton, 1966), p. 45.
32. Roger Chickering, *The Great War and Urban Life in Germany* (Cambridge, Cambridge, 2007), pp. 168–172.
33. Chickering, *Imperial Germany at War*, 143.
34. Feldman, 442.
35. Chickering, 146.
36. RWTH, Great War Exhibition of Rationing, 2014.
37. Gielen, *Es stand im Echo*, pp. 30–3 and pp. 45–7.
38. Gielen, *Es stand im Echo*, p. 47.
39. StaA, OB 6–100–9, Medizinal und Sanität, Grippe Akten 1917–24.
40. Arthur Marwick, *Deluge* (London, 1964).
41. Gottfried Benn, 'Wie Miss Cavell erschossen wurde. Bericht eines Augenzeugen über die hinrichtung der englischen Krankenschwester', in Friedrich Felger (Hrs), *Was wir vom Weltkrieg nicht Wissen* (Leipzig, 1930), pp. 113–17.
42. TNA, FO 383 148/117596, War Office letter the Foreign Office, 17 June 1916.
43. TNA, FO 383 148/102329, *Verbalnote*, 19 May 1916.
44. https://www.birtwistlewiki.com.au/wiki/HMHS_St_Denis. The ship in 1908 was named *Munich* until 1914 and worked the Holland–Harwich route. It was renamed and became a hospital ship with 4 officers, 6 nurses and 28 personnel carrying casualties in 108 cots and 109 berths.
45. TNA, FO 383/148/99982/183 Prisoners in Germany, Foreign Office request for confirmation from the US Ambassador in Berlin, 26 May 1916.
46. TNA, FO 383/148/99982/182 Prisoners in Germany, Sir Edward Grey request for clarification, 26 May 1916.
47. Ernest G.B. Maxse (1863–1943) was born in Heligoland when it was a British crown colony. He was the son of the governor, an army officer, and an actress and attended Harrow School. He worked for the Foreign Office, was employed as High Consul in Rotterdam, and often engaged in correspondence with Prime Minister Lloyd George. He regularly sent reports on the opinions of exchanged prisoners about conditions in Germany.
48. TNA, FO 383/148/107910/183 Prisoners in Germany, Return of Incapacitated Prisoners, letter Alan Johnstone, 11 June 1916.
49. Parliamentary Archives, LG/E/3/18/3 Letter, Maxse to Campbell, 4 October

pp. [23–35] NOTES

1916. Refer to: https://archives.parliament.uk/collections/getrecord/GB61_LG_E_3_18_3
50. TNA, FO 383/148/117596, the repatriated list from the War Office (London), 17 June 1916.
51. TNA, FO 383/148/147949, Letter from Adelaide Livingstone, 29 July 1916.
52. TNA, FO 383/210/ 128706, Francis Badham, 22 September 1916.
53. StaA, 4/7/1 Stadt Aachen, Die Arbeiten und Soldaten Akte, 1918–1925, 'An die gesamte Aachener Bürgerschaft', 19 November 1918.
54. Michael Prömpeler, 'Der Wohnungsbau in Aachen von 1920 bis 1918', in AKV Sammlung Crous, *Weststadt Statt Weltstadt: Aachens Grenzerlebnisse 1914–1929* (Aachen, 2014), pp. 198–203.
55. Wolfgang Trees, *Schmuggler, Zöllner und die Kaffeepanzer* (Aachen, 2002), pp. 30–1.
56. There is a memorial plaque to Lieutenant Graff beside the River Meuse in Liège.
57. Ludwina Forst, *Der Mordfall Johann Greber: Tätersuche im besetzten Aachen 1922* (Erfurt, 2005).
58. Klaus Weberskirch, *Anarcho-Syndikalisten an der Wurm* (Aachen, 1999).
59. TNA, FO 371/39131/Case 1739, Ernst Fraenkel report: Occupation of the Rhineland, 1918–30 (1943), p. 10.

2. LETTING GO OF DEMOCRACY

1. Volkhochschule der Stadt Aachen, *Aachen 1933: Die Machtergreifung der Nazis in Aachen* (Aachen, 1987). In 2019, the city placed a *Stolpersteine* (stumbling stone) commemorating his memory beside his former home.
2. Bernhard Poll, *Geschichte Aachens in Daten* (Aachen, 2003), pp. 308–9. Hans Siemons (1930–2006) was from Aachen and was a noted journalist. He wrote a number of local histories referred to throughout this book. In 2003, Oberbürgermeister Jürgen Linden referred to this work as Der 'Poll', in a celebration of its revised publication edited by Hans Siemons.
3. Holger A. Dux, *Das war das 20. Jahrhundert in Aachen* (Wartberg Verlag, 2001), p. 36.
4. Michael Römling, *Aachen: Geschichte einer Stadt* (Tertulla, 2014), pp. 269–70.
5. CMH, The Frank J. Mc Sherry Papers, Civil Affairs 1944–5 (Germany), Box 50, Saul K. Padover/Dewis F. Gittler interrogation Dr Kurt Pfeiffer in Aachen, Ninth US Army, PW Detachment APO 339, 2 February 1945 (hereafter referred as 'McSherry Papers').
6. Lutz-Henning Meyer, *150 Jahre Eisenbahnen Im Rheinland: Entwicklung und Bauten am Beispiel der Aachener Bahnen* (Köln, 1989).
7. Paul Thomes, 'Entrepreneur und Corporate Citizen—zum 150. Todestag von David Hansemann (1790–1864)', in Paul Thomes, Peter M. Quadflieg (Hrsg), *Unternehmer in der Region Aachen—zwischen Maas und Rhein* (Münster, 2015), pp. 96–111.

NOTES

8. Rüdiger Haude, *Grenzflüge: Politische Symbolik der Luftfahrt vor dem Ersten Weltkrieg* (Köln, 2007).
9. Paul Wietzorek, *Das Historische Aachen* (Petersberg, 2013).
10. Michael Heinzel, *Eisenbahn in Ostbelgien* (Gemünd, 2022).
11. Reiner Bimmermann, *Aachener Strassenbahn. Band 1: Geschichte* (Aachen, 1999).
12. Krettek Herberholz, *Strassenbahnen Im Aachener Dreiländereck* (Düsseldorf, 1980).
13. Hans Schweers, Henning Wall, *Eisenbahneen rund um Aachen: 150 Jahre internationale Strecke Köln-Antwerpen* (Aachen, 1993).
14. Jahresbericht der Handelskammer zu Aachen, 1914 (Aachen, 1915).
15. Vicktor Engelhardt, *Waggenfabrik Talbot Aachen: Eine Festschrift zur hunterjahrfeier 1938* (Berlin, 1938), p. 87.
16. Bjorn Schötten, 'Besatzung statt Bomben: Die Folgen des 1. Weltkrieges für die Stadtenwicklung von Aaachen (1914–29)', in Paul Thomes, Tobias Dewes (Hsg), *Aachen 1914–1918: 100 Jahre 1. Weltkrieg* (Aachen, 2016).
17. Vincent O'Connell, '"Left to their own devices": Belgium's Ambiguous Assimilation of Eupen-Malmedy (1919–1940)', *Journal of Belgian History*, 43, 2013, pp. 10–45.
18. Aachener und Münchener Feuer-Versicherungsgesellschaft, Denkschrift zur Hundertjahr-Feier 1825–1925 (Aachen, 1925), p. 60.
19. Arthur Katz-Foerstner, Deutsche Handels- und Indudtrie- Städte, Berlin, Oktober–Dezember 1921, p. 30.
20. *Poll-Chronicle*, p. 293.
21. *Poll-Chronicle*, p. 298.
22. Holger A. Dix, *Das war das 20. Jahrhundert in Aachen* (Celle, 2001), p. 35.
23. *Poll-Chronicle*, p. 297, pp. 303–4, p. 309.
24. Anne Becker and Detlef Mühlberger, 'The Sociology of the Nazi Party in a Catholic County: The 1939 Census of the NSDAP in County Aachen', *Totalitarian Movements and Political Religions*, 6:2, pp. 243–69.
25. Courtesy of Michael D. Miller with the author's thanks. Michael D. Miller, Andreas Schulz, *Gauleiter: The Regional Leaders of the Nazi Party and Their Deputies, 1925–1945*, Vol. 1 (2012).
26. https://www.wolfgang-birkenstock.de/reportage_aachen.html
27. Max Mehler, *Carl Mehler: Feldbriefe* (Aachen, 1910).
28. Arthur Katz-Foerstner, *Deutsche Handels- und Indudtrie- Städte*, Berlin, Oktober–Dezember 1921, p. 24.
29. Hans Siemons, *Kriegsalltag in Aachen* (Aachen, 1998).
30. Blood, *Hitler's Bandit Hunters*, pp. 72–74.
31. *Zur Geschichte Der Industrie und Handelskammer Für Den Regierungsbezirk Aachen In Den Jahren 1929–1954* (Aachen, 1954), p. 28.
32. Company publication, *Waggonfabrik Talbot Aachen: Eine Festschrift zur Hundertjahrfeier 1938* (Berlin, 1938).
33. Talbot *festschrift*, 1938.

34. TNA, FO 1013/717 Aachen Technical College: Denazification, assessment made in 1946 by British Special Branch investigations.
35. Ulrich Kalkmann, *Die Technische Hochschule Aachen im Dritten Reich (1933–1945)* (Mainz, 2003), pp. 445–68.
36. Monika Herzog, *Architectural Guide Vogelsang* (Cologne, 2010).
37. *Der Eifel*, 'Der führer in der Eifel', December 1936 also proclaimed a local readership of 20,000.
38. NS-Documentation Vogelsang, museum display captions.
39. Siemons, *Kriegsalltag*, p. 65.
40. Siemons, *Kriegsalltag*, pp. 66–7.
41. *Poll-Chronicle*, p. 317.
42. Rainer Monnartz, *Die Garnisons- und Militär-geschichte der Städte Aachen, Eschweiler und Stolberg 1814–1960* (Aachen, 2010), pp. 86–90.
43. Refer to Römling, *Aachen—Geschichte einer Stadt*.
44. Elmar Gasten, *Aachen in der Zeit der nationalsozialistischen Herrschaft 1933–44* (Frankfurt am Main, 1993).

3. IN DEFENCE OF THE COMMUNITY

1. Recollections from former nurse Yvonne Gaida.
2. Len Deighton, *Bomber* (2009), p. 6.
3. Siemons, *Kriegsalltag*, p. 9.
4. Wilhelm Deist, 'War Preparations in Nazi Germany', in Roger Chickering, Stig Förster, *The Shadows of Total War*.
5. 'The Strategic Air War Against Germany 1939–1945', Report of British Bombing Survey Unit, 1946 (hereafter referred as BBSU).
6. Martin Middlebrook, Chris Everitt, *The Bomber Command War Diaries: An Operational Reference Book 1939–1945* (Hinckley, 1995), p. 42, hereafter referred to as BCD.
7. David Edgerton, *Britain's War Machine*, p. 13.
8. Noble Frankland, *Bomber Offensive: The Devastation of Europe* (London, 1969), p. 23.
9. Philip W. Blood, *Bird of Prey: Hitler's Luftwaffe, Ordinary Soldiers and the Holocaust in Poland* (Stuttgart, 2021).
10. TNA, AIR 14/281, Plan W.A.5(b), The attack on the Ruhr and its Effect on the Military Lines of Communication in Western Germany, 20 March 1939.
11. TNA, AIR 24/220, Bomber Command Operation Instruction No. 37, Memorandum on the Burning of German Forests, 30 June 1940.
12. Richard Overy, 'Making and Breaking Morale: British Political Warfare and Bomber Command in the Second World War', in *Twentieth Century British History*, Vol. 26, No. 3, 2015, pp. 370–99.
13. Richard Overy, *The Bombers and the Bombed: Allied Air War Over Europe, 1940–45* (London, 2013).
14. Ritchie Calder, *Carry on London* (London, 1941).

15. TNA, FO 898/178, Political Warfare Executive, Directorate of Plans, Richie Calder, Air Raid Morale, 29 July 1941.
16. TNA, FO 898/178, Political Warfare Executive, Directorate of Plans, Richie Calder, untitled memorandum on political warfare and bombing, 23 August 1941.
17. TNA, AIR 14/3760, 'K' Reports Aachen, summary of RAF raids on Aachen 1940–4, drafted from data supplied by the Air Ministry accounts.
18. Arthur E. Slater, 'Bomber Command: British Bombing Policy to December 1940', in *Purnell's History of the Second World War* (Avon, 1974), vol. 1, pp. 297–308.
19. Bernhard Poll (Hrsg), *Geschichte Aachens in Daten, Teil 1: bis 1964* (Aachen, 2003), pp. 327–8.
20. *Poll-Chronicle*, p. 327.
21. William Shirer, *Berlin Diary: The Journal of a Foreign Correspondent, 1934–1941* (New York, 1942), pp. 268–9. The story of Freiburg covered a navigation error by the Luftwaffe that led to German aircraft bombing the city. It is probable the allies made little fuss over the Nazi claims because of the inaccuracies in allied bombing.
22. Shirer, Ibid, pp. 279–302. Shirer probably confused a Handley Page Hampden with a crew of four with the Armstrong Whitworth Whitley with a crew of five.
23. Shirer, Ibid, pp. 302–3.
24. TNA, AIR 24/217 Air Ministry, Bomber Intelligence Summary No. 185, period 02.00 hours to 10.00 hours, 22 May 1940.
25. TNA, AIR 81/525, Casualties, Hampden L4171, 24 May 1940.
26. BCD, p. 49.
27. The death notices from the Red Cross were issued 12–20 June 1940.
28. TNA, AIR 81/769, Casualties, Hampden P1178.
29. Siemons, *Kriegsalltag*, pp. 37–47. *Poll-Chronicle*, pp. 327-8.
30. TNA, AIR 14/2952, Report on Aachen Air-Raid Shelters, May 1945.
31. TNA, AIR 14/2952, British Bombing Research Mission, Report on Aachen Air Raid Shelters, February 1945.
32. Thomas R. Kraus und Paul Thomes (ed.), *Zwangsarbeit in der Stadt Aachen* (Aachen, 2002), pp. 88–100.
33. TNA, FO-30898/C2642, Postal and Telegraph Censorship Report on Germany (No. 3), 5 March 1942.
34. BBSU, pp. 41–2.
35. *Poll-Chronicle*, p. 329.
36. http://ww2today.com/5th-october-1942-coned-and-shot-down-over-cologne Lutterade is believed to have suffered 83 killed, 22 injured, 800 houses seriously damaged and 3,000 homeless.
37. Greenhous et al., *The Crucible of War, 1939–1945: The Official History of The Royal Canadian Air Force* (Toronto, 1994), p. 628.
38. Greenhous, ibid, p. 620.

39. TNA, AIR 14/4465, Despatch War Operations: 2 February 1942–8 May 1945, p. 7.
40. Air Ministry, *The Rise and Fall of the German Air Force* (Air Ministry Pamphlet, No. 248, 1948), p. 185.
41. Georg Tessin, *Verbände und Truppen der deutschen Wehrmacht und Waffen-SS im Zweiten Weltkrieg 1939–1945*, Sechzehnter Band (Osnabrück, 1996), p. 339. Tessin Flakgruppe Aachen auch Rgt. z.b.V., 31.12.43 in der 7. Flak-Div. Köln, 1.12.44 war die Flakgruppe zum Lw.Kdo. West, Flakscheinwerfer-Rgt. 84 (1941/2–1944).
42. Blood, *Birds of Prey*, pp. 432–41.
43. Paul Edmunds (Hrsg.), *Mit Fünfzehn An Die Kanonen* (Aachen, 1975).
44. Edmunds, ibid, pp. 70–113.
45. Nicholas Stargardt, *Witnesses of War: Children's Lives Under the Nazis* (London, 2006), p. 233.

4. WARLORD

1. TNA, FO 371/30901/C10073, War Cabinet, WP (42)482, The Effects of Air Raids on German Civilian Morale, Anthony Eden 23 October 1942. From a Foreign Office minute drafted by Mr Cavendish-Bentinck, 21 October 1942.
2. Robin Prior, *Conquer We Must: A Military History of Britain 1914–1945* (London, 2022), p. 305.
3. Frederick Taylor, *Dresden: Tuesday 13 February 1945* (London, 2005), p. 134.
4. Tom Harrison, *Living Through The Blitz* (London, 1978), p. 13.
5. Harrison was schooled at Winchester College and joined the Foreign Office in 1932 after Cambridge University.
6. Early in his career, Lockhart had worked on a rubber plantation; he passed the Foreign Office examination and was posted to Moscow in 1912 and later was renowned as a British spy.
7. Hawgood later joined the Political Warfare Executive (PWE) and after the war became a professor of history at Birmingham University—his special field being American western history.
8. Michael S. Goodman (ed.), *The Official History of the Joint Intelligence Committee, Volume 1: From the Approach of the Second World War to the Suez Canal* (London: Routledge, 2014).
9. According to Who's Who, 'Max' was based on Dr Otto Carl Köcher (1884), who served as ambassador in Berne from 1937 to 1945. Köcher committed suicide in December 1945 while interned in an American prison camp.
10. From November 1943, Knatchbull-Hugessen's chauffer began selling his secret documents to the German high command, which was discovered by a Foreign Office security officer.
11. TNA, FO 371/30897/C1333, War Cabinet C 1333/29/18 Foreign Office Memorandum on the situation Germany, 15 January 1942.

12. Ibid., file note, Cavendish-Bentinck, 14 January 1942.
13. Ibid., G. Harrison, file note, 15 January 1942.
14. TNA, AIR 20/5952, Aachen: Zone Map Information Chart, 5 June 1942.
15. TNA, FO 371/30895/C3953, JIC (42) 113, War Cabinet, Axis Strength and Policy, 10 April 1942.
16. TNA, FO 371/30901/C7945, Situation in Germany, reports no. 45 and no. 46, 14 August 1942.
17. TNA FO 371/30900/C6086, Conditions in Germany, Spain: From Madrid To Foreign Office, 11 June 1942.
18. TNA, FO 371/30900/C7014, Travel in Germany Today, PWE-Propaganda Research Section, 4 July 1942.
19. TNA, FO 371/30901/C8882, Public opinion in Germany, P.I.D. report No. 53, 11 September 1942.
20. TNA, FO 371/30901/C8969, Situation in Hamburg, 17 September 1942.
21. Richard Overy, *The Bombers and the Bombed*, p. 81.
22. Ralph Barker, 'The 1000 Bomber Raid', in *Purnell's History of the Second World War*, Vol. 2, 1966, p. 817.
23. TNA, FO 371/30897/C197, Situation in Germany, Deterioration of German morale: letter Sawery to Roberts, 7 January 1942.
24. TNA, FO 371/30897/1066, Situation in Germany and at the Russian Front, January 1942.
25. TNA, FO 30896/C1650, Germany: Attitude towards the war, 12 February 1942.
26. TNA, FO 371/30894/C1385, Germany: Intelligence Summary No. 20, 9 February 1942.
27. TNA, FO 371/30896/C1794, Joint Intelligence Sub-Committee report on Axis Strength and Policy in 1942, 13 February 1942.
28. TNA, FO 371/30896/C953, JIC (42) 113 Final, War Cabinet, Joint Intelligence Committee, Axis Strength in 1942, 20 April 1942.
29. TNA, FO 371/30899/3918, Political situation and public morale in Germany, 14 April 1942.
30. TNA, FO 371/30896/C5350, German attitude towards the war, 27 May 1942.
31. TNA, FO 371/30899/C4370, Conditions in Germany: public morale: Royal Air Force attack on Lubeck, 27 April 1942.
32. TNA, FO 371/30901/8538, Germany: Internal Conditions, Postal & Telegraph Censorship Report on Germany (5), 31 August 1842, p. 10.
33. TNA, FO 371/30900/C7754, Situation in Germany, V.A.L. Mallet in conversation with an unnamed Swedish businessman, 19 June 1942—received by FO Whitehall, 8 August 1942.
34. TNA, FO 371/30901/C8538 Postal and Telegraph Censorship, Report on Germany, letters intercepted en route to Chile and Argentina, 31 August 1942.
35. TNA, FO 371/30901/C9354, Situation in Germany, 29 September 1942.
36. TNA, FO 371/30896, JIC (42) 224, War Cabinet, Joint Intelligence Committee, Axis Strength in 1942, 20 June 1942.

37. TNA, FO 371/30900/C7570, Food Conditions in Germany, 1 August 1942.
38. TNA, FO 371/ 30896/C6914, Attitude of the German minister in Lisbon to the war, 10 July 1942.
39. TNA, FO 371/30900/C7570, Germany: Internal Conditions, 5 August 1942.
40. TNA FO 371/30900/C6955, Political Situation and public morale in Germany, July 1942.
41. TNA, FO/371/30896, British Legation, Mexico City, 4 August 1942.
42. TNA, FO 371/30901/C7945, Situation in Germany, reports no. 45 and no. 46, 14 August 1942.
43. TNA, FO 371/30901/C8538, Postal and Telegraph Censorship Report on Germany (No. 5), 31 August 1942.
44. TNA, FO 371/30900/C7570, Food Conditions in Germany, Istanbul, 1 August 1942.
45. TNA FO 371/30901/C9289, War Cabinet, WP (42) 432 German Morale, 26 September 1942.
46. TNA, CAB 66/29/12, Morale in Germany, 26 September 1942.
47. TNA, FO 371/30901/C8779, Germany: Internal Conditions, 10 September 1942.
48. TNA FO 371/30901/C8930, German Morale, letter Roberts to Hawgood, 23 September 1942.
49. TNA, FO 371/30901/9856, Situation in Germany, Greek Prime Minister Communique, 14 October 1942.
50. TNA, FO 371/30901/C9546, Switzerland: Berne Office to Foreign Office, Mr Norton, 3 October 1942.
51. TNA, FO 371/30901/C9362, Germany: Internal Conditions, 29 September 1942.
52. TNA, FO 371/30901/C9546, Germany: Internal, 5 October 1942.
53. TNA FO 371/30901/C9546, Effects of Air Raids on German civilians, PWE, FIC, FO committee on morale and discussion paper, 6 October 1942.
54. TNA FO 371/30901/C9780, The political situation and Public Morale in Germany during the Third Quarter of 1942, 8 October 1942.
55. TNA FO 371/30901/C10073, The Effects of Air Raids on German Civilian Morale, 21 October 1942.
56. TNA, FO 371/30902/C10212, German Morale, 24 October 1942.
57. TNA, FO 371/39092/C11908, morale and Air Raids, 27 November 1942.
58. TNA, FO 371/30902/C12184, Postal and Telegraph Censorship: Report on Germany, 8 December 1942,
59. TNA, FO 371/30902/C12266, PWE, paper Germany Morale Factors and the War Effort, 9 December 1942.
60. TNA, FO 371/30902/C12749, Report on conditions in Germany, V.A.L. Mallet and A. Eden, 21 December 1942.
61. TNA, FO 371/39092/C12115, Foreign Office minute Morale in Germany, 7 December 1942.

NOTES pp. [109–127]

62. TNA, CAB 66/32/39, Morale in Germany, 24 December 1942.
63. TNA, FO 371/30959/C12305, Indications of the German Collapse in 1918, Memorandum by H.K. Grey, 20 December 1942.
64. TNA, FO 371/30959/C12305, Indications of the German Collapse in 1918, second report, JIC (42) 473, the comparison 1918 and 1942, submitted to War Cabinet, 8 December 1942.
65. Patrick Howarth, *Intelligence Chief Extraordinary: The Life of the Ninth Duke of Portland* (London, 1986), pp. 158–9, p. 182.
66. TNA, cab-66-39, various War Cabinet papers for July 1943.

5. FRYING ELVER

1. BCD, p. 407. Several lists claim *Whitebait* was Berlin, but Middlebook advised the decoy raids were against Cologne.
2. TNA, AIR 14/3104, 'B' Forms. July 1943 Night. Teleprints for Aachen raid 13–14 July 1943.
3. TNA, AIR 14/3218, Raid Plots 1943 July, Pathfinder Force, 14 July 1943.
4. Harris, *Bomber Offensive*, p. 71.
5. https://open.spotify.com/episode/3I6cW4eNQBbFDB6jLEZtKw?si=1PuAs8UeSROvkoDlRweKEQ
6. TNA, AIR 20/5962, Aachen: Zone Map Information Sheet, 5 June 1942.
7. TNA, AIR 20/5962, Aachen: Zone Map Information Sheet, 5 June 1942.
8. Wurzburg book.
9. BCD, p. 313—257 participated in the raid, whereas Bomber Command ORB identified 196 aircraft bombed.
10. TNA, HW 16/6 part 1, Police decodes summary period 16 January–15 February 1942, p. 15.
11. BCD, p. 375.
12. BCD, p. 381.
13. AIR 24/257, Bomber Command Intelligence Narrative of Operations No. 645, 14 July 1943.
14. TNA, AIR 14/3218, Raid plots 1943 July, 4 Group, 14 July 1943.
15. TNA, AIR 14/3218, Raid plots 1943 July, 8 (PFF) Group, 14 July 1943.
16. TNA, AIR 24/257, Interceptions/Tactics, Night 13–14 July 1943, 20 July 1943.
17. TNA, AIR 14/3218, Raid plots 1943 July, 6 (RCAF) Group, 14 July 1943.
18. http://www.aircrewremembered.com/coventry-dfc-henry.html
19. TNA, AIR 14/3218, Raid Plots 1943 July. No. 3 Group plot, 14 July 1943.
20. Luftwaffe officer rolls.
21. http://stichting-vliegeniersmonument-giessenlanden-wo2.nl
22. http://lancasterdiary.net/guestbook.php
23. Edmunds, p. 209.
24. Edmunds, pp. 205–8.

25. Rudolf Storpil, 'Deutsche Schicksalsstadt im Westen', *Aachener Anzeiger Politiches Tageblatt*, 17 July 1943.
26. Edmunds, pp. 200–3.
27. Hans Hoffmann, *Aachen in Trümmern* (Düsseldorf, 1984), pp. 50–62.
28. Rudolf Storpil, 'Die Gefallenen des Terrorangreiffs bestattet', AAPT, 22 July 1943.
29. AIR 24/257, Immediate Interpretation Report No.K.1605, 15 July 1943.
30. TNA, AIR 14/3410, BC-ORS Final Reports on Operations, Night Raids Nos. 280–415, March–August 1943, Vol. 3, Aachen 13–14 July 1943, report No. 376.
31. http://filestore.nationalarchives.gov.uk/pdfs/large/cab-66-39.pdf War Cabinet, Summary of Operations of Bomber Command for Fortnight Ending 1200 Hours Sunday, 18 July 1943, WP (43) 338, 26 July 1943.
32. Werner Crempas, 'Die Nacht des Todes, in der Aachen verbrannte', Aachener Nachrichten, 14 July 1993.
33. BCD, p. 407.
34. *Poll-Chronicle*, p. 332.
35. Jörg Friedrich, *The Bombing of Germany 1940–1945*, trans. Allison Brown (Columbia, 2006), p. 246.

6. THE PARALYSED CITY

1. TNA, FO 837/1313 *The Bomber's Baedeker*, Guide to the Economic Importance of German Towns and cities, Foreign Office and Ministry of Economic Warfare, part 1 Aachen—Küstrin, May 1944, pp. 1–4.
2. http://rafweb.org/Biographies/Searby.htm
3. https://www.youtube.com/watch?v=UjH0UwNJ6O4&t=25s
4. Thanks to Dr Dan Ellin (aka @danmadmorgan) for furnishing evidence from RAF Bomber Command 5 Group records, which confirmed the raid was a 'blitz attack'. https://twitter.com/danmadmorgan/status/1778367085074133055?s=61&t=zqKav-q1yQshWAfc4t7LSA
5. TNA, AIR 24/272.
6. TNA, AIR 24/276, Operational Research Section report B165 Summary of Attacks on Aachen, 11–12 April, 5 May 1944.
7. Noble Frankland, *History at War: The Campaign of an Historian* (London, 1998), p. 28 e-book copy.
8. TNA, AIR 24/272, ORS report 577, Bomber Command Report on Night Operations, 11–12 April 1944, ORS report No. 577, 4 July 1944.
9. TNA, AIR 24/276, Night raid report No. 614. Aachen, 24–5 May 1944, 5 September 1944.
10. TNA, AIR 24/276, Night raid report No. 616. Aachen, 27–8 May 1944, 11 September 1944.
11. *Poll-Chronicle*, p. 335.

12. https://open.spotify.com/episode/6hjmPUEEC3k3U2hzPkU21a?si=m2wj_tjQT_CKrb0EmLkp2A
13. Refer to Chapter 11, Schmeer et al trial.
14. TNA, FO 935/122, Captured enemy documents, speech by Kreishandwerkmeister Mort, Aachen, 13 February 1944.
15. TNA, FO 935/178, Captured enemy documents, Chamber of Commerce circular on procedures for repairing bomb damages by industries, 27 July 1943.
16. TNA, FO 935/178, Captured enemy documents, Meeting of the architects, 6 September 1943.
17. TNA, FO 935/179, Captured enemy documents, circular on air raids and foreign workers August–September 1943.
18. TNA, FO 935/178, Captured enemy documents, Meeting of the architects, 4 October 1943.
19. TNA, FO 935/178, Captured enemy documents, Circular to all German firms, 24 November 1943.
20. TNA, FO 935/178, Captured enemy documents, Circular on the repair of railway yards, 24 November 1943.
21. TNA, FO 935/175, Enemy documents, economic conditions in Aachen-Köln area, Conference pertaining to 11 April 1944 air raid, held at Hotel Quellenhof, Aachen, 14 April 1944, translated 24 November 1944.
22. TNA, FO 935/175, Enemy documents, economic conditions in Aachen-Köln area, Conference pertaining to raids 24–5 and 27–8 May 1944, held at Hotel Quellenhof, Aachen, 31 May 1944.
23. TNA, FO 935/175, Enemy documents, economic conditions in Aachen-Köln area, Conference pertaining to raids 24–5 and 27–8 May 1944, held at Hotel Quellenhof, Aachen, 6 June 1944.
24. Rolf-Dieter Müller, *Der Bombenkrieg 1939–1945* (Ch, Links Verlag, 2004) for NDR, 'Der Bombenkrieg', Studio Hamburg Documentaries 2004. See also ZDF, 'Der Feuersturm', 2006.
25. TNA Air 40/731, USAAF Operations No. 607, 6–7 September 1944.
26. Edmunds, p. 197.
27. Jeremy Noakes, *Nazism 1919–1945, Volume 4: The German Home Front in World War II* (Exeter, 1998), p. 640.
28. Helmut Clahsen, *Trümmerfrauen: Angst, Not, Leid und Tod in Aachen und nach dem 2. Weltkrieg* (Aachen, 2014), pp. 8–49.
29. Müller, ibid, pp. 171–7.
30. Channel 4, 'Wings of the Storm', Australian War Memorial, 1986.
31. Roger A. Freeman, *Mighty Eighth War Diary* (London, 1981), p. 320.
32. Poll, Siemons, *Poll-Chronicle*, p. 335.
33. TNA, WO311/442, Ill-treatment of 2 Allied airmen at Aachen on 9 August 1944. See also WO235/217–220 and 688.
34. TNA, FO 935/177, Letter from the President of the Gau Chamber of Economy, July–August 1944, translated by the Foreign Office 29 November 1944.

35. Matthias Uhl, *Die Organisation Des Terrors: Der Dienstkalender Heinrich Himmlers 1943-34*, (Piper e-books) 2020, p. 1317.
36. Noakes, *Nazis: 1919–1945*, p. 642.
37. *Poll-Chronicle*, p. 335.
38. Guido Baumann, Otto Bönnemann, Walter Meven, *Die Tragödie von Aachen: Die Hinrichtung von zwei Kindern* (Aachen, 2003), pp. 16–20.
39. *Poll-Chronicle*, p. 335.
40. H.R. Trevor-Roper, *Hitler's War Directives 1939–1945* (London, 1966), pp. 272–8.
41. *Poll-Chronicle*, p. 336.
42. Peter M. Quadflieg, *Gerhard von Schwerin: Wehrmacht general, Kanzlerberater, Lobbyist* (Paderborn, 2016), pp. 110–50.
43. Heinz Günther Guderian, *From Normandy to the Ruhr: with the 116 Panzer Division in World War II*, (Bedford, 2001), p. 146.
44. ZDF, *The Wehrmacht*, Episode 5, 'The Bitter End', Cinecentrum Production, 2007.
45. Heinz Günther Guderian, *From Normandy to the Ruhr: with the 116 Panzer Division in World War II*, (Bedford, 2001),, p. 148.
46. Sönke Neitzel, *Tapping Hitler's generals: Transcripts of Secret Conversations, 1942–1945* (Barnsley, 2007), Klaus-Dietmar Henke, *Die amerikanische Besetzung Deutschlands* (München, 1995).
47. Christoph Rass, René Rohrkamp, Peter M. Quadflieg, General *Graf von Schwerin und das Kriegsende in Aachen. Ereignis, Mythos, Analyse* (Aachen, 2007).
48. Bernhard Poll, *Das Schiksal Aachens Im Herbst 1944* (Aachen, 1962).
49. Guido Baumann, et al, ibid, pp. 42–3, the Schack letter was copied in full.
50. David K. Yelton, *Hitler's Volkssturm: The Nazi Militia and the Fall of Germany, 1944–1945* (Kansas, 2002), p. 13.
51. Noakes, volume 4, p. 647.
52. Guido Baumann et al., ibid., pp. 23–5.

7. THE STALINGRAD OF THE WEST

1. 'Battle for Aachen', *After the Battle*, No. 42 (London, 1983) p. 25. *After the Battle* was a popular quarterly journal that traced World War II battlefields by visiting key points or comparing wartime photographs to present-day scenes and surviving sites of interest. It relied on the Charles Whiting/Wolfgang Trees interpretation of the battle.
2. https://en.wikipedia.org/wiki/Battle_of_Aachen
3. F.F.G. Williams, *SLAM: The Influence of S.L.A. Marshall on the United States Army* (CMH, TRADOC, 1999), pp. 19–20.
4. S.L.A. Marshall, *Bringing Up the Rear: A Memoir* (San Rafael, 1979).
5. Williams, ibid, p. 31.
6. NARA, RG407-427, Box 24012, records of 2 Information and Historical Service, 3 January 1945. The author would like to thank Dr Roger Cirillo, Col Rtd, for copies of this collection of records.

NOTES

7. NARA, RG, NARA, RG407–427, Box 24012, records of 2 Information and Historical Service, 3 January 1945, Headquarters Third Battalion, 18th Infantry Regiment, 24 October 1944.
8. NARA, RG, NARA, RG407–427, Box 24012, records of 2 Information and Historical Service, 3 January 1945, Headquarters, Captain JP Gurka, Journal for Third Battalion, 18th Infantry Regiment, 31 October 1944.
9. NARA, RG, NARA, RG407–427, Box 24012, records of 2 Information and Historical Service, 3 January 1945, Headquarters, Third Battalion, field order No. 1 issued 24, amended to 18 October 1944.
10. NARA, RG, NARA, RG407–427, Box 24012, records of 2 Information and Historical Service, 3 January 1945, Headquarters 26th Infantry Regiment, Interviews Battle of Aachen.
11. S.L.A. Marshall, *Bastogne: The First Eight Days* (Washington DC, 1946).
12. Friedrich Kösling's reply to Alfred Zerbel's question: What was the reason for the obstinate defense of Aachen from 8 to 21 October 1944, FMS A-991, Königstein, 7 July 1950.
13. TNA, WO208 3433 MI9, Captured generals, Gerhard Wilck, October 1944.
14. TV episode, 'To the Bitter End'.
15. Bernhard Poll, *Das Schicksal Aachens Im Herbst 1944* (Aachen, 1962).
16. Blood, *Hitler's Bandit Hunters*, pp. 225–8.
17. Roger Cirillo, 'The Market Garden: Allied Operational Command in Northwest Europe, 1944', unpublished PhD thesis, Cranfield University, 2001, p. 494.
18. Eisenhower, p. 355.
19. Omar N. Bradley, *A Soldier's Story* (New York, 1951). Reading a digitised copy of Bradley's manuscript, it's possible to identify the keywords in his text. The most prominent being 'Eisenhower' (295 references), 'Montgomery' (165 references), 'Hodges' 129 references and 'Collins' 90. Of the Germans, there were 39 references to 'Hitler', 41 for 'Rundstedt', 30 'Rommel' and 10 for 'Model'. In contrast, there were only 20 references to 'Aachen' and no reference to the MGO scandals that happened under his command.
20. Omar N. Bradley, *A General's Story* (New York, 1981). He referred to 'Eisenhower' 302 times, 'Montgomery' 117 times and 'Aachen' 17 times, but without reference to either the MGO or Oppenhoff.
21. S.L.A. Marshall, *Bringing Up The Rear: A Memoir* (San Rafael, 1979), pp. 164–5 and pp. 172–4.
22. Chester Wilmot, *The Struggle for Europe* (London, 1952), p. 481, see also p. 548.
23. Charles B. MacDonald, *The Siegfried Line, part of United States Army in World War II* (CMH, 1961), p. 281.
24. Russell F. Weigley, *Eisenhower's Lieutenants: The Campaigns of France and Germany, 1944–1945* (Bloomington, 1981), p. 359.
25. Bradley (1951), p. 233.
26. Weigly (1981), p. 364.
27. Wolfgang Trees, Charles Whiting, *Die Amis sind da! Wie Aachen 1944 erobert wurde* (Aachen, 1975).

28. Lt Col D.M. Daniel, Infantry, Capture of Aachen, 1946–7, Carl Manuscript, p. 6.
29. James H. Cash (Colonel), 'The Operations of the 1st Infantry Division and 30th Infantry Division in the Aachen Offensive 2–21 October 1944 (Rhineland Campaign), Fort Benning, 1948–9.
30. 'Report of Regimental Activities for the Month of October 1944', European Theater of Operations: 26 Infantry Regiment, 1st Infantry Division, October 1944, D767. 681.A2A2dU.
31. Captain Monte M. Parrish, 'The Battle of Aachen: Ana Analysis of City Fighting Tactics', US Army Infantry School, Fort Benning, 30 June 1972.
32. Lt Col Derrill M. Daniel, The Capture of Aachen, Fort Leavenworth, 1946–7, Carl Manuscript Collection.
33. The original: *Die deutschen Soldaten in Aachen erleben den gleichen mitleidslosen Opfergang wie die Kämpfer von Stalingrad.*
34. https://www.youtube.com/watch?v=KiBqZH-guwo&t=1167s
35. I would like to thank Michael Miller for supplying copies of Herbert Rink's SS personnel records.
36. Rudolf Lehmann & Ralf Tiemann, *The Leibstandarte IV/1* (Manitoba, 1993), referred to Kampfgruppe Diefenthal, from Leibstandarte SS Adolf Hitler, later known as 1. SS Panzer-Division, as the commanding formation for SS-Obersturmführer Hubert Rink commander of I. Bataillon, Panzer-Grenadier Regiment 1.
37. Rudolf Lehmann & Ralf Tiemann, *The Leibstandarte IV/1* (Manitoba, 1993), referred to Kampfgruppe Diefenthal, from Leibstandarte SS Adolf Hitler, later known as 1. SS Panzer-Division, as the commanding formation for SS-Obersturmführer Hubert Rink commander of I. Bataillon, Panzer-Grenadier Regiment 1.
38. Peter S. Kindsvatter, *American Soldiers: Ground Combat in the World Wars, Korea, and Vietnam* (Kansas, 2003), p. 238.
39. https://www.fdmuseum.org/about-the-1st-infantry-division/medal-of-honor-recipients/cpt-bobbie-e-brown/
40. Murray Illson, 'Bobbie E. Brown, Medal of Honor Winner is Dead', *New York Times*, 11 November 1971, p. 51.

8. RESTORING DEMOCRACY

1. NARA, RG331, Allied Operational and Occupation Headquarters, SHAEF, General Staff, G-5 Division, Information Branch, Historical Section, 1943 to July 1945. Box 150, Historical Reports, US First Army, jackets 1–3: Note to SMGO 1st Infantry Division from Lt Col Albert A. Carmichael, Commanding Detachment FIG2: Appointment of Burgomeister, 31 October 1944.
2. Perry Biddiscombe, *Werwolf! The History of the National Socialist Guerrilla Movement 1944–1946* (Cardiff, 1998), pp. 36–9.
3. NARA, RG331, Allied Operational and Occupation Headquarters, The Adjutant

General's Office, Department of the Army, Historical Report—First US Army, March 1945. The attention to Luftwaffe uniforms was an indication of how far SS covert operations, during the Battle of the Ardennes, was treated as a security warning by the US Army.

4. NARA, RG331, Allied Operational and Occupation Headquarters, US I Infantry Division, G-2 Periodic Report No. 140, Annex F, The New Mayor of Aachen—Franz Oberhoff [sic].
5. NARA, RG407–427, Box 24012, records of 2 Information and Historical Service, 3 January 1945.
6. NARA, RG331.
7. NARA, RG331, Allied Operational and Occupation Headquarters, SHAEF, General Staff, G-5 Division, Information Branch, Historical Section, 1943 to July 1945. Box 150, Historical Reports, US First Army, jackets 1–3.
8. NARA, RG331, Allied Operational and Occupation Headquarters, SHAEF, General Staff, G-5 Division, Information Branch, Historical Section, 1943 to July 1945. Box 148, First US Army, jackets 1–3. 16 November 1944: Military Government Conference, 9–10 November 1944, document 5668, pp. 528–50.
9. NARA, RG331, Allied Operational and Occupation Headquarters, SHAEF, General Staff, G-5 Division, Information Branch, Historical Section, 1943 to July 1945, Box 148, Historical Reports, First US Army, jackets 1–3, Lieutenant E.G. Milton, Highlights of a Conversation between Mr Robert Murphy and the Bishop of Aachen and the Oberburgermeister of Aachen, 23 November 1944.
10. NARA, RG331, Allied Operational and Occupation Headquarters, SHAEF, General Staff, G-5 Division, Information Branch, Historical Section, Box 150, State of Public Safety in Aachen, 11 December 1944.
11. Saul K. Padover, *Psychologist in Germany: The Story of an American Intelligence Officer* (London, 1946), p. 102,
12. Similar ideas were expressed in Friedrich Hayek, *The Road To Serfdom* (1944), which was brilliantly contradicted by the more fundamental political exposé by Herman Finer, *The Road to Reaction* (1945).
13. McSherry Papers, Ninth US Army, PW Detachment, 'The Political Situation in Aachen', 3 February 1945.
14. Arthur D. Kahn, *Experiment in Occupation: Witness to the Turnabout—Anti-Nazi to Cold War, 1944–1946* (Pennsylvania, 2004), pp. 36–7.
15. Lyn H. Nicholas, *Rape of Europa: The Fate of Europe's Treasures in the Third Reich and Second World War* (New York, 1995).
16. F.S.V. Donnison, *Civil Affairs and Military Government Central Organisation and Planning* (HMSO London, 1966), p. 230.
17. Walker Hancock, 'Experiences of a Monuments Officer in Germany, in the *College of Art Journal*, Vol. 5. No. 4 (May 1946), pp. 271–311, Smithsonian 1977, and 'The Spoils of War', BBC Timewatch 1991.
18. Hermann Weisweiler, *Stefan Buchkremer. Flammenritter, Domretter und Fotograf* (Aachen, 1997).
19. Hancock, 'Experiences of a Monuments Officer in Germany', pp. 272–6.

20. Hancock, 'Experiences of a Monuments Officer in Germany', pp. 279–80. The details contrast with the museum's webpage—https://www.reiff-museum. rwth-aachen.de/home/home_engl.html—which claims: 'The zenith of the museum was ended abruptly after the beginning of the 2nd World War. With the popularization of photography, a collection of copies seemed more and more old-fashioned. In consequence of this change many works were given away, sold or stored in dark basements, where they were buried in oblivion.'
21. Smithsonian, 1977.
22. Hancock, 'Experiences of a Monuments Officer in Germany', pp. 290–1.
23. Hancock, 1946.
24. Hancock, 'Experiences of a Monuments Officer in Germany', p. 307.
25. TNA, WO 219/3494, G-5 Division Records, SHAEF, OPS Branch Internal Affairs, MFA&A Reports on state of care of preservation of etc removal of by Germans, period 15 September 1944 to 3 February 1945.
26. Historical report, G-5 Section, US First Army, 1–30 November 1944, Historical reports, p. 450.
27. McSherry Papers, Ninth US Army, PW Detachment, 'The Political Situation in Aachen', 3 February 1945.
28. NARA, RG331, Allied Operational and Occupation Headquarters, SHAEF, General Staff, G-5 Division, Information Branch, Historical Section, 1943 to July 1945. Box 148, First US Army, jackets 1–3. 16 November 1944: Military Government Conference, 9–10 November 1944, document 5668, March 1945, pp. 528–50.
29. Earl F. Ziemke, *The U.S. Army In The Occupation Of Germany,1944–1946*, Army Historical Series, CMH 1975.
30. Ulrich Kalkmann, *Die Technische Hochschule Aachen im Dritten Reich (1933–1945)* (Aachen, 2003).
31. TNA FO 935/121 Aachen odd documents.
32. Wolfgang Trees, Charles Whiting, *Unternhemen Karneval: Der Werwolf-Mord an Aachens Oberbürgermeister Oppenhoff* (Aachen, 1982).
33. Eisenhower, pp. 473–4.
34. Kahn, ibid, p. 178.

9. BRITISH MILITARY OCCUPATION

1. Giles MacDonagh, *After the Reich: The Brutal History of the Allied Occupation* (New York, 2007), pp. 59–60.
2. Arthur Harris, *Bomber Offensive* (London, 1947), p. 252.
3. TNA, AIR14/2958, BC-ORS, A Brief Survey of the Effects of Air Attack on the City of Aachen, March 1945,
4. TNA, AIR 14/3502, British Bombing Research Mission, Brief Survey oft he Effects of Air Attack on the City of Aachen, March 1945.
5. TNA, AIR 14/4465, Despatch on War Operations: 22rd February 1942 to 8 May 1945, Air Chief Marshal Arthur Harris, October 1945.

NOTES

6. Overy, p. 63, p. 147.
7. FM Lord Alanbrooke, *War Diaries, 1939–1940* (London, 2001), p. 668.
8. Harold MacMillan, *War Diaries: Politics and War in the Mediterranean January 1943– May 1945* (London, 1954), pp. 765–6.
9. TNA, Air 14/3560, Planning Committee Bombing Research, 20 July 1945.
10. TNA, AIR 14/1252, PUBLICATIONS—Sir Arthur Harris Despatch—Reports on Air Operations of the War Against Germany and Italy.
11. Victor Gollancz, In Darkest Germany (London, 1947), p. 73 and p. 98.
12. TNA, WO 171/7953, RB Aachen, war diary 227 MGD, 5 May 1945.
13. TNA, WO 171/7953, RB Aachen, war diary 227 MGD, Colonel Matthews report and notes, 18 May 1945.
14. TNA, WO 171/7953, RB Aachen, war diary 227 MGD, movement orders, 22 May 1945.
15. TNA, WO 171/967, 311 Det Mil Gov war diary and strength record, 1–31 May 1945.
16. F.S.V. Donnison, 1961, p. 208.
17. TNA, WO 171/7953, RB Aachen, war diary 227 MGD, Colonel Matthews report, 25 May 1945.
18. TNA, WO 171/7953, RB Aachen, war diary 227 MGD, Colonel Matthews notes to liaison officer, 25 May 1945.
19. TNA, WO 171/953, 227/311 Detachment Civil Affairs.
20. TNA, WO 171/953, 227 MG, Report period 16 June–1 July 1945, RB Aachen, Colonel Leslie, 3 July 1945.
21. TNA, WO 171/953, 227/311 Detachment Civil Affairs Aachen, Monthly Report Food, Agric, Forestry, Lt Col McConkey, Appendix, 30 June 1945.
22. McSherry papers, Headquarters Ninth US Army, PW Detachment, Josef Hirtz interrofgation, 2 February 1945.
23. Andreas Lorenz, *Arisierung und Wiedergutmachung* (Aachen 2023), p. 166.
24. Gitta Sereny, *The German Trauma: Experiences and Reflections 1938–2000* (London, 2000), p. xix.
25. TNA, WO 309/942, Heimbach airmen, Brief for Investigation, 3 May 1946.
26. TNA, WO 309/942, Heimbach airmen, Brief for Pathologist, Haystack Arrest Report, 6 July 1946.
27. TNA, WO 309/942, Heimbach airmen, Brief for Pathologist, Major A.S. Stone, Royal Artillery, 11 July 1946.
28. TNA, WO 309/942, Heimbach airmen, Deposition Josef Rademacher, Captain Aptaker, 20 July 1946.
29. The only time the airman was identified, but no one asked for his name.
30. TNA, WO 309/942, Final summary of justice, 21 September 1946.
31. TNA, WO 309/104, Brady-Phillips War Crimes tribunal prosecution file, August–September 1946.
32. TNA, WO 309/1525, War Crimes Trial—Aachen Case, 26 July 1946.
33. TNA WO 235/218, Brady-Phillips—the case file and exhibits.

10. IMPOSING THE RAJ

1. TNA, WO 252/252, Inter-service Topographical Department: The town of Aachen, September 1944.
2. TNA, FO 153/22, Mr Lawther Case, transcript of the *Sunday Times* article, 12 March 1939.
3. TNA, FO 153/22, M. Lawther Case, John E. Evan, General Secretary, letter to Lord Halifax at the Foreign Office, 14 March 1939.
4. TNA, FO 153/22, Letter A.B. Hutcheon, Foreign Office, to Evan, 20 March 1939.
5. TNA, FO 153/22, Mr Lawther Case, Foreign Office despatch No. 21, sent 22 March 1939.
6. TNA, FO 153/22, Mr Lawther Case, Letter to Halifax from J.E.Bell on 24 March 1939. Bell signed off as 'a most obedient, humble Servant'.
7. TNA, FO 153/22, M. Lawther Case, letter Zollfahndungsstelle, Aachen, to the Consul-General, 25 March 1939.
8. TNA, FO 153/22, Mr Lawther Case, Parliamentary question from Samuel to Butler, 27 March 1939.
9. TNA, FO 153/22, Mr Lawther Case, German replies sent tot he Foreign Office, 1 April 1939.
10. TNA, FO 153/22, Mr Lawther Case, letter RAB Butler to Lawther, 6 April 1939.
11. TNA, WO 171/953, Legal: Monthly report to 29 June, Appendix B, Major Hirst, 3 July 1945.
12. TNA FO 1060/19, MGO Courts RB Aachen, register of court sentences.
13. TNA FO 1060/2123, Register of thr Military Government Court at Aachen, June–December 1945.
14. TNA, FO 1073/2 FIS 1946–8.
15. TNA, FO 1073/2, Frontier Inspection Service Aachen, File No. 6, Jan. 1946–Dec. 1947, Frontier Control question issued by the Control Commission in Berlin, 11 January 1946.
16. TNA, FO 1073/2, Frontier Inspection Service Aachen, File No. 6, Jan. 1946–Dec. 1947, German Customs Frontier Control—Reconnaissance of RB Aachen Frontier, 6 March 1946.
17. TNA, FO 1073/2, Frontier Inspection Service Aachen, File No. 6, Jan. 1946–Dec. 1947, German Customs Frontier Control—Reconnaissance of RB Aachen Frontier, 6 March 1946.
18. TNA, FO 1073/2, Frontier Inspection Service Aachen, File No. 6, Jan. 1946–Dec. 1947, Frontier Control—RB Aachen Border, Monthly Report No. 1, 25 June 1946.
19. TNA, FO 1073/2, FCS Aachen, Report for January 1947.
20. TNA, FO 1073/2, FCS Aachen, Report for January 1947.
21. TNA, FO 1073/2, FCS Aachen, Report for January 1947.

22. F.S.V. Donnison, Civil Affairs and Military Government Northwest Europe 1944–6 (London: 1961), pp. 373–4.
23. TNA, FO 1013/17, Aachen technical college, letter from Mr A.V. Askwith CSI Chief Inspector of Education and controller of Internal Aaairs and Communications in Hq Mil Gov to Colonel F.H.S. Pownall, Commander RB Aachen.
24. TNA, FO 1013/17, Aachen technical college, Squadron Leader Stall to Lieutenant Colonel H.J. Walker, Staff Officer 1, 20 February 1946.
25. TNA, FO 1013/17, Aachen technical college, Report on the Technische Hochschule, Aachen, 20 February 1946.
26. TNA, FO 1013/17, Aachen technical college, letter from Lt Col Black to A.V. Askwith, 23 February 1946.
27. TNA, FO 1013/17, Aachen technical college, student resolution, 20 February 1946.
28. TNA, FO 1013/17, Aachen technical college, Askwith letter to Black, 26 February 1946.
29. TNA, FO 1013/17, Aachen technical college, Control Commission Letter, 21 February 1946.
30. TNA, FO 1013/17, Aachen technical college, Dr Lerner RB Aachen, 28 February 1946.
31. TNA, FO 1013/717, Aachen technical college, Proklamation An Die Vernunft!, 20 February 1946.
32. TNA, FO 1013/17, Aachen technical college, Internal Affairs Officer Düsseldorf to Askwith, 7 March 1946.
33. TNA, FO 371/70715, Reports of Lecturers to Semester Courses, University Summer Vacation courses in the British Zone of Germany, 1948, G. Murray, undated.
34. TNA, FO 1013/17, Aachen technical college, Personnel of Technische Hochschule Aachen, undated and unattributed list of re-screening results.
35. TNA, FO 371/70715, Reports of Lecturers to Semester Courses, Report on the International Course Aachen, August 1948, Dr A.C. Crombie, University of London, August 1948.
36. TNA, FO 371/70715, Reports of Lecturers to Semester Courses, 'German Universities', *The Times*, MRD Foot, 11 September 1948.
37. TNA, FO 371/70715, Reports of Lecturers to Semester Courses, F.T. Calvert letter to MRD Foot, 21 September 1948.
38. TNA, FO 371/70715, Reports of Lecturers to Semester Courses, Final Consolidated Report, October 1948.
39. Helmut König (Hrsg), *Der Fall Schwerte im Kontext* (Wiesbaden, 1998), pp. 14–38.
40. TNA, FO 1073/22, FIS Monthy Reports 1947–8, part two, report 16 November 1948, by G. Maund, Controller General, Frontier Control Service for October 1948.

pp. [282–294]   NOTES

41. TNA, FO 1073/22, FIS Monthly Reports 1947–8, part two, report 15 January 1949, by Mr Jago, Acting Controller General, Frontier Control Service for December 1948.
42. Wolfgang Trees, Charles Whting, Thomas Omansen, *Drei Jahre nach Null: Geschichte der britischen Besatzungszone* (Düsseldorf, 1989).
43. WDR (West Deutsche Rundfunk), 'Auf Verbotenen Pfaden' (2006).
44. TNA, FO 1073/2, FIS Aachen, Report for January 1947.

11. ORDINARY PEOPLE

1. Josef Grohé (1902–1988), Gauleiter of Aachen-Cologne, speech in the Cologne Messe, 28 September 1941.
2. https://oecher-platt.de
3. Andreas Lorenz, *Arisierung und Wiedergutmachung* (Aachen 2023), pp. 157–69.
4. Centre Charlemagne/Couvenmuseum, *Der Krieg Ist Aus: Politik, Alltag und Medien in Aachen* (Aachen, 2019), Helmut Irmen, 'Erste Prozesse Gegen Nationalsozialiszen in Aachen', pp. 91–100.
5. Richard J. Evans, 'Coercion and Consent in Nazi Germany', Raleigh Lecture on History, The British Academy 2007, pp. 151, 53–81.
6. PWB—thesis.
7. Martin Cüppers et al, *Fotos aus Sobidor: Die Niemann-Samlung zu Holocaust und Nationalsozialismus* (Berlin, 2020).
8. In 1954, a leaflet was circulated in the region that May had been murdered. A legal process was instigated to assess the real story and May was exhumed. In 2019, a *Stolperstein* was laid beside his former home (Muffeter Weg 57), see http://www.bertram-wieland-archiv.de/index.php/aktuelles/presse/63-stolperstein-fuer-aachener-widerstandskaempfer-arthur-may
9. HStaD Regierung Aachen, file 22757, Regierungs Präsident Bischoff, document 25, Hilfspolizei in Preussen: Ein Erlass Görings. Published in the Kölnische Zeitung 24 February 1933.
10. HstaD, file 22757, Regierungs Präsident Bischoff, document 101, Hilfspolizei in Westen, 14 March 1933. Not a Nazi equivalent of the neighbourhood watch!
11. HStaD Regierung Aachen, file 22757, document 34 and document 57.
12. HStaD Regierung Aachen, file 22757, document 34 and documents 86–7. According to document 108, they were eventually provided with formal guidelines for medical assistance duties in March 1933.
13. HStaD Regierung Aachen, file 22757, document 45.
14. HStaD Regierung Aachen, file 22757, document 71.
15. HStaD Regierung Aachen, file 22757, document 97.
16. NARA, R-175/12, 1.Polizei-Revier Aachen was still operational in 1943–4.
17. TNA, WO 208/3648, Report on Interrogation of Kurt Happel by Captain H.K. Kettler, LDC, 24 September 1944.
18. NARA, IRR 319, US Third Army Interrogation Section, 'Gestapo in Aachen', 19 July 1945.

19. Statistik des Deutschen Reichs, *Volkszählung: Die Bevölkerung des Deutschen Reichs nach dem Ergebnissen der Volkszählung 193, Heft 5, Die Glaubenensjuden im Deutschen Reich* (Berlin, 1936), p. 15.
20. http://jewishencyclopedia.com/articles/2-aachen and http://germansynagogues.com/index.php/synagogues-and-communities?pid=63&sid=76:aachen
21. Römling, *Aachen—Geschichte einer Stadt*, p. 276. Otto Blumenthal has been honoured in the new central building with a memorial plaque.
22. Götz Aly, *Beneficiaries*, pp. 123–5.
23. Otto Frank, *The Diary of Anne Frank* (Pan, 1968).
24. TNA, H16, Enemy Alien Registration Cards.
25. Detlev J.K. Peukert, *Inside Nazi Germany: Conformity, Opposition and Racism in Everyday Life* (London, 1987), p. 135.
26. Refer to Kraus & Thomes, *Zwangsarbeit*, pp. 264–292.
27. TNA, FO 371/30898/C1898, British Legation, Stockholm, 19 February 1942.
28. Its probable that Aretz was actually referring to Mozart's 'Leck mich im Arsch', which has come to mean 'kiss my arse'.
29. A more correct translation might have been 'mess', 'filth' or 'scandal'.
30. Zenner evidence.
31. Herbert Lepper, *Von der Emanzipation zum Holocaust—Die Israelites Synagogengemeinde zu Aachen, 1802–1942*, Bd.1 (Aachen, 1994).
32. Ulrich Kalkmann, *Die Technische Hochschule Aachen im Dritten Reich (1933–1945)* (Aachen, 2003).
33. J. Noakes and G. Pridham, *Nazism 1919–1945, 2: State, Economy, and Society 1933–1938* (Exeter, 1995), p. 553.
34. Leon Poliakov, *Harvest of Hate* (London, 1960), p. 29.
35. NARA, IRR 319, Box 37, Aachen, Detailed Interrogation Report, Personalities in Aachen and Vicinity, 12 July 1945.
36. Seetzen, according to Dr Nicholas Terry of Exeter University, was a high flyer who eventually served with *SS-Einsatzgrupen D*, the infamous killing unit, and committed suicide at the end of the war.
37. Robert Gellately, *Gestapo and Society* (KK), p. 109.
38. Gellately, ibid, p. 63.
39. Franz Seidler, Das *Nationalsozialistisches Kraftfahrkorps und die Organisation Todt im Zweiten Welzkrieg* (Munchen, 1984), pp. 632–3.
40. J. Noakes and G. Pridham, *Nazism 1919–1945, 2: State, Economy, and Society 1933–1938* (Exeter, 1995), p. 555.
41. Siemons, pp. 58–9.
42. Lorenz, ibid, p. 166.

REFLECTIONS

1. TNA, Prem 11/1163, Sir Winston Churchill's visit to Aachen, Germany, extract from Churchill's speech, 10 May 1956.

2. Danchev, Alex and Daniel Todman (eds), *Alanbrooke, War Diaries 1939–1945* (London, 2001), p. 668.
3. BBC, *Churchill: Despair*, episode 4, narrated by Martin Gilbert, 1992.
4. Lord Moran's diary, *Winston Churchill: The Struggle for Survival 1940–1965* (London, 1966), pp. 695–6.
5. Blood, *Hitler's Bandit Hunters*, p. 62.
6. *Manchester Guardian*, 3 May 1956, cited in Moran, p. 696.
7. 'Churchill a "great European" to get Charlemage Prize in Germany', *The Londonderry Sentinel*, 5 May 1956.
8. 'Churchill and Charlemagne', *The Spectator*, 18 May 1956, p. 5.
9. Richard Toye, *Churchill's Empire* (London, 2010).
10. Richard Breitman, Official Secrets: *What the Nazis Planned, What the British and Americans Knew* (New York, 1998).
11. Blood, *Hitler's Bandit Hunters*, pp. 57–64.
12. TNA, HW16/6, Zip/MSGP/44/8 April 1943, German police decodes, 7 March–7 April 1943.
13. Middlebook, *BCD*, p. 201.
14. Paul Brickhill, *The Great Escape* (London, 1950).
15. TNA, WO 208/5381, The London Cage by Colonel Scotland, case file opened 6 August 1954.
16. TNA, LCO/2/7288, Access to War Crimes Trials and Court Papers. Various Chancellery notes from Mr Boggis-Rolfe, subject Lord Russell of Liverpool, 8–10 April 1958.
17. TNA, CAB 21/4942, Publication of Memoirs by Field Marshal Lord Montgomery, 24 October 1958.
18. TNA, DE 257/27 Criticisms on the 'Montgomery Story' in 1958.
19. TNA, WO 32/17350 Questions arising from The Memoirs of Field Marshal Montgomery, 1958.
20. F.H. Hinsley with E.E. Thomas, C.F.G. Ransome and R.C. Knight, *British Intelligence in the Second World War Volume 1: Its Influence on Strategy and Operations* (HMSO, 1979).
21. David Stafford, *Churchill, and the Secret Service* (London, 1995).
22. Richard Deacon, *A History of the British Secret Service* (London, 1980).
23. David Reynolds, *In Command of History: Churchill Fighting and Writing the Second World War* (London, 2005), p. 163.

SELECT BIBLIOGRAPHY

Total War:

Calvocoressi, Peter, Guy Wint and John Pritchard, *Total War: The Causes and Courses of The Second World War*, (Middlesex, 1972, second edition 1989).
Chickering, Roger, and Stig Förster, *Great War, Total War: Combat and Mobilization on the Western Front, 1914–1918*, (Cambridge, 2000).
——, *The Shadows of Total War: Europe, East Asia and the United States, 1919–1939*, (Cambridge, 2003).
——, *A World at Total War: Global Conflict and the politics of destruction, 1937–1945*, (Cambridge, 2005).

Aachen and local histories:

AKV Sammlung Crous, *Weststadt Statt Weltstadt: Aachens Grenzerlebnisse 1914-1929*, (Aachen, 2014).
Centre Charlemagne/Couvenmuseum, *Der Krieg Ist Aus: Politik, Alltag und Medien in Aachen*, (Aachen, 2019).
Baumann, Guido, Otto Bönnemann, Walter Meven, *Die Tragödie von Aachen: Die Hinrichtung von zwei Kindern*, (Aachen, 2003).
Bieberstein, *Lüttich-Namur*, (Oldenburg, 1918).
Bimmerman, Reiner *Aachener Strassenbahn. Band1: Geschichte*, (Aachen, 1999).
Clahsen, Helmut, *Trümmerfrauen: Angst, Not, Leid und Tod in Aachen und nach dem 2. Weltkrieg*, (Aachen, 2014).
Dix, Holger A., *Das war das 20. Jahrhundert in Aachen*, (Celle, 2001).
Edmunds, Paul (Hrsg.), *Mit Fünfzehn An Die Kanonen* (Aachen, 1975).
Gasten, Elmar, *Aachen in der Zeit der nationalsozialistischen Herrschaft 1933–1944*, (Frankfurt am Main, 1993).
Gielen, Viktor, *Es stand im Echo: Aachen 1914–1932*, (Eupen, 1986).

SELECT BIBLIOGRAPHY

Herberholz, Krettek, *Strassenbahnen im Aachener Dreiländereck*, (Düsseldorf, 1980).

Hoffmann, Hans, *Aachen in Trümmern* (Düsseldorf, 1984).

Kalkmann, Ulrich, *Die Technische Hochschule Aachen im Dritten Reich (1933–1945)*, (Mainz, 2003).

König, Helmut (Hrsg), *Der Fall Schwerte im Kontext*, (Wiesbaden, 1998).

Poll, Bernhard, *Das Schicksal Aachens Im Herbst 1944*, (Aachen, 1962).

Lepper, Herbert, *Von der Emanzipation zum Holocaust—Die Israelites Synagogengemeinde zu Aachen, 1802–1942*, Bd.1. (Aachen, 1994).

Quadflieg, Peter M., *Gerhard von Schwerin: Wehrmacht general, Kanzlerberater, Lobbyist* (Paderborn, 2016).

Rass, Christoph, René Rohrkamp, Peter M. Quadflieg, *General Graf von Schwerin und das Kriegsende in Aachen. Ereignis, Mythos, Analyse* (Aachen, 2007).

Römling, Michael, *Aachen: Geschichte einer Stadt*, (Tertulla, 2014).

Ruhland, Herbert, *Der Erste Weltkrieg und die Menschen im Vierländerland: Leben und Leiden der Bevölkerung vor und nach dem Krieg*, (Eupen, 2018).

Schweers, Hans / Henning Wall, *Eisenbahnen rund um Aachen: 150 Jahre internationale Strecke Köln-Aachen-Antwerpen*, (Aachen, 1993).

Siemons, Hans, *Kriegsalltag in Aachen*, (Aachen, 1998).

Thomes, Paul/Tobias Dewes, *Aachen 1914-1918: 100 Jahre 1.Weltkrieg*, (Aachen, 2016).

Thomas R. Kraus/Paul Thomes, *Zwangsarbeit in der Stadt Aachen*, (Aachen, 2002).

Trees, Wolfgang, *Schmuggler, Zöllner und die Kaffeepanzer*, (Aachen, 2002).

Trees, Wolfgang, Charles Whiting, *Die Amis sind da! Wie Aachen 1944 erobert wurde*, Aachen, 1975).

Trees, Wolfgang, Charles Whiting, *Unternhemen Karneval: Der Werwolf-Mord an Aachens Oberbürgermeister Oppenhoff*, (Aachen, 1982).

Trees, Wolfgang, Charles Whting, Thomas Omansen, *Drei Jahre nach Null: Geschichte der britischen Besatzungszone*, (Düsseldorf, 1989).

Weberskirch, Klaus, *Anarcho-Syndikalisten an dem Wurm*, (Aachen, 1999).

Secondary histories:

Biddiscombe, Perry, *Werwolf! The History of the National Socialist Guerrilla Movement 1944–1946*, (Cardiff, 1998).

Blood, Philip W., *Hitler's Bandit Hunters*, (Arlington, 2006).

———, *Bird of Prey*, (Stuttgart, 2021).

Bradley, Omar N., *A General's Story*, (New York, 1981).

———, *A Soldier's Story* (New York, 1951).

Breitman, Richard, *Official Secrets: What the Nazis Planned, What the British and Americans Knew*, (New York, 1998).

SELECT BIBLIOGRAPHY

Brickhill, Paul, *The Great Escape*, (London, 1950).

Chickering, Roger, *The Great War and Urban Life in Germany*, (Cambridge, Cambridge, 2007).

Cüppers Martin et al, *Fotos aus Sobidor: Die Niemann-Samlung zu Holocaust und Nationalsozialismus*, (Berlin, 2020).

Danchev, Alex, and Daniel Todman (eds), *Alanbrooke, War Diaries 1939–1945* (London, 2001).

Deacon, Richard, *A History of the British Secret Service*, (London, 1980).

Deighton, Len, *Bomber*, (2009).

Donnison, F.S.V., *Civil Affairs and Military Government Central Organisation and Planning*, (HMSO London, 1966).

Ehlert, Hans / Michael Epkenhans / Gerhard P. Gross, *The Schlieffen Plan: International Perspectives on the German Strategy for World War*, (Kentucky, 2014).

Feldman, Gerald D., *Army, Industry and Labor in Germany 1914–1918*, (Princeton, 1966).

Frank, Otto, *The Diary of Anne Frank*, (Pan, 1968).

Frankland, Noble, *History at War: The Campaign of an Historian*, (London, 1998).

Goodman, Michael S. (ed.), *The Official History of the Joint Intelligence Committee, Volume 1: From the Approach of the Second World War to the Suez Canal*, (London, Routledge, 2014).

Harrison, Tom, *Living Through The Blitz*, (London, 1978).

Henke, Klaus-Dietmar, *Die amerikanische Besetzung Deutschlands*, (München, 1995).

Horne, John and Alan Kramer, *German Atrocities 1914: A History of Denial*, (Yale, 2001).

Howarth, Patrick, *Intelligence Chief Extraordinary: The Life of the Ninth Duke of Portland*, (London, 1986).

Hinsley, F.H. with E.E. Thomas, C.F.G. Ransome and R.C. Knight, *British Intelligence in the Second World War Volume 1: Its Influence on Strategy and Operations*, (HMSO, 1979).

Kahn, Arthur D. *Experiment in Occupation: Witness to the Turnabout—Anti-Nazi to Cold War, 1944–1946*, (Pennsylvania, 2004).

Kindsvatter, Peter S., *American Soldiers: Ground Combat in the World Wars, Korea, and Vietnam*, (Kansas, 2003).

MacMillan, Harold, *War Diaries: Politics and War in the Mediterranean January 1943–May 1945*, (London, 1954).

MacDonogh, Giles, *After the Reich: The Brutal History of the Allied Occupation*, (New York, 2007).

MacDonald, Charles B., *The Siegfried Line, part of United States Army in World War II*, (CMH, 1961).

SELECT BIBLIOGRAPHY

Marshall, S.L.A., *Bringing Up The Rear: A Memoir*, (San Rafael, 1979).

Marshall, S.L.A., *Bastogne: The First Eight Days*, (Washington DC, 1946).

Martin Middlebrook, Chris Everitt, *The Bomber Command War Diaries: An Operational Reference Book 1939–1945*, (Hinckley, 1995).

Marwick, Arthur, *Deluge*, (London, 1964).

Müller, Rolf-Dieter, *Der Bombenkrieg 1939–1945*, (Ch, Links Verlag, 2004).

Lord Moran's diary, *Winston Churchill: The Struggle for Survival 1940-1965*, (London, 1966).

Nicholas, Lyn H., *Rape of Europa: The Fate of Europe's Treasures in the Third Reich and Second World War*, (New York, 1995).

Noakes, Jeremy and G. Pridham, *Nazism 1919–1945, 2: State, Economy, and Society 1933–1938*, (Exeter, 1995).

Overy, Richard, *The Bombers and the Bombed: Allied Air War Over Europe, 1940–45*, (London, 2013).

Padover, Saul K., *Psychologist in Germany: The Story of an American Intelligence Officer*, (London, 1946).

Poliakov, Leon, *Harvest of Hate*, (London, 1960).

Peukert, Detlev J.K., *Inside Nazi Germany: Conformity, Opposition and Racism in Everyday Life*, (London, 1987).

Preston, Diana, *A Higher Form of Killing*, (London, 2015).

Prior, Robin, *Conquer We Must: A Military History of Britain 1914–1945*, (London, 2022).

Reynolds, David, *In Command of History: Churchill Fighting and Writing the Second World War*, (London, 2005).

Richie, Alexandra, *Faust's Metropolis: A History of Berlin*, (London, 1998).

Seidler, Franz, *Das Nationalsozialistisches Kraftfahrkorps und die Organisation Todt im Zweiten Weltkrieg*, (Munchen, 1984).

Sereny, Gitta, *The German Trauma: Experiences and Reflections 1938–2000*, (London, 2000).

Shirer, William, *Berlin Diary: The Journal of a Foreign Correspondent, 1934–1941*, (New York, 1942).

Stargardt, Nicholas, *Witnesses of War: Children's Lives Under the Nazis*, (London, 2006).

———, *The German War: A Nation Under Arms 1939–1945*, (London, 2015).

Stafford, David, *Churchill, and the Secret Service*, (London, 1995).

Taylor, Frederick, *Dresden: Tuesday 13 February 1945*, (London, 2005).

Toye, Richard, *Churchill's Empire*, (London, 2010).

Trevor-Roper, H.R., *Hitler's War Directives 1939–1945*, (London, 1966).

Verhey, Jeffrey, *The Spirit of 1914: Militarism, Myth and Mobilization in Germany*, (Cambridge, 2000).

SELECT BIBLIOGRAPHY

Weigley, Russell F. *Eisenhower's Lieutenants: The Campaigns of France and Germany, 1944–1945*, (Bloomington, 1981).

Williams, F.F.G., *SLAM: The Influence of S.L.A. Marshall on the United States Army*, (CMH, TRADOC, 1999).

Wilmot, Chester, *The Struggle for Europe*, (London, 1952).

Yelton, David K., *Hitler's Volksturm: The Nazi Militia and the Fall of Germany, 1944–1945*, (Kansas, 2002).

Ziemke, Earl F., *The U.S. Army In The Occupation Of Germany, 1944–1946*, Army Historical Series, (CMH, 1975).

INDEX

Aachen, 2, 39, 49, 126, 167
Aachen, air raid precautions and bunkers, 71–4, 78, 151, 156–7, 162–3, 167–8, 174, 178, 188–91, 193–4, 200, 270–1
Aachen, Charlemagne, cathedral, Catholicism, 216, 286–7, 294, 321–2
  relics and antiquaries, 47, 49, 56
  Velden, Johannes van der, Bishop of Aachen, 198
  Bruchkremer, Stephan, 137, 213, 215–16
  St Adalbert church, 130, 131
  St Peter's Church, 279
Aachen, county and former territory
  Dreiländereck, (3 countries corner), 11–2, 14
  Eupen, 13, 26, 31, 35, 120, 198, 204, 219, 279, 280, 292, 317
  Heimbach, (Aachen County district), 241–6
  Monschau, 26, 34, 42, 80, 154, 234–6, 242, 262, 278–9, 294

Aachen, industry and economy, Aachener Feuer-Versicherungs-Gesellschaft, 34
  Aachener-Münchener Fire Insurance Company, 39
  Chamber of Commerce (IHK), 24–5, 27, 34, 38, 40, 45–6, 147–8, 160, 208, 295, 316, 318
  economy, 19, 40–2, 295
  Great Crash (1929), 27, 37, 40–1
  Hansemann, David, 3, 34–5
  Hotel Quellenhof, 26, 150, 151, 162, 174, 179, 187, 188, 189
  industrialisation and democracy, 5, 10–11, 34–7
Aachen, newspapers,
  Aachener Anzeiger Politiches Tageblatt (AAPT), 64, 308
  Aachener Arbeiterer Zeitung, 32, 288–9
  Aachener Nachrichten, 136–7, 286, 328
Aachen, Karlspreis, 165, 322–3
Aachen, Oberbürgermeister, (the City Mayors)

INDEX

Veltman, 9
Fawick, 24–8
Kütgens, Dr. (temporary), 160, 162, 164, 166, 214
Oppenhoff, Franz,(aka Mr Selwyn), 197–200, 204, 206, 207–11, 237, 238
Oppenhof, assassination, see also Unternehmen Karneval (Operation Carnival), 197–8, 218–22
Oppenhof, installed as 'mayor', 198, 208
Aachen, Influenza epidemic, 19
Aachen, Jews, Holocaust and victims,
  Jews, 46, 285–7, 293, 294–6, 297–8, 319–20, 217, 314
  Kristallnacht (November 1938), 199, 286–7, 312–20, 329
  Hirtz family, Holocaust victims Hirtz, August, 286
  Hirtz, Josef 'Bubbi', 237
  Hirtz, Julius, 286
  Hirtz, Otto, 286
  Hirtz, Wally, 319, 329
Aachen, police
  Bach, Kriminalrat Richard, 293–4
  Gasborn Police Station, 301, 302, 304
  German police, order police, frontier police, 28, 205
Aachen, Political parties and organisations
  political party system, 41–2
  Centre Party, (Zentrum), 30–32
  Communist Party, 32, 266, 271
  Social Democratic Party (SPD), 41, 42, 91, 209, 269
Soldiers and Workers Council (SWC), 24–5
Aachen, railways, 10–1, 56–7, 34–5, 89–92, 234
  Aachener Industriebahn AG, 36
  Aachen–Monschau railway, 26
  Aachen–Herbesthal railway, 150
  Aachen–Maastricht railway, 35
  railopolis, 34, 56–7, 89, 327
Aachen, Rathaus, 28, 127, 130, 136
Aachen, schools, 14–15, 79, 152, 154, 295
Aachen, Technical University (TU), today RWTH, 9, 32, 35, 38, 46, 174, 214, 216–17, 265, 266, 267–9, 273–5, 295, 312, 329
Aachen, war crimes, social crimes,
  Herren, Johann, child victim of Nazi, 163
  Schwartz, Karl, child victim of Nazi killing, 163
  Smuggling, 16–8, 27–8, 32–4, 47, 257, 260, 261–5, 277–83
  Juvenile crime, 33, 258–60, 282–3
Adenauer, Konrad, Oberbürgermeister of Cologne, 28–9, 43, 323–4
Allied Military Occupations of Aachen 1918–1950
  Belgian occupation (1918–29), 7, 11, 13–14, 16–17, 25–9, 40, 41–2, 139, 279, 328
  British military occupation

INDEX

(1945–47), 63–4, 100–1, 105, 158, 229–30, 230–2, 232–7, 237–9, 239–46, 247–54, 257, 265–6, 286–7, 328

Matthews, R.C., Colonel British Army, 231–2, 232–3

Crimes Against Humanity Case (1947), 287, 300–11

War Crime case, 1946, 58, 116–17, 137, 155–6, 158, 164, 238, 239–46, 247, 287

Brady-Phillips case, 158, 240–1, 248–50

mass observation of German morale, 86, 92–109

US Army Military Occupation (1944–45), 33–4, 145, 199, 200–5, 220

Aachen-MGO Detachment, 232–3

Stout, Georg L., 212, 213, 214, 216, 218

'Monuments Men'—Allied Art and Antiques Detachment, 211–12

Padover, Saul, (US Army Intelligence Officer), 34, 206–11, 218–22, 237–9, 274

Swoboda, Lee M, Major, US Army, CAO, 209–10

historical branch, 169–79

MGO officers, 199, 200–5, 208, 210, 213, 217, 219, 220, 221, 232–3, 238, 258–9, 271

Military Police battalion, 205

Psychological Warfare officers, 205–6

Allied war crimes prosecution, 239–46

Altendorf, Oberleutant Rudolf, 124

Anglo-German relations, 19–29
  Prisoner exchange, 20, 21
  Maxse, Ernst G.B., 22
  St Denis, HMHS, 21

Armies, Foreign (refer to US Army):
  Belgian Army, 2, 16, 26, 27, 264
  British Army, 227, 230, 240–1, 247, 280, 292, 299, 325, 328 277

Belgium, 18, 201, 260–1, 262, 263, 265

Brown, Bobbie E. (US Army Captain), 183, 190–6

Calder, Ritchie, (Journalist and PWE director), 60–1

Cavell, Edith, 20

Churchill, Winston Spencer, War cabinet, 83–5, 86–7, 89–92, 92–109, 109–31, 156
  Boniface intelligence, 324
  Karlspreis, 1956, 322–3

Cologne, 2, 11, 27–8, 35, 39, 43–4, 75–6, 77–8, 96–7, 100, 103, 107, 119–20, 136, 152–6, 158–60, 172, 177, 181, 216, 235, 249–50, 257, 273, 278, 280

Foot, MRD, British historian, 275–6

Foreign Office, UK, 20, 68, 74, 85–7, 102–3, 106, 108, 109, 116, 145, 227, 256–7, 273–4, 276, 300, 323

363

INDEX

Cavendish-Bentinck, Joint-Intelligence Committee, 87–9, 95, 98, 101, 104, 107–8, 109–12
Eden, Anthony, 83–5, 85–9, 101, 106, 108
FOCD, 85–6, 87, 92, 103, 110, 112, 113
Hawgood, Dr. John, 87, 94–5, 99, 103, 110
Joint Intelligence Committee (JIC), 85, 87, 93–4
Political Intelligence Department (PID), 85, 87, 91–2, 94, 95, 103, 106
'1918 syndrome', 85–7, 102–3, 106, 108, 109, 145, 227, 256–7, 273–4, 300
Political Warfare Executive (PWE), 60, 86, 87, 91, 107–8
Roberts, Sir Frank, 86–7, 93, 95, 102–3, 104, 105, 112
France, 4, 18, 19, 30, 38, 40, 43, 56, 77, 90, 96, 121, 123, 124, 143, 201, 230–1, 321
Frank, Anne, 3, 296–7, 329
Grandfather, Holländer, Abraham, 296
Grandmother Holländer, Edith Abel, 296

Genocide, 5, 112, 287, 327
German Army, senior officers
Arnim, Sixt von, German General, 2, 25
Schwerin, Gerhard Graf von, German General, 162, 163–5, 166, 175, 177, 185
Rommel, Erwin, Field Marshal, 161, 164, 166
von Rundstedt, Field Marshal, 161, 162, 165–6

Wilck, Gerhard, German Army, Commandant of Aachen, 3, 162, 166, 175–7, 178–9, 185, 186, 187–90
German Army formations—Armies, Corps Divisions, Brigades, Regiments, Battalions
Fifth Panzer Army, 162–3
7th Army, 177, 189
LXXXI Armeekorps, 164, 187, 189
1st Panzer Division, 178, 187
3rd Panzer Grenadier Division, 177
7th Flak Division (Cologne), 77
12th Infantry Division, 185
14th Infantry Brigade, 13
116th Panzer Division, 162, 165, 175, 177–8
246th Infantry Division, 176
246 Volksgrenadier Division, 171, 175
108th Panzer Brigade, 177, 185
506th Heavy Panzer Battalion, 177
514th Reserve Heavy Flak Detachment 78
Harris, Arthur, (Marshal of the Royal Air Force) 76, 88, 92, 113, 117, 227–30
Hindenburg, Paul von, President of Weimar, 31, 38, 111
Holland, (Netherland), 16–17, 18, 261, 288, 292, 296, 311

Imperial Germany and army, 1–2, 12, 38, 109
Second Army, 12–13

INDEX

Fourth Army, 2, 25
Xth Corps (Maas-Armee), 12–13
27th Infantry Brigade, 13
29th Infantry Brigade (First Army), 13
34th Infantry Brigade, 13
39th Infantry Regiment, 48
Franco-Prussian War, 10
Great War, Liege, 11, 12–16, 27, 34–5, 38, 40, 180, 183, 201, 257, 262–3
Imperial Germany, collapse of
Collapse, (1918), 1–2, 19
Hohenzollern, Wilhelm, Kaiser, II, 1, 9, 24, 70–1
Ludendorf, Erich (Quartermaster-General), 12–13
Lutow 1 Königliches Preussiches Infanterie-Regiments von Lutzow (1. Rheinisches), 10, 13, 16, 1915–17, 16–19
Neufchâteau, Battle of, 16
Schlieffen Plan, 10, 11, 12, 17

Junkers, Hugo, (Professor and aircraft designer), 35, 46, 219

Lawther, William, British Trade Unionist, 256–7
Liverpool, Lord Russell (British War Crimes Prosecutor), 325
Luftwaffe, 37–8, 57–8, 63, 67–8, 77–80, 93, 125, 129, 154, 157–8, 163, 176, 247–9, 253
Eisenbahn-Flak Longerich, 78
Eilendorf Battery, 154–5
Elisenbrunnen for the Luftwaffenhelfer (LWH), 152

Flakgruppe Aachen, 78
5/889 Reserve light flak detachment, 78
Fliegeralarm, 156, 157
Gefechtsstand der Kölner Luftabwehr, 77–8
Heinz Rökker, fighter pilot, 157
Luftschutzraum (public basement shelters), 68–73
Luftwaffnhelfer, 79, 80

Marshal, S.L.A. (Slam), US Army Historian, 169, 174, 181–2, 196
Military operations, WW2
ground war, 162, 171–2, 177–8, 179, 180, 184, 187, 190
Arnhem, Battle of, 180
Bulge, Battle of the, 182
Falaise, Battle, Pocket (12–21 Aug 1944), 161, 180, 190
Rhineland, Battle of, 11, 27–8, 44, 47, 48, 56–8, 62, 73, 91, 102, 107, 119, 136, 156, 168, 202–4, 216, 290–1
Montgomery, Bernard Law, British Field Marshal, 181–2, 326–7

Nazi extermination and concentration camps, 288, 296, 297
Belsen, 259, 269
Belzec, 319
Buchenwald, 292, 317
Dachau, 300
Sachsenhausen, 288, 292, 317
Sobibor, 288, 319–20, 329
Theresienstadt, 46, 286, 296, 319

365

INDEX

Nazi Party, SS and Organisations
Aachen-Cologne Nazi Gau, 44, 148, 150, 292
Nazi Party, Aachen, 31, 43–4, 46, 49–50, 76, 119–20, 153, 163, 183, 201, 207–8, 210, 238, 246, 255–6, 258, 268, 288, 290–2, 295, 302, 310, 313–17, 318
Frömbken, Adolf, Aachen's first Nazi party leader, 43–4
Goebbels, Josef, 44, 111, 126, 147, 251, 272, 313
Göring, Hermann, 44, 57–8, 77, 79, 119, 144, 219, 289
Heydrich, Reinhard, SS Chief of Reich Security, 292, 313
Himmler, Heinrich, Chief of SS, 111, 148–9, 159, 165, 179, 197, 203, 220, 250, 290–1, 313
Hitler Youth (HY), 47, 80, 81, 152, 213, 268
Hitler, Adolf, 33, 42, 83, 93, 101, 108, 111, 161–2, 164, 165
Jansen, Quirin, Oberbürgermeister of Aachen, 44, 73, 78, 132–3, 144, 147, 160, 216, 300, 307–8
Nazi Gauleiter, 42–4
Nationalsozialistische Führungsoffiziere (NSFO), 175
Nationalsozialistisches Kraftfahrkorps (NSKK), 316–17
Nuremberg Race Laws, 294–5
Ordensburgen, Vogelsang— Nazi political school, 47, 161

Rink, Herbert, SS Officer, 185–6, 187–90
SA, 45, 46, 132, 289
SS, Gestapo and SS-Police institutions, 111, 301, 313–17
Schmeer, Edmund, 44–5, 127, 132–3, 145, 159, 162, 164, 166, 300, 301, 302, 303–11, 315, 318
Schmeer, Hugo, 45, 145
Schmeer, Rudolf, 43–4
Speer, Albert, 94, 149–50
Völkischer Beobachter, 91
Zenner, Carl/Karl SS-Brigadeführer and Chief of Aachen Police, 47–8, 247, 291–2, 293, 300, 301, 302, 303, 304–8, 310–11, 315, 317

RAF, Air Ministry, Aircraft and Operations
Aachen Survey mission, 62–6, 117–19
Air Warfare doctrine and directives, 56–7, 58, 76–7, 84–5
Air Ministry, 61, 62, 64, 65, 75–6, 77, 120, 229, 324
'Arson' Raid, (12–13 July 1943), 116, 128, 133–7, 141, 145, 147, 329
Bennett, Don, Air Vice Marshal, 142
'Blitz' raid (11 April 1944), 60–1, 142–4
Bomber Command (RAF), 53, 56–60, 62, 64, 68, 74, 76–7, 84–5, 92, 96, 115–17, 118–23, 131, 134, 137, 168, 227, 30
Bottomley, RAF Air Marshal, 59

INDEX

British Bombing Research Mission, 68
Broadhurst, Harry, (Air Marshal) 66
Butt Report (1941), 84–5, 92
Bombing Survey reports, 60, 62, 85, 92–3
Cochrane, Ralph, Air Chief Marshal, 142
Harris, Arthur, RAF Marshal, 76–7, 92, 227–30
Johnson, Johnny, RAF engineer, 65, 157
master bomber concept, 141–2
'Musical Parramatta', 115, 116
No. 6 (RCAF) Group, 115, 123
operational Research, 92–3, 134, 227
Pathfinder Force, 141–2, 229
Ruhr bombing raids, 58–9, 62, 119, 135, 143, 175, 182, 291
Saundby, Air Vice-Marshal Robert, 117
Searby, John H., Air Commodore, 142
Slater, Arthur E., 62
squadrons, 59, 65, 120, 121, 76, 115, 123–5
RAF Aircraft
  Armstrong Whitleys, 120
  Avro Lancaster, 116
  De Haviland Mosquitoes, 115–6, 121, 143
  Handley Page Halifax, 115, 122, 124, 125
  Short Stirlings, 116
  Vickers Wellingtons, 115

Schreiber, Heinrich, (soldier, smuggler, stonemason), 277–80, 328
SHAEF—Supreme Headquarters Allied Expeditionary Force, 211, 218, 265–6 G5, 216, 218
General Mc.Sherry, 211, 222
Shirer, William, (journalist, author), 62–4, 70
Stalingrad, Battle of, 5, 108, 111, 167–96

Total War, 2–5, 33, 83–4, 116, 159, 324–329
'The Siegfried Line', (Westwall), 47, 48–9, 56, 78, 168, 170–1, 180, 181, 183–4, 191, 321

US Army, senior officers and commanders
  Bradley, Omah, General US Army, 181–2, 184–5
  Carmicheal, Lt Col, Albert A, 204 209
  Collins, Lawton, 180, 182–3
  Corlett, Charles, US Army general, 184–5
  Corley, John Thomas, Lieutenant Colonel US Army, 173, 186, 189–90
  Daniel, Derrill M., Lieutenant Colonel US Army, 174, 186
  Eisenhower, Dwight D., 180–1, 182, 221–2
US Army military formations— Armies, Corps Divisions, Brigades, Regiments, Battalions, 12–13, 68–9, 199, 205, 208, 212, 220–2, 231, 302, 306–9, 313, 314, 315, 317 328
  12th Army Group, 180, 182

INDEX

First Army, 202, 212–13,
    217, 218, 220
Third Army, 293
VII Corps, 170–1
XIX Corps, 171
IXth Tactical Air Force, 171
1st Infantry Division, 170, 180
18th Infantry Regiment, 172,
    185, 190, 194, 195
26th Infantry Regiment, 172,
    173, 179, 200

USAAF 379th Heavy
    Bombardment Group, 158
United States Holocaust
    Memorial Museum
    (USHMM), 312
US Diplomat, Murphy, Robert
    Daniel, 204, 211

Warsaw Uprising, 164–5

Zuckerman, Solly, 229